Reviewing before the *Edinburgh* 1788-1802

Reviewing before the *Edinburgh*

1788-1802

Derek Roper

METHUEN & CO LTD, LONDON

First published in Great Britain 1978
by Methuen & Co Ltd
11 New Fetter Lane,
London EC4P   4EE

© 1978 by Derek Roper

Printed in the USA
ISBN 0 416 16780 2

To my Parents

Contents

Illustrations

Preface

This book began to take shape many years ago when, browsing through volumes of the eighteenth-century Reviews, I found much intelligent writing and plausible criticism. The account of these journals given in the literary histories was disparaging, even contemptuous. It seemed worth while to collect an adequate sample of review articles and see how often a reasonable appraisal was made, and by what methods. This work, together with a chapter on the organization, staffing, and practices of the Reviews, made the substance of a thesis presented at Oxford in 1959. Since that time the more famous Reviews of the early nineteenth century have been made the subject of several studies and anthologies, and their criticism has been related to eighteenth-century traditions—notably by J. H. Alexander in *Two Studies in Romantic Reviewing* (Salzburg, 1976). Some of the articles I discussed have been reprinted in the useful "Critical Heritage" series, and in Donald H. Reiman's *The Romantics Reviewed* (New York, 1972). But no work has yet been published whose purpose is to set such articles in context, to evaluate them, and to reach some general conclusions about the performance of these earlier Reviews. It is hoped that the present volume, a revised and expanded version of my earlier study, may fill that gap.

During the fifteen years covered by this work these Reviews were at the height of their influence and development. As it happened, this was a period of intense literary and political activity. In 1788 Gibbon is com-

11

pleting his *Decline and Fall;* in 1802 Jeffrey is savaging the Lake poets; in between come the debate on the French Revolution, the rise of the Gothic romance, and much else. It has been a time-consuming pleasure to read all these works (I have skimped on the thirteen volumes of Anderson's *British Poets*), and I have tried to keep my experience of them in mind when discussing the reviews. To assess the performance of a journal some quantitative check is necessary; the principles I have tried to observe in separating the more from the less satisfactory articles are described at the end of chapter 1.

This study deals with the five main Reviews published in this period: the *Monthly Review,* the *Critical Review,* the *English Review,* the *Analytical Review,* and the *British Critic.* Miscellanies such as the *Gentleman's Magazine* and *Monthly Magazine* have been excluded, even when these carried review sections. This has partly been a matter of space, but it is also true that the reviewing in the magazines was much less full and comprehensive than in the Reviews proper. Also excluded (save for a brief discussion in chapter 4) are the *Antijacobin Review and Magazine,* which is not a critical journal but a vehicle for government propaganda; and ephemeral publications such as the *Literary Review* (1794-95). Even with these limitations, the following pages should give a fairly adequate notion of the contemporary reviewing climate, and of the reception given to individual authors.

Academic obligations are recorded below. Here I should like to thank my wife, for sharing an existence of which these Reviews have long been a part.

D.S.R.

Sheffield, 1976

Reviewing before the
Edinburgh
1788-1802

1
The Reviews

The spurious criticism of periodicals, notoriously kept alive by publishers to promote the sale
of their own books, was, virtually, all that existed.

Cambridge History of English Literature

Reviewing, it seems, began in Athens about 140 B.C.;[1] but the first
periodical devoted to accounts of new books was the *Journal des Sçavans,*
begun at Paris in 1665. This journal consisted almost entirely of summaries
of scholarly or scientific works, and the first half of the eighteenth century
saw the appearance of several English periodicals of the same type. Their
aim, as defined by Michael de la Roche in the Preface to *Memoirs of
Literature* (1710-14), was "to give readers an universal account of the state
of learning." In a consciously enlightened age these abstract-journals kept
serious readers informed about the progress of knowledge in all fields.
They also served to guide scholars and professional men to developments in
their own subjects at a time when specialised journals were very few. They
saved time, and, being vastly cheaper than the books they summarized,
they saved money. With the growth and prosperity of the middle classes

and the steady spread of education, the market for such journals should have been rising; yet the English ones at least tended to be short-lived, none finding a stable readership large enough to give it adequate support.

When Ralph Griffiths published the first number of the *Monthly Review* in May 1749 he probably had no intention of departing very far from the established pattern. Griffiths was not a man of great learning: he was a bookseller, short of capital, known as the writer of a catchpenny account of the rebellion of '45 and the publisher of *Fanny Hill*.[2] No other abstract-journal was being published in London at that moment, and Griffiths saw his chance to set up a profitable sideline. But the *Monthly Review* proved more interesting than its predecessors in two respects. First, it dealt not only with learned works but with poetry, novels, drama, and the *belles-lettres* generally, which earlier journals had largely ignored.[3] Indeed, by July 1749 Griffiths had decided to try and provide a comprehensive account of all new books and pamphlets, with a special section of short notices for the slighter works.[4] Second, in an increasing number of cases the *Monthly* supplied criticism as well as summaries and extracts. Griffiths defined his policy cautiously as "to enter no farther into the province of criticism, than just so far as may be indispensibly necessary to give some idea of such books as come under our consideration";[5] but this elastic criterion permitted many kinds of review. Though some of the early articles were pure abstracts, most gave at least a brief general appraisal of the work in hand. Some thorough pieces of reviewing, in the full modern sense of the term, can be found as early as 1750;[6] and as Griffiths drew in more expert contributors the critical level of the articles improved. These two developments made the *Monthly* more entertaining, more popular, and more useful than its predecessors, and helped to give it the wide readership that earlier journals had lacked.[7]

In a few years Griffiths found it worth while to give up other bookselling and publishing activities and devote all his time to the Review.[8] This single-mindedness must have played its part in the continued success of the work; so must Griffiths' commercial shrewdness, and his skill in finding good reviewers. An early contributor was Smollett; and it was Smollett who in 1756, with much bombastic advertisement, launched the *Monthly*'s most serious competitor, the *Critical Review*. From time to time other Reviews were started. Some introduced small novelties, but for the most part they, like the *Critical*, followed the successful pattern established by Griffiths. Each dealt with as many works as possible, with a "Catalogue" of shorter notices for the less important; each gave prominent attention to learned works, but also reviewed poetry and other literature; each used a method based on summary and illustrative quotations, but with a proportion of critical comment that varied from Review to Review and from article to article. Some of these journals were conducted with enterprise and skill, but the *Monthly* remained supreme until the coming of the *Edinburgh Review* in 1802.

In the period covered by this study these Reviews stood at the height of their power and prestige. The "cultural explosion" of the eighteenth century[9] had meant a vast increase in the number of persons eager to learn about books. This rising market not only brought prosperity to the *Monthly* and *Critical*, but supported other successful Reviews: between 1793 and 1796 five notable Reviews were being published, none of which had a life of less than ten years. *Monthly* and *Critical* had now settled into a peaceful co-existence, the touch of Grub Street no longer visible in their concerns. Griffiths, who had started the *Monthly* with only three ill-assorted assistants,[10] could call on the services of a large group of experts writing in from all parts of the country. Between 1788 and 1802 James Mackintosh and Richard Brinsley Sheridan were writing for the *Monthly* on politics; the great Dr. Burney on music; his son Charles Burney II, "one of the most distinguished English scholars of his generation," and Thomas Burgess on classical literature; Thomas Holcroft, William Taylor of Norwich, and John Wolcot ("Peter Pindar") on modern literature; John Gillies on history; Abraham Rees, William Wales, and Robert Woodhouse on mathematics; Thomas Beddoes, John Leslie, Lockhart Muirhead, Joseph Planta, and John Rotherham on the sciences; William Marshall (then "at the height of his career as one of the leading authorities") on agriculture.[11] "Dr. Griffiths," a venerable figure, still edited the *Monthly* with assistance from his son George Griffiths; and through the period of the French Revolution, as through the American War of Independence, he directed the Review in the spirit of "an Old *Whig*, and a consistent *Protestant*."[12] Prudence and patriotism, however, restrained the *Monthly*'s politics during the Napoleonic years, and George Griffiths signalled a rise in the social scale by becoming a Colonel of Volunteers.

Less is known about the editing and staffing of the other Reviews, but it is likely that neither the *Critical* nor the *English* enjoyed such firm centralised control as the *Monthly*. The printer Archibald Hamilton, who had been concerned in the *Critical* from the beginning, seems to have been chief proprietor and chief editor from the departure of Smollett in 1763 until a few years before his own death in 1793.[13] Printed for A. Hamilton" continued to appear on the title page until 1799, when the name became "S. Hamilton"; this suggests that the financial interest passed first to one grandson, Archibald Hamilton III, and then to another, Samuel. Southey contributed to the *Critical* from 1797 until 1804, and from May 1799 refers to Samuel Hamilton as the editor.[14] It seems to have been the custom for one of the contributing scholars to act as assistant or co-editor to the reigning Hamilton. During the 1780s some such position seems to have been held by the Shakespearean George Steevens;[15]

in 1794-96 by Dr. George Gregory;[16] about 1802 by the Orientalist John Mason Good;[17] at another period by the antiquarian John Pinkerton.[18] Three famous contributors during the early years of the *Critical* were Johnson, Hume, and Goldsmith. Among the later reviewers were Charles Burney I, who wrote for the *Critical* before graduating to the *Monthly*;[19] Coleridge,[20] Samuel Parr,[21] and William Taylor.[22] For thirty years the *Critical* took the Tory side (when this could be identified) in controversies, but from 1791 onwards moved towards the Foxites and was soon more Whiggish than the *Monthly*. This change may have been due in part to the influence of the bookseller George Robinson, who acquired a stake in the *Critical* about the year 1774.[23]

The *English Review* — a journal owned, edited, and in great part written by Scots — was founded by John Murray I in January 1783.[24] Its first editor was Gilbert Stuart, a well-known historian who had earlier reviewed for the *Monthly*; after Stuart's death in 1786 the leading spirit in the Review was William Thomson, who became proprietor in 1794.[25] Other contributors were James Currie, the biographer of Burns;[26] William Godwin,[27] Thomas Holcroft,[28] John Obadiah Justamond,[29] John ("Zeluco") Moore,[30] and John Whitaker.[31] Murray took pains with the Review and is glimpsed writing to Sir Robert Liston in Turin for foreign articles, and to John Leslie about "a paper on electricity."[32] Holcroft wrote a section of theatre criticism, but this feature was dropped after the first five numbers. Thomson's supplement on "National Affairs," however, was expanded and diversified. The *English Review* was not a great success financially, and suffered from the death of Murray in 1793 at a time of increased competition among the Reviews.[33] In 1796 the *English* was absorbed into the *Analytical Review*, where Thomson continued to write his supplement on current affairs.

The originator of the *Analytical* was Thomas Christie, a young man of considerable learning, energy, and charm who had studied medicine in Edinburgh and London.[34] Christie's aim was to return to the method of the abstract-journals and give, not an opinion, but an "analysis" or digest of each work reviewed; possibly too he would have liked all articles to be signed, for in his Prospectus he writes disapprovingly of anonymous criticism.[35] His enthusiasm won the support of the Unitarian bookseller Joseph Johnson, and the *Analytical* was launched in May 1788. Its method represented a compromise between Christie's ideals and current practice: some criticism was to be given, but the Review was to "have more of the analytic cast in it than any other"; and articles were signed, but only with letters or ciphers which would reveal the author to the initiated. In the event the *Analytical* won a reputation not for its abstracts but for its opinions, which were more radical both in politics and in religion than any other journal. Among its contributors were John Aikin,[36] James Currie,[37]

Henry Fuseli,[38] Alexander Geddes,[39] Mary Hays,[40] Joshua Toulmin,[41] and Mary Wollstonecraft.[42] Cowper contributed at least ten articles to the early numbers.[43] Most of the editorial labour fell upon Johnson: Christie spent much time in Paris between October 1789 and August 1793, and in October 1796 he died while on a business visit to Surinam. But Johnson's corps of reviewers was less dispersed than Griffiths'. Several of the most active contributors, like Fuseli and Mary Wollstonecraft, were close friends of the editor and regular visitors to his house in St. Paul's Churchyard; and the *Analytical* was very often first in the field with its review. In July 1798 Johnson was convicted of selling Gilbert Wakefield's *Reply to the Bishop of Llandaff* (1797), now found to be seditious.[44] The government had probably been glad enough to seize this chance of putting out of action the publisher of an obnoxious Review and other radical works.[45] Confined to the Rules of the King's Bench Prison from November 1798 to August 1799, Johnson was compelled to transfer the Review to other hands;[46] and a new series under fresh management was announced in January 1799. In this last phase a leading contributor and perhaps a financial backer was the Unitarian Anthony Robinson,[47] whose friend Henry Crabb Robinson was also writing for the Review.[48] Six months later the *Analytical* uttered a last defiant message to the forces of reaction, and expired.

In the very different political climate of 1791-92 a group of Tory churchmen had canvassed support for a new Review, to counteract "what may be called *a monopoly of the press.*"[49] By June 1792 an editor and a publisher had been found and in May 1793 the *British Critic* made its appearance, backed by the subscriptions of well-wishers and by Pitt's secret-service money.[50] The philologist Robert Nares edited the *British Critic* until 1813 with the assistance of William Beloe, a classical scholar and miscellaneous writer; the Review was owned jointly by Nares, Beloe, and the publishers, F. and C. Rivington.[51] The *British Critic* drew contributors as well as readers away from the liberal Reviews, among them the physicist Jean André de Luc[52] and the orientalist Joseph White,[53] both of whom had written for the *Monthly*. John Whitaker had reviewed for the *English* for payment, but from 1793 to 1796 wrote for the *British Critic* "gratuitously, and merely to support it as an orthodox and constitutional journal of literature";[54] another reviewer who declined payment was Samuel Partridge.[55] The economist John Brand,[56] the astronomer John Hellins,[57] Thomas Percy of the *Reliques*,[58] and William Vincent, the headmaster of Westminister,[59] all contributed to the new Review; so probably did Thomas Maurice, the historian of India, and Thomas Rennell, Master of the Temple.[60] Tory support and some good articles in the early numbers soon gave the *British Critic* a sale equal to that of the long-established *Critical Review.*[61]

By contemporary standards the *Monthly, Critical,* and *British Critic,* at least, achieved a wide circulation. The only sales figures available for the 1790s are those given by C. H. Timperley for 1797: *Monthly,* 5,000; *Critical,* 3,500; *British Critic,* 3,500; *Analytical,* 1,500.[62] No authority is given for these figures, but that for the *Monthly* seems roughly in line with the documented expansion of 1749-76, when the printings rose from 1,000 to 3,500;[63] and the others bear a plausible proportion. Their combined total equals one-sixth of the contemporary reading public, if we accept Burke's estimate of this at 80,000.[64] The sale of the *Monthly* was surpassed by no periodical of the day, and was equalled only by the *Monthly Magazine.*[65] Much larger figures were to be achieved by the *Edinburgh* and *Quarterly,* but not for many years: in 1803 sales figures for the *Edinburgh,* then reckoned a dazzling success, were around 2,000, and in January 1805 its initial printing was still only 4,000 copies.[66] Even the *Analytical,* which by 1797 was doing relatively badly, had a sale nearly equal to that of the *London Magazine* of Lamb, Hazlitt, and De Quincey in the greatly expanded market of 1821-25.[67]

Some of the more famous purchasers of these Reviews can be identified from the evidence of sale catalogues. Subscribers to the *Monthly* included William Beckford, Hugh Blair, Edward Gibbon, Thomas Hollis, and probably Laurence Sterne. *Critical* readers included Thomas Day (author of *Sandford and Merton*) and William Dodd (clergyman and forger). William Hayley and Thomas Hollis owned complete sets of Johnson's *Analytical.* Horace Walpole subscribed to the *British Critic* from political and patriotic motives. From 1756 to 1763 the radical Wilkes took in the Tory *Critical,* but in his later conservative years he switched to the Whiggish *Monthly.* Warren Hastings began subscribing to the three extant Reviews on his return from India in 1785; at his death the bound volumes of the *Monthly, Critical,* and *English* at Daylesford extended to the mid-1790s, while several hundred numbers of the *Monthly* and *Critical* still awaited the binder. Southey's library included the *Monthly* complete to 1815 and the *Critical* to 1793, making together 238 volumes. This total was far surpassed by Samuel Parr, whose collection in 1825 included complete sets of the *Monthly, Critical,* and *English;* twenty volumes of the *Analytical*; and the *British Critic* complete to 1813, when it suffered a change of editorship of which Parr disapproved.[68]

Less famous but more typical subscribers known to us from bookplates or other evidence include landowners great and small;[69] clergymen (including two bishops) and scholars;[70] professional men[71] and commercial men.[72] These upper- and middle-class readers gave the Reviews their solid core of support, and it is these "country squires, rusticated peers, and provincial doctors" whom Horner reports as beginning to turn to the *Edinburgh* in 1804.[73] Even the copies of these private subscribers must usually have been read by more than one person: friends sometimes had standing arrangements to read each other's Reviews. But a still wider and a very in-fluential audience was reached through educational institutions and learned societies. Some of the universities used their position under the Copyright Act of 1709 to collect sets of the Reviews:[74] Glasgow and St. An-drew's each received the *Monthly, Analytical,* and *British Critic* in this way, Edinburgh the *Monthly, Critical,* and *Analytical,* and Cambridge the *Monthly* and *Analytical.* King's College Aberdeen acquired free numbers of the *Analytical,* and Marischal College of the *Monthly;* but Trinity Col-lege Cambridge purchased the *Monthly* regularly from its own funds. The Dissenting academies had of course no rights under the Copyright Act and must usually have paid for their Reviews. Though most of their libraries are now dispersed, it is known that Exeter Academy and Coward College took in the *Monthly.*[75] The London Institution took in the *Analytical.*[76] The Royal College of Physicians at Edinburgh subscribed to the *Monthly* and the *British Critic;*[77] the Writers to the Signet at Edinburgh and the Society of Lincoln's Inn, to the *Critical.*[78]

The Reviews reached an even wider public through the subscription libraries, literary societies, and book clubs which flourished in the latter part of the century. The Leeds Library, founded by Joseph Priestley and others in 1768, took in the *Monthly, Critical, Analytical,* and *British Critic;*[79] Worcester Library the *Monthly, Analytical,* and *British Critic;*[80] Bristol Library Society the *Critical, Analytical,* and *British Critic.*[81] "Dr. Shepherd's Library," a civic library formed round a nucleus of books presented to the town of Preston in 1761, took the *Monthly* and later the *British Critic.*[82] The Norwich Public Library and the Halifax Circulating Library took the *Monthly,*[83] Gloucester Permanent Library and Hull Subscription Library the *Critical,* [84] and Warwick Library the *British Critic.*[85] Among the more ambitious provincial literary societies, the Mon-trose Natural History and Antiquarian Society took in all five Reviews;[86] the Newcastle Literary and Philosophical Society only the *Analytical,*[87] and the Liverpool Athenaeum the *British Critic.*[88] In the simpler type of club which existed solely to buy books a Review was almost a necessity, and could greatly influence the members' choice of purchases. The pioneering Liverpool Library had begun in 1758 as a book club taking in the *Monthly Review;*[89] thirty years later the Cirencester Book Club was still at this stage of development, and seems to have taken the *Monthly* regularly.[90] A reader who had joined a country book club about 1802 recalled later that among the "many good books" the club owned was "a long series of. . . Monthly and Critical Reviews."[91] In 1798 the Rev. J. Kennedy remarked that in the book clubs "few publications are purchased until the lords para-mount of literature, the Reviewers, have fixed on them the seal of their ap-probation."[92]

Through these clubs, or by the aid of friendly arrangements for passing

copies through several hands, these journals carried literary news into the
quietest villages and to persons of modest means and education. Cowper,
waiting in 1782 for the *Monthly* to review his poems, wrote in mock
anguish to William Unwin:

> Here are watchmakers, who themselves are wits, and who at present
> perhaps think me one. Here is a carpenter, and a baker, and not to
> mention others, here is your idol Mr. Teedon [the schoolmaster],
> whose smile is fame. All these read the *Monthly Review,* and all these
> will set me down for a dunce, if those terrible critics show them the
> example. But oh! wherever else I am accounted dull, dear Mr.
> Griffiths, let me pass for a genius at Olney![93]

Yet the same journals crossed both the Channel and the Atlantic; volumes
of the *Monthly* were shipped to Sir Horace Mann at Florence; and when
the Lycée at Paris "reopened under revolutionary auspices in January, '91
. . . three hundred subscribers studied the *Monthly Review.*"[94] Their influence was not under-estimated by contemporaries. Wordsworth was convinced that reviews could materially affect the immediate sale of a book,
and Southey estimated that a favourable notice of *Madoc* in the *Critical*
would make him "half an edition the richer man."[95] Publishers already
advertised their wares by displaying well-chosen quotations from reviews,
and some authors were not above citing them as testimonials.[96]

Such influence could not have been achieved if the Reviews had not
been fairly well esteemed in their day. This is further shown by the calibre
of their contributors, and by the comments and reactions of contemporaries. Johnson, himself a *Critical* reviewer, had praised both *Monthly*
and *Critical* for their fairness; Reynolds had noted the good writing to be
found in them.[97] Burke thought it worth while to rewrite several passages
of his *Philosophical Inquiry into . . . the Sublime* (1756) so as to meet or
rebut criticisms made in the Reviews by Goldsmith and others.[98] The
fullest and most explicit tribute was paid in 1795 by Samuel Parr, who contributed to several Reviews, was dependent upon none, and subscribed to
them all:

> Of the share which I have already taken, and may hereafter take
> in these periodical publications, I can never be ashamed. I might
> plead the example of many scholars both at home and abroad, far
> superior to myself in vigour of intellect, and extent of erudition. But
> I wish rather to insist upon the utility of the works themselves, and
> upon the opportunities which they furnish to men of learning, for
> rendering some occasional service to the general cause of literature.
> There is no one Review in this country, but what is conducted with
> a considerable degree of ability; and though I decline the task of
> deciding upon their comparative excellence, I have no hesitation in
> saying that all of them deserve encouragement from learned men.

They much oftener assist than retard the circulation of books — they much oftener extend than check the reputation of good books — they rarely prostitute commendation upon such as are notoriously bad.[99]

Naturally complaints were also lodged, usually by injured authors or political opponents; sometimes too by oppressed or disenchanted reviewers. "The Critical is so miserably bad," Southey writes to William Taylor in October 1799, "that indolently as I write myself, I am almost ashamed to be in such company." Yet two years later Southey and Taylor are agreeing that to become a reviewer would be valuable literary training for Southey's brother Henry. "If I get Phillips to receive his voluntaries in the Monthly Magazine, he will know that trash will *do,* and will take the less pains; and he will know that it will do *at any time,* and procrastinate; but in the Critical neither of these excuses will avail." Taylor also guesses that a new Review would not be likely to succeed, for "both the Monthly and the Critical are in the main well conducted."[100]

On this last point Taylor was wrong: within a year of his remark the *Edinburgh Review* was launched, and with it a new style of journalism that became immensely popular. Ten years later the *Edinburgh* and *Quarterly,* Whig and Tory journals on the new pattern, dominated the scene as the *Monthly* and *Critical* had dominated it for so long. An encyclopaedia article of 1813 notes that the *Monthly* has been "the ablest work of its kind in Europe," but suggests that it now receives "the civility due to age" rather than "the homage extorted by transcendent merit."[101] The old Reviews were not, in fact, eclipsed so swiftly and completely as such remarks imply. Ten years later the *Monthly* was being praised in *Blackwood's* for its impartiality and its first-rate articles,[102] and it continued to appear until 1845, missing its century by four years. The *British Critic* remained commercially profitable long after the *Quarterly* was established, and survived until 1843, becoming in its final phase the house organ of the Oxford Movement. Even the *Critical,* which had suffered from a disastrous fire in 1803 and from still more disastrous changes of policy, maintained itself until 1817. These journals continued to attract good contributors and print good articles, and their circulations were probably respectable by eighteenth-century standards. But in the early nineteenth century literature was a growth market, and the older Reviews did not take their share of the growth. By comparison with the *Edinburgh,* the *Quarterly,* and *Blackwood's,* their readership and influence was small. As they died they were forgotten. Wordsworth's generation was the last that could have remembered, had it cared to, their eighteenth-century achievements.

In our own century few writers have paid serious attention to these journals. Scholars whose projects have demanded some account of reviewing before the *Edinburgh* seem to have glanced into them hastily, if at all, and then fallen back upon legend:

Indeed, these ancient tomes are daunting even to the most stubborn reader; the *Literary,* the *Critical,* the *British,* where are they? . . . It is true that genuine men of letters, like Smollett, Johnson, or Cowper, are found contributing to them; but, in general, their contents were menial work, ill-paid, partisan, uncritical, and in form seldom presentable.[103] (1912)

Men wanted to know about books, and events, and to find them discussed; yet, till the eighteenth century had struck, it is hardly too much to say that able, honest and independent literary criticism was unknown. The spurious criticism of periodicals, notoriously kept alive by publishers to promote the sale of their own books, was, virtually, all that existed.[104] (1915)

[These Reviews] were poor stuff in themselves, so feeble that the *Edinburgh Review,* when it came, seemed something wholly different . . . .Before 1802 the higher possibilities of periodical literature had barely been conceived. . . .That is to say, there were magazines on the level of the Erasmus Darwins, and Hayleys, and their dull generation.[105] (1928)

During the eighteenth century . . . the bookseller, a semi-piratical figure. . . , saw to it that reviewing was governed by a simple principle; his own books were praised to the skies ("puffed" was the word), and those of his rivals plentifully smirched with mud. . . . As the eighteenth century ebbed away, periodical writing seemed to be dying with it. The two chief publications were, not to put too fine a point upon it, corpses left over from the age of Johnson. There was the Whig *Monthly Review* . . . and the Tory *Critical Review.*[106] (1953)

[William Taylor and] other able men were engaged in reviewing by the turn of the century; Southey, Parr, Mackintosh. But they as well as the scores of hacks and penny-a-liners were completely dependent on the mercy of editors in their turn dependent on booksellers who financed the reviews in order to advertise the books they printed and sold. This meant that praise and blame were almost invariably bestowed on the basis of commercial rather than literary criteria.[107] (1957)

Most of the critical journals of the time were either what amounted to publishers' organs, written by hacks who sneered or rhapsodized at their employers' bidding, or unscrupulous instruments of party politics, buttering or slashing up a book in accordance with its author's political affiliations.[108] (1970)

None of these passages suggests much first-hand knowledge of the Reviews so confidently described. These have for the most part remained unread except by scholars seeking particular articles; and the articles have sometimes been misunderstood through inadequate knowledge of the Reviews.[109]

Most of the conventional account of eighteenth-century reviewing can be traced back, through Forster's *Life of Goldsmith,* to early polemical writings whose very authors hardly expected them to be taken literally. Much picturesque invective was hurled against the *Monthly* by Smollett as he strove to establish the rival *Critical.* From the moment of issuing his prospectus, Smollett transmitted an image of the *Monthly* critics as a set of "obscure Hackney Writers, accidentally enlisted in the Service of an undistinguishing Bookseller"; "wretched Hirelings, without Talent, Candour, Spirit, or Circumspection," and "subservient to the most sordid Views of Avarice and Interest."[110] Three years later Smollett was still putting out the same propaganda: the *Monthly* reviewers are "a parcel of obscure hirelings, under the restraint of a bookseller and his wife."[111] When in 1848 John Forster came to describe Goldsmith's connection with the *Monthly Review,* he unfortunately took this invective at its face value. Forster was not a careful student of the Reviews,[112] and Smollett's propaganda fitted in well both with the picturesque anecdotes about Goldsmith that had been circulating for nearly a century and with Forster's instinct to create a "scene of suffering." Griffiths is therefore portrayed as a tyrant, his contributors as obscure hirelings, and Goldsmith's articles as "a lively interruption to the ordinary *Monthly* dulness."[113] Forster's book was read when the Reviews were not; it was and, at first or second hand, still is influential. Benjamin Nangle has pointed out how even for a careful scholar like Birkbeck Hill, Forster's special pleading was able, in 1887, "completely to erase the judgements of two such critical contemporary minds as those of Johnson and Boswell."[114] In 1899 Lewis E. Gates gave an account based largely on Forster of the Reviews as "merely booksellers' organs . . . written for the most part by drudges and penny-a-liners, who worked under the orders of the bookseller like slaves under the lash."[115] In 1957 John Clive gave in his turn a sketch of reviewing before the *Edinburgh* (quoted above) which owes its ideas and some phrases to Gates.[116] In 1961 Christopher Devlin drew on the same tradition for his contemptuous account of the *Monthly* and *Critical,* and of "the callous, cantankerous, bloodsucking Griffiths . . . in whose clutches poor Goldsmith writhed for so long."[117]

Despite their real shortcomings—which are rather different from those they are usually charged with—the eighteenth-century Reviews deserve much more attention than they have yet had, or than the above-quoted passages invite. Our judgement should at any rate be based on facts and on their performance, not on literary legends or generalisations at third hand. The following chapters attempt an assessment of that performance over a period of fifteen years—from just before the French Revolution to the coming of the *Edinburgh Review.* The rest of the present chapter will discuss, first the alleged, next the real limitations of these journals.

The first of two charges commonly brought against these Reviews is that they were written by "hirelings" or "hacks." If the term *hack* meant simply a paid writer, it would apply to most reviewers of all times, save only contributors to modern scholarly journals. If it meant one dependent on his writings for all or most of his income, it would apply to a minority of the known reviewers in the 1790s, most obviously to Southey and Mary Wollstonecraft: but we do not now think of such writers as necessarily contemptible or incompetent. In the above passages, however, *hack* has strong connotations of "mere scribbler," "literary prostitute." Each of the reputable writers found contributing to the Reviews has been regarded as an altogether exceptional case. Saintsbury mentions that the *Monthly* and *Critical* "employed some really eminent hands, notably Smollett and Goldsmith," but in the same paragraph accepts the convention that most reviewing was "hack-work"; Jacob Zeitlin feels sure that "the *Critical Review* did not employ many writers of Southey's calibre," and William Haller regrets that his hand "is probably not in every case to be distinguished from the dull fists of other [*sic*] hacks";[118] Clive knows that Parr, Mackintosh, Southey, and William Taylor wrote for these Reviews, but proceeds undeterred to generalise about the "scores of hacks and penny-a-liners." Hacks, it seems, are the reviewers one cannot identify. But the area available for mythmaking has shrunk. Since 1955 the names of almost all the *Monthly* reviewers between 1749 and 1815 have been made accessible in the two Indexes compiled by Benjamin Nangle. From these it is clear that even in 1756 and 1757, when Smollett's rhetoric about the "obscure hirelings" was at its height, Griffiths was drawing upon an impressive team of contributors, most of them men of learning or talent who can never have been dependent on Griffiths for their bread.[119] Taking the First Series of the *Monthly* as a whole, Nangle justly comments that "the miserable hacks of legend . . . prove to be in fact among the most eminent scholars in the kingdom." Probably none of the other Reviews could quite match the staff of the *Monthly*: yet they reviewed the same books, and survived the competition for years. More than thirty contributors to these other Reviews have already been named in these pages, and they are men of considerable qualifications. Should it not be assumed that many other contributors, still unidentified, were similarly qualified? And that *hacks* has outlived its usefulness as a blanket description of reviewers in this period?

The second charge brought against these Reviews is that they were biased, especially by commercial factors: the proprietor's "own books were praised to the skies . . . and those of his rivals plentifully smirched with mud"; they were "mere booksellers' advertisements." Such statements suggest a wealth of evidence. Yet only one review out of many thousands published during the century has been shown to earn this description. Griffiths was the publisher of *Memoirs of Fanny Hill,* and in the first year of the *Monthly*'s existence he wrote and printed a short article defending the novel from the charge of immorality.[120] There is one other documented example of commercial influence, but of a rather different kind, bringing no particular benefit to any editor or proprietor. Having written the introduction and prefaces to Richard Brookes's *New and Accurate System of Natural History* (1763), Goldsmith wrote two reviews of the book which he "placed" with the *Monthly* and *Critical*; and the publisher Newbery expressed his appreciation by a cash payment.[121] These examples prove, what might have been guessed, that abuses did occur. They do not come near to justifying the traditional view that abuse was universal.

Not only is the evidence for this view meagre, but the stereotype of the bookseller-editor-advertiser is difficult to apply, especially in the latter part of the century. Once the success of the *Monthly* was established, Griffiths ceased to sell or publish books; his Review could be contrasted with Constable's *Edinburgh* or Murray's *Quarterly* in its freedom from "base Bibliopolic influence." Among the other Reviews the usual pattern was for a bookseller to own only a share of the concern and leave its editing to other men, who might also be part-owners. Thus George Robinson, part-owner of the *Critical*, left the editing to Archibald or Samuel Hamilton and their learned assistants; John Murray I owned a share in the *English*, which at his death passed to the editor William Thomson (who thus became sole proprietor); Francis and Charles Rivington owned between them a third share in the *British Critic* but left the editing to Nares and Beloe, each of whom held another third share.[122] It is true that once Christie had lost interest in the *Analytical* this Review was both owned and edited by the bookseller Joseph Johnson; but Johnson's integrity, and his dislike of even legitimate advertisement, were proverbial.[123]

It seems likely enough that a *Critical* reviewer dealing with one of Robinson's publications, or an *Analytical* reviewer with one of Johnson's, would feel that a certain tact was called for, and in some cases look optimistically at the work under review. To that extent they were no differently placed from reviewers in the *Edinburgh* or *Quarterly* faced with books published by Constable or Murray. But I do not think booksellers' influence during the 1780s and 1790s amounted to much more than that. Only a little reflection is needed to show how unlikely it is that gross interference took place. These Reviews were not, as the usual accounts seem to imply, distributed free to innocents. They were sold competitively, to the more educated part of the public, at a considerable price.[124] The publisher of each was well-known;[125] and each article in each Review began by stating the publisher as well as the author, title, and price of the work reviewed.[126] Systematic abuse of the kind so often described would therefore have been self-detecting, self-defeating, and fatal to the sale of the Review. No reader would have continued to pay thirty shillings a year—the equivalent of many times that sum in modern currency—for a journal which existed to praise its proprietor's works and vilify all others. The notion that these Reviews were simply puffing-machines must therefore be discarded, and unsupported charges of commercial bias should be treated with great caution, even when found in the gossip of the period.[127]

This is not to say that booksellers were selfless men. Those who published Reviews did so in the first place because a popular Review was itself a highly profitable enterprise.[128] Beyond this immediate motive, booksellers benefited generally from the Reviews because they encouraged the sale of books. A bookseller sold other men's publications as well as his own; and in the case of a large wholesaler like Robinson, supplying to bookshops all over the country, this was an important part of his trade.[129] A review which created interest in any book was therefore creating profit for all booksellers. In these conditions it is not likely that one of them would use his Review to attack all books except the minority that had appeared under his own imprint. The danger was rather that the general tone of criticism would be too favourable. Walter Scott, indeed, remembered that this had been the case, in a more plausible account of the faults of these Reviews than has been offered by later critics:

> The common Reviews, before the appearance of the Edinburgh, had become extremely mawkish; and, unless when prompted by the malice of the bookseller or reviewer, gave a dawdling, maudlin sort of applause to everything that reached even mediocrity. The Edinburgh folks squeezed into their sauce plenty of acid, and were popular from novelty as well as from merit.[130]

For what it is worth I am inclined to agree that the critics most often erred on the side of leniency, especially when dealing with poetry. My guess, however, is that this was caused less by commercial motives than by the perennial tendency of frequent reviewing to erode the critical standards of the reviewer. Also, Scott exaggerates: among the notices examined below the favourable do outnumber the adverse, but only by about two to one (149:74), which does not seem excessive when the literature dealt with includes all the best writing of the period. And uncritical leniency, where it exists, seems at least no worse a fault than indiscriminate severity—the "universal efforts at blackguard"[131] Scott found in the Reviews after new fashions had been set by the *Edinburgh*.

Commercial factors were probably less of a threat to fair reviewing than personal relationships. The literary world was small, so that Coleridge could write in 1796: "It is hardly possible for an author, whose literary acquaintance is even moderately large, to publish a work which shall not be flattered in some one of the reviews by a personal friend, or calumniated

by an enemy.'"[132] It is certainly a striking coincidence that when two out of
four reviewers of the last instalment of the *Decline and Fall* can be identified, one turns out to be Gibbon's friend Gillies and the other his enemy
Whitaker. Occasionally an editor might try to turn known friendships to
account, as when Johnson and Goldsmith were given the chance of reviewing each other's works in the *Critical*.[133] More often such arrangements
were pressed upon the editor by contributors anxious to oblige their
friends. The elder Charles Burney was closely connected with the *Critical*
between 1771 and 1785, and his works were reviewed in that journal by his
allies—sometimes under Burney's supervision.[134] Scott's *Border Minstrelsy*
was dealt with in the *British Critic* by George Ellis, with whom Scott was in
friendly correspondence. William Taylor reviewed *Thalaba* in the *Critical*
at Southey's instance; and Whitaker, after much solicitation from his
friend Polwhele, reviewed Polwhele's works first in the *English Review* and
later in the *British Critic*.[135] One instance has been alleged of a still
stronger personal bias: on the evidence of style, Eudo C. Mason believes
that the *Critical* reviewer of Fuseli's *Remarks on Rousseau* (1767) was
Fuseli himself.[136]

The first point to be made about such abuses is that they were not
peculiar to the Reviews of the eighteenth century. John O. Hayden has
pointed out some of Jeffrey's "disingenuously favorable reviews of works of
his friends" in the *Edinburgh*; and a more famous instance of self-review
than Fuseli's is provided by Scott, who in collaboration with his friend Erskine reviewed *Tales of my Landlord* in the *Quarterly*.[137] (Scott himself
proposed this arrangement to Murray, who was virtually certain of Scott's
authorship and was a publisher both of the *Tales* and the Review.) Second,
though doubtless these abuses were too frequent, they were probably much
less so than contemporary gossip would suggest. Writers were quick to
assume that bad notices were the work of enemies, and conjectures were
often aired as though they were certainties. Anna Seward was mistaken in
thinking that *Gebir* had been reviewed by its author in the *Critical*, and
Wordsworth was probably quite wrong to believe that C.V. Le Grice
persecuted all Coleridge's friends there;[138] the "hostile hand" Southey
detected in the *Monthly*[139] was that of John Ferriar, a conservative
critic but otherwise no enemy of Southey; Burney had no grounds
whatever for suspecting Sir John Hawkins of reviewing his own work in the
Critical, and only the slenderest evidence for believing that Burney's *General History of Music* was reviewed there by William Jackson of Exeter.[140]
Last, a personal interest in the work under review does not always give rise
to bad criticism. Ellis's review of *Border Minstrelsy* is more satisfactory
than the one by Muirhead, Taylor's review of *Thalaba* gives a better account of the poem than either of those written by Jeffrey, and Scott's self-
review in the *Quarterly* is a valuable, well-balanced piece of work. But it

is not likely that all reviewers, thus tempted, showed such integrity.

To publish biased criticism was to risk the reputation of the Review. Editors were aware of this risk, yet had sometimes to weigh it against the risk of offending a useful contributor by excluding his eulogy of a friend's book, or by printing an offensive review of work by the contributor himself. Of all editors Ralph Griffiths probably had the least need to be accommodating in such ways. From a study of the editorial correspondence, Nangle concludes that Griffiths "made a strenuous effort to maintain a high standard of honesty himself, and to ensure impartiality in the reviews," using the following principles:

> He never, so far as he was able to avoid it, allowed a member of the staff to review his own works.
> He insisted that members of his staff should not use their opportunities to puff their friends or attack their enemies.
> Voluntary reviews were frequently submitted to the *Monthly*; usually, of course, because the volunteer had some axe to grind. These Griffiths rarely accepted, though they offered him an obvious chance to save money.
> By ensuring complete anonymity . . . he made it possible for members of his staff, men active in social, political, and literary affairs, to write without fear of incurring professional enmities or impairing their social standing.
> He rejected emphatically any proposal which endeavoured to secure by undue influence the insertion of a favourable review.[141]

After a close study of William Bewley's reviewing of Charles Burney's works in the *Monthly,* with the relevant correspondence, Roger Lonsdale concludes that "Professor Nangle's claims for the editorial impartiality of the *Monthly Review* are basically justified." The additional principle he formulates does Griffiths no discredit:

> Griffiths wished to be informed if one of his reviewers proposed to deal with a work by a friend. If he was convinced both of the merit of the book and of the competence and integrity of the reviewer, he apparently had no objections.[142]

One last point of *Monthly* practice may be noted. It more than once happened that a regular contributor to the *Monthly* found his own works severely condemned in that same journal, and in at least one case this led to an estrangement between the contributor and Griffiths.[143] By 1793 Griffiths had apparently developed a policy of forestalling such collisions. His "hint" to William Taylor that a slashing attack on Arthur Murphy's translation of Tacitus would not be welcome, and Taylor's reply, may illustrate how a measure of worldly prudence could be combined with the genuine concern for high standards shared by both editor and contributor. Griffiths wrote:

I doubt not, that in reporting the merits of this work, you will do perfect justice both to the author and the public. One thing I have to mention, *entre nous,* [is] that Mr. M. is *one of us,* and that it is a rule in our society for the members to behave with due decorum toward each other, whenever they appear at their own bar as *authors,* out of their own critical province. If a kingdom (like poor France at present) be divided against itself, "how shall that kingdom stand?" Excuse, good Sir, this hint. You will easily at one glance see the propriety of it, as well as of the conduct to which it bears reference. But I imagine you will find yourself under no temptation to pass any harsh censure on a work that has cost so able a man above twenty years' labour, allowing for professional and occasional literary avocations. Mr. M., I am very sure, will have no objection to any fair and candid criticism, conveyed in the language of urbanity.

Taylor replied:

I have read enough of [Murphy's translation] to think it a very good one. When my opinion happens not to coincide with your wishes, I shall simply decline transmitting it. To conform, is not in me. . . . I am obliged by what you hint of a remuneration. . . . But I must decline all recompense, unless I can retain the entire liberty of refusing at any time every book to which I may happen to feel disinclined, or to think myself unequal. By these means we shall both feel at ease.[144]

The exchange is creditable to both men; and to expect higher standards than this in a parallel situation, then or now, would be naive.

For the other Reviews no such revealing correspondence has survived; but one would expect other editors to have evolved similar policies to Griffiths', for similar reasons. Some doubt has recently been expressed as to the integrity of the *Critical* by J. H. Alexander, who on the basis of half-a-dozen remarks exchanged between Southey and Taylor concludes that "the *Critical Review* was more open to puffing than its main rival."[145] On the next page this is restated, without fresh evidence, as "puffing has been shown to be frequent . . . in . . . the *Critical.*" Four of these remarks refer to the review of *Thalaba* by Taylor, who at this period (1799-1804) chose to contribute to the *Critical* rather than the *Monthly.* It is true that Taylor, like Bewley, was permitted to review his friend's work; but as Alexander himself shows, what he wrote was an excellent piece of criticism — sincere, perceptive, warm in its praise, and sharp in its adverse comments.[146] The phrase "mere puff" is used by Taylor to describe the review he did *not* write. Another of the remarks Alexander cites is Southey's description of a *Critical* notice as "the puff superlative," simply because he thought it too laudatory. Not much can be based on the remaining remark — Southey's claim that he has "*perhaps* and *probably* enough interest in the Critical Review to insert any puff of decent praise and brevity" (my italics). I do not believe that "puffing" was frequent in any of these five Reviews; to insist that it should not occur at all is to apply standards that the reviewing of no period could meet.

To conclude this discussion of bias in the Reviews, mention must briefly be made of political and religious factors. These probably influenced reviewing more often than any other external influences; though bias of this kind is seldom alleged against these journals, probably because it was at least as conspicuous in the *Edinburgh* and *Quarterly*. The period was, of course, one of acute controversies and conflicts. Contemporaries expected these to be treated, not with god-like impartiality, but from a consistent and intelligible point of view. The position taken by each journal has been generally indicated, and is more fully discussed in chapter 4. What must be said here is that by the end of 1791 these positions were generally known and could be allowed for by readers; also that though critics were not less partisan than other men of their day, the best of them remained critics and were not merely propagandists. Even those who wrote propaganda did so from conviction and not for pay. The *British Critic* supported Pitt's government, but was a very different concern from the *Antijacobin Review*, which was manned chiefly by Treasury journalists. Though launched with the aid of a government donation, it seems thereafter to have paid its own way;[147] and some of its contributors reviewed free of charge, out of patriotic or religious motives. Nor has any evidence been found of payments made by the Foxite Whigs to those Reviews which supported the Opposition. Last, despite the strength of political feeling, it should be remembered that even at the height of controversy only a small fraction of the material published in any Review number had to do with politics.

Though our picture of these Reviews is incomplete, the evidence we have strongly suggests that in the last quarter of the eighteenth century they were as ably staffed and as honestly edited as those of any later period. What, then, caused their retreat before the *Edinburgh* and the *Quarterly*? The answer is that the new journals adopted new roles more suited to an age in which both books and readers were becoming very much more numerous. In some respects the new Reviews were more ambitious than the old; in other respects they were less so, for it was the very ambitiousness, in scope, of the *Monthly* type of Review which brought about its demise in the new century.

Superficial comparisons with later Reviews tend to obscure the real character of these eighteenth-century journals. Numbers of the *Monthly* and *Critical* were not meant to be read for entertainment and thrown away. They were conceived as instalments of a continuous encyclopaedia, recording the advance of knowledge in every field of human enterprise. Their sub-titles claim as much: *The Critical Review, or Annals of Literature; The Analytical Review, or History of Literature, Domestic and Foreign.* The word *literature* is used here in its very broadest sense. All the researches, speculations, discoveries, and achievements of that age of progress were recorded in these journals by means of a systematic review of as many new publications as possible—ideally, of all. To comment on the latest poems and novels was a small part of the reviewers' task. They had to summarise and, where possible, evaluate the work of Arthur Young in agriculture, of Mallet and Percy in antiquities, of Linnaeus in botany, of Priestley, Lavoisier, and Humphry Davy in chemistry, of Cook and Bruce in geography, of Jenner in medicine, of Sir William Jones in Oriental studies, of Hume in philosophy, of Adam Smith and Jeremy Bentham in economic and political theory, and of countless minor scientists and scholars in these and other fields. They reviewed the *Transactions of the Royal Society* and of other learned bodies. It is no wonder that Peacock's Mr. Panscope includes the *Monthly Review* among the sources of knowledge he has mastered, together with the *Encyclopaedia Britannica* and *Memoirs of the Academy of Inscriptions.* Indeed, a good run of the *Monthly* is still an extremely useful asset for the historian of literature or of almost any other subject,[148] presenting a great part of the culture of the period as it appeared to that period and within a reasonable compass. Volumes were reprinted from time to time, and complete sets and volumes to make up incomplete sets were regularly advertised;[149] and it was assumed that new volumes would continue to be added until civilisation came to an end. A correspondent of 1793 expresses pleasure at seeing a friend's name going down "to latest posterity in the Monthly Review."[150]

But the ideal of comprehensive reviewing can never have been easy to achieve; and by the end of the century it had become impossible, if only because of the sheer volume of new publications. The number of new titles printed annually had increased fourfold since the *Monthly* and *Critical* had been founded,[151] and journals which had once dealt with between twenty and thirty books and pamphlets each month were now despatching sixty to seventy, sometimes more, and still falling behind.[152] Monthly numbers had increased in size by a third, and in 1790 the *Monthly* began a new series in which volumes were to be bound three times a year instead of twice, with three appendixes of foreign literature instead of two; in 1791 the *Critical* followed suit. In his prospectus of the *Analytical* Thomas Christie suggested that it would be an improvement to review at great length the "truly *standard* works, which add to the stock of human knowledge," and to omit the "trifling and temporary" publications, or simply record their titles. In the event, the *Analytical* reviewed at least as many works as the older journals. When deciding how best to meet the challenge of the *British Critic* in 1793, Griffiths too seems to have considered adopting a more selective approach, for his friend and reviewer William Enfield wrote back opposing any such change:

> Our R[eview] has, I am persuaded, been the only one which has noticed *all* publications: and it must always be a recommendation of a journal of this kind that it does so. If possible, we should not I think give up this distinction. It would be better to give a *single line* to many articles, or even as formerly the bare titles, than to omit them entirely.[153]

Comprehensiveness was too much a part of the encyclopaedic character of these Reviews to be easily renounced, especially since renunciation seemed certain to give an advantage to rivals.

This tradition of reviewing all new publications bore very hard on critics in certain fields, notably in politics, verse, and prose fiction. Much of the increase in book production came from the manufacture of cheap novels. Enfield himself protested to Griffiths in October 1795:

> from the great number of novels sent me in the *two last* parcels, I conclude that a hint I dropt some time ago has escaped your attention. I have no objection to be lounging now and then an hour in Lane's shop: but to be shut up for several days together in his warehouse is to an old man an irksome confinement.[154]

Young men as well as old could suffer, as Coleridge discovered a year later:

> I am almost weary of the Terrible, having been an hireling in the Critical Review for these last six or eight months — I have been lately reviewing the Monk, the Italian, Hubert de Sevrac & &c & &c — in all of which dungeons, and old castles, & solitary Houses by the Sea Side, & Caverns, & Woods, & extraordinary characters, & all the tribe of Horror & Mystery, have crowded on me — even to surfeiting.[155]

In December 1797 Southey announced with some pride that he was "now engaged in the poetical department of the *Critical Review*," but added: "You would be astonished at the load of trash they send me."[156] By 1803 astonishment must have abated:

> Habeo, Deus unicus scit quantos libros revidere! libros magnos, libros medios, libros parvos, libros cujusque generis, quos omnes necesse est sine mora occidere ex.[157]

In these conditions an energetic *débrouillard* like Southey was of more use to editors than a dilatory genius like Coleridge; and in fact Coleridge's engagement with the *Critical* probably lasted less than a year, while

Southey stayed on for five, earning something like four hundred pounds by "killing off" new publications.[158]

The economics of literary reviewing requires closer inspection. Reviewers then, as later, were paid at an agreed rate for each "sheet" of copy contributed, a sheet being sixteen printed pages. Works were assigned them by editors who had already looked over the volumes and decided in doubtful cases what scale of treatment was required.[159] An epic poem, or even a Gothic romance by a popular author, might be given first place in the monthly number;[160] but most novels, volumes of verse, and political pamphlets were inevitably allocated to the "Catalogues," where the notices averaged less than a page in length.[161] A reviewer of modern literature might thus have to deal with sixteen or more such works before he had filled his sheet and earned his fee, which was usually either two or three guineas.[162] In a novel of 1794 by Holcroft a well-educated young man who has tried to earn money by reviewing declares:

> I entered on my new office with great determination; but I soon discovered that, to a man of principle, who dare neither condemn nor approve a book he has not read, it was a very unproductive employment. It is the custom of the trade to pay various kinds of literary labour by the sheet, and this among the rest. Thus it frequently happened that a book, which would demand a day to peruse, was not worthy of five lines of animadversion.[163]

To one of Holcroft's quixotic, somewhat rigid mind it may well have seemed sheer knavery to pronounce upon the trashiest book without having first read it from cover to cover; others probably got through the rubbish very quickly, and concentrated their efforts on the few works that showed some possibility of talent. Even so, there was a real danger that minor achievement would be overlooked amid the flood of mediocrity. A year before publishing the above narrative Holcroft had himself reviewed Wordsworth's *Evening Walk* and *Descriptive Sketches* in a group of five works destined for the Catalogues; he made some damaging adverse criticisms, but missed the touches of imaginative observation and poetic promise.[164] Coleridge had reason when he undertook never to review more than one work for any one number of *The Watchman*: "I shall not carry with me to the perusal of unexpected excellence the ill-humour or disgust occasioned by having previously toiled thro' pages of frippery or dullness."[165]

Three guineas a sheet does not seem high pay when compared with the ten guineas—soon, sixteen guineas—paid by the *Edinburgh*.[166] Griffiths does not seem to have been generous in money matters, and could probably have afforded to give a lead by raising his fees; under his son's editorship payment rose to five guineas by 1809.[167] It is quite misleading, however, to attribute the success of the later Reviews to high pay. Three guineas did not seem such miserable payment at the time: Whitaker was "staggered" to be offered this fee after having written for the *English* for two guineas and the *British Critic* for nothing.[168] The eighteenth-century Reviews commanded plenty of talent, as we have seen, and whatever fees he had offered Hamilton could hardly have found two likelier reviewers of modern literature than Coleridge and Southey. The reviewers' complaint was not against their low pay but against their obligation to deal with masses of mediocre books. It is true that had payments been higher each reviewer would have had to cope with fewer books to earn a given fee. But until the ideal of comprehensive reviewing had been abandoned, large numbers of bad books had to be dealt with somehow; if the existing reviewers had handled fewer works, more hands would have had to be taken on. Thus an editor who doubled his fees might at the same time have had to double his staff. The only practicable means of easing the burden for reviewers of literature, and of making full use of the talent many of them possessed, was for editors to adopt a much more selective approach to the works chosen for review.

The most important innovation made by the *Edinburgh* was precisely that. In their preliminary advertisement Jeffrey and his friends renounced all claim to comprehensive coverage, wishing their journal "to be distinguished, rather for the selection, than for the number of its articles."[169] This virtue was firmly based on necessity: the four young men who planned their first number so light-heartedly had not the resources to produce anything on the *Monthly* pattern if they had so desired. The final number of the *Analytical* had reviewed sixty-five works; in October 1802 the *Monthly* reviewed forty-four, the *Critical* sixty, and the *British Critic* seventy-seven. The *Edinburgh,* which as a quarterly might have been expected to deal with three times as many works as these monthly journals, reviewed twenty-nine. But the success of this first number made it clear that a Review could be highly selective and still attract plenty of support. As the fame and circulation of the *Edinburgh* increased, selectivity was seen to be a prime advantage, and the number of articles in each of its numbers was reduced to a mere dozen. That success was not the result of high fees can be seen from the fact that for the first three numbers contributors received no payments at all, and were expecting none.[170] High fees came later, when the decisive break with the tradition of comprehensive reviewing had already been made.

Though selectivity greatly improved the lot of reviewers, it threw upon editors a correspondingly heavy burden: that of deciding which few books out of so many should be noticed. Under the earlier system as many books as possible had been seen by the editor and then read more closely by the reviewer, giving some chance at least that important new writing would be

identified. What method of screening new books was practised by Jeffrey
and Gifford I do not know; but it is remarkable that of the important new
writers who appeared between 1802 and 1820—Jane Austen, Byron,
Hazlitt, Hunt, Keats, Scott, Shelley—none was first recognised in the
Edinburgh or the *Quarterly*.[171] Similarly, all but a handful of new works
by known writers were reviewed in the smaller periodicals before the big
quarterlies noticed them. Even when allowance has been made for the fact
that a monthly Review can be quicker off the mark than a quarterly, it
looks as though the smaller Reviews did more than their share in finding
new talent and initiating discussion. Once game had been started it was
easy enough for the hawks of the *Edinburgh* to fly at it—a pattern set,
perhaps, by Jeffrey's first attack on the "Lake School" in 1802. At all
events, it was an advantage to readers that the *Monthly,* the *Critical,* and
the *British Critic* survived until well into the nineteenth century, and that
they and other small Reviews could provide between them the coverage
that the quarterlies lacked.[172]

A second limiting feature of the eighteenth-century Reviews was their
conservative interpretation of their function. John O. Hayden complains
that "little attempt was made to go beyond providing readers with an idea
of the content and relative worth of recent publications—the merest practical function of reviewing."[173] To describe and evaluate new books was indeed the main business of reviewers, then as now, and where they did these
things well it seems unreasonable to condemn them for not performing
some undefined but loftier functions. A more exact description of their approach is given by J. W. Robberds:

> Custom had not, in those days, authorized a reviewer to place the title
> of a book at the head of an article, as a text or pretext to introduce
> a new pamphlet of his own. He was expected to make the author,
> and not himself, the most prominent object of attention, to give an
> epitome of the work which he announced, to scan its merits and
> defects, and to extract appropriate passages in support of the judge-
> ment which he uttered.[174]

This tradition of reviewing obviously did not provide for long original
essays of the kind Macaulay contributed to the *Edinburgh Review*—essays
which, as Robberds implies, were reviews in name only. It is also true that
more space was usually given to the display of a book's content than to the
investigation of its relative worth.

From the abstract-journals the Reviews inherited the practice of summarising the work under review and of giving substantial extracts. To this
was added a proportion of criticism that varied considerably from one article to another. For long works a favourite method was what might be
called the "guided tour," in which the reviewer first gives a short statement

of the scope and nature of the book and then works his way through it, summarising, quoting, and occasionally criticising. At the end comes an attempt to cast the balance of its merits and defects, or perhaps only a brief general verdict. It needs to be said that this was and remains a perfectly adequate method of reviewing many non-controversial works of scholarship and science. John Clive offers as "typical of the sort of review published in the *Monthly* and the *Critical*" a sentence from the closing paragraph of one of these guided tours:

> We have thus resumed and concluded our examination of this highly useful and interesting work, noting such passages and observations as seemed necessary to convey some suitable ideas of its extent, variety, and merits.[175]

Clive not only omits the specific criticism which follows this sentence,[176] but also fails to mention that it comes from a competent account of George Shaw's *General Zoology* (1800-1802) which is not at all unlike some of the scientific articles in the *Edinburgh;*[177] indeed, for fourteen years the reviewer, Lockhart Muirhead, wrote simultaneously for both the *Edinburgh* and the *Monthly.*[178]

When such methods were applied to works of literature, it must be admitted that the results were sometimes unsatisfactory. In this field critical discussion mattered more than paraphrase, and the "guided tour" might or might not be the best way of presenting such discussion. But despite some inadequate reviews it can be said that on the whole the reviewers of literature recognised the need for criticism and supplied it in reasonable measure. The following table shows the average length of the reviews given by each journal to the new poetry, novels, and romances dealt with in the present study, and the proportion of critical discussion:[179]

	POETRY		NOVELS AND ROMANCES	
	Length of Review	*Length of Criticism*	*Length of Review*	*Length of Criticism*
Monthly	2,100 words	900 words	1,500 words	850 words
Critical	2,000 "	500 "	2,200 "	600 "
English	1,600 "	500 "	1,300 "	400 "
Analytical	1,100 "	300 "	1,700 "	400 "
British Critic	1,600 "	700 "	2,050 "	700 "

By modern standards these figures represent articles of generous length, and except perhaps in the *Analytical* the length of critical discussion also compares favourably with that of most modern literary reviewing.[180] When *Lyrical Ballads* first appeared the *Monthly* gave it an eight-page review, including nearly two thousand words of criticism; the *Critical* gave a seven-page review, including five hundred. It is not easy to think of a periodical in general circulation today in which a small, anonymous volume of verse would be dealt with on such a scale.[181] As will be seen, the overall proportion of criticism to summary and quotation varies considerably from one Review to another: in the *Critical* and *Analytical* it is 1 : 4, in the *English* 1 : 3, in the *British Critic* 3 : 8, and in the *Monthly* nearly 1 : 1.

The reviewing methods of the day could of course be abused. In particular, the practice of giving long extracts gave opportunities to lazy reviewers, who were paid the same rate for quoted as for original material.[182] Samuel Badcock of the *Monthly* pointed out to Griffiths more than one occasion on which their rival had failed to live up to its name:

The Critical Review, which extended this Article to two distinct & large Papers, gave *nothing but extracts* without one single observation of their own. 'Tis very easy to be a Reviewer on such Terms! — I would call them Transcribers, not Critics.[183]

The *critical* Reviewers, as they call themselves, have been content to be *mere Transcribers* both of Steevens's & Malone's Publications. — They have more Need of the Hand than of the Head.[184]

The fault Badcock rightly condemns is the absence of criticism and not the presence of substantial extracts. These, if well chosen, could obviously be useful, and the very fact that editors were willing to pay for them at the full rate shows that neither they nor their readers regarded them as inferior material. Conscientious reviewers took pains to find quotable passages, which were usually meant to show the author at his best. Pearne regrets having had to cut out "many good things of the author's" from his unfavourable review of Burke's *Reflections;*[185] Enfield complains of having hunted all through one book without finding "a passage which our readers would bear to read";[186] the *British Critic* introduces an extract from *St. Leon* with the comment that it is "as little exceptionable as any."[187] Southey took credit for printing "some of the most exquisite poetry in the language" in his review of Landor's *Gebir,*[188] and was rebuked by Lamb for not having displayed the "elaborate beauties" of the *Ancient Mariner.*[189] The practice of giving long extracts was retained by all Reviews until well into the nineteenth century, though not always with such kindly intentions.[190]

Between 1789 and 1802 the reviewers seem almost always to have made some attempt at criticism when dealing with works of literature. But in some cases the criticism is too brief or too general to be satisfying, not only in the Catalogues but in the main review sections as well. This fault too Badcock had detected, even in the pages of the *Monthly Review*. To Griffiths he wrote frankly in 1782:

> Your poetical Department is very generally disliked. It consists of
> mere general Observations. There is nothing pointed, acute, or dis-
> criminating. [Criticism] requires cool Judgement, Acuteness, and
> Taste. The Mind should be quick to espy and delicate to feel. . . .
> The Critic is not barely to *hit off* a good Thought. He is to produce
> a Chain of good ones. He must compare—He must argue; he must
> *pursue* Argument.[191]

A review ending in "mere general Observations" doubtless sometimes
means that the writer has been too lazy, too busy, or too incompetent to
produce anything more detailed. But it should also be noted that men differed about the extent to which criticism was desirable in the Reviews.
Badcock's opinion may be contrasted with that of Boswell, who in 1791
writes slightingly of reviewers who

> instead of giving an accurate account of what has been done by the
> authour whose work they are reviewing, which is surely the proper
> business of a literary journal, . . . produce some plausible and
> ingenious conceits of their own, upon the topicks which have been
> discussed.[192]

Very similar views are expressed by Thomas Christie in the prospectus of
the *Analytical Review:*

> The true design of a Literary Journal is, in our opinion, to give such an
> account of new publications, as may enable the reader to judge of them
> for himself. Whether the writers ought to add to this their own judg-
> ment, is with us a doubtful point. If their account be sufficiently ac-
> curate and full, it seems to supersede the necessity of any addition of
> their own.

Nor was the *Analytical* the only work founded with the intention of restor-
ing as far as possible the methods of the abstract-journals: in 1797 the
Monthly Epitome, later sub-titled *Readers their Own Reviewers,* began a
life of nine years. In 1801 Southey wrote to Taylor that reviewing "ought to
be merely analytical, or according to . . . fair and written canons of
criticism."[193] It is not surprising that reviewers should sometimes have
limited the scope of their criticisms in a period when it was doubted
whether they should criticise at all.

These ultra-conservative interpretations of the reviewers' function
become intelligible when it is remembered that these journals were not
conceived primarily as organs of opinion. Though they had perforce to be
different things to different men, the prevailing ideal was that of an objective chronicle of cultural progress; and from this point of view controversial opinion was no more desirable in the Reviews than in the en-
cyclopaedias to which they have previously been compared. This ideal

probably came close to being fulfilled in the realms of science and pure scholarship, where objective summaries were useful and where expert, authoritative treatment could be given to matters of fact. In religious and political affairs disputes were inevitable; but most journals had at least a consistent point of view derived from the doctrines of a church or party, doctrines which it was believed time would vindicate. It was in the field of literature that the ideal of the objective chronicle was hardest to achieve. Though men still paid their respects to the notion of universal "canons of criticism," these were in practice elusive. Developments in literature and criticism since mid-century had made the Augustan synthesis look old-fashioned, yet nothing had so far evolved that was coherent enough to take its place. The tendency was for criticism to become more a matter of individual response: but this was at variance with the impersonal and objective ideals of the Reviews. Certainly no criticism that might be considered eccentric could be approved by these journals, whatever might be tolerated in the less austere world of the magazines.[194] The best the Reviews could do was to mask the personal and fallible nature of literary judgement by maintaining an unbroken front of references to the collective wisdom of corps," by preserving consistency,[195] and by avoiding anything too controversial. These were not favourable conditions for sustained flights of imaginative criticism.

The decisive part played by Jeffrey and the *Edinburgh Review* in bringing about a change in these conditions has always been recognized. The *Edinburgh* was from the first a journal of opinion, embodying new conceptions of reviewing at the opposite extreme from those represented by the *Analytical.* When attending to the work under review it very often retained the methods of summary, extracts, and the "guided tour"; but the important feature of most articles was opinion, usually aggressively and often voluminously stated, and sometimes only slenderly connected with the work in hand. The new selectivity made ample space available for original writing. Jeffrey reviewed *Thalaba* for both the *Monthly* and the *Edinburgh,* and in each his account of the poem occupies about ten pages; but whereas in the *Monthly* he added less than two pages of critical discussion, in the *Edinburgh* he could introduce his account by a nine-page essay, of doubtful relevance, on the new "*sect* of poets."[196] In his own way Jeffrey tried as hard as his predecessors to mask the fact that fallible personal opinion was being offered. The eighteenth-century Reviews sometimes assumed an authoritative manner; the *Edinburgh* contrived to create "an impression of omniscience."[197] As for the desired effect of objectivity, Jeffrey achieved this in his review of *Thalaba* and in other literary articles by appealing, with an air of supreme confidence, to supposedly universal and timeless standards. In so far as these have coherent existence they represent a much more conservative, Augustan taste than that to which Jeffrey owned in private.[198] Authoritative and instructive, yet entertaining and in-directly flattering to readers by its satire, the *Edinburgh* soon won a wide public; and its success encouraged other Reviews to be less chary of giving "ingenious conceits of their own." By the second quarter of the century it was taken for granted that the Reviews should serve as channels for opin-ion, discussion, and new writing, and as such they played an important part in the intellectual life of their age. Thus the founding of the *Edin-burgh* was the most important step in the evolution of reviewing since Ralph Griffiths began the *Monthly* fifty-three years before.

Nevertheless, to accept conventional accounts of a golden age of periodical criticism that began in 1802 is to set the eighteenth-century Reviews in a false perspective. Whatever view is taken of particular con-troversies and of the philosophy or psychology of Francis Jeffrey, one's chief feeling about the early literary reviewing of the *Edinburgh* and *Quarterly* must be regret for opportunities wasted. Six or seven great writers — fore-most among them Wordsworth, Coleridge, Keats, and Jane Austen — came before critics who had the attention of a larger public than critics had ever known and practically unlimited space in which to develop their ideas. The *Edinburgh* ridiculed Wordsworth and Coleridge for at least twenty years;[199] the *Quarterly*, politically more sympathetic, did not begin counter-operations until 1814 and soon gave them up.[200] When Keats's turn came it was the *Quarterly* which ridiculed him and the *Edinburgh* which made a belated and unsatisfactory defence.[201] The vogue Jeffrey had created for slashing attacks was as harmful to the development of good criticism as the new, enlarged scope of reviewing was potentially beneficial. As for Jane Austen, the *Quarterly* missed her first three novels but then made amends by two appreciative notices;[202] the *Edinburgh* ig-nored her altogether. It is true that Byron and Scott were generally praised, as were Rogers, Campbell, and Felicia Hemans. But these poets had already made their way as popular favourites and stood in no need of commendation; Shelley, who did need it, was attacked by both major Reviews.[203] The success with which these Reviews are said to have main-tained "the essential lines of communication between criticism and original writing"[204] is not, to say the least, obvious, either from a summary record of their judgements or from a reading of their most frequently reprinted articles.

John O. Hayden notes that "on many counts, the secondary Reviews pro-vided criticism superior to that of the *Edinburgh Review* and the *Quarterly Review*";[205] and it may well be that the *Edinburgh* benefited literature more by the criticism it stimulated in other periodicals, including those carried on from the eighteenth century, than by its own. Unfortunately its aggressive style of journalism was also imitated by other Reviews, so that even journals which had praised *Lyrical Ballads* were by 1807 ready to take up the cry against the "Lake School."[206] When Hazlitt, himself a slashing reviewer for the *Edinburgh,* compares the reviewing climate of 1821 with the "calm peaceable period" before 1802, his praise for the methods and manners of the earlier critics is apt enough, though playfully expressed:

> The writers [in the *Monthly Review*], instead of "outdoing termagant or out-Heroding Herod," were somewhat precise and prudish, gentle almost to a fault, full of candour and modesty.
>
> "And of their port as meek as is a maid!"
>
> There was none of that Drawcansir work going on then that there is now; no scalping of authors, no hacking and hewing of their Lives and Opinions, except that they used those of Tristram Shandy, GENT. rather scurvily; which was to be expected. All, however, had a show of courtesy and good manners. The satire was covert and artfully insinuated; the praise was short and sweet. We meet with no oracular theories; no profound analysis of principles; no unsparing exposure of the least discernible deviation from them. . . . The former laconic mode was well adapted to guide those who merely wanted to be informed of the character and subject of a work in order to read it: the present is more useful to those whose object is less to read the work than to dispute upon its merits, and go into company clad in the whole defensive and offensive armour of criticism.[207]

The present writer too admits to finding the style of the eighteenth-century Reviews more appropriate and agreeable than that of their successors. Even when the judgements of Jeffrey, Croker, Lockhart, and the others are reasonable and their comments relevant, the patronising tone and amazing verbosity of many articles do not endear them to modern taste.

It is by their criticism, however, that the eighteenth-century Reviews must be judged. The following chapters will attempt to show how the *Monthly,* the *Critical,* the *English,* the *Analytical,* and the *British Critic* dealt with literature that was, or in some cases seemed, of importance between 1788 and 1802. "Literature" has been interpreted in a broad enough sense to include the major works of political and religious controversy discussed in chapter 4, as well as Gibbon's *Decline and Fall* in chapter 5. No reviews of a given work have been ignored, though interesting articles are allowed more prominence than dull ones. Full references to the reviews discussed are to be found in Appendix A. In this appendix, and sometimes in the text, a distinction has been made between "satisfactory" reviews and others. A satisfactory review is one which takes the work under review with the right degree of seriousness and points out real and important merits or faults. To illustrate: the *Monthly* seems to have overrated Rogers's *Pleasures of Memory* and to have given inadequate prominence to Maria Edgeworth's *Castle Rackrent,* and neither review has been counted as satisfactory; but in dealing with Charlotte Smith's *Old Manor House* both

Monthly and *Critical* made substantial and accurate criticisms and both reviews have been counted as satisfactory, even though one is preponderantly favourable and the other adverse. This method of division is crude and inevitably, in part, subjective. I can only say that some such assessments are necessary if any kind of quantitative check is to be kept on my conclusions, and that I have tried to make them fairly. As far as possible they have been supported by quotations, especially in the case of the satisfactory reviews. These are marked by an asterisk in Appendix A. Interested readers can therefore test the standards which have been applied to these articles, and to the reviewing of this period as a whole.

2
The Reviewing of Poetry

The school of Pope has had its day; a taste has been
introduced for the rude but more vigorous effusions
of our ancestors.

Southey in the *Critical Review*, January 1799

In his Preface to the *Oxford Book of Eighteenth-Century Verse* David
Nichol Smith recommends readers to forget the usual critical catchwords,
to lay aside the terms *classical* and *romantic,* and to see the period as one
neither of decadence nor of preparation but of achievement. That is certainly how it was seen by most readers and writers of the 1790s. Poetry and
the understanding of poetry were felt to have shared in the general advance of civilisation and knowledge throughout the past century. Thomson, Gray, Collins, Mason, Cowper, Akenside, Charlotte Smith—though
there might be room for controversy about the particular merits of each,
these poets were seen, not as sappers undermining an Augustan citadel,
but as colonists who had brought fresh territory under cultivation, or made

49

neglected land fruitful. The same is true of the Wartons, Young, Hurd, and the many writers on aesthetic philosophy. Almost all the literary developments that used to be called "pre-Romantic" were welcomed by the eighteenth-century Reviews.[1]

Seen against this background, Jeffrey's attacks upon Wordsworth and Coleridge in the *Edinburgh Review* — attacks which served as models for other persecutions, and did much to create a less tolerant critical climate — seem all the more surprising. Do they represent a genuine and inevitable reaction to Wordsworth's innovations, such as most readers must have felt even if Jeffrey had never written a line? Coleridge thought not: he admitted that Wordsworth's Preface to the 1800 edition of *Lyrical Ballads* was provocative, but considered that had it not been for this Preface and for Jeffrey's intervention the poems would have aroused no hostility. Left to themselves they would quietly have won a gradually increasing understanding and admiration from "not a few" readers.[2] This theory can be neither proved nor disproved; but a close reading of some reviews of poetry from the days before Jeffrey's reign began may help to show how far it is plausible, and to explain how relations between the leading poets and the reviewers can thereafter have taken such a turn for the worse.

This chapter will also illustrate more generally the opinions and achievements of reviewers of poetry in this period. As the previous chapter shows, their chief difficulty lay in having to deal with large quantities of mediocre verse. A second difficulty lay in the worn critical vocabulary of the age. "Correctness," Joseph Warton had written as early as 1756, "is a vague term, frequently used without meaning and precision"; the same is true in this period of *nature* and *elegance,* and portentous words like *genius* and *inspiration* were also liable to abuse.[3] To gloss such terms would not always be possible, nor fortunately is it necessary. The reviewer with something to say generally makes his meaning clear enough by means of discussion, specific comment, and illustration.

Collections by Anderson, Ellis, and Scott

For the ordinary reader of the mid-eighteenth century the age of poetic enlightenment seemed to have begun about a hundred years before. From the preceding dark age three luminaries indeed shone forth, Shakespeare, Milton, and (more faintly) Spenser; but lesser writers were for the most part unknown. It was these writers who in the latter half of the century attracted increasing interest from scholars and antiquarians, whose numerous editions and anthologies eventually made possible that rehabilitation of earlier poetry which was to be so important for the new age.[4] This process was strongly in evidence between 1789 and 1802; but the fact that even readers of advanced tastes could characterise all poets from Chaucer to Cowley by such general epithets as "elder" and "earlier" shows that is was still far from complete.

Progress towards a truer historical perspective was aided by the creation of a *corpus poetarum*. In 1777 the publishers of Johnson's *English Poets* had planned a collection of verse reaching back to Chaucer. Eighteen years later their project was realised, though by other hands, in Robert Anderson's *Complete British Poets* (Edinburgh, 1792-95). Its thirteen bulky volumes contained a vast quantity of verse, from Chaucer to Chatterton; Johnson's biographical prefaces were reprinted, and new ones supplied by Anderson. Wordsworth and Coleridge were among the many who made good use of this collection.[5]

British Poets received favourable and, from a contemporary viewpoint, competent notices in the *British Critic* and the *Critical*. The *British Critic* welcomed the movement to revive pre-Restoration poetry:

> It is true that, generally speaking, these poets are inferior to their successors in the choice of their subjects; in the art of conducting them; in a delicate imitation of the ancients; in grace and perspicuity of expression; in harmoniousness of versification; and in every poetical attribute which lies within the province of taste; but they do not yield to them in any of the qualities of a vigorous and enthusiastic mind. In originality of conception, in fertility of imagination, in frequency and strength of reasoning, or in depth and variety of learning, they are equalled by few, and excelled by none of their rivals.[6]

Sir John Davies is praised for his effective imagery, correct, easy and expressive language, and musical verse; Hall, here compared with Juvenal, is admired for his original and descriptive epithets and for the easy harmony sometimes found in his verse; the two Fletchers are commended for genius and learning, and, though the *Purple Island* of the elder is condemned on the general grounds of its being an allegory, the *Piscatory Eclogues* are praised for their "native graces and simple ornaments." Though the reviewer's understanding of "early" poetry does not go beyond that of most cultivated admirers in this period, he does attempt critical discriminations at first hand:

> Many straggling beauties are certainly to be met with in [Daniel and Browne]; . . . but to get at these the reader is forced to traverse a long and cheerless waste of rhyming prose. Their chief excellence is in their easy language; but the latter author, though ingenious, is quaint and puerile in an extreme degree, and the former has written much more than his industry could support, with the vigour belonging to his native genius.

The *Monthly* reviewer, Samuel Rose, concerns himself largely with Anderson's biographical sketches and offers little criticism of the poetry. But Southey's review in the *Critical*[7] not only places *British Poets* in its historical context but gives a lively summary of the young poet's critical opinions, and some hints of his own ambitions. After deploring the neglect of "early" writers since the time of Pope, Southey boldly claims that

> . . . the school of Pope has had its day; a taste has been introduced for the rude but more vigorous effusions of our ancestors; and it is from comprising the early writers that the present collection derives its great and distinguished value.

There follows a rapid sketch of the history of English poetry from the reign of Edward III onwards, with special praise for the Tudor poets:

> At the court of Henry VIII appeared the earl of Surry, who was distinguished by a correctness of taste unexampled and long unfollowed. He was succeeded by Sackville Lord Buckhurst, who was possessed of a genius which seemed to promise that he would become the Dante of England. The golden age of our poetry ensued; and Spenser arose. From his time to the middle of the last century, English poetry did not advance; but, except in the drama, it can scarcely be said to have been retrograde.

The continuation of Southey's sketch deserves to be quoted at length:

> The period between Milton and Pope may be called the dark age of English poetry. After Pope we find no more such trash, as by the privilege of gentility formerly passed for poems. Under Elizabeth our poetry was like a mountain brook, rough indeed and broken, but delighting the traveller with whatever is great, magnificent, and sublime. After the Restoration, it was the stream that passes by a city and receives its filth. With Pope it became like his own Thames, smooth, beautiful, and majestic.
> The taste, however, which Pope introduced, was calculated rather to make mediocrity tolerable, than to produce excellence. We were sinking to the tame and tiresome regularity of French poetry; the stream began to stagnate like a Dutch canal. Young, Thomson and Akenside, rose to excellence; but a sad rabble of versifiers appear in the collection at this period. The Wartons led us back to a better school. The pupils of that school are now the candidates for fame; and it is for the next age to decide upon the present.

In discussing the importance of preserving early poetry, Southey adopts a "historical estimate" of the kind Arnold was later to disparage:

The minor poets of the early ages are not to be estimated by the publications that now swarm. . . . When reading and writing were no common accomplishments, it indicated some talents to venture on composition. We think all should be published to a certain period, perhaps to the aera of Cowley.

Like Percy in the *Reliques,* Southey also commends early poetry as material for social history:

If, however, it should be deemed necessary to exclude some, we are decidedly of the opinion that all who were popular in their own times should be admitted. They characterise the taste and history of their respective ages, and should therefore be re-edited, though their fame may be no longer great.

Some omissions from Anderson's collection are regretted, particularly of Hawes, Langland, Marlowe, the *Pharonnida* of Chamberlayne, and the *Athenaid* of Glover. "The list of modern poets is sufficiently extensive: we could willingly have spared a volume of them to have made room for older and better company."

Southey concludes his review by describing the pride such a collection of poetry must inspire in an Englishman, and by comparing the achievements of English and other poets in various fields. Homer, he admits, is unrivalled, but so in his own kind of epic is Milton; no English poet has equalled Virgil or Tasso, but Spenser is at least as great as Ariosto. In lyric poetry, however, Southey finds that Dryden, Gray, and Collins have been surpassed by Klopstock. Shakespeare remains supreme in the drama, though Mason and Horace Walpole challenge competition in their own dramatic genres, and much is to be hoped from Joanna Baillie.

The remaining species of poetry are of inferior merit: in these, Britain yields to no country. Pope is at least equal to Boileau. Akenside, Young and Thomson are without competitors; and our minor poets are as numerous and valuable as those of any other country. Of living writers this is not the place to speak. The Pantheon of Glory admits only the dead.

Southey, whose *Joan of Arc* had just gone into a second edition, had hopes of being admitted into that Pantheon.

The fact that Anderson's publishers were willing to go back to Chaucer, whereas Johnson's eventually included no poet earlier than Cowley, suggests that the intervening eighteen years had seen a very considerable increase in the readership of pre-Restoration poetry. This was largely due to the numerous anthologies published by antiquarians like George Ellis in the last quarter of the century. Ellis, like Anderson, had hoped to carry out the original scheme of Johnson's booksellers; but he ran short of materials, and the first edition of his *Specimens of the Early English Poets* (1790) contained only lyric verse of the sixteenth and seventeenth centuries.[8] Such verse was extremely popular with the revivalists. Elizabethan poetry seemed to offer more authentic passions and fresher imagery than that of their own age; it certainly employed richer language and a greater variety of verse forms.

In 1790, however, the reviewers showed no great enthusiasm for Ellis's *Specimens*. The unidentified author of a Catalogue notice in the *Monthly* feared

> that the modern reader, whose taste is refined by the works of Pope, and others of our later bards, will be apt to consider the merit of the present volume, as consisting more in the extremely elegant manner in which it is printed, than in the poetry which is copied from most of the writers in the preceding list [which includes Surrey, Wyatt, Gascoigne, Shakespeare, Sidney, Daniel, Beaumont, Fletcher, Marlowe, Raleigh, Jonson, Drummond, Drayton, Donne, Shirley, Carew, Randolph, Davenant, Wotton, Cartwright, Suckling, Cowley, Waller, Milton, Dryden, and Sedley], and from others whose names we have passed in silence. Those of SHAKESPEARE, MILTON, DRYDEN, &c. can never be mentioned with too much respect; but there are *some* in this collection, who do not seem altogether worthy of the very honourable company into which they are introduced.

The *Analytical* and *Critical* gave vague, mild praise, the first declaring that Ellis's "little pieces" might vie with the Anthologia of any age or country, the second simply describing the volume as a pleasing companion. But the *English* made the *Specimens* a pretext for attacking the whole movement for the revival of earlier poetry. Such verse, the reviewer asserts, must grow less attractive every day as its language becomes more obsolete, and its "coarse and harsh expressions" must disappoint modern readers.

> Many are, perhaps, prejudiced enough to fancy themselves touched with these testimonies of age, and value them as the precious rust of an ancient coin, that helps to obscure information and puzzle conjecture. Others, with less reverence, will consider them as the faded frippery of a great-grandmother's wardrobe, which has lost its colour, its strength, and its utility.

Most early poetry is deficient in metre and harmony; and

it is not enough to be told, that there is much fine imagery and sound morality contained under these rude forms; still it may not be poetry; to constitute which there must be an harmonious arrangement and colouring of these loose materials. If it be answered, what can you expect from such rude ages? we reply, that we do not expect this, and . . . we do not expect poetry.

Here the contempt for antiquarianism, the insistence on critical standards, would have been more impressive if the reviewer had shown closer contact with the "early poetry" he disparages.

The second edition (1801) of the *Specimens* was expanded from one volume to three, with introductory essays that together formed a "Historical Sketch of the Rise and Progress of the English Poetry and Language." Short poems from the Old English period to the seventeenth century were now included. This more ambitious version drew increased attention from the reviewers, though strangely enough most of their remarks were directed to poems which had been included in the first edition; the Old and Middle English poems were passed over in silence.

A substantial and favourable review came from Southey in the *Critical*.[9] Comparing the new *Specimens* with Anderson's collection, he remarks:

> In Dr. Anderson's edition of the British Poets, there has been either too much done or too little; he has included too many authors for a selection, and not enough for a complete *corpus poetarum*. Our oldest poets should be published at length—they have all their value, as the historians of manners. . . . But there exist many writers of the middle age of our poetry, whose re-publication never can be expected; of those poems which *happen* to be in Dr. Anderson's collection, there are many whose length and dullness will deter even assiduous readers. The fine passages which they contain might be threaded on an analysis of their works; these pearls should be dug out of the pool and strung together. In this manner should the long poems of Daniel be treated; the Edward III and the Henry II of May; the long pastoral of Browne, &c.

Southey's only complaint is that Ellis's selections are not always representative:

> The specimens of Warner and Sylvester convey a very inadequate idea of their *mannerism:* from Randolph, from Wither, from Quarles, they must have been selected with random carelessness.

(Though this is an overstatement, it is true that Ellis chose what seemed most likely to please contemporaries rather than what was most characteristic of the poet, so that Donne is represented by 'Go, and catch a falling star.") Southey takes the opportunity of discussing Quarles, Wither, and other poets in whom he was interested, of again praising Chamberlayne's *Pharonnida*, and of impressing the reader with his own expertise. ". . . we are aware of the toil and patience necessary in these studies."

The *British Critic* reviewed Ellis's second edition in two instalments. In the first, the reviewer discusses the revival of interest in earlier poetry without seeming wholly to approve of it. Patriotism, piety, and historical interest suggest themselves as motives for this pursuit, and the possibility that such poetry has literary value is the last to occur. Still, it does occur:

> Nor must it be forgotten, that these antiquarian researches have enlarged the stores of elegant amusement, by reviving the popularity of some poets, who are not merely the objects of curiosity for their antiquity, but of admiration for their excellence.

The reviewer's discussion of Elizabethan poetry is very cautious:

> [The Elizabethan age] has been sometimes called the poetical age of England, and . . . perhaps may justly be so distinguished, if we have respect rather to the *productive* than to the *guiding* powers of the poet; if we bestow the greatest praise on those excellencies which peculiarly characterize English poetry; if poetical honour and fame belong more to great works of genius, than to regular productions of art, and faultless models of taste.

But by the time the second instalment was written the critic had clearly read and enjoyed the anthology, and comes down firmly on the side of the Elizabethans. Gascoigne, Turberville, and Greene are found harmonious and pleasing; Southwell's poems "breathe a sober and pensive morality, very remote from the affected passion and romance of his age"; Spenser's minor poems and Hall's and Drummond's satires are all praised. Carew and Suckling are even more highly commended, while Lovelace's poems "are among the greatest ornaments of this work." Even Crashaw and Cowley are said to display much genius, though in a vicious style. The *Specimens* will delight every reader of taste:

> and if there be any, whose appetite we have not already provoked, their case must be hopeless. All attempts to practise upon them must be unavailing. Their heads must be inaccessible to criticism, and their hearts insensible to poetical beauty.

The only adverse criticism is in a sense a Romantic one, for the reviewer accuses the Elizabethan sonneters of insincerity:

> when we see *every* poet in love, we know that it is no longer a sentiment, but a fashion. From the accession of Elizabeth to the Restoration, perhaps as much ingenuity was employed by poets in counterfeiting

love, as had two or three centuries before been extended by schoolmen in the erection of systems of philosophy, and with a very similar issue, as far as relates either to the pleasure of the reader or the durable reputation of the author.

The *Monthly* reviewer, Dr. John Ferriar, was interested in Elizabethan poetry and had published papers on Massinger;[10] but his account of Ellis's second edition is disappointing, for it consists only of extracts with some valueless general remarks.

Scottish and Border ballads formed a class of poetry so far removed from the Augustan ideal that after praising "Chevy Chase" in the *Spectator* Addison had felt obliged to forestall the charge of being "too singular." But interest in these ballads had never quite died out, as is shown by the appearance of several small Scottish collections in the first half of the century; and after the publication of Percy's *Reliques* in 1765 they came increasingly to be admired by ordinary readers, as well as by antiquarians and Scots. Walter Scott's *Minstrelsey of the Scottish Border* (Kelso and Edinburgh, 1802-3) thus appealed to a taste which had already been created. None the less, Scott is cautious about claiming literary merit for his ballads; though he commends some in his introduction for their rude energy and pathos, he suggests that others will be read for their historical value, or simply for the stories they contain.[11]

In the *British Critic* Scott's work was reviewed by Ellis himself, who had already exchanged friendly letters on antiquarian subjects with Scott.[12] Ellis puts his main emphasis on the pieces Scott had classified as "Historical Ballads," and dwells on their documentary value:

> The great political events of each reign are to be found in every historical abridgement; but we here behold a delineation of the scenes on which they took place, the minor incidents by which they were accompanied, the impressions they made on the actors, with all the modifications which they received from passion and from national prejudice.

"The Fray of Support" and "A Lyke-Wake Dirge," however, are praised for their literary qualities. "Both are singularly uncouth and savage; but their wildness has a terrific effect, which would perhaps be diminished, if they were more easily intelligible." In the "Romantic Ballads" Ellis finds a variety of interest and an element of the "marvellous" which are sure to attract the general reader. The later ballads, he thinks, will be less popular, since they differ from the early ones "at least as much as a hero in a coat and waistcoat differs from a hero in complete armour." Ellis warmly commends Scott's industry, patience, and learning.

The *Critical* reviewer, who may have been William Taylor of Norwich,[13] declares that Scott has done for Scotland what Percy had done for England, and with equal taste and dexterity. He does not discuss the antiquarian value of the ballads, but praises their picturesque qualities and their stimulating effect on the imagination. They will gratify, he declares, the common taste among civilised men for finding every ancient building and picturesque spot made more romantic by association with some marvellous adventure; and they will provide material for future poets and for the decoration of yet unwritten metrical romances. "Nations must have their mythologists: when the priest grows rational, the poet takes up the task of delusion."

The *Monthly* reviewer, Lockhart Muirhead, showed little interest in either the antiquarian or the literary qualities of the ballads. "The illustration of the peculiarities of border manners, as they modified the feudal spirit of the times," he declares, "required not much expenditure of time or paper." His comment on Scott's Introduction is that "a review of family feuds and barbarous inroads, though penned with elegance, can convey little of either instruction or pleasure to the bulk of readers." He finds a few of the ballads, such as "Annan Water," to be simple and moving, but

> it is seldom, however, that our patience is rewarded by melting strains; nor does either genius or elegance seem to have presided at the birth of most of the popular ditties which Mr. S. has so painfully accumulated.

Muirhead declines to join Scott in regretting that many such compositions have been lost, and prefers the modern imitations included in the collection to "those coarse strains which indicate the once untutored state of Caledonia." He hopes that in future Scott will employ his pen on more important subjects. The general effect of this review is to belittle, even to ridicule *Border Minstrelsy*: it pays some general compliments to Scott's diligence, taste, and learning, but also includes much petty fault-finding. Muirhead was Principal Librarian at Glasgow University and was soon to become its first Professor of Natural History. Nationality was his only obvious qualification for reviewing Scott's book, and even this may have worked to Scott's disadvantage: the phrase about "the once untutored state of Caledonia" seems to deprecate a preoccupation with Scotland's picturesque and primitive past.

These reviews display a wide range of attitudes towards the revival of earlier poetry — indifference, hostility, appreciation of its historical interest, enthusiasm for its literary merit; but since nine of the fourteen notices are favourable, it would seem that on the whole the Reviews encouraged the movement. Ellis's *Specimens* of 1790 received short, unenthusiastic notices, but the other three publications were reviewed at length and (Muirhead's notice apart) treated with respect. The best reviews are those in the *British Critic,* for they at least attempt some revaluation of the poems and ballads collected. With Percy and Ellis among its contributors, this Review was well placed to assist in the antiquarian revival. The *Critical* provides three lively and relevant essays, though none contains much specific criticism; the *Monthly* gives a very poor performance.

Thomas Warton and Smart

Through his prose writings Thomas Warton did as much as any man to revive interest in earlier English poetry; but despite his revival of the sonnet and his taste for the "phrase that time has flung away," Warton's own verse belongs in essentials to the Augustan tradition. Warton held the Laureateship and a Chair of Poetry at Oxford. Smart, a much more original poet, lived and died a needy vagrant and has often been represented as a victim of his age, more particularly of its reviewers.[14] Posthumous collections of both men's work appeared in the same year, giving critics an opportunity for comparison and revaluation.

Most items in Warton's *Poems on Various Subjects* (1791) had been printed before, which is presumably why the *Analytical* did little more than announce the volume. Both *Monthly* and *Critical,* however, gave full reviews. The *Monthly* reviewer, Dr. Charles Burney, took this occasion to compare Warton's poetry with that of Smart, whose active and loyal friend Burney had been for more than twenty years:

> On the whole, if we were obliged solemnly to give our opinion on oath concerning the degree of *originality* in our four poets of the present age, Gray, Mason, Smart, and Warton, — we should place Smart at the head of all for invention, and Warton the last. . . .Poor Smart, careless, hasty, and needy, was never solicitous, nor at leisure, to polish. Warton's taste in poetry was truly classical and elegant; his versification was nervous and correct; his reading was extensive; and his knowledge of rural nature was seemingly acquired from an actual survey of her works: — but there is an original and appropriate stamp impressed on the best productions of Smart, Mason, and Gray, which instantly informs a reader of taste to whom they severally belong. There are, however, poems by the late Laureat, though of considerable length and excellence, that might have been written by others; and which would never, when seen or heard for the first time, excite the exclamation "this is TOM WARTON!"

Warton's best poems, Burney suggests, are "cast in the mould of some gifted predecessor," often of Milton: "*The Pleasures of Melancholy* . . . is a beautiful Miltonic poem, abounding with bold metaphors and highly-coloured pictures," and the imagery of the "Ode on the Approach of Summer" is so obviously Miltonic that Warton should have described it as an

Imitation. "His imitations of Milton, like the pictures of Raphael copied by Giulio Romano, are *perfectly copied:* but still they are copies." But to other poems Burney gives warm praise: the spirit, force, and fancy of the "Ode for Music," he declares, "will give pleasure to an Englishman as long as the present language remains intelligible." He admires Warton's descriptions, particularly those of Gothic scenes, and finds that the "Gothic pictures and embellishments" of the Birthday Odes for 1787 and 1788 "give that kind of mellowness to these poems, that time confers on medals and productions of the pencil."

The *Critical* gives an excellent characterisation of Warton's poetry:

> Mr. Warton possessed a classic taste with a Gothic Muse. . . . his Poems show a strong predilection for the days of chivalry and romance; and even every New-year's Ode goes back with a fond partiality to the tales of other times, and speaks of crested chiefs and tissued dames, and wisard spells, and castles frowning with lofty battlements; but his ear was formed to the correct harmony of more modern times; and the turn of his genius was rather chaste and elegant than wild or sublime. Most of his Poems bear strong marks of imitation, and he has sometimes not scrupled to borrow, not only epithets and peculiarities of expression from the elder poets, but sometimes whole lines with little or no variation [examples follow]. There is, likewise, in these Poems a sprinkling of obsolete words, agreeable, perhaps, to those who are very conversant with our earlier authors, but which, in the opinion of those who love nature and simplicity, gives to composition rather an affected quaintness than any real grace. Such are *besprent, chosen imps, scant, pensive eld,* &c. The traces of imitation which we have remarked, may, perhaps, serve to show that our author was one who rather caught the flame of poetry by reflection, than from strong original genius; notwithstanding which, his productions contain many pleasing and elegant pieces, and he well deserves to be honourably ranked among the class of our minor poets.

The reviewer prefers "The Triumph of Isis," quoting its invocation to Oxford; he also praises "The First of April" for its beautiful and accurate descriptions, the Birthday and New Year Odes, and the humorous "Progress of Discontent." "The Pleasures of Melancholy" he finds "by no means one of the best." He also gives much observant detailed criticism, as in his comment on the line "The due clock swinging slow with sweepy sway": "Of *sweepy sway,* it is difficult to say what it is, except that is is *alliteration.*"

The Poems of the Late Christopher Smart (Reading, 1791) contains none of Smart's best and most distinctive work, but includes a number of good poems of the second class which reveal him as a vigorous and original poet. The *Monthly* reviewer was again Dr. Burney, who declared that the old dispute between Smart and the *Monthly* was now dead and buried: "real merit must have foul play, indeed, if it does not, at length, burst from accidental and temporary clouds, and shine forth with fresh lustre." Burney finds it inexplicable that Smart has not been included among Johnson's *English Poets*. Recalling earlier *Monthly* notices of Smart's poems, he emphasises the more favourable comments and in particular the "diffuse praises" awarded to *A Song to David*. Turning to the *Poems* under review, Burney describes "Care and Generosity" as "one of the most beautiful allegories that has ever been imagined"; pronounces Smart's ballads to be stamped with originality, wit and pleasantry; and finds that the "Epitaph on the Rev. Mr. Reynolds" breathes the true spirit of poetical pathos. The Fables he thinks the best in the language after Gay's, and superior even to Gay's in originality, wit, and humour. Smart's faults, Burney declares, are those of "redundant genius," and are amply compensated for by his beauties:

> His errors are those of a bold and daring spirit, which bravely hazards what a vulgar mind could never suggest. Shakespeare, Milton, and Dryden, are sometimes wild and irregular; and it seems as if originality alone could try experiments. Fowls of feeble wing seldom quit the ground, though at full liberty; while the eagle, unrestrained, soars into unknown regions.

These remarks seem intended as a defence of the Smart who wrote *A Song to David* rather than of anything published in 1791.

The *Analytical* gave a poor review, describing the volume as interesting and valuable but preferring the humorous pieces. The *English* followed the *Monthly* in declaring that Smart's genius had been unduly neglected. Some of his pieces, the reviewer asserts, concentrate "the very soul of poetry"; of those now appearing, the "Ode to Ill-Nature" and "Ode on St. Cecilia's Day" are preferred. Some stanzas of the latter work are found "sublimely poetical."

In these reviews Warton is accurately placed as a pleasant minor poet, and it is the obscure Kit Smart who is awarded such terms as "genius" and "sublime." Two of the three articles favourable to him were written by his friend Burney, and if Griffiths had sent the *Poems* to, say, John Ferriar, a different picture might have been given. None the less, Burney's praise is sincere—little was to be gained by praising a dead man—and in keeping with his general views on poetry; and his "critical taste" on this occasion was commended by Griffiths.[15] That the *Monthly,* followed by the *English,* should have published such enthusiastic comments is enough in itself to refute the legend of an "allegiance to the Augustans" on the part of these journals.

For his dead friend's reputation Burney wrought better than he knew, or

has yet been generally realised. His complaint that Smart had been excluded from Johnson's *English Poets* was heard by Robert Anderson, who
reprinted the whole of the 1791 *Poems* in vol. 11 (1795) of his *British Poets*.
In his introductory account of Smart Anderson drew heavily on Burney's
review, much of which (including the peroration contrasting "fowls of feeble wing" with the eagle that soars into unknown regions) he copied ver-
batim. From Anderson the same laudatory comments passed into vol. 5 of
the *Cabinet of Poets* (1808),[16] and into Alexander Chalmers's expanded
version of Anderson, the *English Poets* of 1810. Neither Anderson nor
Chalmers could find a copy of *A Song to David* for reprinting; but
Chalmers did his best by giving the twenty-eight lines from that poem
which had been quoted and praised by the *Monthly* in April 1763 (*English
Poets*, 16: 10-11). Thus it was in great part owing to the much-maligned
Monthly reviewers that Smart's name and some of his work were kept in
circulation until the renewal of interest brought about by Browning in
1887.

Burns and Bloomfield

Burns is a major poet and Bloomfield a good minor one, yet their work
might never have found a public if they had written before the establishment of the cult of the inspired peasant. Implicit in this cult were a
preference of the primitive to the civilised, of genius to correctness and of
passion to wit. Burns, however, is in his own style a very witty poet, and the
work of both men gives ample proof of intelligence and conscious skill. The
chief test for the reviewers was to avoid misrepresenting Burns and Bloomfield in terms of the peasant cult, whether they themselves approved of this
cult or not.

The *Monthly* was the first London Review to notice *Poems, Chiefly in
the Scottish Dialect* (Kilmarnock, 1786), though a notice in the *Edinburgh
Magazine* and Henry Mackenzie's paper in the *Lounger* had appeared a
little earlier. The reviewer, James Anderson, had himself been a farmer
and usually reviewed agricultural books; he was also a Scot, though he concealed this fact and pretended that some notes which he supplied in the
course of his article had been provided by a friend who understood the
language. In a very favourable review Anderson contrasted Burns with the
race of "polished *versifiers*":

> His simple strains, artless and unadorned, seem to flow without effort,
> from the native feelings of the heart. They are always nervous,
> sometimes inelegant, often natural, simple, and sublime. The objects
> that have obtained the attention of the Author are humble; . . . yet his

verses are sometimes struck off with a delicacy, and artless simplicity, that charms like the bewitching though irregular touches of a Shakespear.

Anderson praises "To a Mouse" and "To a Mountain Daisy" for their "delicate tenderness," and "Hallow-e'en" for its antiquarian interest; but the poem he most admires (and quotes in full) is "The Cotter's Saturday Night," as "a beautiful picture of that simplicity of manners, which still, we are assured, on the best authority, prevails in those parts of the country where the Author dwells." Burns is at his best, too, "in the sportive, humorous strain"; his mind is not well enough stocked with "brilliant ideas" for success in "Songs, Odes, Dirges &c." (This remark probably refers to poems in Burns's more conventional literary style, such as "Man was made to mourn, a Dirge"; "Winter, a Dirge"; "To Ruin.") He is recommended to use less antiquated verse forms, and it is regretted that his dialect and frequent references to provincial customs will hinder the enjoyment of English readers. In conclusion, this farmer-reviewer compares the Kilmarnock volume to a carelessly winnowed heap of wheat: "Some grain of a most excellent quality is mixed with a little chaff, and half ripened corn."

The *English* reviewer was almost certainly another Scot—Dr. John Moore, now best remembered as the author of *Zeluco*.[17] Hailing Burns as "a *natural,* though not a *legitimate,* son of the muses," he ranks him far above earlier peasant prodigies like Stephen Duck. Moore prefers the humorous and satirical pieces, and describes the "Address to the Deil," "Holy Fair," and others as masterpieces of this kind; he notes too that these poems are original, whereas the more solemn ones tend to be derivative. He warmly praises "The Cotter's Saturday Night," "To a Mouse" and "To a Mountain Daisy," but finds "Hallow-e'en" to be poorly executed in spite of its interesting subject: "A mixture of the solemn and the burlesque can never be agreeable." His summary contains both just and unjust criticism:

> The stanza of Mr. Burns is generally ill-chosen, and his provincial dialect confines his beauties to one half of the island. But he possesses the genuine characteristics of a poet; a vigorous mind, a lively fancy, a surprizing knowledge of human nature, and an expression rich, various and abundant. In the plaintive or pathetic he does not excel; his love poems . . . are execrable; but in the midst of vulgarity and common-place, which occupy one half of the volume, we meet with many striking beauties that make ample compensation. . . . His situation, however, is critical. He seem to possess too great a facility of composition, and is too easily satisfied with his own productions. Fame may be procured by novelty, but it must be supported by merit.

The *Critical* gave a short notice which praises Burns with warmth, but reads like a *précis* of the *Monthly* review and contains no evidence that the critic has actually seen the Kilmarnock volume.

Despite their modest length and a tendency on Anderson's part to over-stress Burns's "artlessness," the *Monthly* and *English* reviews of his first publication are generally sensible and perceptive. Fourteen years later, reviewing Currie's edition of *The Works of Robert Burns* (Liverpool, 1800), the critics gave this poet much more space but less satisfactory criticism. Most of their attention went to Burn's life, as set out in Currie's Introduction: Samuel Rose in the *Monthly* devoted his entire review to this subject, referring readers in search of criticism to Anderson's review of 1786, while the *British Critic* deplored at great length Burns's moral failings and democratic sympathies. Such criticism as appeared tended to assimilate Burns to the "peasant poet" stereotype by representing him as the untutored poet of strong emotions. Thus the *Critical* declares:

> He wrote under the impulse of strong feelings; and for this reason his reader is, as it were, carried away by the torrent of his impassioned eloquence. Whether he indulge in the sportive sallies of wit and humour, or pour out his sorrows in the accents of melancholy, we recognise the indelible characters of truth and nature, and we rejoice when he rejoices, and weep with him when he weeps.

This reviewer does, however, recognise that judgement must have played some part in the creative process:

> In how many instances do we find the splendid productions of uninstructed genius tarnished by occasional improprieties of expression, and other philological inaccuracies! How strong must have been the intellect of Burns, which, exercising itself upon the scanty materials supplied by his poverty and retirement, could produce such maturity of judgement as is displayed, not only in his remarks on other authors, but more particularly in his own compositions!

But the *British Critic* adopts the theory of emotional inspiration in full. After quoting in full the song "Scots, wha ha'e wi' Wallace bled," the reviewer pours scorn upon those "who consider the artifices of style as the principal merit of poetry," and declares that

> those who regard the power of inspiring passion as the noblest ex-cellence of an ode; who know that passion has no leisure for elegance; that it is hardly reconcileable with that refinement of thought, or pro-fusion of imagery, which are the principal causes of obscurity; that im-passioned language is simple, negligent, abrupt, vehement, full of repetition, confined to its object, and, though often disorderly yet more than clear, because peculiarly significant; those who have formed such a taste . . . will perhaps not blame us for saying, that we think this song scarcely inferior in spirit and energy to any English Ode that has ap-peared since *Alexander's Feast.*

The theory here invoked owes something to eighteenth-century interpretations of Longinus; but is is an ultra-Romantic critic who asserts that emotion is better when not recollected in tranquillity, and that thought is a
principal cause of obscurity. (The use of such a well-contrived poem as
Dryden's for comparison is puzzling, and in context bathetic.) This
reviewer also emphasises the "peasant" qualities of Burns, whom he calls
an "uninstructed and unpolished rustic."

On 19 January 1802 Robert Bloomfield wrote to the Earl of Buchan:

> The illustrious soul that has left us the name of Burns, has often been
> lowered down to a comparison with me; but the comparison exists more
> in circumstances than in essentials. That man stood up with the stamp
> of superior intellects on his brow, a visible greatness; and great and
> patriotic subjects, which only have called out action, and the powers of
> his mind, which lay inactive while he played calmly and exquisitely the
> pastoral pipe. . . . I am not Burns, neither have I his fire to fan nor to
> quench, nor his passions to control.[18]

These remarks are not only modest but, so far as the comparison goes,
true. Bloomfield, who began life on a Suffolk farm and later became a
shoemaker, showed character and intelligence in making effective use of
his talent; but it is a smaller talent than Burns's, confined mainly to the
sensitive and observant rendering of scenes from country life. The best of
his quiet and pleasant poems is the first, *The Farmer's Boy* (1800), which
describes in couplet verse the work of the changing seasons.

In the *Critical* Southey[19] deliberately avoids reference to Bloomfield's
background until he has given the reader a chance to judge his work on its
own merits, by presenting several long extracts. He grasps the nature of
Bloomfield's talent:

> This poem abounds with beautiful lines of accurate and minute descrip-
> tion. . . . Objects that would have escaped common writers are here
> noticed, and so brought before the eye that every reader recognises the
> truth of the picture; and even trite circumstances appear original in the
> discriminating language of the poet. Thus, in describing the plowman
> at his work, he says,
>
> > "Strong on the wing his busy followers play,
> > Where writhing earth-worms meet th'unwelcome day."
> >
> > "Stopt in her song perchance the starting thrush
> > *Shook a white flower from the black-thorn bush,*
> > Where dew-drops thick as early blossoms hung,
> > And trembled as the minstrel sweetly sung."

Southey points out that the poem is not an imitation of Thomson, and that
the cycle of the boy's occupations "gives a wholeness and originality to the

plan." Bloomfield, he finds, has the eye and the feeling of a poet.

The *British Critic* was also favourable, but slightly patronising, and uncertain whether special standards were not required to judge the work of a peasant poet:

> If this Poem be considered as the production of an uninstructed and unassisted author, without even the ordinary aids of education and improvement, it must unquestionably be termed a great and extraordinary curiosity. If viewed with a severe and critical eye, various errors and defects will frequently present themselves; but there is certainly much poetical feeling, many accurate and interesting descriptions, a warm and vigorous imagination, and versification far more melodious and happy, than could possibly have been expected from a writer of very limited reading, and from a poet of very little experience . . . . The writer's observations will not be found to have been very extensive; but they have the merit of great accuracy, and he appears to have attended to many minute circumstances of rural simplicity, which would probably have escaped a loftier and more capacious mind.

Here the right points are made, but clumsily: the excessive astonishment (to borrow Graham Hough's words, "as though a Trobriand islander were to write *The Golden Bough*") and the absence of irony from the last clause show, at least, no prejudice in favour of peasants. The *Monthly* too was favourable, but its review is too vaguely phrased to have any critical value.

By 1802, when Bloomfield's *Rural Tales, Ballads and Songs* appeared, *The Farmer's Boy* was in its fifth edition. The *British Critic* seems to have assigned *Rural Tales* to a different reviewer, who shows much more enthusiasm. Bloomfield is now described as "a genuine Child of Nature," and in this review the word *natural* is worked very hard:

> The author here relates Tales, in themselves pleasing, in the language of beautiful simplicity, and natural poetry; or pours forth pastoral Songs, full of pleasing ideas, in a style exactly suited to their expression.

"Market Night" contains a "natural and pleasing picture of conjugal tenderness," drawn with genuine feeling and animation; "Richard and Kate" is "full of the simple beauties which result from the plain and true expression of the best natural feelings." Almost all the poems are praised, and there is no adverse criticism. Though responsive to Bloomfield's charm, this critic is too undiscriminating, and too ready to assume that poetry is simply an overflow of "the best natural feelings."

Southey,[20] in the *Critical*, was more judicious. After commenting that Bloomfield now has the difficult task of maintaining a high reputation, he points out several faults. The story of "The Miller's Maid" he blames for resembling "the trick of novel-mongers." Of "Market-Night" he writes:

Mr. Bloomfield sometimes deviates in this poem from his usual truth. A farmer's wife does not apostrophise the winds and the echo, —nor call upon the guardian spirits. . . . Every-day rhymers can write thus; but it is in such passages as the following we discover that the poet is delineat-feelings which he understands.

> "Where have you stay'd? put down your load,
> How have you borne the storm, the cold?
> What horrors did I not forebode—
> *That beast is worth his weight in gold.*"

On the whole, Southey finds, the standard of *The Farmer's Boy* has been maintained. The *Monthly,* in a tardy review, notes the truth and simplicity with which Bloomfield paints the manners of the labouring poor, but hints at "several faults which would require animadversion under different circumstances"; and the reviewer adds that it is no real kindness to Bloomfield to compare him with Dryden.[21]

Burns and Bloomfield were well served by the Reviews: in the *Monthly* Anderson gave Burns warm praise when his name was little known in England, and in the *Critical* Southey did the same for Bloomfield. All the reviews in this section are predominantly favourable, though Burns is properly given the larger share of praise and space. The longest reviews are those of Currie's edition of Burns, but these also contain the smallest proportion of good criticism: far too much attention is given to Burns's life, and the *British Critic* misrepresents his poetry as the product simply of emotional inspiration. The same is true of this journal's account of *Rural Tales,* in which everything is explained by "nature." Southey, in dealing with Bloomfield, deliberately avoids biographical irrelevance; his criticisms are not developed at length, but are accurate and well-illustrated. The *Monthly* gives a cautious, non-committal, and undistinguished performance, except for Anderson's review of the Kilmarnock volume.

Rogers and Campbell

By the end of the eighteenth century the heroic couplet had been used by so many poets, for such different effects, that is was almost impossible to handle this form in an original way. Pope remained the great exemplar of couplet mastery, and his kind of verse still had a direct and powerful influence on many poets, not always to their benefit. Of these, two of the latest were Samuel Rogers and Thomas Campbell. Partly because of the appeal of their themes, these distinctly minor poets were extremely popular with both readers and reviewers in the early nineteenth century,[22] when Wordsworth and Coleridge were still comparatively neglected.

The poem by which Rogers made his name was *The Pleasures of Memory* (1792). His descriptive passages recall *The Deserted Village* in their relaxed verse and quiet melancholy; but in his generalising and reflective passages he tries to achieve something of the antithetical "point" and allusiveness of the *Essay on Man*. The result, at its worst, corresponds fairly closely to the description in Hazlitt's lecture "On the Living Poets":

> He is an elegant, but feeble writer. He wraps up obvious thoughts in a glittering cover of fine words; is full of enigmas with no meaning to them; is studiously inverted, and scrupulously far-fetched; and his verses are poetry, chiefly because no particle, line, or syllable of them reads like prose. . . . It is a tortuous, tottering, wriggling, fidgetty translation of everything from the vulgar tongue, into all the tantalizing, teasing, tripping, lisping, *mimminee-pimminee* of the highest brilliancy and fashion of poetical diction.

Nothing as forceful as this appeared in the Reviews: indeed, the reviewers were generally more susceptible to the appeal of Rogers's themes than critical of his verse. All admired the description of the old mansion with its tapestry, stained glass, and other Gothic features, and the nostalgic recollections of childhood games; all transcribed one or other of these passages, and the *Monthly* reviewer printed both. Nevertheless the *Critical* made a few sharp comments on the looseness of Rogers's thinking and the vagueness of his imagery:

> We do not thoroughly approve of the heart's being styled a "martyr", nor of "flying in the shepherd dance." This word seems rather pressed into the service in another place. The negroe slave is described as expecting after death to wake again on Congo's shore, and
>
> > "Beneath his plaintain's ancient shade, renew
> > The simple transports *that with freedom flew.*"
>
> Again,
>
> > "The school's lone porch, with reverend mosses gray,
> > Just tells the pensive pilgrim where it *lay.*"
>
> Should we not have had *stood* instead of *lay,* if the rhyme would have admitted it?—Some few expressions are rather confused.
>
> > "That hall, where once, in antiquated state,
> > The chair of justice held the grave debate."
>
> The chair of justice, figuratively speaking, might *hear,* but those who urge their complaints against each other before it, properly speaking, "hold the debate."

This criticism is very much to the point, though it would perhaps have seemed sheer pedantry to a later generation that found Dryden and Pope "classics of our prose." Despite these comments the *Critical* judged that the beauties of the poem outweighed its faults, and declared that Rogers's description of the old house "speaks to the heart." The *English* praises the poem in general terms, though the reviewer does criticise Rogers's weakness for alliteration:

The second part opens with these lines —

"Sweet Memory, wafted by thy gentle gale,
Oft up the *t*ide of *t*ime I *t*urn my sail." &c. &c.

Allured by the alliteration, we are almost *t*empted to *t*urn our *t*ail.

(Rogers apparently enjoyed this joke.[23]) The *Analytical* gave the poem only mild, vague praise. The most favourable notice of all appeared in the *Monthly,* where William Enfield admired both Rogers's choice of subject and his treatment and declared:

Correctness of thought, delicacy of sentiment, variety of imagery, and harmony of versification, are the characters which distinguish this beautiful poem, in a degree that cannot fail to ensure its success.

This hardly seems adequate criticism, though Rogers's biographer, writing nearly a century later, finds it "a perfectly just account of the poem."[24] The *Monthly* reviewers may have been well-disposed towards Rogers, because of his close connections with the Dissenters at Newington Green; but we need not suppose anything insincere about Enfield's review, for he had praised Rogers's early anonymous "Ode to Superstition" and read it aloud to his family.[25]

It was *The Pleasures of Memory* which suggested to Campbell the theme of *The Pleasures of Hope* (Edinburgh, 1799) — a performance that earned him the title of "the Pope of Glasgow."[26] Hazlitt describes this poem as being "of the same school" as Rogers's and denounces it in much the same terms. But despite the similarities, *The Pleasures of Hope* has a sweep and vigour which Rogers's poem lacks, and reveals Campbell's power of creating stirring rhythms and sonorous phrases. After 1799 Campbell wrote only two short poems in couplet verse, and his talents found their fullest scope in the less exacting metres of "Hohenlinden" and "The Battle of the Baltic."

All reviews were favourable, though perceptive adverse criticsim also appeared in the *Critical* and *British Critic.* The *Analytical* praised Campbell's zeal for "liberty," but was reluctant to pass judgement on his poetry. The *British Critic* urged him to "beware of the cant of Condorcet and Godwin," yet went on to give a fair review of the poem. This reviewer finds that Campbell has treated his subject "with much genius, and, in general, with good judgement; certainly with a very singular splendour and felicity of versification." Much of this article consists of sharp-eyed criticism of detail:

Some expressions . . . are to be classed among the felicities of inventive genius, being at once just, novel, and very highly poetical; such as "the circling march of sound," and this line,

"Or yield the lyre of Heav'n another string."

The allusion has some obscurity, but it has still more beauty, and therefore is worth investigation. We must . . . remark, that *march*, though excellently applied in the expression just noticed, is among the cant terms of the day, and is so used in other parts of this Poem. Thus,

"The *march* of Genius, and the pow'rs of man."

And,

'—to sound the *march* of time."

Some good lines are singled out and quoted—among them the famous "Like angel-visits, few and far between"—and in conclusion Campbell is earnestly recommended to cultivate his talents and to maintain a strict and severe self-criticism.

Alexander Hamilton, who reviewed *The Pleasures of Hope* in the *Monthly*, specialised in geography and Oriental affairs and seldom dealt with verse. His article is favourable but vague: passages are described as "very poetical," "a pleasing picture," and so on, and the poem is said to prove Campbell's capacity for "genuine and sublime poetry." The *Critical*, in a more exact review, noted that the poem was free from the usual faults of beginners and that the verse was "correct and stately." The reviewer also perceived Campbell's tendency to bombast: "We are sometimes reminded of Dr. Darwin's versification, and of characteristic bulk rather than sublimity of conception." Two turgid passages (lines 58-60, 587-94) are then quoted with the accurate comment that ". . . the words are ponderous and the images gigantic; but they do not partake of sublimity." In the apostrophe to the Polish patriots, however, the critic finds "a glow of feeling, . . . from which much may be hoped."

Both *The Pleasures of Memory* and *The Pleasures of Hope* were over-praised by the reviewers, whose standards of couplet-writing were not high (though by Augustan standards the same may be said of Byron). None the less, close criticism and accurate comment appeared in three articles: the best is the notice of Campbell's poem in the *British Critic*. The *Monthly* and *Analytical* each contributed two poor reviews.

Landor

Walter Savage Landor's *Gebir* and *Crysaor* are quite unlike any poems written by his contemporaries. Though influenced to some extent by Milton, they owe a much larger debt to the Greek and Latin poets whom Landor admired, particularly in their terse language. *Gebir* is an Oriental tale, but has none of the exotic richness of Southey's *Thalaba:* Landor strove for an austere dignity and precision. Its descriptions have "a vivid clearness of outline, which recalls the best classic art."[27] Such poems could never have been widely popular, and their appeal was still further restricted by obscurity arising from over-conciseness. Landor's method of publication also worked against him: after issuing a volume of early verse at London under the title *The Poems of Walter Savage Landor,* he published *Gebir* and *Crysaor* anonymously at Warwick. Thus the discernment of the reviewers was put to a severe test.

Landor's *Poems* (1795) are mostly exercises on familiar themes in couplet verse; the most interesting is "The Birth of Poesy," a reshaping of material from Landor's classical reading. Some of the shorter poems expressed his radical opinions. The *Analytical* found promise in the volume:

> though we do not find in these poems the traces of that patient industry, which fixes the stamp of faultless accuracy upon every line, we discover many proofs of ready invention, bold fancy, a good acquaintance with ancient poetry, and a copious command of poetical language.

The separate pieces are favourably described, though the plan of "The Birth of Poesy" is found obscure. The *British Critic* deprecated Landor's opinions but praised his poetry:

> The author is evidently a young and negligent writer, but is certainly not destitute of poetical talent. The Birth of Poesy shews a lively fancy, but betrays evident marks of haste, and occasional imbecility.
>
> > "His arm encircled now her polished waist,
> > Hers *mantling higher* his glowing neck embraced."
>
> We are frequently disgusted with expletives, and with words of one syllable, against all authority, protracted into two; yet we are not seldom gratified with such lines as these [canto 1, lines 177-80 and canto 2, lines 199-216].

James Bannister in the *Monthly* gave a dull and disparaging review, pronouncing Landor's genius to be wild and eccentric rather than strong and vigorous. But the *Critical*, though it joined in the complaint against the obscurity of "The Birth of Poesy," found Landor's a promising volume:

> what he has given us contains a good deal of pleasing description and smooth versification; and if his powers were more concentrated, —if he chose to exercise judgment as well as fancy, and to give to his pieces that effect which can only be produced by a steady adherence to a judicious and well-digested plan, —we doubt not but he would produce something worthy the attention of the public.

On the whole this was as favourable a reception as the volume deserved, and Landor afterwards wrote that the *Poems* "every-where met with as much commendation as was proper."[28]

Gebir—published anonymously at Warwick in 1798, badly printed and paper-bound—remained in obscurity for a year before Southey's review appeared in the *Critical*. Southey was very much excited by the poem,[29] but in reviewing it gave more space to extracts than to criticism, hoping perhaps that its merits had only to be seen to be recognised. He found the story "strange indeed, and told in language sometimes uncouth, but abounding with such beauties as it is rarely our good fortune to discover"; and after paraphrasing the narrative and illustrating it by ample quotations, he declared:

> The story of this poem is certainly ill chosen and not sufficiently whole; and the language is frequently deficient in perspicuity. These are the faults of Gebir. Of its beauties, our readers must already be sensible. They are of the first order; every circumstance is displayed with a force and accuracy which painting cannot exceed. . . . We have read [this anonymous] poem repeatedly with more than common attention, and far more than common delight.

In February 1800 Coleridge wrote to Southey "You have made a Sect of Gebirites by your Review," adding his opinion that "it was not a *fair,* tho' a very kind, Review."[30] He had not been able to trace the author or to find any of his books in London.

To this "sect of Gebirites" none of the other reviewers, it seems, belonged. Five months after Southey's review appeared John Ferriar, in the *Monthly,* damned the poem with the faintest of praise:

> An unpractised author has attempted . . . the difficult task of relating a romantic story in blank-verse. His performance betrays all the incorrectness and abruptness of inexperience, but it manifests occasionally some talent for description. He has fallen into the common error of those who aspire to the composition of blank-verse, by borrowing too many epithets and phrases from our incomparable Milton.

After complaining of the obscurity of the narrative, Ferriar declares that the author "may produce something more worthy of approbation, if he will labour hard, and delay for a few years the publication of his next performance." In the same month the *British Critic* gave a strange piece of impressionistic criticism:

> Turgid obscurity is the general character of the composition, with now and then a gleam of genuine poetry, irradiating the dark profound. The effect of the perusal is to give a kind of whirl to the brain, more like distraction than pleasure; and something analogous to the sensation

produced, when the end of the finger is rubbed against the parchment of the tambourine.[31]

"After all," wrote Landor in his unpublished *Postscript,* "I do not wonder that they barked at *Gebir* — he came disguised and in tatters." Not unnaturally he thought Southey's a "masterly" review, but was fiercely indignant at Ferriar's "insolence." Scornfully challenging the *Monthly* reviewer to write twenty lines as good as the worst twenty lines in *Gebir,* or to find three more "spirited and classical" pages in the work of any contemporary, he supposed that he would be met with the work of Charles Pybus or Luke Booker — two small poets whom the *Monthly* had recently praised.[32]

Landor's next original publication was *Poetry by the Author of Gebir* (1802). In this volume the most important item is "The Story of Crysaor," a blank-verse narrative describing the punishment of a mythical king who had arrogated to himself privileges due only to gods. The poem is less obscure than *Gebir,* and Sidney Colvin calls it "Landor's finest piece of narrative writing in blank verse."[33] Unluckily Landor placed at the forefront of this volume some inferior verse written as early as 1795, for a poem which was to have been called "The Phocoeans." The *Monthly* ignored the work, and both the *British Critic* and the *Critical* condemned it; neither Review distinguished between the merits of the early fragments and of the later, completed poem. Recalling its notice of the "strange unintelligible poem," *Gebir,* the *British Critic* comments:

> We were then inclined to give the author credit for some poetical abilities; but since, after four years, he still produces only noise and nonsense, we relinquish all our hopes of him.

If the poem means anything, the reviewer declares, it means mischief; but fortunately it is too obscure to be dangerous. The *Critical* was merely abusive. "We know not the *age* of this gentleman; but we can easily perceive that his *wisdom,* at least, is on the wane."

These reviews are disappointing: the critics were encouraging towards Landor's early, conventional verse, but only Southey appreciated either of the original poems which followed. Landor's republicanism, his dislike of kings and authorities, shows itself to some extent in all three publications, and obviously helped to arouse the suspicions of the *British Critic.* But the political significance of these poems is not great: the *British Critic* praised Landor's first volume, and the Foxite *Critical* condemned the third. The generally unfavourable reception of *Gebir* and *Poetry, by the Author of Gebir* was caused chiefly by the obscurity of the first, and by the fact that even "The Story of Crysaor" demands closer attention than readers who had first wrestled with "From the Phocoeans" would be likely to give it.

Thomas Moore

Unlike Landor, Moore presents no difficulties to the understanding: his early poems are gay little trifles which do not pretend to be anything else. He was often attacked for "immorality,"[34] but in his first two volumes the treatment of what he calls "a subject so simple as love"[35] seems trivial rather than dangerous—dewy lips, rosy cheeks, sparkling eyes, with only here and there a touch of real sensuality among these generalised fancies. His wit too is playful rather than profound. Most of Moore's early poems are in short, lyrical verse forms and use rapid rhythms; Shelley admired his verse,[36] and wrote lyrics in the anapaestic metre that Moore had done much to popularise.

Despite its learned Preface, *Odes of Anacreon, Translated into English Verse* (1800) reads like a collection of Moore's own poems, since he had often modified the substance as well as the spirit of the original. Howard Mumford Jones writes that "in the absence of any important reviewing medium, the book had to make its way by word of mouth";[37] but in reality it received three very favourable notices, the first at least of which appeared early enough to help its sale. The *Critical* praised the "taste" of Anacreon, alleging that this kept his poems from being offensive even where they lacked moral refinement, and found the same quality in Moore's versions:

> Mr. Moore seems to have a clear perception of the peculiar graces of the original, and has not been unsuccessful in transfusing them into his native language. His versification is at once polished and easy; and he has imitated, as far perhaps as it was possible in a translation, that concise simplicity of phrase which renders the odes of Anacreon so attractive.

The reviewer notes several of the additions made by Moore to the sense of the original, but praises most of them as being in Anacreon's own spirit and manner. Thus in Ode XV,

> The second line of the couplet,
>> "On his harp then sink in slumbers,
>> Dreaming still of dulcet numbers,"
>
> has not the shadow of an archetype in the original: but he who can condemn such a beauty must have a frozen heart.

The Ode as a whole is said to have been "exquisitely translated." Moore's work is "chaste, elegant, perspicuous and lively," and his prefatory "Anacreontic" shows him able to handle the lyre with a master's ease.

In the *Monthly,* Dr. Charles Burney concentrates on the musical qualities of the translation. He congratulates Moore in general on his success, but complains of harsh lines and "unlyrical words," and prefers Fawkes's translation of Ode VI as being smoother than Moore's.[38] The *British Critic* replied by printing both versions of this Ode and declaring that Moore's was very much the better; this may be true once it is accepted that Moore, in this critic's words, aims at "an expansion of the author's sentiments by an elegant paraphrase", not a literal translation. The same reviewer pronounces that Moore has the talents of an original poet, and that some of his versions surpass their originals. As further proof of Moore's powers he refers to *The Poems of Thomas Little*, which had appeared before this belated review. But the critic objects to an occasional diffuseness and to a superabundance of epithets — "a very general error with poets of the present day." He concludes:

> The author is certainly a young man of elegant taste, and of a lively, though not sufficiently regulated imagination. If he learns . . . to restrain that imagination within due bounds, and to apply it to subjects of more importance, and of a more moral tendency (instead of ringing perpetual changes upon "dimples and smiles, kisses and blisses, racy tides, and sparkling bowls") few poets of the present day will equal, and perhaps scarcely any excel, him.

Jeffrey's well-known *Edinburgh* review of *Anacreon* appeared in the number for July 1803. It scores over the earlier reviews by being in the form of a long, readable essay, and by some just criticism of the "tinsel" in Moore's poetry; though in pointing out his superabundance of epithets Jeffrey had been anticipated by the *British Critic*. But in his other main criticisms Jeffrey is less just than the earlier reviewers. His condemnation of the work on moral grounds as "calculated for a bagnio" seems excessive now and, if we may judge by the initial reception of *Anacreon*, was excessive then. He demonstrates with great thoroughness that Moore's is not a close translation, and apparently finds this intolerable; he may have the *Critical* in mind when he writes:

> There are some gentle readers of poesy . . . whose feelings are abhorrent from the most moderate restrictions on the liberty of translation. These personages entreat . . . that full scope should be given to all possible improvements; and they love to repeat (after their harmless and kindly manner), that it is unjust to reprove him who increases the sum of our pleasure. . . . Those readers for whom the classics wrote, seldom wish to see their favourite authors converted into vehicles of modern sentiments.

But to point out (as the *Critical* and *British Critic* did) that Moore's work is an "elegant paraphrase" and can be enjoyed as such seems more reasonable in a reviewer than to affect Jeffrey's kind of indignation. Jeffrey's treatment of *Anacreon* is obviously influenced, if not controlled, by a desire to keep up the "slashing" reputation won by the review of *Thalaba*.

The Poetical Works of the Late Thomas Little (1801) contains *jeux d'esprit* and short love-poems, half-sensual, half-sentimental, on themes which recall Anacreon and the Latin love-poets, but are treated with an extreme simplicity that is Moore's own. (The original edition included some "schoolboy improprieties" which were later expurgated.) The *Critical* was the first Review to attack Moore on moral grounds:[39]

> The age in which we live has imposed upon him the necessity of employ-ing decent language; but few ages have ever been disgraced by a volume more corrupt in its whole spirit and tendency. . . . The Monk had its spots; — this is leprous all over.

The reviewer none the less pays high compliments to the literary merits of the poems, which he declares "abound in wit, and discover a power of language and a simplicity which have rarely been equalled." The *Monthly* review was by Ferriar, who, as a reader of Rabelais,[40] made light of the im-proprieties and even over-praised the volume:

> It is with unusual pleasure that we here find ourselves called to review the productions of a real favourite of the Muses. We acknowledge in these poems the fire of genius, the feeling, the taste, and the precision, which are characteristic of those authors
>
> "Who, from the Ancients, like the Ancients write."
>
> . . . although some of the poems may be such as rigid virtue must disap-prove, decency of expression has been carefully consulted; and nothing occurs which can disgust a general reader of poetry.

Ferriar finds in these poems "tenderness and simplicity; — genuine simplici-ty, which gives force to expression, by divesting language of every superfluous decoration." The emphasis on "genuine" may be intended to contrast Moore's poems with the short pieces by Southey that Ferriar had also reviewed. The pronouncements of the *British Critic* are confusing, as though the reviewer had realised that he had been too hasty in praising this volume in the course of his review of *Anacreon:*

> though many of the Poems have little but smoothness of versification to recommend them, and some of them are, in a high degree, excep-tionable, yet there are several which display spirit as well as elegance, and some which not only are consistent with morality, but beautiful-ly enforce it.

The reviewer then quotes "To a Boy, with a Watch" — one of the very few poems that would support his last statement.

Moore was clearly much more to the taste of the eighteenth-century reviewers than Landor: ample justice was done to his talent, even when his *Thomas Little* volume was being criticised on moral grounds. Ferriar's defence of that volume is rather unsatisfactory, seeming as it does to imply that so long as no four-letter words are used only "rigid virtue" can object. But one must be grateful for a critical approach that does not condemn all literature that might shock young girls.

The Della Cruscans and William Gifford

To us who do not read them there is something slightly mythical about the Della Cruscans; but in the late 1780s and early 1790s they made a strong impact on English poetry. Robert Merry ("Della Crusca"), Hannah Cowley ("Anna Matilda"), and their friends had great talent for self-advertisement, and their verse achieved wide circulation through *The World* and *The Oracle,* through the more important *European Magazine,* and in their own collections and anthologies. Some of what they wrote was merely dull, but much was bad in a way that appealed to the unsettled taste of the age — by its emotionalism, its parade of sensibility, its "gaudiness and inane phraseology," and its strong or surprise effects that now seem absurd. These features of Della Cruscan poetry can be related to wider cultural changes, and no doubt much bad poetry of the 1790s would have shown the same tendencies if these writers had never lived. Nevertheless, there are enough indications of specific influence on the earliest writings of Wordsworth, Coleridge, and many lesser poets[41] to make it seem that here if anywhere was an occasion when the Reviews should have fulfilled their role as guardians of the public taste. This section will examine the response of each Review in turn to the main Della Cruscan publications: *The Poetry of the World* (vols. 1-2, 1788; reprinted with additions as *The British Album,* 1790; vols. 3-4, 1791); *The Poetry of Anna Matilda* (1788); *Diversity, a Poem, by Della Crusca* (1788); and *The Laurel of Liberty* (1790), a poem in praise of the French Revolution that Merry published over his own name. The reception given to the two satires by which William Gifford is generally supposed to have crushed the Della Cruscans[42] — *The Baviad* (1791) and *The Maeviad* (1795) — will also be discussed.

Most of the *Monthly* reviews of Della Cruscan poetry were written by a clergyman, Christopher Moody. They are very favourable, and almost wholly uncritical: Moody's usual method is to introduce each publication with some handsome compliments, to follow these by long extracts, and finally to declare that minute criticism of such poetry would be invidious. His review of *The Poetry of the World* (volumes 1 and 2) contains the statement:

Della Crusca, who, we must confess, has pleased us most, appears to be a gentleman, a scholar, and a poet; and several of his pieces claim a distinguished place in the class of modern poetry.

In the same article Merry is described as "a modern poet of eminence." Reviewing *The Poetry of Anna Matilda*, Moody is "agreeably disappointed"[43] to find that the author, contrary to her previous promise, is still writing verse; and though he objects to the line "He only knows adroitly how to trill" (intended as a compliment to Merry's poetic talents) he declares that her volume will be read with pleasure. In his review of *Diversity* he approves Merry's decision to ignore the rules of "regular" lyric poetry laid down by Mason, since

> great geniuses are to be considered as sovereign princes, enjoying independent jurisdiction, and not to be shackled and restrained by the ordinances and decrees of each other. The creative mind is a law to itself, and should be permitted to mark its own way, and direct its own course.

Notwithstanding some small faults, *Diversity* is pronounced "the production of a true poet." Moody likewise admires many poems of *The British Album,* including the absurd "Interview" describing the fateful meeting of Della Crusca and Anna Matilda. In reviewing volumes 3 and 4 of *The Poetry of the World* he praises the managers of Bell's newspaper "for the exertions which they have made to rescue newspaper poetry from disgrace, by inviting some acknowledged favourites of the Muses to decorate their pages"; and, listing the contributors, he finds that such names promise the reader entertainment.

Confronted by *The Baviad,* Moody admitted that

> even those poets, who are far from being destitute of genius, discover an extreme aptitude to overlook sense, for the sake of a pleasing flow of words; and to mistake fustian and bombast for elevated diction and true simplicity.

But while hoping that Gifford's satire would help to correct such errors, he finds this writer "apt to be intemperate and undiscriminating," and comments:

> We do not approve . . . of that ill-natured fastidiousness, which, for the sake of some defect, would deny all praise; nor can we be pleased with the tone of sovereign contempt which this author assumes, in speaking of the productions of some modern writers.

His final verdict is that Gifford is "certainly too severe," especially in his ungallant strictures on the female poets. His comment on *The Maeviad* is similar:

If the writers, whom he so satirically criticises, were so contemptible, the Baviad was satire enough, and the repetition of the stroke must be of the nature of Falstaff's valour in stabbing the dead Hotspur. This looks like ill-nature, particularly when it is united with harsh and ungentleman-like expressions: and remarkably so when speaking of ladies, as is sometimes the case in the notes to this new Dunciad.

Considered as a defence of the poets he had previously admired, this is remarkably weak; but Moody has obviously lost confidence in his earlier opinions, and is trying to disguise the fact that Gifford has done what he, as an official guardian of the public taste, should have done some years before. That he recognises the power of Gifford's satire is evident from the phrase "this new Dunciad," and from the implication that the Della Cruscans are dead.

One *Monthly* reviewer, however, did not fail in his duty. Some months before *The Baviad* appeared, Thomas Pearne of Peterhouse gave an excellent analysis of Merry's poetry as represented by *The Laurel of Liberty:*

> Mr. Merry's art is too visible. . . . From a want of *sufficient real* labour, there is, in parts of his poem, a *great deal* of *apparent* labour, difficulty, and toil, to attain what he cannot reach. Hence, at times his harsh, forced, and inverted constructions; his imperfect expressions; his uncouth elisions; his flat and prosaic sentiment, and diction; and hence too, at other times, his quaint affectation; his obtrusive finery; his obscure and remote conceits; his accumulated and mixed imagery; and the whole train of what, in theatrical language, are called *clap-traps.*

These charges are solidly backed up by quotations; thus, in discussing Merry's affected language, Pearne writes:

> When Mr. Merry calls the sun, the *lord of lustre,* and talks of *lawny vales; gleamy meteors; streamy warblings; paly shrowds; pearly panoplies;* and *lightless crowds;* we do not approve; but when he soars a flight higher, and entertains us with *tissued rays; gauzy zephyrs; filmy rains;* and *gossamery tears;* we do not understand. . . . This pretty tinsel excites no ideas in our minds; nor, we believe, in any minds, but such as run away with sound, and conceive it to be sense.

Pearne's is clearly the one satisfactory review of the Della Cruscan poets to appear in this journal.

Blame for this generally disappointing performance must be divided between Moody and his editor. Had Griffiths sent the Della Cruscan volumes to a more competent reviewer of poetry, the *Monthly,* doyen of the Reviews, would have been well placed to give a lead in exposing the pretensions of these poets. That he did not do so may have been partly from an unwillingness to oppose what he believed to be a general verdict in their favour. Pearne was given *The Laurel of Liberty* to review, not because Griffiths was dissatisfied with Moody's articles, but because Pearne was at that time reviewing publications on the French Revolution. His notice would have been still more severe had it not been for the need to preserve an element of "consistency" with the earlier articles; and Griffiths softened the effect still further by adding some compliments to Merry for his generous attitude towards Burke. Pearne approved of these additions, but disagreed with Griffiths's estimate that Merry was "the reigning favourite with the public." Only Pearne's side of this correspondence survives; it confirms one's respect for his critical and independent judgement.[44] On Griffiths's behalf it must be said that he did, after all, publish Pearne's review, the general effect of which remains overwhelmingly unfavourable.

Divided counsels may also have been at work in the *Critical*, for its reviews are usually indecisive. On *The Poetry of the World*, for example, its comment is:

Many [poems] are undoubtedly extremely elegant, and we frequently meet with striking and original thoughts happily expressed; but our admiration of them is by no means as exalted as Mr. Topham's appears to be. We will not, however, detract from their general character by objections which may be urged against particular passages.

Similarly, while pointing out some "truly ridiculous" passages in Merry's play *Ambitious Vengeance* (included in volume 1 of *The Poetry of the World*), he qualifies this censure by praising the "spirit and energy" of others. The *Critical* was likewise reluctant wholly to condemn *Diversity*. After quoting the opening, in which Genius and Rapture are personified, the reviewer observes:

There is, we think, great splendour of imagery in this passage, and some lines are not destitute of genuine poetic fire; but the fire sometimes scorches instead of warming; and our sight is dazzled, not enlightened. It appears in part evidently dictated by "Genius," but the "maniac Rapture" seems likewise to have had a share in this unequal composition.

The first really hostile review in the *Critical* is of *The Laurel of Liberty*, which is condemned for its unqualified approval of the French Revolution. This journal greeted *The Baviad* with approval:

Our author, a little inhumanly, with one blow of his caestus, is eager to destroy the whole corps; and if his wholesome reprehension will contribute to check the flimzy conceits, and the insipid nonsense which is at present called . . . poetry, he may be acquitted of any very great offence.

The Maeviad was likewise pronounced to be keen and spirited, though the *Critical,* now Foxite in its politics, makes one thrust at the Tory satirist:

> We must, however, admonish the author of the Maeviad, that folly has now been chastised sufficiently; let him next endeavour to produce some work of merit, which may stand the test of that criticism by which he tries the productions of others.

Though the *Critical* did little to "chastise folly" when it was necessary, it joined in the attack once *The Baviad* had appeared.

The *English* attacked the Della Cruscans almost from the first. Its only favourable review was that of *The Poetry of the World,* and even in this article the reviewer shows himself alive to the characteristic defects of Della Cruscan poetry:

> There is a great command of numbers in their poems, much imagery and poetical enthusiasm; but that enthusiasm is not everywhere under the guidance of judgement and good taste; the orgasm is sometimes so violent as to carry the poet far beyond the precincts of common sense.

He quotes some examples of exaggeration and absurdity, with amusing comments. *The Poetry of Anna Matilda* is criticized more severely: the author is said to possess some fancy, but to be shamefully inaccurate and ignorant. In "Invocation," for example,

> Anna Matilda, being in a violent perspiration, invokes the zephyr. . . . But no person, whose poetical creed is orthodox, can believe that her prayer was heard. The abode of the soft, the gentle, the genial zephyr, is in the *West;* whereas this lady calls him from the *North,* and from some outlandish country named "the Artic". . . . It was even a singular mercy that Boreas did not break forth, all streaming with rain and rattling with ice, and give her such a drenching as had effectually cooled her constitution.

Roy Clark calls this article "a really withering criticism," and justly remarks that "such a review, characterized by humorous ridicule, was much more appropriate than Gifford's lumbering couplets."[45] The *English* employed similar banter upon *Diversity:* the obscurity and excessive ornamentation of this ode are contrasted with the effective simplicity of Dryden, and after much detailed and sometimes ironical criticism the reviewer summarizes:

> The writer certainly possesses talents for poetry; but he wants chastity and sobriety in his composition; his thoughts are not seldom far-fetched,

his pathos is too *pretty,* and the labour of art frequently too apparent. . . .
We would recommend to Della Crusca to lay aside much of his gorgeous
trappings; we would advise him to woo the maid *Simplicity.*

This journal continues to comment on Merry's absurdities and affectations
in its review of *The Laurel of Liberty.* When his lines on the French revolutionaries are quoted —

> For by their *efforts* is this *axiom* known,
> That when they have the will, the strength's their own —

the reviewer's italics hint that axioms are usually grasped without effort;
and of Merry's apostrophe to the philosophers

> By whose strong arms the letter'd lightnings hurl'd,
> Have pierc'd the hov'ring shadow of the world.

he remarks: "We leave this passage to the *initiated,* for our unenlightened
minds cannot reach such *excessive sublimities!*" Merry's weaknesses are
diagnosed as "a deficiency of judgement, and too violent a passion for ornamentation." Yet when *The Baviad* appeared the *English* was not undiscriminating in its approval. While the reviewer agreed with Gifford that
"a pompous and glittering phraseology, a substitution of sound for sense,
. . . is the predominant failing of modern authors," and praised the genius
of Gifford's poem, he also found in it "a degree of acrimony, and a want of
politeness, which we cannot approve," and added that "to give no other
proof of the demerit of an author [Jerningham] than harsh and illiberal
abuse, is totally unjustifiable." Of all five Reviews the *English* has the best
record for criticising the Della Cruscans.

The *Analytical* paid these poets little attention. Mary Wollstonecraft
gave a brief, rather favourably worded account of *Diversity,* and she or
another reviewer praised the *The Laurel of Liberty* for its matter but not
its manner:

> The sentiments, we acknowledge, afforded us more pleasure than the
> rhymes in which they were conveyed; for affectation is, we think, some-
> times suffered to creep into the style, and an unnecessary pomp of
> words often tickles the ear without moving the heart, or leaving any
> striking idea in the mind.

By the time the *British Critic* was founded, the Della Cruscans had ceased
to publish, but a favourable notice of *The Maeviad* in that journal showed
that it was at least capable of wisdom after the event:

When the Baviad made its appearance, public taste was menaced with no little danger. An inundation of poetic compositions had been poured upon the public, in which, under the plausible mask of well-flowing lines, the tritest sentiments were so bedizened with the frippery of affectation, conceit, and vanity, that the votaries of common sense gazed in silent astonishment, and were induced, though almost ashamed to ask of one another, if "more was not meant than met the ear."

The critic declares that *The Baviad* cannot easily be matched among English satires since *The Dunciad*, and that *The Maeviad* shows a poet capable of almost any undertaking.

Thirty years later, Scott remembered that Gifford had "squabashd at one blow a set of coxcombs who might have humbugd the world long enough" (*Journal*, 17 January 1827). This remark appears to do little credit to the reviewers, but it is not quite true. The only critic who showed enthusiasm for the Della Cruscans was the egregious Moody in the *Monthly;* and his praise was finally offset by the admirable criticism of Pearne. The *English* attacked their style of writing from the first; the *Critical* gave some praise, but also sensible adverse comment; the *Analytical* largely ignored them. *The Laurel of Liberty* came in for hostile comment from the three Foxite Reviews as well as, more expectedly, from the *British Critic*. Since this poem was given preponderantly unfavourable notices a year before *The Baviad* appeared, it looks as though Gifford was swimming with a tide that had already turned. Once he came upon the scene, the reviewers aknowledged the truth of his satire, though they also noted that righteous indignation was made the pretext for indulging a vein of brutality.

Early Poems of Wordsworth and Coleridge

Jeffrey's long-continued attacks on the "Lake School" are so well known that even today, when texts or summaries of most of the earlier reviews are easily accessible,[46] Wordsworth and Coleridge are still habitually thought of as coming to maturity in a climate of critical hostility. Thus of "Goody Blake" F. W. Bateson can write "even the reviewers liked it," as though such favour were quite exceptional and gave proof of the poem's "Augustan" qualities.[47] It will already be clear that to speak of a general "allegiance to the Augustans"[48] is quite misleading, though naturally some critics were less advanced in their tastes than others. It should also be remembered that when the *Edinburgh Review* was founded, Wordsworth and Coleridge had been before the public as poets for nine and eight years respectively, in which time Wordsworth had published three volumes of verse, Coleridge four, and the two men jointly one; and *Lyrical Ballads* had long since been thoroughly reviewed. Despite obvious differences, it will be convenient to consider the reception of the separate early works of these two poets in one section.

The desire to record with exact truthfulness the impressions made by natural scenes and objects is a recurrent feature of Wordsworth's poetry from "The Vale of Esthwaite" onwards. The chief positive quality of *An Evening Walk* (1793) and *Descriptive Sketches* (1793) is exact observation imaginatively rendered; of *An Evening Walk* Wordsworth said in 1843 that there was not an image in it that he had not observed. But in both poems fresh description is diluted by conventional phrasing — men and fields becoming swains and lawns — and personifications and other formal devices abound. Epithets such as *sombrous, foamy,* and *paly,* borrowed from Erasmus Darwin or the Della Cruscans, also occur.[49] Thus the poems combine one of Wordsworth's characteristic virtues with some very poetic diction and some gaudy, if not inane, phraseology.

Both poems were published by Johnson, and the *Analytical* gave the earliest notices, taking a balanced view of their merits and defects. The reviewer sees that the "diversified pictures of nature" in *Descriptive Sketches* "could only have been produced by a lively imagination, furnished by actual and attentive observation with an abundant store of materials"; but he finds that a connecting narrative is needed, and that at times Wordsworth's meaning is obscured by "a certain laboured and artificial cast of expression." In *An Evening Walk* the same critic notices "distinct and circumstantial views of nature" which "discover the eye of a diligent observer, and the hand of an able copyist." The *Critical* also praised *An Evening Walk* for "new and picturesque imagery" that "would not disgrace our best descriptive poets," quoting several apt passages, and accurately pointed out the debt to Langhorne in the description of the soldier's wife (lines 241-300 in the 1793 text). But a less perceptive reviewer seems to have dealt with *Descriptive Sketches,* which the *Critical* condemned for its harsh and prosaic lines, ill-chosen (though sometimes "glowing") imagery, and feeble and insipid decription. The notices in the *English* were perfunctory.

Thomas Holcroft[50] of the *Monthly* was cast into a gloom by Wordsworth's title-pages:

More descriptive poetry! . . . Have we not yet enough? Must eternal changes be rung on uplands and lowlands, and nodding forests, and brooding clouds, and cells, and dells, and dingles? Yes; more, and yet more: so it is decreed.

It is not surprising that this surfeited reviewer did less than justice to what was good in Wordsworth's early poems. Yet he discharged the negative functions of a critic very effectively by spelling out the point previously made by the *Analytical* about their "laboured and artificial" language:

> Return delights! with whom my road beg*un*,
> When *Life rear'd* laughing *up her* morning *sun*;
> When Transport kiss'd away my April tear,
> "Rocking as in a dream the tedious year."

Life *rearing* up the sun! Transport kissing away an *April* tear and *rocking* the year as in a dream! Would the cradle had been specified! Seriously, these are figures which no poetical licence can justify. . . . Mr. Wordsworth is a scholar, and, no doubt, when reading the works of others, a critic. There are passages in his poems which display imagination, and which afford hope for the future: but, if he . . . will critically question every line that he has written, he will find many which, he must allow, call loudly for amendment.

Holcroft's review may well have had important consequences. Wordsworth almost certainly read this article and was galled by it, for on 23 May 1794 he wrote to William Mathews: "They [the two poems] have been treated with unmerited contempt by some of the periodical publications, and others have spoken in higher terms of them than they deserve."[51] He also mentions that he has been revising the poems. In future editions these lines from *An Evening Walk* were omitted; and the opening of *Descriptive Sketches,* which Holcroft discussed in similar terms, was severely revised. It is possible that Wordsworth's historic rejection of "gaudiness and inane phraseology" began at the moment when he perceived the truth of Holcroft's criticisms.

Coleridge, at Jesus College, was more enthusiastic about *Descriptive Sketches* than Holcroft had been: "seldom, if ever," he wrote later, "was the emergence of an original poetic genius above the literary horizon more evidently announced."[52] His own early poems were different in kind from Wordsworth's, and very diverse in their qualities. His chief interests were religion, philosophy, and politics, and his aim was probably to combine his opinions about all three in an elaborate philosophical poem: several of his more ambitious early works seem rehearsals for this enterprise. At the same time he was developing the less formal style of his "conversation-poems," modelled on Cowper's *Task.* By 1798 Coleridge had written good poetry of both kinds, though his public manner was still occasionally marred by bombast and his more personal poems by effusiveness and sentimentality. Neither kind of writing prepared readers for "The Ancient Mariner."

Coleridge came before the reviewers with some advantages denied to Wordsworth. His political and religious opinions, though individual and continuously developing, were very much of a kind to win favour from the Foxites and Dissenters who in 1794 still controlled four out of the five Reviews. This favour was reinforced by personal contacts. A great stroke of luck was his meeting in September 1794 with George Dyer — a Christ's Hospital and Cambridge man of an earlier generation, and a fellow Unitarian. Dyer liked Coleridge and his poetry, and since he reviewed for both the *Critical* and the *Analytical* he could at least make sure that Coleridge's early works were not overlooked by these journals; in fact the first few notices in the *Critical* were probably written by Dyer himself.[53] Two other Unitarian well-wishers were Dr. John Aikin, whom Coleridge may have met at Bristol through John Prior Estlin, and his sister Mrs. Barbauld, whom Coleridge visited in August 1797 and again in October 1798. Aikin reviewed two of Coleridge's works in the *Monthly*, and to him and his sister may be tentatively assigned reviews of two other works in the *Analytical*.[54] Last, if Coleridge's statement is to be credited, his friend Francis Wrangham reviewed for the *British Critic;* and though the evidence is not strong, Wrangham may have been responsible for two favourable articles in 1799.[55]

The Fall of Robespierre (Cambridge, 1794) is described as "an historical drama," and is certainly better regarded as a dramatic poem than as a play. The second and third of its three acts were written by Southey, though his name did not appear on the title-page. The work attempts to dramatise contemporary French affairs somewhat in the manner of *Julius Caesar;* it expresses strong enthusiasm for the cause of French liberty, and ends with the alarming prediction that, now that Robespierre is overthrown, France

> . . . shall wield
> The thunder-bolt of vengeance — she shall blast
> The despot's pride, and liberate the world!

Compared with Wordsworth's early poems *The Fall of Robespierre* seems a facile piece of work, yet all three notices were favourable. The *Critical* reviewer, who seems almost certain to have been Dyer, pointed out the difficulties of treating such a subject and gave Coleridge high marks for his attempt:

> It affords ample testimony, that the writer is a genuine votary of the Muse, and several parts of it will afford much pleasure to those who can relish the beauties of poetry. Indeed a writer who could produce so much beauty in so little time, must possess powers that are capable of raising him to a distinguished place among the English poets.

Dyer thought the first act the best but also admired the closing lines, and pronounced the drama as a whole to be "a very agreeable specimen of Mr. Coleridge's poetical talents." The *Analytical* review is likely to have been written by Dr. John Aikin,[56] who disapproved of "the practice of exhibiting recent events in a dramatic form," but judged Coleridge to be "tolerably successful in his attempt to imitate the impassioned language of the french orators"; the closing lines are quoted to illustrate his "talent for dramatic declamation." The *British Critic* gave a review short enough to be quoted in full:

> Mr. Coleridge has aimed at giving a dramatic air to a detail of Conventional speeches, which they were scarcely capable of receiving. The sentiments, however, in many instances are naturally, though boldly conceived, and expressed in language, which gives us reason to think the Author might, after some probation, become no unsuccessful wooer of the tragic muse.

Since all three reviewers saw promise in *Robespierre*, it is a pity that they did not discuss the work more fully; even Dyer's piece, which is the longest, suffers from a lack of specific criticism.

The lectures Coleridge published in 1795 as *A Moral and Political Lecture, Conciones ad Populum,* and *The Plot Discovered* won praise from the liberal Reviews (modified by cautions about the "vehemence" or "violence" of his language) and disapproval from the *British Critic.*[57] By 1796 he had won some reputation as an active speaker and writer on the antiministerialist side, and had widened the circle of his personal contacts. He had also developed considerably as a poet. *Poems on Various Subjects* (1796) contained the "Religious Musings"—Coleridge's most highly wrought piece so far, on which he "rested for all his poetical credit"[58] — and an early conversation-poem, "The Eolian Harp." Also included were the "Monody on the Death of Chatterton," a group of political Epistles, the juvenile "Songs of the Pixies," and shorter poems such as "To a Young Ass," "To an Infant," and "To the Nightingale." Twenty years later Coleridge remembered that this volume had been well received, although critics had objected to "obscurity, a general turgidness of diction, and a profusion of new coined double epithets."[59] His memory was accurate. All the reviews were gratifying except for the first, which appeared in the *British Critic;* and even that journal gave only a few words of mild praise mildly qualified, and pronounced the volume free from subversive tendencies "apart from the violent rant to Lord Stanhope."[60]

The reviewers on the liberal side saw Coleridge as an unconventional but highly imaginative poet. Most of them regretted the unconventionalities and set them down to carelessness; but John Aikin in the *Monthly* saw them almost as signs of genius. Coleridge's bent, he finds, is for "boldness and novelty of conception, strength of figure, and sublimity of sentiment":

> Not that we mean to represent him as unqualified for producing
> pictures of beauty and elegance, or for depicting the soft and tender
> emotions; of both of which there are such striking examples in his
> works, that the sweet and the pathetic may be reckoned peculiarly
> congenial to his nature: but even in these the manner of an original
> thinker is predominant; and as he has not borrowed the ideas, so he
> has not fashioned himself to the polish and correctness of modern
> verse. Such a writer may occasionally fall under the censure of criti-
> cism: but he will always be, what so few proportionally are, an
> interesting object to the genuine lover of poetry.

Aikin finds the "wild irregular strain" of "Chatterton" appropriate to its
theme, and some of its touches very moving and fanciful; he also finds
"pleasing imagery" in the "Songs of the Pixies." But his warmest admiration goes to "Religious Musings":

> its subject, and the manner of treating it, place it on the top of the
> scale of sublimity. . . . Often obscure, uncouth, and verging to
> extravagance, but generally striking and impressive to a supreme
> degree, it exhibits that ungoverned career of fancy and feeling which
> equally belongs to the poet and the enthusiast. The book of Rev-
> elations may be a dangerous fount of prophecy, but it is no mean
> Helicon of poetic inspiration.

Aikin then quotes lines 277-322, with the comment: "Who will deny genius
to such conceptions . . . ?"

From the *Critical* a friendly review was perhaps to be expected: not only
was Dyer, it seems, once more the reviewer, but Coleridge himself had
recently joined the staff of the Review.[61] Yet the article reads like an honest
piece of criticism, and though it gives the same sort of account as the
Monthly review its total effect is rather less adulatory. After praising Coleridge's "fine invention, and . . . lively imagination," the passion and
energy of his poems, and his "enthusiastic love of liberty," Dyer discusses
his faults in some detail. The irregular metre of "Chatterton" is "not, in
our judgment, consistent with the laws of poetry"; and in other pieces "the
versification is not always sufficiently polished, and, by not having the
pause and accents in the proper place, grates upon a correct ear." Dyer objects to some archaisms borrowed from Shakespeare and Spenser, and also
to some new coinages:

> The liberty too taken by Mr. Coleridge of coining words, and the
> impetuosity of a most powerful imagination, hurry him sometimes
> into what his readers will call bombast.[62] For example —

-----yea, and there
Unshuddered, unaghasted, he shall view
Ev'n the seven spirits, who in the latter day
Will shower hot pestilence on the sons of men.

After some more criticism of Coleridge's verse, Dyer proceeds to a favourable but not unfair summing-up:

Mr. Coleridge's blemishes are such as are incident to young men of luxuriant imaginations, which time and experience will, we doubt not, enable him to correct. His beauties are those of a very superior genius: — a richer line than the last of the three following we scarcely ever remember reading:

O! aged women, ye who weekly catch
The morsel tossed by law-forc'd charity,
And die so slowly, that none call it murder.

The *Analytical* gave a shorter but essentially similar account of Coleridge's volume:

The poems [have] very different degrees of merit: some of them appear to have been elaborated with great pains; others, to have been the negligent productions of a momentary impulse. The numbers are not always harmonious; and the language, through a redundancy of metaphor, and the frequent use of compound epithets, sometimes becomes turgid: but every where the writer discovers a lively imagination, and a ready command of poetical language. The general character of the composition is rather that of splendour than of simplicity; and the reader is left more strongly impressed with an idea of the strength of the writer's genius, than of the correctness of his taste.

This reviewer did not think the Epistles very successful, and seemed uncertain what to make of "Religious Musings": he describes it as "a pretty long poem, in blank verse, chiefly valuable for the importance of the sentiments which it contains, and the ardour with which they are expressed." The *English*[63] put rather more emphasis on the faults of the volume:

Mr. Coleridge is neither deficient in imagination nor in poetical expression, but there is a want of correctness and polish discernible throughout the publication; and his poetical *furor* sometimes leads him to the confines of absurdity. He is fond of coining new words, and much too profuse of compound epithets.

Among the coinages cited are "unshudder'd," "unaghasted," "unclimbing," and "imbrothelled"; among the compound epithets are "storm-vex'd," "soul-jaundiced," "gloom-pampered," and "tempest-shatter'd." As an instance of the absurdity into which Coleridge sometimes strays the reviewer quotes the line "But Love, who *heard* the *silence* of my thoughts," while he illustrates the poet's "genius, tenderness and humanity" by giving stanzas from the "Epistle to Sara."

Apart from the perfunctory notice in the *British Critic,* this is a good group of reviews: Coleridge was delighted by the praise, and was disposed to agree with some of the criticisms of his diction. On 4 July 1796, when all the Reviews except the *English* were out, he wrote to Estlin: "The Reviews have been wonderful—The Monthly has *cataracted* panegyric on my poems; the Critical has *cascaded* it; and the Analytical has *dribbled* it with very tolerable civility. The Monthly has at least done justice to my Religious Musings."[64] Later that day he repeated the first part of this remark to Poole and added: "as to the British Critic, they *durst not* condemn and they would not praise—so contented themselves with 'commending me, as a *Poet*[']—and allowed me 'tenderness of sentiment & elegance of diction.' "[65] One of the main adverse criticisms of the reviewers—that of too great a readiness to coin new words—simply confirmed what Coleridge had previously suspected. On 5 May 1796, before any reviews had appeared, he wrote to Poole:

> There are . . . instances of vicious affectation in the phraseology of ["Religious Musings"]—'Unshudder'd, unaghasted' for instance.—Good Writing is produced more effectually by rapidly glancing thro' language as it already exists, than by an hasty recourse to the *Mint* of Invention.[66]

These two coinages were criticised both by the *Critical* and by the *English,* and the passage was subsequently revised.[67] In the second edition (1797) of his *Poems* Coleridge publicly made "his acknowledgments to the different reviewers for the assistance which they have afforded him in detecting his poetic deficiencies."[68]

Coleridge's *Ode on the Departing Year* (Bristol, 1796) is written in his more public style, and shows a characteristic interfusion of religious and political ideas. It describes a vision in which the Spirit of the passing Year recounts, in Heaven, the events it has seen on earth, and the Spirit of the Earth implores God to punish Britain—"the bloody island." Coleridge wrote the poem in three days under difficult conditions,[69] and despite its vigorous dramatic movement and some good phrases it is not one of his best poems: the tone is sometimes shrill and sometimes (as at the close) embarrassingly smug. The language too still showed some of the faults of which Coleridge himself was aware.

Only two Reviews noticed the poem, one favourably and the other adversely. In the *Monthly* John Aikin[70] continued to "cataract praise," and though he noticed the effects of haste he recognised that the poem was a topical one: the "departing year" would not wait for Coleridge to write at leisure. This ode, he implied, was "the *genuine* offspring of enthusiasm," not of "the *imitated* enthusiasm of a cold and artificial imagination":

> The writer before us . . . will not be thought, by any one who is acquainted with his former compositions, defective in that first essential of sublime poetry, *ardent conception;* and the present effusion, faulty as it may be from extravagance in some parts, and from haste in others, will never be read without the emotions which true genius alone can call forth.

Aikin quotes the first two strophes, confident that they will "excite a desire in the real lovers of poetry to peruse the whole." The *Critical* changed its emphasis towards Coleridge's work, making the same kind of criticisms as before but more prominently and more sharply: either Dyer had decided that Coleridge's poetry was in urgent need of discipline, or a new reviewer had taken over.

> We are sorry to say that he too frequently mistakes bombast and obscurity, for sublimity. The poem certainly possesses some nervous lines; but in general we dare not applaud. We are displeased at finding such a number of affected phrases as a *bowed mind—skirts* of the departing year, which is rather a vulgar figure, notwithstanding the *"blanket"* of Shakspeare may be brought forward to keep him in countenance.
> *Foeman—lidless—recenter—bedim—strangeyed destruction—marge —warfield—frost-winds—uncoffin'd—cum multis aus,* are affectations. . . . Pegasus is a fiery steed; and when spurred, as he seems to have been on the present occasion, he is apt to fling his rider in the dirt: *sat verbum.* The above strictures are by no means meant to discourage, but to *reform.* Poetical Enthusiasm should take Reason for her companion.

In support of these criticisms the *Critical* quotes the same two strophes that the *Monthly* had held up for admiration.

Aikin's review may have been encouraging, but his commonplaces about "enthusiasm" and "true genius" cannot count for much as criticism. The *Critical* reviewer is more specific, his charge of "bombast" has some justification, and his criticisms of Coleridge's diction cannot be dismissed out of hand unless we also dismiss Wordsworth's plea for poetry in "the real language of men." But his examples suggest an undiscriminating pedantry: "strange-eyed destruction," an offensively glittering phrase, is lumped in with some harmless archaisms and with two imaginative original metaphors ("a bowed mind," "recentre my immortal mind") which in context are admirable. This critic is less successful in pointing to real faults of diction than the *English* reviewer of *Poems on Various Subjects,* and though Coleridge later removed some of these expressions[71] from the ode it is doubtful whether the result was an improvement.

Coleridge's quarto pamphlet of 1798 shows him nearly at the peak of his achievement as a poet. Though different in their styles, the three poems it contains all show development towards a simpler, yet more sensitive language than that of their earlier counterparts — a change which owes something to the reviewers as well as to Wordsworth. "Fears in Solitude" expresses once more Coleridge's fear that divine retribution may overtake Britain for her crimes in Europe and Africa, but is a more mature poem in thought and style than the "Ode on the Departing Year." "France, an Ode" sets forth his changed feelings towards France and the French Revolution after Napoleon's invasion of Switzerland, moving towards the view that all changes in the "forms of power" are in vain — at least unless accompanied by spiritual regeneration, such as may result from communion with nature. Humphry House describes this ode as "one of the best achievements of the whole political poetry of that period."[72] "Frost at Midnight," which House calls "one of the finest short poems in the language,"[73] is less directly concerned with politics; but all three may be seen both as "chapters of integrative autobiography"[74] and as bridges between the world of intimate thought and feeling and that of public events.

Christopher Moody succeeded John Aikin as the reviewer of Coleridge's poems in the *Monthly;* Southey, who had already written a fairly severe piece on *Lyrical Ballads,* probably reviewed it for the *Critical;*[75] and the articles in the *Analytical* and the *British Critic* may perhaps have been written by Mrs. Barbauld[76] and by Francis Wrangham.[77] None of these reviewers really rose to the occasion: they praised the poems but apparently did not recognise their altogether outstanding quality, nor did they criticise in any detail. The simplification of language was noticed, apparently with approval, by the *Analytical:* "Mr. C. is unusually sparing of imagery; . . . what imagery he has given us is unusually free from extravagance." Otherwise the only comment on this point came from Moody, who noted the absence of "an exploded though elegant mythology" but went on to censure some lines as "very prosaic" and the diction as "not always sufficiently nice." It is unfortunate that Coleridge's new poems came before Moody, who, almost alone among the reviewers, positively enjoyed the glittering effects of the Della Cruscans.

Coleridge's opinions came in for more discussion than his poetry. The *Analytical* summarised his themes with approval; the *Monthly* noted his wish "to consecrate his lyre to truth, virtue, and humanity"; the *Critical* observed that "without being a ministerialist, Mr. Coleridge has become an alarmist," while from the other side of the fence the *British Critic* lamented "his absurd and preposterous prejudices against his country."

"Fears in Solitude" received more attention than the other poems and was quoted at greater length, probably because it stood first in the volume. After quoting lines 41-129 Moody comments: "There is so much truth, with so much serious, pointed, and suitable exhortation, in these lines, that we feel it a duty, more for the sake of the public than of the author, to solicit their perusal." Moody summarises "France" without criticism, beyond describing the last stanza as "a beautiful address to Liberty." Southey, by contrast, thought the close of this poem "very ridiculous," and asked of the last four lines "What does Mr. Coleridge mean by liberty in this passage? or what connexion has it with the subject of civil freedom?" This reminds one of "What were they going to do with the Grail when they found it, Mr. Rossetti?", though Southey's question is rather more pertinent and the answer not obvious.[78] The *British Critic* likewise noted some loose rhetoric in the poem: quoting lines 25-27,

> *Bear witness for me*, how I hoped and feared!
> With what a joy my lofty gratulation
> Unawed I sung, *amid a slavish band*,

the reviewer remarked:

> It is not apparent who is to bear witness for the poet, and we are sorry that one who sings so well should be obliged to *sing amid a slavish band*. We should like to know where *this slavish band* existed. There are none of that description in this country.

The first objection merely shows careless reading, but the second does point up a certain falseness in Coleridge's presentation of himself as a lonely revolutionary poet among tyrants and slaves.

"Frost at Midnight" did not pass quite unnoticed. The *Analytical* thought its opening lines did great honour to Coleridge's feelings as a husband and father, and the *British Critic* preferred this poem as being free from political absurdities: "a few affectations of phrasing, are atoned for by much expressive tenderness, and will be avoided by the author's more mature judgment." Southey declared the poem to be "very beautiful," but found that "the lines respecting the film occupy too great a part of it." Coleridge eventually reduced this passage, lines 15-23 of the final text, by five lines. Moody describes "Frost at Midnight" as "a pleasing picture of virtue and content in a cottage," but objected to its original ending: "The last line . . . is extremely flat, and gives the idea of an exhausted muse." Here again Coleridge seems to have benefited by the criticism: in all subsequent editions the six lines which originally ended the poem were omitted, a revision described by House as "one of the best artistic decisions Coleridge ever made."[79] In fact, though all the reviewers praised Coleridge's 1798 volume, they were much more successful in pointing out its minor faults and weaknesses than in explaining its merits.

On the whole, the reception of Wordsworth and Coleridge's early poems may be described as friendly and helpful. Two of the four Reviews noticed the merits as well as the defects of *An Evening Walk* and *Descriptive Sketches,* and though Holcroft's criticism of these poems was sharp, it was accurate and salutary. The goodwill of the Dissenting, anti-ministerial Reviews towards Coleridge sprang partly from personal contacts, and from the wish to help forward a young writer with the right sort of opinions. His work received some deserved praise and some accurate detailed criticism; but political discussion obscured the real stature of "Frost at Midnight," and "The Eolian Harp" passed unnoticed. Nine of these eighteen reviews may be said to provide satisfactory criticism — three each in the *Analytical* and *Critical,* two in the *Monthly,* and one in the *British Critic.*

Lyrical Ballads

Since *Lyrical Ballads* is in some ways a revolutionary work, one easily supposes that its appearance outraged a literary establishment. Current reference books tell us so,[80] and a famous passage in Hazlitt seems to confirm it:

> The change in the belles-lettres was as complete, and to many persons as startling, as the change in politics, with which it went hand in hand. There was a mighty ferment in the heads of statesmen and poets, kings and people. . . . The world was to be turned topsy-turvy; and poetry, by the good will of our Adam-wits, was to share its fate and begin *de novo.* It was a time of promise, a renewal of the world and of letters; and the Deucalions, who were to perform this feat of regeneration, were the present poet-laureat and the two authors of the Lyrical Ballads.[81]

This account implies both a revolution and a reaction, and the reaction Hazlitt has in mind is Jeffrey's long persecution of the "Lake School" in the *Edinburgh Review;* elsewhere he refers to Jeffrey's "treatment of the Lyrical Ballads at their first appearance." But their first appearance was in October 1798; that of the *Edinburgh,* in October 1802: and between these dates no *furore* took place. Despite Wordsworth's fairly frequent lamentations, *Lyrical Ballads* went through four editions and sold more copies than any work of his was to do for another thirty years;[82] and recent scholars have noticed that the earliest reviews were by no means hostile. The theory of an unappreciative establishment dies hard, however, and since the reviewers of 1798 did not actually announce that the Romantic Movement had begun, it has been possible to speak of their "neglect" of *Lyrical Ballads,* or of their "apathy."[83]

When the reviews are placed in context, such comments are seen to be utterly unreasonable. *Lyrical Ballads* came before the critics as a small anonymous volume of no particular prestige. Its "Advertisement" was somewhat provocative, and its contents uneven in quality. Wordsworth had not yet, to use his own phrase, created the taste by which he was to be relished. Nevertheless, the reviews given to *Lyrical Ballads* average six pages in length, much more than was usually given to volumes of verse — twice the space given to Rogers's *Pleasures of Memory,* or Moore's *Thomas Little* volume. All reviewers expressed strong interest, and their reaction was generally favourable. The *Monthly* bestowed praise and blame in roughly equal proportions, the *Analytical* was preponderantly favourable, and the *British Critic* gave almost nothing but warm praise. The only review in which adverse criticism predominated was that in the *Critical,* written by the third member of the supposed Lake School, Robert Southey.[84] His was the earliest review to appear; but except for one comment on "The Ancient Mariner" repeated in the *Analytical,* no critic seems to have followed his lead.

Southey outlines the "experiment" described in Wordsworth's Advertisement, and comments severely on several of the experimental poems. After praising those of a more orthodox kind, he pronounces:

> The "experiment," we think, has failed, not because the language of conversation is little adapted to "the purposes of poetic pleasure," but because it has been tried upon uninteresting subjects. Yet every piece discovers genius; and, ill as the author has frequently employed his talents, they certainly rank him with the best of living poets.

The *Analytical* passed no general judgement on the volume, but praised many of the poems. In the *Monthly* Dr. Burney took a judicious view of the "experimental" poems:

> Though we have been extremely entertained with the fancy, the facility, and (in general) the sentiments, of these pieces, we cannot regard them as *poetry,* of a class to be cultivated at the expence of a higher species of versification, unknown in our language at the time when our elder writers, whom this author condescends to imitate, wrote their ballads. . . . None but savages have submitted to eat acorns after corn was found. — We will allow that the author before us has the art of cooking his acorns well, and that he makes a very palatable dish of them for *jours maigres:* but, for festivals and *gala* days,
>
> > *Multos castra juvant, & lituo tubae*
> > *Permistus sonitus.*

He also makes the just criticism that some of Wordsworth's poems are moving largely because of the pathos of their content: "we have been as much affected by pictures of misery and unmerited distress, in *prose.*"[85] Two tendencies in the poetry which Burney criticises are the turning away from civilised society to rural solitude (which he seems to suspect of being a Rousseauistic affectation) and the preoccupation with social outcasts. Of such poems as "The Convict" and "The Dungeon," both rather conventionally humanitarian poems which were dropped from later editions of *Lyrical Ballads,* Burney writes that "candour and tenderness for criminals seem pushed to excess." After commenting briefly on each poem in the volume, criticising in a good-humoured tone and making many favourable remarks, Burney concludes that

> so much genius and originality are discovered in this publication, that we wish to see another from the same hand, written on more elevated subjects and in a more cheerful disposition.

The most favourable review, perhaps by Wrangham, appeared in the *British Critic:*[86]

> The attempt made in this little volume is one that meets our cordial approbation; and it is an attempt by no means unsuccessful. The endeavour of the author is to recall our poetry, from the fantastical excess of refinement, to simplicity and nature. . . . we do not often find expressions that we esteem too familiar, or deficient in dignity; on the contrary, we think that in general the author has succeeded in attaining that judicious degree of simplicity, which accommodates itself with ease even to the sublime. It is not by pomp of words, but by energy of thought, that sublimity is most successfully achieved; and we infinitely prefer the simplicity, even of the most unadorned tale in this volume, to all the meretricious frippery of the *Darwinian* taste.

Among Wordsworth's poems, the most warmly commended was "Tintern Abbey." Southey wrote:

> On reading this production, it is impossible not to lament that [the author] should ever have condescended to write such pieces as the Last of the Flock, the Convict, and most of the ballads. In the whole range of English poetry, we scarcely recollect any thing superior to a part of the following passage [lines 65-111].

Burney described the poem as

> the reflections of no common mind; poetical, beautiful, and philosophical: but somewhat tinctured with gloomy, narrow, and unsociable ideas of seclusion from the commerce of the world: as if men were born to live in woods and wilds, unconnected with each other! Is it not to education and the culture of the mind that we owe the raptures which the author so well describes, as arising from the view of beautiful scenery, and sublime objects of nature

enjoyed in tranquillity, when contrasted with the artificial machinery and "busy hum of men" in a city? The savage sees none of the beauties which this author describes. . . . He has no *dizzy raptures* in youth; nor does he listen, in maturer age, "to the still sad music of humanity."

Southey also found "The Female Vagrant" to be "admirable," and the *British Critic* called it "a composition of exquisite beauty." Wordsworth's more experimental poems won varying degrees of praise. Southey disliked "The Idiot Boy," of which he wrote:

No tale less deserved the labour that appears to have been bestowed upon this. It resembles a Flemish picture in the worthlessness of its design and the excellence of its execution.

Burney, on the other hand, was enthralled:

The Idiot Boy leads the reader on from anxiety to distress, and from distress to terror, by incidents and alarms which, though of the most mean and ignoble kind, interest, frighten, and terrify, almost to torture, during the perusal of more than a hundred stanzas.

The *British Critic* agreed that this poem, "though it descends quite to common life," was "animated by much interest, and told with singular felicity"; and the *Analytical* numbered it among the particularly pleasing poems. "Goody Blake" was less well received: Southey feared that by vouching for the truth of such a story Wordsworth was encouraging superstition, and the *British Critic* voiced similar fears, while Burney deduced from it some unsatisfactory social implications:

The hardest heart must be softened into pity for the poor old woman; —and yet, if all the poor are to help themselves, and supply their wants from the possessions of their neighbours, what imaginary wants and real anarchy would it not create? Goody Blake should have been relieved out of the *two millions* annually allowed by the state to the poor of this country, not by the plunder of an individual.

Yet the *Analytical* liked the poem and quoted it in full. Of "The Thorn," Southey remarked that ". . . he who personates tiresome loquacity, becomes tiresome himself";[87] but the *British Critic* found in this poem "many beauties," and the *Analytical* also admired it. "The Mad Mother" was commended by the *Monthly* and *Analytical*, and "The Forsaken Indian Woman" by the *Monthly* and *British Critic*. Burney's comments show him happiest when he can assimilate Wordsworth to earlier poetic traditions:

Lines on the first mild day of March abound with beautiful sentiments from a polished mind.

Simon Lee, the old Huntsman, is the portrait, admirably painted, of every huntsman who, by toil, age, and infirmities, is rendered unable to guide and govern his canine family.

Anecdote for Fathers. Of this the dialogue is ingenious and natural: but the object of the child's choice, and the inferences, are not quite obvious.

Among Coleridge's contributions, it is well known that "The Ancient Mariner" completely baffled Southey:

We are tolerably conversant with the early English poets; and can discover no resemblance whatever, except in antiquated spelling and a few obsolete words. This piece appears to us perfectly original in style as well as in story. Many of the stanzas are laboriously beautiful; but in connection they are absurd or unintelligible. Our readers may exercise their ingenuity in attempting to unriddle what follows [lines 301-22 of the 1798 text]. We do not sufficiently understand the story to analyse it. It is a Dutch attempt at German sublimity. Genius has here been employed in producing a poem of little merit.[88]

Coleridge's poem has of course some relation to the "German sublimity" of poems like Bürger's *Lenore,* and the *Analytical,* whether following Southey's lead or independently, made the same comparison: "In our opinion it has more of the extravagance of a mad german poet, than of the simplicity of our ancient ballad writers." Burney was perplexed but not wholly unappreciative, and put more emphasis on what he could discern of the merit of the poem:

The author's first piece, *The Rime of the ancyent mariner,* . . . is the strangest story of a cock and a bull that we ever saw on paper: yet, though it seems a rhapsody of unintelligible wildness and incoherence, (of which we do not perceive the drift, unless the joke lies in depriving the wedding guest of his share of the feast,) there are in it poetical touches of an exquisite kind.

The *British Critic* likewise found "many excellencies, and many faults" in the poem: the story of the wedding guest is said to be "well-imagined," and the beginning and end of the poem to be striking and well-conducted; "but the intermediate part is too long, and has, in some places, a kind of confusion of images, which loses all effect, from not being quite intelligible." "The Nightingale" won praise from Burney, who described it as "Miltonic, yet original; reflective, and interesting in an uncommon degree," and from the *British Critic,* which more perceptively compared the form of the poem to that of *The Task.*

Second editions were not normally noticed by these journals, and despite the addition of a second volume only one full review appeared of *Lyrical Ballads* (1800). This review was by John Stoddart, a friend of Wordsworth and Coleridge, who had paid a long visit to each of the poets during the autumn of 1800. Though not a regular reviewer, Stoddart wrote his account of the new edition as soon as it was in print—probably at Wordsworth's suggestion—and offered it to the *British Critic*, in which journal it was published after some small alterations had been made.[89] John Wordsworth, who had seen Stoddart's article in manuscript, feared it was "too much of a panegyric" to be acceptable; but the version that appeared was not markedly more favourable than the *British Critic's* review of the first edition, in which Stoddart had had no hand. As before, both Wordsworth's intentions and his achievement were approved. Stoddart found that the now-famous Preface contained "much penetrating and judicious observation," though "written in some parts with a degree of metaphysical obscurity";[90] and he quoted many of Wordsworth's remarks with approval, including his contention that the language of poetry ought not be different from that of prose. Of the new poems he preferred "Michael" (which was still being written during Stoddart's visit to Grasmere), "The Brothers," and "The Old Cumberland Beggar," and he quoted in full "Strange fits of passion I have known." Stoddart praises the "purity" of the language in which these poems are written:

> As to the subjects, it must be owned that their worth does not always appear at first sight; but, judging from our own feelings, we must assert, that it generally grows upon the reader by subsequent perusal.

In conclusion, Stoddart warmly commends Wordsworth's efforts to bring poetry back to a more natural style and to "a simple language, expressive of human passions":

> We will not deny that sometimes he goes so far in pursuit of his simplicity, as to become flat or weak; but, in general, he sets an example which the full-dressed poet of affectation might wish, but wish in vain, to follow. He would correct Mr. W. as the dancing-master of Hogarth would correct the attitude of Antinous.[91]

A brief announcement of this second edition appeared in the *Monthly* for June 1802. The unidentified writer (whose style resembles Moody's) declares that it is unnecessary to enlarge on the criticisms of the previous review:

> Suffice it, therefore, to observe that we deem the present publication not inferior to its precursor; and to express our hope that this will

not prove the last time of our meeting with this natural, easy, sentimental Bard, in his pensive rambles through the wilds and groves of his truly poetic, though somewhat peculiar, imagination.

Taking these reviews together, one must agree with John Hayden that "they can scarcely have been a hindrance" to the success of *Lyrical Ballads*.[92] In the light of subsequent events it is ironical that the least favourable review should have been written by the other "Lake poet." But to suppose that Southey should have leapt to the defence of his fellow-Romantics would be expecting him to act up to a version of literary history that was not yet current. It was not until 1802 that *Lyrical Ballads* needed such defence. Though Southey was well aware of recent developments in literary taste, he expected them to go forward without persecution, assuming that "the school of Pope has had its day."[93] This naturally did not preclude differences of opinion among the new poets; and on *Lyrical Ballads* Southey spoke his mind freely, in the abrupt, dogmatic style that marks all his critical utterances at this period. He could not foresee that four years later he, Wordsworth, and Coleridge would be lumped together as "the new school," and beaten with the rod of a sham Augustanism. It remains to consider the question of personal bias; and it seems to me that Professor Simmons exaggerates when he describes the review as "largely founded on personal malice."[94] Southey may possibly have been prejudiced against Wordsworth by Lloyd's gossip,[95] but had no reason to harbor malice or any other strong feeling towards him. It is true that since November 1797 he had been on very distant terms with Coleridge, whom he suspected of having parodied his poetry in the *Monthly Magazine*.[96] Resentment may explain his grudging reference to the "laboriously beautiful" stanzas of "The Ancient Mariner," and his choice of what he considered a particularly baffling passage as a specimen. But his main complaint against the poem — that the story was unintelligible — seems to have been voiced by every contemporary critic except Charles Lamb.[97] On other matters Southey's judgements are at least defensible. He did justice to "Tintern Abbey," quoting one of its finest passages, and to several smaller poems. He recognised the "genius" of the authors, and placed them in the front rank of modern poets. His dislike of "The Thorn" and "The Idiot Boy" has been shared by many impartial critics. His private letters show that the opinions expressed in this article were sincerely held.[98] Probably no criticism from Southey's pen, at this time, would have satisfied Wordsworth;[99] but if he had been more appreciative of "The Ancient Mariner," this would have been an acceptable review.

The account of *Lyrical Ballads* in the *Analytical*, though generally favourable, is slight. The remaining three reviews are satisfactory. Dr. Burney's article in the *Monthly* is proof in itself that the old order was capable of adjusting to the arrival of the new without undue fuss. The only real distortion is a tendency to scrutinize Wordsworth's poems for social and political implications and to discuss these instead of the poem, so that "The Last of the Flock" leads to a consideration of agrarian laws. Of the several comments that have been made on this review, Dr. Lonsdale's seems the fairest: "It is surely to his credit that, at the age of seventy-three and with a literary acquaintance which stretched back to James Thomson, he should have responded with such interest and enthusiasm to the basic quality of the volume."[100] The solidly favourable reviews in the *British Critic* (and on a smaller scale in the *Antijacobin Review*[101]) show that conservatives did not associate the volume with revolution in the way Hazlitt later did. In fact, this group of articles supports Coleridge's view that if later critics had not focussed public attention upon a few passages that were open to ridicule, *Lyrical Ballads* would have had no difficulty in making its way in the world.

Southey

Between 1794 and 1801 nine verse publications written wholly or partly by Southey came before the reviewers, but the reception of the earlier works need only be briefly summarised. The favourable notices given to Coleridge's *Fall of Robespierre* (1794), in which Southey had a large though unacknowledged share, have already been discussed. *Poems, by Robert Lovell and Robert Southey* (Bath, 1795), a slim volume treating picturesque and nostalgic themes in conventional verse, received mixed but on the whole encouraging reviews.[102] *Joan of Arc* (Bristol, 1797), the "epic" Southey had written in six weeks at the age of nineteen, was treated respectfully and at length by the *Monthly, Critical,* and *Analytical*.[103] All three reviewers disapproved of the "ill-placed vanity" shown in the Preface, where Southey gives the impression of boasting of the speed with which he wrote the poem; but they admired his "noble, liberal, and enlightened sentiments" and, in general, the poetic quality of his work. Forty years afterwards Southey gave a just account of these reviews:

> The chief cause of its favourable reception was, that it was written in a republican spirit, such as may easily be accounted for in a youth whose notions of liberty were taken from the Greek and Roman writers, and who was ignorant enough of history and of human nature to believe, that a happier order of things had commenced with the independence of the United States, and would be accelerated by the French Revolution. Such opinions were then as unpopular in England as they deserved to be; but they were cherished by most of the critical journals, and conciliated for me the good-will of some of the most influential writers who were at that time engaged in periodical literature, though I was personally unknown to them.

They bestowed upon the poem abundant praise, passed over most of its manifold faults, and noticed others with indulgence.[104]

The *British Critic,* which had praised the *Poems* of 1795 and pronounced Southey to be "fairly qualified" for the epic project which he announced in that volume, now hinted that there was much to disapprove; but it refrained, perhaps for the sake of "consistency," from making any real attack on the poem. The three Foxite Reviews also commended the revised edition of *Joan of Arc* that appeared in 1798.[105] Southey had now achieved an impressive, indeed an inflated, reputation; and his position in the literary world was strengthened by contacts with men like Dr. John Aikin, and by his post "in the poetical department of the *Critical Review.*"[106] But the political opinions that had brought Southey somewhat exaggerated praise were soon to prove an unreliable asset.

The following paragraphs will discuss the reception of the short poems published by Southey in several collections between 1797 and 1800, and of his *Thalaba* (1801). These articles are little known, and only four of the seventeen are included in the recent "Critical Heritage" volume;[107] but they show important developments in the public criticism of Southey's work that were later taken over by the reviewers of Wordsworth and Coleridge. Southey's short poems of this period are in some respects as "advanced" as the *Lyrical Ballads.* Some deal with subjects from humble life in "the language really used by men," and in these poems Southey's radical and humanitarian views are again in evidence. Others versify miraculous legends from such sources as Mandeville's *Travels* and Heywood's *Hierarchies of the Blessed Angels.* But despite his industry and up-to-dateness Southey's poetic talent was a minor one, and whether from carelessness or deeper psychological causes he was often unable fully to exploit it. He was therefore vulnerable to criticism, especially after the praise that had been lavished on *Joan of Arc.*

The first volume of Southey's *Poems* (1797) contained four "Botany Bay Eclogues." The first and fourth of these ("Elinor" and "Frederic") are uninteresting blank-verse monologues, but the second and third are fairly successful attempts to make use of the idiom of common speech. Though a touch of genre can still be detected, they differ from previous rustic dialogues in that the effect intended is not comic:

> Talk of hardships! what these are the sailor don't know;
> 'Tis the soldier, my friend, that's acquainted with woe,
> Long journeys, short halting, hard work, and small pay,
> To be popt at like pigeons for sixpence a day!—
> Thank God! I'm safe quartered at Botany Bay.
>
> ("John, Samuel, and Richard")

The volume also included verses against the slave trade; two legendary tales in the ballad stanza, "Donica" and "Rudiger"; and three poems remembered chiefly for their parodies in the *Anti-Jacobin*—"Inscription for the Apartment in Chepstow Castle," "The Soldier's Wife," and "The Widow."

The three Foxite Reviews praised the humanitarian purposes of the volume, but concentrated on the poems of more conventional form. The *Analytical* pronounced:

> Of the Botany-Bay eclogues, the first is peculiarly sweet; poor Elinor! she is Penitence itself! The others exhibit in more familiar language the situation and employment of our transports on that distant shore.

The *Critical* agreed that "Elinor" was "very affecting," and found in the volume "the same animated description, the same spirit of benevolence, and the same love of virtue, that pervaded Mr. Southey's former poems." (The easy cant of benevolence and virtue was soon to be derided by the *Anti-Jacobin*.) In the *Monthly* Dr. Aikin applied himself more seriously to Southey's *Poems,* and gave a warning almost Wordsworthian in its solemnity:

> Of the lyric compositions [Southey] speaks in terms of disparagement which may lead us to wonder that they should have been admitted; nor can we forbear to repeat a hint which we formerly ventured to give this youthful writer,—that a little more deference for the public, and a greater sensibility towards his own permanent fame, would be useful in directing the efforts of his genius. The poetical character, surely, is not that slight and trivial thing which is not worth the pains of acquiring or keeping. If poetry be not the first of all the energies of the human mind, as some of its votaries have deemed it, there is, at least, enough in it to found an immortal name, and to afford delight and instruction to whole ages and nations. Neither is it probable that a truly poetical genius can, with much advantage, substitute another pursuit as a basis for reputation and profit. Poetry is a trifle to trifling poets and trifling readers:—but no one ever excelled in it who treated it as a trifle.

But despite its "negligence and inequality," Aikin found in the volume "that vivid force of imagination, and that warm colouring of expression, which essentially distinguish the POET from the artificial measurer of syllables"; and he chose "Elinor" to illustrate "the sort of music, which the touch of genius can draw from this wild instrument." The *British Critic* transposed Aikin's warning into a less sympathetic key:

> There is every appearance that Mr. Southey writes at all times, and on all occasions, and publishes all he writes. He is certainly not without

poetic talents; but till he shall have learned, that time for correction is as necessary, to the most brilliant genius, as leisure for writing, he never will atchieve the legitimate title of a poet.

The reviewer quotes the first four lines of "The Soldier's Wife" with the comment "Fiddledum, diddledum." In this short review we can hear the first rumbling of the critical landslide that was so severely to batter, indeed temporarily to bury, the Lake poets. Four months later the *Anti-Jacobin* began publication, and took Southey for one of its chief victims; its well-known parody "The Soldier's Friend," which appeared in the fifth number, showed that the *British Critic* review had been remembered by Canning and Frere. The parody ends with the lines:

> Reason, philosophy, "fiddledum diddledum,"
> Peace and Fraternity, higgledy, piggledy,
> Higgledy, piggledy, "fiddledum diddledum."

Despite the scholarly quotation-marks, the source of the quoted phrase has not, I think, previously been noticed.[108]

In 1799 Southey added to his *Poems* a second volume, which showed that although he considered *Lyrical Ballads* a failure he was willing to try similar experiments himself.[109] His six "English Eclogues" all deal with humble life: "The Funeral" and "The Ruined Cottage" are in the first person and comparatively formal in style, but the other four are dialogues in the idiom of common conversation. "Jaspar," "The Cross-Roads," and "The Sailor who Served in the Slave Trade" are all moral tales in the ballad stanza dealing with sensational themes of murder and suicide (Southey had complained that Wordsworth's experiment had been tried upon uninteresting subjects). A certain lack of subtlety in the content of these poems is matched by careless technique, and the speech-rhythms of the dialogues are often at war with Southey's metre. "The Rose," "Henry the Hermit," and "The Old Woman of Berkeley" display Southey's fondness for miraculous legends, and pieces such as "The Complaints of the Poor" show his continuing humanitarian sympathies.

Even the Foxite journals found Southey's new poems hard to digest: probably the *Anti-Jacobin* had alerted them to weaknesses in his work. The *Analytical*, though generally favourable, demurred at the language of the "English Ecologues":

> The great difficulty of writing a dialogue between two countrymen would be the choice and preservation of appropriate language: it is obviously indispensable that the language . . . should be equally remote from vulgarity and refinement. Vulgarity would disgust us by its coarseness, and refinement by its unsuitableness to the characters introduced. We rather question whether the first twenty lines of Mr. S.'s

first eclogue ["The Old Mansion"] have not too much colloquial familiarity. . . . On the whole, however, we are pleased with these deviations of our author from the vulgar track of bucolic poetry.

The *Critical* praised the volume in general terms, but its remarks about particular poems were unenthusiastic; most of the Eclogues were judged to be "too familiar in their style and manner to afford much gratification to the admirers of poetry." This reviewer drew a not very illuminating comparison between "The Old Woman of Berkeley" and Bürger's *Lenore* — "because I suppose," Southey wrote to Taylor, "there is a horse in both, and of the same breed perhaps."[110]

In the *Monthly* a development took place that had ill consequences for the Romantic poets. The sympathetic Dr. Aikin was replaced by the much more conservative Dr. Ferriar, who surprised Southey by the first full-scale hostile review he had ever received and persecuted him through three successive *Monthly* articles. Ferriar attacked both the conversational language and the use of legendary themes:

> Seduced by the brilliant but dangerous excentricities of Cowper, . . . Mr. Southey has attempted to make the Muse descend a step lower, and has, in reality, brought her to the level of prose. To this error, he has joined an excessive fondness for obsolete phrases and turns of expression. Thus, instead of attempting to polish his strains, and to clothe his ideas in the most poetical garb which our language at present affords, his efforts are perpetually reverting to an imitation of the rudest productions of the last two centuries.

Printing passages from the "Metrical Letter," "The Cross-Roads" and "The Grandmother's Tale" as prose, Ferriar defies his readers to restore Southey's lineation.[111] "The Sailor" and "Jaspar" he recommends to the *Cheap Repository*,[112] "since the moral is excellent, and the versification is well adapted to the taste of the lower classes of society." For Southey's sources and models in earlier literature — including Bunyan — Ferriar shows contempt. He dismisses "Henry the Hermit" as a silly monkish legend; he cannot imagine why Southey based "The Rose" on a story from Mandeville instead of using a classical fable; and of "The Old Woman of Berkeley" he remarks that when the Devil flew away with the old lady he should have taken Southey's poem with him. Ferriar concludes by declaring that Southey is wasting his talents:

> Let Mr. Southey look up to the classic models, instead of the monkish trash which he has studied, and he will find reason for congratulating himself on his change of objects.

Here at last we have what looks like the reaction of an Augustan establishment to the new poetry: an appeal to the classics, a demand for poetic diction, a view of poetry as something for the educated rather than "the lower classes of society." But Ferrier is no more entitled than Burney or Aikin to be regarded as the typical literary man of his age. His undiscriminating contempt for the ballads, his dismissal of earlier literature as "monkish trash," the elegant couplet verse that he himself published[113]—all show his taste to be markedly conservative; and Southey's *Poems*, unlike *Lyrical Ballads,* contained nothing that might have inclined him "to be pleased in spite of his own pre-established code of decision." In condemning many of them as careless and unmetrical he was simply being accurate; and his review was not, in March 1800, anything more than the response of a particular, old-fashioned sensibility to a rather inferior collection of poems. The ponderous style of his condemnation is partly to be explained by Southey's reputation: the poet of *Joan of Arc* could not be briefly dismissed in the Catalogue. Ferrier could not, however, have reversed the *Monthly's* favourable policy towards Southey in such a drastic fashion without editorial support, and it is a question why Griffiths allowed the reputation of his journal for "consistency" to be thus endangered. Quite apart from Griffiths's own opinion of Southey's work, which is unguessable, two reasons suggest themselves. One is that after the *Monthly's* failure to put the Della Cruscans in their place had been shown up by Gifford, Griffiths was anxious not to spare the weak sides of any fashionable new poet, or coterie of poets. The other is that since 1796 he had been attempting to steer a safe course in politics, and from November 1797 onwards Southey had been marked out by the *Anti-Jacobin* as a writer whom it would be dangerous to favour. Ferrier's review is obviously a sincere piece of work, but Griffiths might well have toned it down before publication if it had not been for these extraneous factors.

Southey contributed more than fifty poems to the two volumes of the *Annual Anthology* (1799-1800), of which he was the originator and editor. Though his name did not appear in these volumes, his connection with the *Anthology* was advertised in the *Monthly Magazine* in January 1800 and seems thereafter to have been an open secret, a fact he later regretted.[114] Most of the pieces Southey included in volume 1 (1799) should be classified as light verse, though they show a continuation of his earlier interests. Many are legendary tales of the kind that had offended Ferrier: among these were "King Henry V and the Abbott of Dreux," "Bishop Bruno," and "The Pious Painter." Two poems deal with popular superstitions, thus combining Southey's interest in the poetry of humble life and language with his fondness for the miraculous: "The Well of St. Keyne" and "St. Michael's Chair." Others, like "Musings on a Scarecrow," are facetious. In a more serious vein are "The Last of the Family" (another "English Eclogue") and "The Dancing Bear," which reaffirms Southey's detestation of the slave trade. Many of these poems were left-overs from the volumes

Southey published over his name, and the general standard is not high: "The Holly Tree" is probably the best, "You are old, Father William" the worst.

The first two reviews show the mildly favourable response we should expect for an unpretentious miscellany in which a few pleasant poems can be found. The *British Critic* found it "ingenious and agreeable," and quoted "The Well of St. Keyne" in full; the reviewer, probably unaware of Southey's hand in the volume, declares tolerantly that in the work of young writers he is neither surprised nor offended to find "high-flown notions of liberty." The *Critical* disliked the humorous poems, and commented on the legendary tales that "poetical talent might be more judiciously employed than in embalming the ridiculous fictions of dark times." However, this critic praised "The Holly Tree," despite its "quaintness," for its novelty and sound moral, and described "The Last of the Family" as "a successful example of the author's talent in using a familiar vehicle of sympathy and instruction without falling into . . . prosaic flatness." But in April 1800, one month after reviewing Southey's *Poems*, Ferriar returned to the charge, and there is no doubt that he was aware of Southey's connection with the *Anthology:*

> Some of these poems are evidently written to satirize the prevailing faults of modern bards; but others are placed by their side, which are so serious and yet so similar in their structure, that we feel a perplexity like that of the manager who asked an author . . . "Pray, Sir, is this your tragedy, or your comedy?"

Ferriar makes some accurate general criticisms of the imitation ballads of the day:

> It seems to be imagined . . . that the merit of old ballads consists in their quaintness; and that to adopt their obsolete phraseology is to appropriate their beauties. This is an unfortunate mistake. The authors of those compositions wrote the best language with which they were acquainted.

(It is interesting that this review should have appeared just before work began on the second edition of *Lyrical Ballads,* for which Coleridge removed the more obvious archaisms from "The Ancient Mariner.") Less perceptively, Ferriar commends the ballads of Gay and Goldsmith as examples of simplicity and feeling truthfully expressed in "the modern style." Many of Southey's poems are severely criticised. To "The Last of the Family" Ferriar raises the same objection that Southey himself had raised against Wordsworth's "The Thorn": "Mr. S. has proved so very correct in his imitation of the gossipping of Farmer James and Farmer Gregory, that he has taken off much from the gravity, as well as of the interest of the

piece." In conclusion Ferriar promises to use his utmost endeavours to expose "affectation" in poetry, whether in the form of strained refinement or
of vulgar simplicity; and hopes to see "more estimable originality, and less
of the *bizarre"* in the next volume of the *Anthology*. Though much of Ferriar's criticism is just, these remarks (and to some extent the whole review)
suggest a campaign of the kind that was soon to become all too familiar;
nor does he discriminate closely, "The Holly Tree" being briefly condemned along with a number of other poems.

Southey's contributions to volume 2 of the *Annual Anthology* (1800)
were of a much higher standard, perhaps because the cream had not been
skimmed off for use in his own publications; some of these poems represent
his best achievement in the kinds of poetry with which he had been ex-
perimenting since 1796. "St. Juan Gualberto" and "Bishop Hatto" are the
most effective of his legendary tales; "The Wedding" is the best of the
"English Eclogues"; and "The Battle of Blenheim" is probably the best-
known of all his poems, certainly his best piece of humanitarian propaganda. This improvement in quality was not reflected in the reviews. The
British Critic found the volume "an agreeable miscellany," but preferred
the humorous poems. The *Critical* praised "The Battle of Blenheim,"
which, it declared, "archly conveys, in strains of poetic simplicity, a most
affecting moral"; but condemned "The Wedding" for "that carelessness,
or rather that affectation of carelessness, which we have often had occasion
to notice and reprobate of late as absurd and pretended attempts at genuine simplicity and ease." Ferriar failed to recognise the "estimable
originality" that he had called for. He announced that since "Mr. Southey
and his friends" had ignored previous warnings, he would give them up for
lost: he would notice only the few poems that had some merit. These did
not, apparently, include anything of Southey's[115] except "St. Juan
Gualberto," in which Ferriar found two good stanzas (xxxvi-xxxvii). The
combination of insensitivity and critical arrogance shown here is almost
unique in the literary reviews of this period; all that can be said in Ferriar's
favour is that he is as good as his word, makes a short job of his article, and
gives no protracted exhibition of real or imaginary faults.

It is clear that the short poems Southey published between 1797 and
1800 damaged his reputation with the reviewers, and called forth the kind
of criticism that is noticeably absent from reviews of *Lyrical Ballads*. It will
also be seen that when Jeffrey came to work up his collective caricature of
the "new school of poetry" in the *Edinburgh Review* for October 1802,
most of the materials were ready to his hand. It is virtually certain that he
knew Ferriar's articles, and not only because they appeared in the leading
Review of the day. Some time in the spring of 1802 Jeffrey had himself
joined the staff of the *Monthly*, and had been given *Thalaba* to review;

and it was almost inevitable that he should look up earlier articles on Southey to see what line the *Monthly* had taken. In putting the main weight of his own attack upon the "slovenliness and vulgarity" of the new poets' language, Jeffrey was following Ferriar's lead.

Apart from Ferriar, the most important precedents for Jeffrey's treatment were provided by the *Anti-Jacobin* and the *Antijacobin Review;* and it may be worth while to sketch the part played by these journals in the development of the "Lake School" myth. The existence of a school of poets subversive both in politics and literature was postulated as early as 20 November 1797, in the first number of the *Anti-Jacobin:*

> We shall select from time to time from among those effusions of the *Jacobin* Muse which happen to fall in our way, such pieces as may serve to illustrate some one of the principles on which the poetical as well as the political doctrine of the NEW SCHOOL is established.

The editor, William Gifford, hoped perhaps to repeat his satirical coup against the Della Cruscans; but in the event the *Anti-Jacobin* made little use of the "school" and excelled in parodying individual writers. Among these, of course, Southey was the most notable victim, and the only one to be included by Jeffrey in the "Lake School." But on 9 July 1798, in the final number of the *Anti-Jacobin,* the notion reappeared in lines 334-37 of "New Morality'—a satirical poem by Canning, Frere, Gifford, and George Ellis. These lines mention five Jacobin poets, though only four are named:

> As ye five other wandering Bards that move
> In sweet accord of harmony and love,
> C--DGE and S--TH-Y, L--D, and L--BE and Co.
> Tune all your mystic harps to praise LEPAUX!

Politically Coleridge and Southey were fair game, but the "Jacobin" element in Charles Lloyd's writings amounted to very little and in Lamb's it was non-existent.[116] The idea of a school had been made more plausible, however, by a number of overlapping joint publications that spread guilt by association: Coleridge and Southey had collaborated in *Robespierre* and *Joan of Arc,* Lamb and Lloyd in *Blank Verse* (1798); Lamb and Lloyd had also contributed verse to Coleridge's *Poems* (1797). And George Dyer had linked together these four men and Wordsworth in a footnote to *The Poet's Fate* (1797), a poem urging young writers to "join Pantisocracy's harmonious train."[117] If, as seems likely, Dyer's note inspired the passage in "New Morality," his attempt to give his friends a lift had unfortunate consequences. Through the *Anti-Jacobin,* and through the collected *Poetry of the Anti-Jacobin* which began to appear in 1799, the satire achieved a much wider circulation than Dyer's poem; and it proved a godsend to the *Antijacobin Review*. These lines from "New Morality" were engraved by Gillray at the foot of a pull-out print published in the *Antijacobin Review* on 1 August 1798. In September the same four names were strung together in a poem called "The Anarchists." Wordsworth (who, if Dyer's note was the source, must have been the unnamed fifth bard) came under attack at the end of 1799, when John Gifford reported that he and Coleridge had been abroad to imbibe the "abominable principles" of German philosophy. (The factitious nature of these attacks is shown by the fact that when *Lyrical Ballads* came anonymously for review, this journal failed to detect the Jacobin taint and received it with enthusiasm.)[118]

Thus disseminated, the idea of a "new school," though far from dominating criticism as it did later, gained a certain currency. It was given further credibility by Southey's *Annual Anthology*, to which Coleridge, Lamb, and Lloyd were contributors. Though Southey was still the most conspicuous of these poets, Coleridge was favourably mentioned by the *Critical* in October 1800 as "the founder of a distinct school in poetry"; and Wordsworth, named as the author of the second edition of *Lyrical Ballads*, was awarded the same honour by the *Monthly Mirror* in June 1801.[119] These writers were now well enough known to be worth attacking, and the experimental side of their work—particularly of Southey's—had already come in for some sharp criticism. The targets were set up for another satirical coup, in a more up-to-date style than the couplet verse of Gifford's *Baviad*.

Southey's *Thalaba* seemed to Jeffrey a good pretext for assailing the whole group, even though it marked a new departure for Southey and did not fit in at all well with the kind of essay Jeffrey had decided to write. He ignored Lloyd (who had made a separate peace with the *Antijacobin* reviewers), but brought in each of the other four poets; his spelling "Lambe" suggests that he knew of this writer chiefly through the *Anti-Jacobin* and *Antijacobin Review*. In attacking the supposed school for its "splenetic and idle discontent with the existing institutions of society," Jeffrey was treading a path worn smooth by those two journals. In deriding their affected simplicity and prosaic language, he was expanding Ferriar's criticisms of Southey. In his account of their "sources" he drew freely on the work of earlier critics, especially those in the *Monthly*. Thus Burney had found some of Wordsworth's poetry "unsociable," and called his "Yew-Tree" a "seat for Jean-Jacques." The *Anti-Jacobin* had linked the extravagance of *Sturm und Drang* drama with the "new system" in philosophy and literature.[120] Several critics, including Ferriar, had recognised Cowper's influence. Ferriar had also condemned Southey's use of the "quaint" language of older poets. Like the well-known writer on Chinese Philosophy, Jeffrey simply "combined the information"; and in the very act of repeating these second-hand charges, he has the impudence to accuse his victims of lacking originality!

The productions of this school, we conceive, are so far from being entitled to the praise of originality, that they cannot be better characterised than by an enumeration of the sources from which their materials have been derived. . . . 1. The antisocial principles, and distempered sensibility of Rousseau. . . . 2. The simplicity and energy (*horresco referens*) of Kotzebue and Schiller. 3. The homeliness and harshness of some of Cowper's versification, interchanged occasionally with the *innocence* of Ambrose Philips, or the quaintness of Quarles and Dr. Donne.[121]

Not even the new collective name that was one of Jeffrey's few original contributions to the criticism of these poets makes its appearance in this review; for Jeffrey did not publicly associate them with the Lakes until 1807, and the terms "Lakers" and "Lake School" date respectively from 1814 and 1817.[122]

Viewed as a piece of rhetoric, Jeffrey's essay on the new *"sect* of poets" is well-organised, eloquent, and entertaining. Only by courtesy can it be called criticism. The real achievements, and indeed the real failures, of these poets are kept at a distance. Three years before, Jeffrey had read *Lyrical Ballads* and been "enchanted";[123] now he takes from it only a few details that can be made to look comic, together with a distorted sentence from Wordsworth's "Advertisement" of 1798. No doubt his response to these poets was a mixed one, yet the new Review pattern gave him ample room in which to distinguish and discriminate if he had so chosen. But to write a lively attack was a surer means of giving his first number the desired *éclat*. For this purpose, it was enough to combine and amplify the less favourable comments already in circulation.

Thalaba the Destroyer (1801) is a good poem of its kind, and certainly Southey's best in this period. The story, like that of the *Arabian Nights*, exists chiefly for the sake of the episodes it can be made to carry; but these are dramatically handled, and the descriptions—both of the simple life of the nomads and of the dwellings and enchantments of the sorcerers—are extremely well done: "pastoral charms and wild streaming lights" was Coleridge's phrase for them. Neither the episodic structure nor the *vers libre*, however, was calculated to please critics who had been increasingly inclined to find fault with Southey's poetry; and additional offence was given by a Preface that referred disparagingly to the "jew's-harp twing-twing" of the Augustan couplet. The *British Critic,* in an early review, proclaimed that "a more complete monument of vile and depraved taste no man ever raised." The reviewer declares that Southey has now completed the process of writing himself down, and marvels that "the writer of this wretched stuff has the vanity to censure the approved verse of his country." As in Wordsworth's case, we may guess that the Preface generated at least as much indignation as the poetry.

The next two Review articles on *Thalaba* appeared a year later; both were from the hand of Jeffrey. who had no scruples about reviewing the same work anonymously and at length in two publications. No two articles could better illustrate the difference between the old style of reviewing and the new. The *Monthly* review, which one would guess to have been written first though it appeared a month later, is duller but a good deal fairer. Jeffrey's introductory remarks give equal weight to the merits and defects of the poem:

> It is not easy either to class or to appreciate this singular performance. It has many faults and many striking beauties. It is irregular and splendid, improbable and interesting, and at once extravagant and elaborate. . . . The hand of a poet is discernible throughout, but it changes its instrument and its tone rather too often; and it blends the Lyric and Dramatic style with the sober strain of the Epic, rather more copiously than the strict rules of harmonious composition will admit. — The versification corresponds with the irregularity of the whole structure.

Then follows a "guided tour" of *Thalaba*, with "favourable specimens" introduced by favourable remarks: thus the descriptive passages in Book 3 (which in his *Edinburgh* article Jeffrey found redundant) are here said to show "much vivacity and poetical painting." Jeffrey then proceeds to his summing-up:

> That [*Thalaba*] contains poetical beauties of the first order, we conceive to be sufficiently proved by some of the quotations which we have already exhibited. . . .That there are faults in the composition, however, and some of them very glaring, the same specimens will testify; and there are others which are more apparent on a consideration of the whole work.

There follow two paragraphs of adverse criticism: Jeffrey complains of improbability, inconsistency, an excessive reliance upon the supernatural, and faulty metre ("It is now too late, we apprehend, to introduce a new style of versification into the English language"). But his conclusion again sets Southey's "genius" in equal balance with his faults:

> On the whole, we conceive that this work contains more ample and decisive proofs of the author's genius and capacity for poetical impressions, than any of his former publications: but at the same time, we are sorry to observe that it affords no indications of his advancement towards a more correct taste or a more manly style of composition. Together with much that must please readers of every description, it contains not a little that will offend those whose suffrages Mr. Southey should be most ambitious of securing.

Here neither Jeffrey's method nor his general estimate of the poem can be

called unfair, though he is more articulate about the defects of the poem
than its merits. The same cannot be said of his review in the *Edinburgh*.
The reader of this article is first entertained by nine pages of irrelevant
satire against the new "*sect* of poets." He then reads six pages of adverse
criticism of *Thalaba,* an amplification in harsher terms of the penultimate
two paragraphs of the *Monthly* article ("The subject of this poem is almost
as ill chosen as the diction: and the conduct of the fable as disorderly as the
versification"). Only on the sixteenth page does he find that *Thalaba* has
"passages of very singular beauty and force" and "a richness of poetical
conception." Neither these compliments nor the three pages of approved
extracts that follow can remove the impression that the poem as a whole is
a ridiculous failure; and the conclusion of the review associates the poem
once more with the "peculiar manner" of the "new school." It is
remarkable that in his *Monthly* review, which is eleven pages long, Jeffrey
had not found it necessary to mention the new school once.

The *Critical* review of *Thalaba* appeared late in 1803. Though it was
written by Southey's friend William Taylor,[124] more space is taken up by
adverse criticism than by praise, and in many of his criticisms Taylor
agrees with Jeffrey's *Monthly* article. Thus he finds the hero
"uninteresting," and the other characters too "supernatural in their turn of
mind" to create sympathy. He complains too of an excess of the
marvellous: "Where the most gordian knot of difficulty can be untied with
an amulet . . . that anxiety is seldom excited, which human energy struggl-
ing with difficulty never fails to inspire." Unlike Jeffrey, however, Taylor
shows himself fully appreciative of Southey's descriptive poetry, in a
passage that shows something of Wordsworth's dislike of "poetic diction":

> Thomson and Cowper are among the best of our describers, but they
> are surely left behind by the descriptions in Thalaba: there is here no
> pedantry, no Latin verbiage incapable of exciting pictures in the mind,
> no substitutions of personified abstractions to definite sensible action.

But he acutely remarks that among such scenery the characters tend to be
lost, like figures in a painter's landscape. As to the diction and verse,
Taylor finds that Southey has been too lavish and too various:

> All the fountains of expression are brought together, and gush,
> with sousing vehemence and drifting rapidity, on the reader; who ad-
> mires, but not at ease, and feels tossed as in the pool of a cataract, not
> gliding as on a frequented stream.

His article surpasses Jeffrey's *Monthly* review chiefly by its enthusiasm, its
suggestion that the difficulties of the poem can and should be overcome:
"after repeating the perusal, when an outline of the story is mapped in the
mind. . . , the poem will be frequently interrupted, to give vent to interjec-

tions of applause, and . . . thrilling exultations of delight." He makes one thrust at the *Edinburgh:* quoting in full Khawla's invocation of Eblis (Book 9), he taunts:

> Greeks! Latins! come with your pythonesses! Where is there a description like this? Edinburgh reviewers, tamers of genius, come and vaunt couplets and habitual metres, and show us an effect like this! Ghost of Boileau, scowl! We will enjoy.

Yet Taylor's general verdict balances the talent of the poet against the defects of the poem very much as Jeffrey does in the *Monthly:* "Perhaps no work of art so imperfect ever announced such power in the artist — perhaps no artist so powerful ever rested his fame on so imperfect a production — as Thalaba."

Southey was the Jonah of the Lake poets. Having himself written the least friendly review *Lyrical Ballads* received, he published inferior but superficially similar work in "prosaic" language which brought repeated attacks from Ferriar; his criticisms of "The Idiot Boy" and "The Thorn" rebounded upon his own "English Eclogues." His somewhat inept poems on social and political themes drew devastating satire from the *Anti-Jacobin,* and his collaborations inspired his enemies to set up the target of a "new school" of poets with subversive literary and social doctrines. Jeffrey took over these lines of attack, and applied them to Wordsworth as well as to Coleridge and Southey; and his elaborate, scornful, patronising articles harried all three poets for another twenty years. It has often been alleged that the publicity he gave Wordsworth's poetry must have been beneficial: this comforting belief is not borne out by the sale of Wordsworth's volumes.[125]

Despite good articles by Aikin and Taylor, Southey's own poetry does not show the reviewers at their best, for it was first over-praised and later undervalued. At each stage politics played some part; the Foxite journals first saw this rising poet as an asset, then quickly came to regard him as a liability. Critics were more successful in pointing out the weaknesses of the early experimental poems than in recognising the merit of some later ones. As for *Thalaba,* since not even William Taylor could wholly approve of it, it seems that this poem at least really was too daring in technique for its day.[126]

Nevertheless, it may fairly be claimed that the Reviews of this period were more tolerant and open-minded about poetry than the *Edinburgh* and its successors were to be for many years. They encouraged the revival of earlier poetry; praised Smart; welcomed Burns; and gave Moore, Wordsworth, Coleridge, and the early Southey more favourable notices than they were to get from the major periodicals of the early nineteenth century. Most of the volumes dealt with in this chapter are works of some merit; the only ones dealt with harshly by the reviewers were the later publications of Landor (whom they found obscure) and Southey. The praise given to the Della Cruscan poets by the *Monthly*, however, shows that leniency could be carried to excess.

The reviewers could be critical as well as kind: fifty-one of the 113 articles discussed here may be called satisfactory pieces of criticism. The *Critical* has the best record in this field, with rather more successful than unsuccessful notices (18:15); the *British Critic, Monthly, Analytical* follow in that order, while the *English* contributed too few poetry reviews in these years to provide a fair sample. Even the satisfactory reviews usually contain more summary and quotation than criticism, though the proportion varies among the journals. The *Monthly* and *British Critic* give almost as much space to critical comment as to "analysis" and extracts. But the *English* gives, on average, twice as much space to summary and quotation as to criticism; the *Critical* three times as much; and the *Analytical* four times as much. Detailed and thoughtful criticism is nevertheless not uncommon. Setting aside the collections that were given the scale of treatment appropriate to scholarly publications,[127] the average review of a new volume of verse is rather more than four pages long and includes about 600 words of criticism.

Reviewers in the "poetical department" nearly always recognised their duty to criticise and did not pretend that a well-illustrated summary would suffice. So far as we can tell, their criticism was usually free from extraneous bias. No instances occur here of favourable treatment for the publisher of the Review, or for fellow reviewers; in several cases the opposite is seen to occur.[128] Politics sometimes influenced the reviewers' judgement, as in all other periods, but their verdicts went counter to political allegiances perhaps as often as not. Coleridge was probably right in thinking that personal relationships were the likeliest source of bias. Of these 113 articles, forty-four are by reviewers whom we can name with a fair degree of certainty; and of these, nine had some kind of relationship with the author whom they reviewed. Yet eight of these nine reviews are good ones, as though friendship had caused the reviewer to make a special effort.[129]

The rate of success achieved by these critics is certainly not contemptible, and if the quantity of poetry they had to deal with is taken into account, it may be called reasonably good. Where they failed it was because what they wrote was obtuse, or irrelevant, or inadequate, or inexact—the faults to which reviewers as a class are at all times liable. They did not fail through bias, corruption, or a misunderstanding of their function. Nor did they make the work under review the pretext for a display of saleable ferocity. Such few expressions of contempt as occur are brief.

A place should perhaps be found in future literary histories for John Aikin, M.D. and John Ferriar, M.D.[130] Aikin was the most forward-looking and sympathetic reviewer that Coleridge and Southey found for many years, and to him they owed half-a-dozen encouraging articles in the leading Review of the day. These articles are consistent with the views on literature set out in several of his *Letters of a Father to his Son* (1793-1800). It was a bad day for these poets when Aikin was replaced in the *Monthly* by Ferriar—one of the few reviewers of the period who show what William Smith Ward calls an "allegiance to the Augustans."

BP301.1

Beard

(No. VII. for JULY, 1798.)

THE

Analytical Review,

For JULY, 1798.

Being the FIRST NUMBER of VOL. XXVIII.

Printed for J. JOHNSON, in St. Paul's Church-Yard;

And MURRAY and HIGHLEY, Fleet-Street,

Where any preceding Numbers may be had.

CONTENTS of this NUMBER

Front cover of the *Analytical Review* for July 1798
(Original soft-paper wrapper)

Dr. Ralph Griffiths, owner and editor of the *Monthly Review*
(Engraved by W. Ridley, from an unidentified
portrait, for the *European Magazine*, 1803)

Dr. William Enfield, contributor to the *Monthly* and *Analytical*
(Silhouette engraved by Anker Smith for Enfield's
posthumous *Sermons on Practical Subjects*, 1798)

George Dyer, contributor to the *Critical* and *Analytical*
(Engraved by Elizabeth Cristall from the
portrait by J. Cristall)

Robert Southey, *Critical* reviewer
(Drawing by Robert Hancock, 1798)

Dr. John Aikin, *Monthly* **reviewer**
(Engraved by Englehart, from an unidentified
portrait, for Lucy Aikin's *Memoir of John
Aikin*, 1823)

Dr. John Ferriar, *Monthly* **reviewer**
(Engraved by Bartolozzi from the drawing by J. Stothard)

3
The Reviewing of Fiction

To a refined and sensible people, — says Mr.
Rousseau, — instruction can only be offered in the
form of a novel. . . . Whether reviewers are graver
than the rest of mankind; whether they do not ac-
cord to the above-mentioned sentiment of John
James; or whether they do not think us yet sufficiently refined and sensible; it is certain the whole
corps, *una voce,* exclaim against this favor'd
species of composition. Some, I believe, because
they think, les Sages, les Marivaux, the Fieldings,
the Smolletts, are dead and buried, and will not rise
again; others, because novels, as novels, do poison
the minds of young ladies; and young ladies do
poison young gentlemen; and so there is danger of
an universal sanies, from this corrupted and cor-
rupting cause.

Robert Bage, Preface to *Man as He Is* (1792)

In 1788, as so often since, the future of the English novel seemed doubtful.
Seventeen years had passed since the death of Smollett, and only Fanny
Burney had produced anything remotely comparable with the famous
novels of the mid-century; while bad novels abounded. The increased demand for light reading had given rise to a new industry, and faced with its
products the reviewers sometimes felt that the decline of the novel was ir-

reversible. "We are indeed so sickened with this worn-out species of composition, that we have lost all relish for it," writes John Noorthouck of the *Monthly*, who later begs young writers: "let not the rare success of two or three masters in this species of composition, tempt you to sink into the lowest class of literary drudges, for poor pay, and public contempt."[1] In the same journal Thomas Ogle, dealing with a story translated from the German, "soon found that, whatever country gave it birth, a novel was a novel; that it was still the same unnatural, ridiculous, tedious, and stupid, composition."[2] Such impatient remarks may be excused, for novels formed the most burdensome part of the reviewer's task. They were numerous without being varied: a journal might easily make the mistake of reviewing the same novel twice.[3] Most ran to three volumes, some to five. The policy of comprehensive reviewing meant that not even the most trivial could be ignored, as almost all novels were later ignored by the *Edinburgh* and *Quarterly*. A critic had to read at least enough of each one to be sure of its "moral tendency"; but the resulting article was usually short and therefore unremunerative. It is not surprising that a conscientious reviewer like William Enfield should have asked Griffiths to send him as few novels as possible.[4]

Yet even at its lowest ebb the novel was not excluded from the comprehensive coverage of literature provided by the Reviews. This in itself helped to foster the development of prose fiction, as Robert D. Mayo has argued:

> The fact that busy, learned and cultivated readers of the *Monthly* and *Critical* should be asked to give a small but fairly regular part of their attention to new fiction season after season, year after year, for more than half a century was no small advantage to the genre as a late-comer on the literary scene. It helped beyond any other single agency (outside the obvious merits of the better novels themselves) to ensure for prose fiction a recognized place in the total eighteenth-century consciousness. It was also a guarantee of ultimate respectability from which the nineteenth-century novelists vastly benefited.[5]

Moreover, whatever they might think of the examples they were faced with, most reviewers at most times believed in the possibilities of the novel as a form. Thomas Holcroft, who was both a novelist and a reviewer, gives a dignified reply to the remark by Bage quoted at the head of this chapter:

> When we consider the influence that novels have over the manners, sentiments, and passions, of the rising generation, —instead of holding them in the contempt which, as reviewers, we are without exception said

to do, — we may esteem them, on the contrary, as forming a very essential branch of literature. That the majority of novels merit our contempt, is but too true; and, for the reason above given, it is a truth of a serious and painful nature. The very end of a novel is to produce interest in the reader, for the characters of whom he reads: — but, in order to produce this interest, it is necessary that the novel writer should be well acquainted with the human heart, should minutely understand its motives, and should possess the art, without being either tedious or trifling, of minutely bringing them to view. This art is so little understood by the young ladies who at present write novels, which none but young ladies and we, luckless reviewers, read, that it is not wonderful that they should have incurred a considerable share of neglect from us: — but when a novel has the power of playing on the fancy, interesting the affections, and teaching moral and political truth, we imagine that we are capable of feeling these beauties, and that we have liberality enough to announce them to the world.[6]

The flood of cheap fiction did not slacken in the last quarter of the century; but several excellent novels also appeared, and their merits were usually recognised. When confronted with such works, the reviewers could pay very handsome compliments to the novelist's art. No genre, writes one, "has a more legitimate claim to an ascendancy over the human mind than a well-written novel"; to produce such a work is "a more difficult and glorious feat in literature than the turning of a thousand sonnets"; and the novel is "a species of composition, the laws and appropriate merits of which it might become an Aristotle to investigate and pronounce upon."[7]

The criteria most frequently applied were those of "nature" and morality. By *nature* the reviewers implied their preference for realism, as it was understood in that age: a novel, they considered, should be a heightened representation of contemporary life, with plausible characters and a not-too-improbable plot. Thus *Henry and Isabella* is described as giving "a truly agreeable picture, coloured according to nature"; three novels entitled *Eleonora, Euphemia,* and *Louisa* all earn the praise of "natural incidents"; and the "natural" characters of Richard Graves's *Plexippus* and Charlotte Smith's *Young Philosopher* are contrasted with the "caricatures" of inferior novels.[8] This traditional view of the novel was justified by reference to the practice of Richardson, Fielding, and even Smollett. Such standards were not always adequate to deal with the "novel of purpose" that flourished in the 1790s; and to the Gothic romance they were largely irrelevant. Thus demands were made upon the open-mindedness of the reviewers, as well as upon their faith and vigilance. Their concern for "morality" has been found excessive, and is strongly censured by Ernest Baker:

> The influence of the reviews often became thoroughly mischievous through the obstinate prepossessions of the reviewers. Instead of applying canons of imaginative art . . . the reviewers insisted that every story must enforce a moral lesson. . . . The *Critical,* the *Monthly,* and the rest of the reviews, when they dealt with fiction, uniformly acted upon these principles, insisting upon the most rigid and indeed the most stilted morality.[9]

To put moral considerations foremost was of course a characteristic of many writers in that age, including Johnson, Coleridge, Southey, Godwin, Fanny Burney, and Mary Wollstonecraft — all of whom wrote reviews. Yet the age was not barren of criticism. Doubtless the reviewing of novels sometimes called forth a needlessly protective attitude on behalf of the young girls who were supposed to read them; but here too the reviewers were simply acting and thinking as men of their time. George Steevens, an editor of the *Critical,* wrote a crushing moral indictment of *Manon Lescaut* in a private letter to the luckless translator, who had sent him a copy.[10] Good criticism could be, and was, written despite such preoccupations. But a distinction should be made between the brief notices of the Catalogues and the more elaborate main reviews. In the Catalogues, dealing for the most part with cheap fiction to which "canons of imaginative art" could not seriously be applied, reviewers often did little more than separate the harmless from the possibly harmful. When criticising better novels they could take a broader view, as examples in this chapter will show.

In novels as in poetry the period was one of experiment, and therefore challenging to the critics; but the reviewers of novels had certain advantages. It is usually easier to convey one's experience of a good novel than of a good poem. Moreover, nature and morality are more useful criteria than correctness and elegance, for the principles implied ·are fundamentally sound. Even a romance must have its own kind of truth to life, though it will not give the effect of a transcript, and the evaluation of a novel almost inevitably raises moral issues. Not all reviewers interpreted these principles so broadly; but it is generally true that the appreciative critic in this field was less hampered by outworn notions and phrases than the critic of poetry.

Charlotte Smith

Romance is a useful term for forms of fiction which, unlike the true novel, do not aim at the direct representation of real life.[11] From the mid-seventeenth to the mid-eighteenth century the romance, exemplified by *The Grand Cyrus* and other marvellous stories, was in disrepute. "The special characteristic of all these romances . . . was their falseness and unreality, all that was imaginary and impossible in them, all that was contrary to the more rational view of life which was beginning to dominate men's minds."[12] The word *romantic* came into our language to express these qualities, and it is understandable (though often inconvenient) that the major cultural development which began in the later eighteenth century should be known as the Romantic movement. Men turned with renewed interest to tales of chivalry and enchantment; they even created new romances, preserving in many cases the medieval costume and background. In the following century the "Gothic" romance declined, but other varieties sprang up and still flourish.

Not all reviewers distinguished between the romance and the novel proper; and even those who allowed the romance to be a separate genre with laws of its own often regarded it as a childish and obsolete one. The type of story that stimulates terror by supernatural or quasi-supernatural devices was obnoxious to the spirit of the Enlightenment. Holcroft puts the case against such stories succinctly in the *Monthly Review:*

> Of all the resources of invention, this, perhaps, is the most puerile, as it is certainly among the most unphilosophic. It contributes to keep alive that superstition which debilitates the mind, that ignorance which propagates error, and that dread of invisible agency which makes inquiry criminal. . . . The good writer teaches the child to become a man; the bad and the indifferent best understand the reverse art of making a man a child.[13]

When *The Castle of Otranto* appeared in 1764 John Langhorne, in the same Review, had praised its dramatic power but regretted that its appeal should be restricted to "those who can digest the absurdities of Gothic fiction, and bear with the machinery of ghosts and goblins." The *Critical* had comdemned the tale outright: "The publication of any work, at this time, in England composed of such rotten materials, is a phænomenon we cannot account for."[14] Clara Reeve's *Old English Baron* (1777), a less extravagant romance, had been received with slightly more favour,[15] and Sophia Lee's *The Recess* (1783-86) had won praise for its elaborate historical background.[16] But in the 1780s most critics still frowned upon a kind of writing that not only violated the canon of "nature," but dealt in "the strange luxury of artificial terror."

At this point they were confronted by a writer who could combine romance and realism. Charlotte Smith[17] describes her own works as novels: her minor characters are "drawn from nature," often with satirical heightening; her backgrounds are of contemporary life, and her dialogues, and touches of concrete detail, sometimes suggest the more fully developed realism of later novelists. Yet, with all this, she is the forerunner and corrival of Ann Radcliffe. Almost all her novels contain episodes of mystery, suspense, and nocturnal alarm, often in a setting of Gothic architecture. Her lavish use of picturesque scenery in the earlier novels anticipates that of her famous successor. Finally, the leaven of the daydream is strongly at work: her heroes and heroines are dream figures, like Emily and Valancour, and their adventures are governed by no strict standard of probability.

Charlotte Smith's first novel was *Emmeline, the Orphan of the Castle* (1788). Its setting is in contemporary Britain, and its plot, evolved from the conflict of love and duty, supposed illegitimacy and propriety, resembles that of Fanny Burney's *Cecilia.* But the heroine is exposed to the influence of two castles, in Ireland and Wales; and at Mowbray, in the dead of night, she is alarmed by "a rustling, and indistinct footsteps near her room."[18] Other terrifying incidents follow: a pursuit through a long dark gallery, a candle blown out, a voice that replies but is not that of the person addressed. . . . A new and still unobtrusive feature of the novel is its careful description of ancient buildings and of romantic wooded scenery.[19]

The reviews were generally favourable. "Charlotte Smith, after tripping not ungracefully among the shrubbery of Parnassus, [20] has attempted to tread the more elevated and arduous paths of the mountain, and done it, so far, with success," wrote the *English* reviewer; in the *Monthly* Andrew Becket paid a similar compliment; the *Critical* found *Emmeline* nearly, if not quite, as good as *Cecilia.* The Gothic element in the novel attracted no comment. The *Critical* and *English* concentrated on the realistic aspect of Charlotte Smith's art, praising her characters and plots: "The story is well imagined, and the incidents so well conducted that every one hastens on the event," wrote the *Critical,* while the *English* noted that "she seems to aid at natural strokes of *character,* not bizarre dashes of caricatura." Mary Wollstonecraft places *Emmeline* above the common run of novels, but her *Analytical* notice none the less criticises the work severely by the standards of "nature" and morality:

> The false expectations these wild scenes excite, tend to debauch the mind, and throw an insipid kind of uniformity over the moderate and rational prospects of life, consequently *adventures* are sought for and created, when duties are neglected, and content despised. We will venture to ask any young girl if Lady Adelina's theatrical contrition did not catch her attention, while Mrs. Stafford's rational resignation escaped her notice?

This judgement may be thought unduly harsh: Lady Adelina's story forms only a minor episode in a novel that contains few "wild scenes." Andrew Becket takes a juster view when he declares that *Emmeline* resembles the calm and pleasing landscapes of Claude Lorraine rather than the wild, magnificent scenery of Salvator Rosa. The picturesque descriptions won praise from all four reviewers: Mary Wollstonecraft found that the most natural feelings in the novel were those described as being inspired by romantic scenery, and the *Critical* observed that ". . . the scenes are often drawn with great beauty. Mrs. Smith excels in landscape-painting." All four critics recognised Charlotte Smith's talent, and the *Critical* and *English* gave well-balanced reviews.

Charlotte Smith's second novel, *Ethelinde; or The Recluse of the Lake* (1789), was modelled on her first; as the *Analytical* remarked, "the two heroines might be taken for twin sisters." *Ethelinde,* however, stands closer to the romances of Ann Radcliffe. The plot is looser, the descriptions (this time of the English Lake district) are more frequent and prominent, and the episode in which the heroine, alone in a tapestry-hung room, believes that she sees her father's ghost[21] is worked up with much care.

The Reviews were again very favourable. The *Analytical* apparently refers to the scene in the tapestry room when it remarks that some incidents are "mere stage tricks," but no other objections were raised on this score. Warm praise was again bestowed upon the picturesque descriptions. The *Analytical* declared that Charlotte Smith saw nature with a poet's eye: "Her picturesque views of the lake claim the warmest praise; indeed, all her landscapes are drawn by pencil of taste, that can feel and describe the evanescent graces, which . . . escape the notice of common, blunt organs." The *Critical* found the descriptions "some of the best parts of the work," and Becket in the *Monthly* wished the author had given more of them: "As her imagination is really poetical, she sometimes considerably heightens our British scenery, and almost brings the Thessalian Tempe to our view." But the Reviews were not undiscriminating. "The story wants a grand point of interest," remarked the *Analytical,* "and innumerable misfortunes are so entangled together, that sympathy must be worn out, and give place to sheer curiosity, long before the close of the fifth volume." The *Critical* observed that the story was "scarcely progressive," and would have liked to see the five volumes reduced to three. The insipidity of the heroine was also discussed. The *Critical* noted that almost her only trait was "a tender affec-tionate softness," and that as a person she was less significant than other characters. The *Analytical* was more direct: "The heroine is too often sick, and rather inspires love than respect." Becket found Ethelinde too perfect to be natural. By contrast, the minor figures — Tom Davenant, the Newendens, the Chestervilles, the Maltravers, realistic characters in Fielding's manner — were discussed with enthusiasm. These are three unusually detailed and successful reviews.

Celestina (1791) has one gloomy castle in the south of France, but no supernatural episode occurs there. In other respects the work has even more of the romance than Charlotte Smith's other novels. Celestina's birth and upbringing are more mysterious and less probable even than those of Emmeline, plausibility is often sacrificed for the sake of a strong scene or a change of setting, and the plot is finally resolved by the sudden, causeless transfer of hitherto unshakeable affections. Landscapes are introduced from England, Switzerland, Provence, the Pyrenees, the Hebrides, and the Scottish Highlands.

If we may judge by the Reviews, it was with *Celestina* that Charlotte Smith reached the height of her reputation. The *Monthly, Critical,* and *English* introduce the work with much preliminary pomp; the *Critical* describes Charlotte Smith as the rival of Fanny Burney, and the *English* sees these two women, with Sophia Lee, as the heirs of Fielding and Smollett. The *Monthly* and *Critical* comment on Thorold's sudden change of heart, but overlook other improbabilities; Enfield in the *Monthly* even notes a "general air of probability," and the *English* is pleased to find "no unnatural effects produced by particular causes." The characters are generally praised, and the *Critical* accepts with only a slight touch of irony that since "the hero and heroine must be of course faultless," characterisation must be sought among the minor figures. Both *Monthly* and *Critical* admire the pathos of the final *éclaircissement:* the *Critical* reviewer confesses to having more than once been obliged to remove his spectacles (conventional properties, like the "grey beards" officially worn by reviewers). Mary Wollstonecraft was again more exacting, and her notice alone is preponderantly unfavourable. She objects to the "romantic adventures, and artificial passions, that novel reading has suggested to the mind of the author," and wishes "that with Mrs. Smith's abilities, she had the courage to think for herself, and not view life through the medium of books." But she joins in the praise of the descriptions, finding "a degree of sentiment in some of her delicate tints, that steals on the heart, and made us *feel* the exquisite taste of the mind that had guided the pencil." The *Monthly* and *Critical* also warmly commended the landscapes, and the *English* agreed that "the fair author's *forte* is certainly the poetic and descriptive."

The reader who judges *Celestina* by its truth to life must agree with Mary Wollstonecraft's strictures; the more flexible critic will disregard the label "A Novel" and accept the semi-romantic convention within which *Celestina* is written, as in effect the *Monthly, Critical* and *English* reviewers did.

Charlotte Smith's fourth work of fiction, *Desmond* (1792), is a "novel of purpose" expressing sympathy with the French Revolution, and was discussed largely in terms of its political content. But with *The Old Manor House* (1793) this author returned to her formula of an improbable love story in a realistic setting. Mrs. Rayland is a more plausible figure than the

Marchesa di Vivaldi, but Monimia is immured at Rayland Hall as romantically and improbably as Ellena at the Convent of San Stefano. Nor are Gothic terrors wanting: the Hall is believed to be haunted, and two scenes of nocturnal alarm take place as the result of sinister noises beneath the chapel.[22] These are later found to have been caused by smugglers, in the same way that the haunting of the Chateau Villefort in *Udolpho* (1794) is explained by the activities of pirates.

With the exception of the *Critical,* the Reviews were very favourable. Three of the five critics mentioned the improbabilities of the story, but were not seriously perturbed: the romantic adventures of Orlando and Monimia were generally found acceptable, and the work was even praised for its realism, though examples of this quality were necessarily drawn from the background and from minor characters. Enfield's criticism in the *Monthly* is representative:

> This young pair, Orlando and Monimia, who find opportunities for frequent interviews, entertain a tender and innocent attachment for each other. The principal business of the piece is to exhibit the embarrassments which attend their concealed passion. . . . The narrative, if not in every particular guided by probability, is however too well filled up with incident to suffer the reader's attention to flag. The characters are drawn with strength and discrimination, and speak their own appropriate language.

The *British Critic* found that Orlando's adventures in England, if not those in America, were made to appear probable, and the *English* thought the story "adapted to the level of domestic life." Charlotte Smith's characters were generally admired, the favourites being Mrs. Rayland, Mrs. Lennard, Dr. Hollybourn, and General Tracy; Enfield particularly approved of the manner in which the "inferior ranks" were portrayed. This critic also enjoyed the setting: "one of those spacious antient halls, or manor houses, which fill the warm imagination with romantic ideas, and which at once invite and favour adventure."

The *Critical* reviewer alone, standing fast to his canons of nature and morality, refused to accept the tacit conventions of the work. After discussing the criteria of the true novel he summarises the plot of *The Old Manor House* in terms that invite us to imagine it taking place in real life; he naturally finds it both immoral and absurd. He emphasises the weaknesses of the plot, the improbability of the incidents, and the magical resolution of all difficulties at the conclusion. He condemns even more strongly the "moral tendency" of the story: Orlando indulges his passion for a girl of low birth, visits her nightly in her *bed-room in the turret* (reviewer's italics), and marries her on a capital of £250; yet in the end ". . . youthful thoughtlessness and intemperance are crowned with success." These objections are logical enough. Yet surely Enfield approaches nearer the spirit in which *The Old Manor House* should be read when he allows its flow of incidents to distract him from its improbabilities, and accepts the "tender and innocent attachment" of Orlando and Monimia at its face value. Indeed, the work is as innocent as a fairy tale.

The *Critical* reviewer might be thought to embody that rational spirit which resisted the progress of romance. Yet it is he who admires the "Gothic" episodes: he describes the more ghostly of the two as "among the most interesting events in the work," quoting it at length, and compliments Charlotte Smith on her "power to arrest and command attention, by a happy description of circumstances and objects awful, terrific, and sublime." The other critics paid no special attention to these episodes.

Charlotte Smith's subsequent novels are of less interest, and their reception need only be briefly summarised. *The Banished Man* (1794) expresses a change of attitude towards the French Revolution, which it violently attacks. These sentiments won little favour from the *Monthly, Critical,* and *Analytical,* and though the *British Critic* approved of them, all reviews of this novel were short. From this date onwards all the Reviews showed less interest in Charlotte Smith's work. For this the chief cause was the undoubted decline in her writing: not even Scott had been able for long to turn out good novels at the rate of one a year, as she had been doing since 1788, and her basic patterns were becoming threadbare. Her excursions into politics had probably done her more harm than good; moreover, she was becoming increasingly obsessed with private grievances. From *The Banished Man* onwards her novels are filled with references to treacherous relations and grasping lawyers: such allusions were invariably condemned by the reviewers, who believed that "private history should not be introduced for public perusal."[23]

In *Montalbert* (1795) Charlotte Smith avoided politics and returned to the formula of a simple heroine of complex parentage, a romantic story, and a realistic setting. The Reviews were favourable, but did not restore her to her former position of importance: notices were even shorter than those of *The Banished Man,* and two appeared in the Catalogues. The story of *Marchmont* (1796) resembles that of *The Old Manor House,* and provoked similar objections from the *Critical:* the Catalogue notices of the *Monthly* and *Analytical* were even less favourable. *The Young Philosopher* (1798), an exposure of social evils as seen by a virtuous young man of Rousseauistic upbringing, was kindly treated by the *Critical* and *Analytical* and more faintly praised by the *Monthly.*

By 1794, the year of *Udolpho,* Charlotte Smith had been surpassed both in her descriptions of romantic scenery and her episodes of "Gothic" suspense. Rather, perhaps, than be outshone where once she ruled supreme, she made little use of these features in her later novels,[24] though

Marchmont has some pleasant landscapes and the most magnificent of her ruined castles. By 1796 there were signs of a reaction among the reviewers against the Gothic romance, and they approved Charlotte Smith's abstinence.

> Mountains, woods, castellated rocks overhanging a lake, luxuriant thickets, glowing sunsets, and midnight storms, if without intermission presented to the reader, cannot but become extremely tedious,

wrote Arthur Aikin in his review of *Montalbert:* the wheel had come full circle since another *Monthly* reviewer, Andrew Becket, wished Charlotte Smith had used her descriptive talent more freely. In 1798 the *Critical* observed, in a review of *The Young Philosopher:*

> Her stories do not agitate like the mysterious horrors of Mrs. Radcliffe; they do not divert like the lively caricatures of Mrs. D'Arblay; but, more true to life than either, they awaken that gentle and increasing interest, which excites our feelings to the point of pleasure, not beyond it.

But these rather negative merits could not save Charlotte Smith from sinking out of favour. The *Critical* review of her last considerable publication, *The Letters of a Solitary Wanderer* (1801), resembles an obituary:

> Genius has its dawn, its maturity and decline. While we admit that Mrs. Smith has possessed this quality in a considerable degree, we must also confess that it now only sparkles in occasional coruscations, and that she often borrows from "meaner spirits of the muses' train," and not unfrequently from herself. . . . Yet, though the discharge of our duty to the public has led us to a somewhat scrutinous criticism on these volumes, we must remember, with kindness and gratitude, the author who has so often interested and entertained us, who has, for a time, checked the tear, or induced a temporary oblivion of the wounded spirit.

The *Monthly* mentioned the work politely but perfunctorily in its Catalogue. Charlotte Smith was well on the way to the status she so long retained of a forgotten favourite.

The reviewers on the whole dealt justly with Charlotte Smith's novels: they were quick to notice her talents, gave her best novels warm praise, and politely but firmly registered her decline. They praised the realistic aspect of her work, but most of them also came tacitly to accept the element of romantic fantasy with which her novels are permeated. They sometimes enjoyed, sometimes criticised her "Gothic" episodes, but paid them no excessive attention. From the first, however, they admired her picturesque landscapes, and the reviews of *Emmeline, Ethelinde,* and *Celestina* show that such backgrounds for fiction were popular well before the appearance of Ann Radcliffe's *Romance of the Forest*. The overworking of this vein by these two writers and others subsequently led to complaints. Twelve of the sixteen notices here fully discussed (those of *Emmeline, Ethelinde, Celestina*, and *The Old Manor House*) may be called satisfactory pieces of reviewing. Taken together, these articles show that Charlotte Smith enjoyed considerable status between 1789 and 1794 even among the "greybeard" reviewers, and that some features of her work certainly prepared the way for the success of Ann Radcliffe.

Ann Radcliffe

Unlike Charlotte Smith, Ann Radcliffe does not term her works novels but romances, thus disclaiming the imitation of "nature" and implying that prose fiction may have other legitimate ends. The Gothic romance, of which she is the most famous and successful exponent, has sometimes been extended as a genre to include all narratives of the period that include scenes of horror.[25] Ann Radcliffe's own kind of romance, however, has been outlined thus:

> A sensitive but spirited girl is brought to a Gothic building and exposed to its influence. She is lonely, helpless, in unhappy circumstances and presently threatened by real peril, and her reasonable fears gradually sap her defences against the unaccountable terrors with which her surroundings and the confused stories of ignorant servants inspire her. Her nerves are subjected to a series of slight, harassing attacks, in which intimations of earthly and ghostly terror are blended.[26]

This genre makes for an exciting narrative, subtly developed, and for studies in the psychology of fear. But though Ann Radcliffe provides both of these, her deeper purpose is to capture the effects on the sensibility of Gothic architecture or of picturesque scenery. The centre of interest lies neither in character nor in plot, but in "the southern landscape, whose fullest effect is to be elicited by the happy musing lovers or by their terror-stricken flight; it is the castle or convent, for complete expression of which we require both the victim and the tyrant."[27]

Ann Radcliffe's first publication, *The Castles of Athlin and Dunbayne* (1789), is a romance of medieval chivalry. It holds the attention in spite of improbable events and two-dimensional characters, and its rapid action shows a narrative power that was to be smothered by the diffuseness of some of the later works. It does not resemble these in pattern: its central figures are not passive heroines, but active men; it has few descriptions, and only the faintest hint of supernatural terror. It does, however, reveal Mrs. Radcliffe's fondness for secret doors and intricate underground passages.

The *Critical* review consists of two sentences:

> There is some fancy and much romantic imagery in the conduct of this story; but our pleasure would have been more unmixed had our author preserved better the manners and costume of the Highlands. He seems to be unacquainted with both.

Andrew Becket's notice in the *Monthly* is also brief:

> To those who are delighted with the *marvellous,* whom wonders, and wonders only, can charm, the present production will afford a considerable degree of amusement. This kind of entertainment, however, can be little relished but by the young and unformed mind. To men who have . . . attained the meridian of life, a series of events, which seem not to have their foundation in nature, will ever be insipid, if not disgustful. The author of this performance appears to have written on the principle of Mr. Bayes, to *elevate and surprise.* By means of *trap-doors, false pannels, subterranean passages,* &c. &c. this purpose is effected: and all this . . . will possibly have its admirers. But though we are not of the number of such readers, we must honestly confess, that this little work is to be commended for its moral; as also for the good sentiments and reflections which occasionally occur in it.

It will be seen that there are degrees of merit even among the shortest Catalogue notices. While the *Critical* gives only vague praise and unimportant criticism, the *Monthly* at least raises the important question of whether an adult taste can find pleasure in the marvellous. Becket gives the classical and conservative answer; later reviewers were to be less confident.

A Sicilian Romance (1790) is one of Ann Radcliffe's best stories. It has numerous Gothic features: a persecuted heroine, an apparently haunted castle, a convent, flights through tunnels and caves, banditti, and rich Sicilian landscapes. Julia is more enterprising and more interesting than Ann Radcliffe's other heroines,[28] and the narrative of her adventures is rapid and full of incident.

Two critics pointed out the unusual merit of the work. William Enfield, reviewing *A Sicilian Romance* together with seven novels in the *Monthly* Catalogue, was brief but appreciative:

> In this tale, we meet with something more than the alternate tears and rapture of tender lovers. The writer possesses a happy vein of invention, and a correctness of taste, which enable her to rise above the level of mediocrity. Romantic scenes, and surprizing events, are exhibited in elegant and animated language.

The *Critical* reviewer seems to have been pleased against his will, but gave more space to *A Sicilian Romance* than Enfield and came to closer terms with it:

This very interesting novel engages the attention, in defiance of numerous improbabilities and "hairbreadth scapes" too often repeated. Perhaps, on a second reading, these might be still more disgusting; but it is an
experiment that we can scarcely venture to try but with modern novels
of the first class. We found the tale . . . very entertaining, and involved
with art, developed with skill, and the event concealed with great dexterity. If our author again engages in this task, we would advise her not
to introduce so many caverns with such peculiar concealments, or so
many spring-locks which open only on one side.

Ann Radcliffe's second romance may be seen as lifting its head above the
flood of anonymous cheap fiction that filled the Catalogues.

Her third publication, *The Romance of the Forest* (1791), appeared
with her name in all editions after the first. It is longer than her previous
works and lacks their unity. The first volume, set in a ruined abbey, is in
the Gothic mode, while the second displays Adeline's resistance to the
Lovelace-like schemes of the Marquis; both volumes can still be found exciting. In the third, the action is for long periods becalmed among tears
and sensibility. With the reviewers this mixture was extremely successful.
By common consent they dealt with *The Romance of the Forest,* not in the
Catalogues, but in the main review sections, and all gave it warm praise. In
the *Monthly,* William Enfield ventured a limited defence of the romance as
a genre:

> The days of chivalry and romance being (ALAS! as Mr. Burke says,)
> for ever past, we must hear no more of enchanted forests and castles,
> giants, dragons, walls of fire, and other "monstrous and prodigious
> things;" — yet still forests and castles remain, and it is still within the
> province of fiction, without overstepping the limits of nature, to make
> use of them for the purpose of creating surprise. By the aid of an inven-
> tive genius, much may still be done, even in this philosophical age, to
> fill the fancy with marvellous images, and to "quell the soul with
> grateful terrors."

The qualification "without overstepping the limits of nature" suggests that
an author may make his forests and castles appear as enchanted as he
pleases so long as, like Mrs. Radcliffe, he eventually supplies satisfactory
material causes for such appearances. Similarly, the *Critical* observes:

> We have [as with *Otranto* and the *Old English Baron*] the ruined abbey,
> a supposed ghost, the skeleton of a man secretly murdered, with all the
> horrid train of images which such scenes and such circumstances may
> be supposed to produce. They are managed, however, with skill, and do
> not disgust by their improbability: every thing is consistent, and within
> the verge of rational belief: the attention is uninterruptedly fixed, till
> the veil is designedly withdrawn.

(Can this phrase have given Mrs. Radcliffe the hint for the famous, literally veiled secret in *Udolpho*?) The *English* agrees that the author has kept within the limits of "nature."

The critics also appreciated her power of creating suspense. "The novel before us engages the attention strongly, and interests the feelings very powerfully," wrote the *Critical,* noting also that ". . . events are concealed with the utmost art, and even suspicion sometimes designedly misled." The *Monthly* commented on her ability "to hold the reader's curiosity continually in suspense, and at the same time to keep his feelings in a state of perpetual agitation"; and praised "the happy manner in which the authoress has concealed the termination of the plot till the last *éclaircissement*." All three reviewers enjoyed "the rapid succession of woody glens, tufted battlements, long-drawn aisles, and scattered fragments of ancient grandeur" (*Monthly*); the *Critical* noted that the picturesque scenes of Savoy seemed "drawn from personal examination,"[29] and the *English* thought most care had been taken with the descriptive passages. All chose picturesque scenes for their extracts.

Both *Monthly* and *Critical* give excellent reviews, but the *Critical* reviewer must have the credit of being the first to deal so fully with a work of this kind. That he was conscious of his own daring is clear from his final paragraph:

> If it may appear, that we have commended this novel with an eager warmth, we can only say, in apology for it, that we have copied our real sentiments. The lady is wholly unknown to us, and probably will ever continue so. We must, however, consider "The Romance of the Forest" as one of the first works in this line of novel-writing that we have seen.

The Mysteries of Udolpho (1794), most famous of all Gothic romances, represents the maturity of Ann Radcliffe's art. It is more than twice as long as the usual novel or romance of this period, but carries its length well despite occasional diffuseness. The romance opens with an idealised picture of domestic life at La Vallée, governed by benevolent principle, sensibility, and taste; this life is later contrasted with the coarse, unfeeling vanity of polite society, and then, more dramatically still, with the violence of robbers and *condottieri*. Udolpho is Mrs. Radcliffe's most impressive castle, vast, ruinous, and full of terrors both imaginary and real; and its tyrant master, Montoni, is a striking prefiguration of the Byronic hero.[30] Emily escapes his grasp and takes refuge with a friendlier family, but these too have their castle, secret, and ghosts. Meanwhile her lover, Valancourt, at Paris, has fallen under the spell of a countess, and his expiatory sufferings give occasion for a display of sentiment and moral principle. Thus all the author's favourite themes are employed.

Udolpho was greeted with enthusiasm, taking first place in the *Critical*[31] for August 1794 and second place in the *British Critic* for the same month. The five reviews discussed here average seven pages in length. George Dyer, writing in the *Analytical*,[32] found that *Udolpho* surpassed the *Romance of the Forest;* Enfield in the *Monthly* found it equally good with that work, the *Critical* less good only because it was too long; the *British Critic* pronounced it "one of the best and most interesting" of Mrs. Radcliffe's works, and the *English* rather obtusely called it "the best composition of this kind to appear since Mrs. Inchbald's Simple Story."

The critics found the same merits in *Udolpho* as in the earlier romances. Enfield describes with approval Ann Radcliffe's technique of producing ghostly effects by what later turn out to be mundane causes:

> Without introducing . . . any thing really supernatural, Mrs. Radcliffe has contrived to produce as powerful an effect as if the invisible world had been obedient to her magic spell; and the reader experiences in perfection the strange luxury of artificial terror, without being obliged for a moment to hoodwink his reason, or to yield to the weakness of superstitious credulity.

The *Critical* and *British Critic* dwell on the same point. The *Critical* also gave lucid testimony to her power of maintaining suspense:

> The same powers of description are displayed, the same predilection is discovered for the wonderful and the gloomy — the same mysterious terrors are continually exciting in the mind the idea of a supernatural appearance, keeping us, as it were, upon the very edge and confines of the world of spirits, and yet are ingeniously explained by familiar causes; curiosity is kept upon the stretch from page to page, and from volume to volume, and the secret, which the reader thinks himself every instant on the point of penetrating, flies like a phantom before him, and eludes his eagerness till the very last moment of protracted expectation.

All reviewers praised the descriptions — "rich, glowing, and varied" — and the *Monthly* and *British Critic* commented on the consistent characterisation. The characters most admired were Emily, Madame Cheron, and Montoni, and Enfield gave an enthusiastic appreciation of the melancholy tyrant.

Some adverse criticism also appeared, the most cogent being that of the *Critical:*

> Curiosity is raised oftener than it is gratified; or rather, it is raised so high that no adequate gratification can be given it; the interest is completely dissolved when once the adventure is finished, and the reader, when he is got to the end of the work, looks about in vain for the spell which had bound him so strongly to it.

The reviewer reasonably concludes that

> four volumes cannot depend entirely on terrific incidents and intricacy of story. They require character, unity of design, a delineation of the scenes of real life, and the variety of well supported contrast.

The *British Critic* likewise comments that "the Mysteries of Udolpho have too much of the terrific: the sensibility is sometimes jaded, and curiosity in a manner worn out." This reviewer anticipates Scott's criticism that Ann Radcliffe's "explanations" are sometimes as incredible as the supernatural itself:

> The endeavour to explain supernatural appearances and incidents, by plain and simple facts, is not always happy; and in particular the strange removal of Lodovico [*sic*] from the chateau of the Count de Villefort, and his being found after a long interval among Banditti in the Pyrenees is improbable in the extreme.

The *Critical* agrees that probability is sometimes violated, but remarks that "the trite and the extravagant are the Scylla and Charybdis of writers who deal in fiction." While admiring the picturesque landscapes, all five reviewers object that they occur too often, and all but the *English* point out that they are too much alike. "The pine and the larch tree wave, and the full moon pours its lustre through almost every chapter," complains the *Critical,* while the *British Critic* observes: "We are sometimes so fatigued at the conclusion of one representation of this kind, that the languor is not altogether removed at the commencement of that which follows."

The most interesting of these articles is that in the *Critical.* George Robinson, one of the proprietors of that Review, was also the publisher of *Udolpho* and had paid the unprecedented sum of £500 for its copyright; but though this article is the longest and most prominently placed of the group, its general effect is less commendatory than any of the others.[33] The reviewer begins with an intelligent short essay on the pleasurable excitements and the inevitable disappointments of Ann Radcliffe's kind of romance as a genre; proceeds to some adverse criticism of detail; and finally, after giving one very long extract in prose and another in verse, ends on a note of rebuke to the author for being "disposed to sacrifice excellence to quantity, and lengthen out a story for the sake of filling an additional volume." The *British Critic* makes some acute adverse criticisms, but these seem to have occurred to the writer as he neared the end of his review, so that he ends with a lower estimate of *Udolpho* than he began with. The *Monthly* appreciates Ann Radcliffe's genuine skills, but seems rather to overrate her characters. The *English* and *Analytical* give uncritical reviews, each containing little more than a summary of the plot introduced and followed by a few general remarks.

The last of Ann Radcliffe's romances to be published in her lifetime was *The Italian, or The Confessional of the Black Penitents* (1797). The story is set in the mid-eighteenth century, and the ruined castle is replaced for purposes of horror by the chambers of the Inquisition. In writing *The Italian* Mrs. Radcliffe seems to have heeded the advice of the Reviews: it is shorter than *Udolpho,* its plot is simpler and more unified, and there is much less picturesque description. Despite these improvements the work is, on the whole, less successful than its predecessor. Its events are so thickly shrouded in uncertainty that the reader loses his grasp of essentials; the author gives the impression of devising, or at least altering, her plot as she goes on; and instead of giving her characters the few simple and striking traits and motives needed for figures in her kind of romance, she spends much time in unconvincing presentation of their thought processes. The writing is also more diffuse than in *Udolpho.*[34]

Reviews of *The Italian* were on average just half as long as those of *Udolpho*; they were also less prominently placed. With the exception of the *Critical* notice, however, they were still favourable. The *Monthly* awarded *The Italian* "a very distinguished rank" in modern fiction, the *Analytical* found it an admirable work, and the *British Critic* judged that its merits would ensure it a high reputation.

Arthur Aikin's review in the *Monthly* is excellent, not least because he explicitly distinguishes between the romance and the true novel:

> The most excellent, but at the same time the most difficult, species of novel-writing consists in an accurate and interesting representation of such manners and characters as society presents. . . . Such is the Clarissa of Richardson, and such is the Tom Jones of Fielding. . . . Next comes the modern Romance; in which, high description, extravagant characters, and extraordinary and scarcely possible occurrences combine to rivet the attention, and to excite emotions more thrilling than even the best selected and best described natural scene. This species of fiction is perhaps more imposing than the former, on the first perusal: but the characteristic which distinguishes it essentially from, and shews its vast inferiority to, the genuine novel, is that, like a secret, it ceases to interest after it can no longer awaken our curiosity; while the other, like truth, may be reconsidered and studied with increased satisfaction.

Aikin concludes that though the romance is an inferior genre it should be judged by its proper criteria: "Whatever is perfect in its kind is better than an imperfect and unsuccessful attempt at any thing higher." Mary Wollstonecraft, in the *Analytical,* seems to agree that some improbability is inherent in the nature of such works. The *Critical* reviewer was Coleridge,[35] who had recently reviewed *The Monk* and was becoming critical of the Gothic genre; by contrast with the other reviewers he puts most of his emphasis on the inferiority of the romance to the novel.

It was not difficult to foresee that the *modern romance,* even supported by the skill of the most ingenious of its votaries, would soon experience the fate of every attempt to please by what is unnatural,
and by a departure from that observance of real life, which has
placed the works of Fielding, Smollett, and some other writers, among
the permanent sources of amusement.

Coleridge also points out that once we know that supernatural appearances
are always to be explained by natural causes, they cease to terrify: "So
many cries 'that the wolf is coming,' must at last lose their effect." Mary
Wollstonecraft makes the same point, but admits that despite this
foreknowledge she succumbed while reading to the charm of suspense:
"the spell, by which we are led, again and again, round the same magic
circle, is the spell of genius." The *British Critic* declares that Mrs.
Radcliffe has made able use of all the advantages offered to "the genius
and spirit of romance" by her subject and setting, but expresses surprise
that such a talented author should confine herself to this kind of writing.

On the figure of Schedoni the *Monthly, Analytical,* and *British Critic* all
bestowed praise. The *British Critic* admired "the rich enchantment of picturesque scenery"; Aikin noted with approval that the landscapes were less
obtrusive than in *Udolpho,* "though still very far from *deficient*"; Mary
Wollstonecraft thought the descriptions "less diffuse" than before, and
Coleridge also thought them less prolix but still more numerous than
necessary. Aikin alone pointed out the improved structural unity of this
romance. His is certainly the best review of the four, and the *British Critic*
is also appreciative. Both Coleridge and Mary Wollstonecraft make interesting remarks, but neither comes to close enough terms with the work
under review.

To summarise the reviewing of Ann Radcliffe's romances, one may say
that ten of the sixteen reviews were satisfactory. Her early works received
less attention than those of Charlotte Smith, partly no doubt because they
were anonymous and brief, partly because they were undisguised romances
and not novels with a romantic element. Even the first two works, however,
were not entirely overlooked, and when *The Romance of the Forest* appeared the Reviews did it ample justice. *The Mysteries of Udolpho* was
given exceptionally long and favourable notices; but three years later *The
Italian* was given less prominence, less space, and generally less praise.
Though *The Italian* is a less successful romance than *Udolpho,* no critic
gives a really good account of its faults, and its reception was almost certainly prejudiced by extraneous factors. Between 1794 and 1797 the Gothic
romance had been handled by very many writers, some inept, some intent
on quick profits, some willing to experiment with or exploit the violent
horrors of the German school. The response of the Reviews to some works
of this last class now needs consideration.

M. G. Lewis and the German School

Ann Radcliffe ceased to publish romances after 1797 because she considered that less fastidious writers had brought the genre into disrepute. Many of these writers dealt in translations or imitations of the German *Schauerromane*, which are thus described by J. M. S. Tompkins:

> The ideal elements of the English romances are wholly lacking; terror is coarsely material and love a theme for jocularity, while the delicacy, dignity and moral scrupulousness of Mrs. Radcliffe's method are replaced by a heavy-handed grotesqueness, a strained emotionalism and violent assaults on the nerves. . . . German terror is frequently hideous, for the authors detail protracted butcheries that bruise the mind to contemplate.[36]

The term "Tales of Terror" is better applied to works of this school than to the gentler romances of Ann Radcliffe.[37]

The vogue for German romances began with the publication, in the same year as *Udolpho*, of *Herman von Unna*, a translation from the German of Carl Gottlob Kramer. This work introduced to English readers the theme of the secret religious tribunal claiming its victims through mysterious agents. The book might have passed unnoticed had not William Taylor, who did much to make recent German literature known in England, made it the subject of a long article in the *Monthly*. Taylor regrets that the more distinguished romances of Goethe, Schiller, and Wieland are not widely known, but judges that *Herman of Unna* will at least have "the full force of originality." His praise recalls that which other critics were giving to Ann Radcliffe's work:

> It delineates the manners of the fifteenth century with considerable fidelity; and although the secret tribunal be painted in colours somewhat too strong and gloomy for historic truth, yet the effect produced by the description of its meetings is truly terrible, and the perpetual recurrence of its incomprehensible interference has all the *marvellousness*, without the *incredibility*, of supernatural agency.

His adverse criticism is acute: such tales, he observes,

> by familiarizing characters of a stronger sinew than are common, crimes of a bolder enormity, and modes of coercion which the tolerance of a polished age had renounced, . . . tend to suggest a revival of the heroic in virtue and vice, and to prepare the general mind for contemplating, with complacence, a sort of characters, the influence of which may not prove very compatible with the "monotonous tranquillity of modern states."

Herman of Unna was apparently popular, for eight months after Taylor's article had appeared the *Critical* gave the work an even longer review. The writer detected some improbabilities and found the tribunal scenes too frequent, but admitted that they were "wonderfully calculated to excite the imagination."

Numerous other translations and imitations followed, and "the chords of terror which had tremulously shuddered beneath Mrs. Radcliffe's gentle fingers were now smitten with a new vehemence."[38] Despite the popular vogue for such works, they usually received short and unfavourable notices. *The Ghost Seer; or Apparitionist* (1795), a translation from Schiller, was reviewed only in two Catalogues: the *British Critic* complained that the expectations aroused by Schiller's name had been disappointed, and Taylor in the *Monthly* admitted that the work was second-rate. Nevertheless, he claimed, it was original:

> It has pointed out a new source of the TERRIBLE, — the pursuit of an influence over the invisible world, — and has given birth to imitations nearly as contemptible as they are multifarious.

Even when a work of this kind found some favour with the reviewers, they seldom allowed it more than a paragraph of praise. The *Critical* review of *The Dagger* (1795), a translation from the German of Carl Grosse, consists of one sentence:

> There is originality in the incidents of this little work — the sentiments are impassioned, — the style glowing, — and, from the dénouement, some useful truths may be extracted.

The *English* agreed that though the events were improbable, at least the moral was excellent. The *British Critic* was less optimistic:

> A dissolute baron, intriguing to the annoyance of his consort's peace, and pursued by all the fiends and phantoms of romantic fiction, however reduced to a virtuous close, affords no very interesting, nor, in our judgement, instructive picture of real life.

In the *Monthly* Taylor wisely avoided moral issues, briefly praised the narrative and characters, and added a work of commendation for another romance by Grosse, *Der Genius*.

Early in the following year appeared M. G. Lewis's *The Monk* (1796), the most famous of the English tales of terror and one of the least inhibited fantasies then written.[39] The main interest of the work is frankly sexual: it describes in some detail the development and gratification of Ambrosio's lust, first for Matilda, then for Antonia. The first partner later turns out to

have been a demon; the second, Ambrosio's sister. Other elements are
sadism, indulged in in several brutal murders, the rape of Antonia, and
the torture of Ambrosio; sacrilege, in the sexual profanation of Ambrosio's
monastery and the adjoining nunnery; and necrophily, in the tale of the
Bleeding Nun and the charnel-house horrors beneath the Convent of St.
Clare. Varied and intensive use is made of supernatural effects, ranging
from prophetic dreams and palmistry to the summoning of Lucifer; two
ghosts are introduced, and the Wandering Jew makes a brief appearance.
Within the narrow limits indicated by this subject matter, *The Monk* is a
successful romance. The action moves rapidly, though the "History of
Count Raymond" forms an irritating digression; the horrors are too varied
to become wearisome; the style is brisk, and the tone often humorous. Indeed, the effect of the work as a whole is exhilarating rather than (as the
horrors would suggest) depressing.

The *British Critic* and the *Monthly* dismissed Lewis's romance very
briefly in their Catalogues. The former notice can be given in full:

> Lust, murder, incest, and every atrocity that can disgrace human
> nature, brought together without the apology of probability, or even
> possibility, for their introduction. To make amends, the moral is
> general and very *practical*; it is, "not to deal in witchcraft and
> magic, because the devil will have you at last!!" We are sorry to
> observe that good talents have been misapplied in the production
> of this monster.

Taylor discusses Lewis's sources and praises some of his verse,[40] but then
pronounces:

> A vein of obscenity, however, pervades and deforms the whole
> organization of this novel, which must ever blast, in a moral view,
> the *fair* fame that, in point of ability, it would have gained for the
> author; and which renders the work totally unfit for general circulation.

The *Analytical* review of *The Monk* has been attributed to Mary
Wollstonecraft;[41] but as will be seen, its judgements are very unlike her
usual, rather strictly moral ones. This critic, far from objecting to obscenity, finds "some scenes to mark the progress of passion very happily imagined," and adds:

> the gradual discovery of Matilda's sex and person . . . is very finely
> conceived, and truly picturesque; indeed the whole temptation is
> so artfully contrived, that a man, it should seem, were he made as
> other men are, would deserve to be d--ned who could resist even
> devilish spells, conducted with such address, and assuming such a
> heavenly form.

His imagination has been caught by Ambrosio's fate: " . . . fancy follows him to Hell, and wishes to see him meet the treacherous Matilda in her own person, and hear his bitter upbraidings. The Monk, in fact, inspires sympathy, because foiled by more than mortal weapons." Yet he observes that it was Ambrosio's pride that really betrayed him. This reviewer also differs from Enfield in his attitude to the Radcliffean pseudo-supernatural:

> the author deserves praise for not attempting to account for super-natural appearances in a natural way. After being awakened to wonder by the rumbling of a mountain, the reader has an unpleasant sensation of being tricked . . . when he perceives only a mouse creep out.

His only adverse criticism is of the interruption caused by Count Raymond's story, and the insufficiently Gothic background.

Coleridge's review in the *Critical*[42] is fairly well known and need only be briefly summarised, though it is longer, more careful, and more penetrating than the others. He begins by discussing the vogue for the horrible and the supernatural, which, though it marks the infancy of German literature, suggests a decline in that of England; though he hopes that the public, "wearied with fiends, incomprehensible characters, with shrieks, murders, and subterraneous dungeons," will soon tire of it. He outlines *The Monk* and acknowledges its merits, praising the character of Matilda as "exquisitely imagined" and the tale of the Bleeding Nun as "truly terrific." The whole romance, he finds, is "distinguished by the variety and impressiveness of its incidents," and by the author's "rich, powerful and fervid" imagination. Its faults are nevertheless more numerous and more important. A romance should entertain, but Lewis's does not: "The sufferings which he describes are so frightful and intolerable, that we break with abruptness from the delusion." He has introduced, not only supernatural marvels — which the mind can temporarily accept — but "moral miracles," or psychological impossibilities, which the imagination rejects. Thus we cannot believe that Ambrosio, in the horrifying vaults beneath the Convent of St. Clare, would still be able to feel such a transient emotion as lust. *The Monk* is obscene: "The shameless harlotry of Matilda, and the trembling innocence of Antonia, are seized with equal avidity, as vehicles of the most voluptuous images." It is also irreligious. Coleridge ends by praising Lewis's verses, and quotes an elegy ("The Exile") which he prophesies "will melt and delight the heart, when ghosts and hobgoblins shall be found only in the lumber-garret of a circulating library."

This is an exceptionally good review; the only possible objection is that Coleridge takes *The Monk* more seriously than it asks or needs to be taken. The *Analytical* review is free from any such fault, and, though far less elaborate than Coleridge's article, it may be taken as a fair one. The other two reviews are short and inadequate.

Only a few more examples of the reviewing of tales of terror need be given: these illustrate the increasing severity of critics from 1796 onwards. Two translations of *Der Genius*, by Carl Grosse, appeared in 1796, and both were unfavourably reviewed. The first, entitled *The Genius: or The Mysterious Adventures of Don Carlos de Grandez*, drew this comment from the *Critical:*

> In imitation of some of his more successful countrymen, . . . the present writer has introduced a sufficient number of ghostly stories and marvellous adventures—in the recital of which, he has not more grossly violated the laws of nature and probability, than those of composition. . . . Events equally ridiculous, unconnected, and uninteresting, are jumbled together, without method or meaning, resembling the wild ravings of a maniac.

The *Analytical* reviewer was almost equally disgusted, and found

> some scenes, of the terrible kind, exhibiting the german force and passion, others affording a monstrous and ludicrous combination of wildness and absurdity, the whole ill-connected and very negligently written.

Taylor in the *Monthly* attempted to be more discriminating: while admitting that these scenes of supernatural horror are ill-connected, he declares that they may "furnish some situations not unworthy of selection by future writers, who possess a less disorderly imagination." When a new abridged translation of *Der Genius* appeared under the famous title *Horrid Mysteries*, the *Monthly* did not notice it, and the only Review to do so awarded it a scathing paragraph. Picking up the translator's remark that "the subsequent pages are, indeed, no pattern of a perfect romance," the *Critical* commented: "no—nor a pattern of any thing else. More gross and absurd nonsense was surely never put together under the name of adventures."

The last tale of terror whose reception we need examine is *Santa Maria: or, The Mysterious Pregnancy* (1797), by Joseph Fox, which well illustrates the degradation of the form that Ann Radcliffe had made popular. The narrator, a monk, explains how he has drugged, raped, and buried alive a number of nuns. The *Analytical* pointed out that a romance should be produced by the "creative powers of mind," not by "the ravings of an extravagant imagination"; Arthur Aikin in the *Monthly* described the work as "a very poor and evident imitation of the style and character of Mrs. Radcliffe's romances"; the *British Critic* commented tartly that "if the wonder-working brains of novelists cannot produce more probable or agreeable fictions, we would advise them to descend for ever to the safer regions of fact." The best review appeared in the *Critical,* and shows what could be achieved by irony even within the limits of the Catalogues:

> Our modern romance-writers appear to be extremely desirous of ascertaining how far it is possible to carry extravagance and absurdity; and the experiment of this author, though not absolutely decisive, approaches as nearly to decision as most of the attempts which we have witnessed. . . . Besides copying, with little variation, the mysteries of all the castles lately built, he introduces the mystery of pregnancy, or . . . *Lucina sine concubitu*—a most delicate subject in a work principally intended for the amusement and instruction of *females!* It would have required abilities of no common kind to conceal the deformity of such a story; but, in the hands of Mr. Fox, it is productive of great disgust. . . .
>
> In the last volume he attempts to make his characters (who are all Italians) speak the language of Shakespeare; and he is successful as far as the source is pointed out by the repetition of "beshrew me," "ever and anon," and such scraps.—As specimens of the *grand* and *sublime* in romantic writing, the reader may take the following passages.
>
> Vol. i. p. 151, "Rodolph eagerly opened the chest—when—!!! to his infinite astonishment and horror, he beheld—a frightful vacuity!!!" These marks of *admiration* are the author's; and the meaning is, in plain English, that Rodolph opened a chest, and was surprised to find it empty.

Doubtless Jane Austen could have taken the hint for a famous scene in *Northanger Abbey,* which was already being written, from many other sources besides this article. But it can at least be said that *Northanger Abbey* came into being at a time when the clichés of the Gothic romance were being satirised from a commonsense viewpoint in the Reviews.

The attitude of the reviewers towards the development of the romance in this period can now be traced. They praised Charlotte Smith's early novels primarily for their traditional qualities, but in doing so came to tolerate certain romantic elements in their composition. Reviews of *Emmeline, Ethelinde,* and *Celestina* show them prepared to accept a degree of improbability in the plot, short episodes of Gothic suspense, and an abundance of picturesque scenery. Closely following these works came Ann Radcliffe's first outstanding success, *The Romance of the Forest;* and both this romance and *The Mysteries of Udolpho* won high praise from the reviewers. Mrs. Radclife's talent was appreciated, and her technique of explaining supernatural appearances by material causes—a concession to "nature"—was at first admired. *Herman of Unna* was also well received; and Varma is right to suggest that "on the evidence of reviews, the year 1794 may be noted as the high-water mark of Gothic fiction."[43]

The tide soon subsided. Even in 1794 the critics were complaining of an excess of picturesque description, and they continued to complain in 1796 and 1797. Mrs. Radcliffe's sham supernatural effects seem to have caused some disappointment to the *Critical* reviewer of *Udolpho* — "curiosity is raised oftener than it is gratified" — and were explicitly criticised by the *Analytical* when reviewing *The Monk*, and by the *Analytical* and *Critical* when reviewing *The Italian*. But most reviewers were not prepared to accept the alternative of the genuine supernatural, which was now being pressed upon them by the German school. William Taylor in the *Monthly* said the best that could be said for the *Schauerromane*, but other critics usually condemned or ignored them. By 1797 the excesses of some writers had driven the reviewers into strong opposition: the canon of "nature" was reasserted, and even Ann Radcliffe received less praise for *The Italian* than for her preceding two romances.

The record of the reviewers in dealing with individual works is fairly good. The most important novels and romances dealt with in these sections are *Emmeline, Ethelinde, Celestina, The Old Manor House*, Ann Radcliffe's five romances, and *The Monk*. Among them these works received 37 reviews, 25 of which can be called satisfactory. Yet little progress was made towards the rehabilitation of the romance as a distinct kind of writing. Throughout this period some reviewers continue to use the terms *romance* and *novel* interchangeably, and to apply the standard of "nature" to both: and even those who, like Coleridge and Arthur Aikin, make a clear distinction between the two genres tend to emphasise the limitations of the romance rather than its possibilities. In mitigation it should be said that the romances brought to their notice were not of the highest order, and that despite subsequent developments and refinements, the romance — supernatural or scientific — is still generally taken to be a form of writing inferior to the true novel.

Bage

Like the romance, the novel of purpose departs from the broadly realistic tradition handed down from the mid-century, though it was easier to justify in terms of current literary theory. Critics had always demanded that a novel should teach, and in the work of Bage, Holcroft, Godwin, and Mary Hays teaching is the foremost consideration. But whereas other novelists reinforced or refined traditional notions of wisdom and morality, these writers canvassed the most advanced political, social, ethical, and religious ideas of the age. They shared enough common ground to be regarded as a distinct school.[44] They disliked monarchy and priesthood; they wished to see society remodelled on more rational lines; they believed that if this were done common men would become very much wiser and more virtuous. The early events of the French Revolution gave great encouragement to these reformers, and the best of their novels were written under its stimulus.

The reviewers had, of course, already encountered fiction with a reforming purpose, notably in works by Voltaire and Rousseau. In theory they approved of the genre. John Berkenhout's review in the *Monthly* of a translation of *La Nouvelle Héloïse* illustrates the usual defence of this kind of writing:

> We confess our difference in opinion from those who consider all romances merely as books of amusement. It is certainly in the power of a moral, sensible, Writer, to convey instruction in any form or guise he shall think fit to assume; and, considering the prevailing taste of the present age, we know not whether, as a novelist, his lessons are not most likely to command attention.[45]

Opinions naturally differed as to whether Voltaire and Rousseau, or Godwin and Holcroft, were "moral, sensible writers." Critics in our period inevitably judged these novels in their light of their own political and religious opinions, which in most cases were in line with the policy of the journal to which they contributed. This does not, however, preclude good criticism: judgement upon such a novel as *Emma Courtney* involves judgement upon its doctrines, and a reviewer of 1796 who pretended to have no opinions on the subject of women's emancipation would be merely evasive. In this section reasoned criticism from an intelligible point of view has been preferred both to *ex parte* judgements, the mechanical pursuit of a "party line," and to unconvincing shows of neutrality.

At the beginning of our period Robert Bage was known as the author of four witty and entertaining novels with strong didactic tendencies: *Mount Henneth* (1782), *Barham Downs* (1784), *The Fair Syrian* (1787), and *James Wallace* (1788). His last two works, *Man as He Is* (1792) and *Hermsprong: or, Man as He Is Not* (1796), are of a similar cast. Bage's chief talent is for crisp, formal dialogue, and these two novels are full of lively discussions of the rights of men and kings, the emancipation of women, the slave trade, religious establishments, and other controversial topics. Characters who take "the liberal side of the question" inevitably get the last word. Besides his mastery of dialogue Bage has the power of creating lively, eccentric, two-dimensional characters, and in both these respects his art anticipates that of Peacock.

The structure of *Man as He Is* resembles that of a morality play. In the centre is Sir George Paradyne, a wealthy young aristocrat who, though intelligent and kind-hearted, finds himself wasting time and money in fashionable dissipation. The other characters fall into two main groups: those who represent the existing vices of society, like Lord Auschamp and Lady Mary, and those who represent the life of simplicity, integrity, and active benevolence, like Mr. Lindsay and Miss Colerain. Among the second group Bage introduces two historical figures, Lafayette and DuLally Tollendal; and in chapter 93 and elsewhere he satirises Burke's *Reflections on the French Revolution*.

The reviews were very favourable. Though *Man as He Is* was published anonymously, the *English* recognised Bage's hand and preferred this novel to his earlier ones; the *Monthly* and *Analytical* recognised its superiority to the general run of novels. All three critics approved of Bage's opinions. Thus the *English* remarks,

> With respect to religion his sentiments are liberal and enlightened; and on the subject of government he is not inclined to accede to the *ius divinum* of kings.

Holcroft, in the *Monthly*, praises Bage for "teaching moral and political truth," and the *Analytical* praises his "strength of mind, and soundness of thinking." Both the *Monthly* and the *English* quote the discussion in chapter 10 in which Miss Carlill exposes the bigotry of the Rev. Mr. Holford. But the critics do not dwell exclusively upon Bage's "sentiments." Holcroft expresses concern lest politics and metaphysics should tire the reader; what he chiefly requires in a novelist, and finds in Bage, is the power of understanding human feelings and motives. He also finds fault with *Man as He Is* for lacking unity, a criticism Bage had anticipated in his Preface. The *Analytical* likewise finds the story "rather a bundle of finely imagined incidents than a regular plot." Both *Monthly* and *Analytical* condemn the weak ending, in which the hero falls ill and thus brings about a change of heart in his mistress. All three Reviews praise Bage's characters; the *Analytical* specially commends the delicate touches that mark their individuality. This Review also comments upon Bage's "pointed" dialogue.

The *Monthly* and *Analytical* give fair reviews, and praise the novel for its real literary merits as well as approving of its doctrines; the *English* has not enough criticism of this kind. The *Analytical* notice, though appearing very late, is the best of the three. Its position, in a group of reviews the last of which bears one of her signatures, suggests that it may have been written by Mary Wollstonecraft.

In *Hermsprong: or, Man as He Is Not*, published anonymously four years later, the mixed character of Sir George Paradyne is replaced by the ideal figure whose name gives the work its title. Educated among the American Indians, Hermsprong is brave, strong, truthful, generous, and free from prejudice. He arrives in England to befriend and be befriended by a few enlightened spirits (Mr. Glen, Mr. Woodcock, Miss Campinet, Miss Fluart), and to oppose the tyranny of Lord Grondale, Dr. Blick, Mr. Corrow, and other entrenched reactionaries. Since Hermsprong has a large fortune and a claim to Lord Grondale's estate, he wins the contest with little difficulty. This is the best known and the most revolutionary of Bage's works. "The book not only shows abundant evidences of the influence of the most extreme political thinkers of his time, but contains numerous direct references to such writers as Rousseau, Thomas Paine, and Mary Wollstonecraft. Here gentle satire of social follies and shams takes on a note of bitterness, and there are passages of vigorous denunciation directed against specific evils in the body politic."[46]

The reviews of *Hermsprong* are disappointing. In the *Monthly* William Taylor commends the hero as "a prominent and fine delineation of the accomplished, firm, frank, and generous man," and states accurately that the novel has more unity than *Man as He Is;* but that is almost the sum total of his criticism. In the *Analytical* the book was reviewed by Mary Wollstonecraft herself, who probably read it with mixed feelings. Despite his generally sympathetic attitude to women's emancipation and his favourable mention of *The Rights of Woman* in chapter 42, Bage must have offended her by addressing his readers in such terms as "the dear sex," and by making his hero treat all women with exaggerated politeness. Thus, after some similar remarks to Taylor's, Mary Wollstonecraft notes only that it is difficult to make a perfect hero interesting, and remarks ambiguously that "the author has a happy mode of recommending mental improvement to a sex he loves, which the *dear creatures* can scarcely find displeasing." Two years after publication a paragraph appeared in the *Critical,* more appreciative than the others but still inadequate, in which the reviewer seems to assume that Bage is a promising new writer:

> This novel must be distinguished from the common sort. The author displays an intimate acquaintance with human nature, and delineates it with the pen of a master. His characters are drawn with just discrimination, and placed in situations where their actions strictly correspond with the original sketch. There is occasionally a little tincture of the new philosophy, as it is called, and a shade of gloom is thrown upon human life; but the writer is not unsuccessful in his humorous attempts; and, upon the whole, the reader has a chance of becoming wiser and better by a perusal of this work, if his taste has not been vitiated by the trifling productions of the age.

It points to a weakness in the eighteenth-century system of reviewing that a novel found to be masterly should still be given only a single paragraph in the Catalogue.

Holcroft

Bage wrote for the most part in isolation; Thomas Holcroft was the senior member of a group of reformers that included Godwin and Mary Wollstonecraft. After some unsuccessful early attempts at fiction, Holcroft had made his name as a dramatist. He had also found regular work with the Reviews: Murray had employed him as dramatic critic for the *English,* and at the time of writing *Anna St. Ives* he contributed frequently to the *Monthly,* with whose editor he was on fairly close terms. His novels, plays, and reviews were made vehicles for the ideas of one "as close as an Englishman could come to being a *philosophe.*"[47]

The heroine of *Anna St. Ives* (1792), an emancipated and courageous girl, has two suitors: Frank Henley, who has all the virtues of Hermsprong, and Sir Coke Clifton, who has humane feelings but unreliable principles. Anna becomes engaged to Clifton so as to win him to her ideal pursuit, the service of mankind; Henley magnanimously co-operates in this scheme. Clifton wearies of lectures and decides to possess Anna without marrying her. His complicated, Lovelace-like schemes are foiled, and Anna marries Henley; the novel closes with the hope that this pair may yet succeed in reforming Clifton by their virtuous example. If we could accept Anna and Henley as real persons we should find them solemn and priggish. Psychological realism has, however, been made to give way to moral syllogism; the resulting work is symmetrical and unified, but also closed and abstract.[48] If it holds our attention it is by the skilful management of some dramatic scenes, the vigour of its several different prose styles, and the earnest force with which Holcroft expounds his moral philosophy.

Anna St. Ives was given a mixed reception. The notice in the *Critical* was the least favourable: evidently the reviewer disliked "the levelling principle, the pretended philosophy of modern times." He does not, however, discuss Holcroft's ideas, but concentrates on the absurdity of the plot. With some truth he observes that "it displays . . . no little defect in judgement to connect these events with the modern reasoning system," and asserts that "if it were the intention of the author to ridicule the new doctrines, he could not have taken a more effectual step." Yet the volume he prefers is the last, with its account of Clifton's schemes of seduction — the most conventional but certainly not the most probable part of the story. The reviewer suggests, unjustly, that the work has an immoral tendency, and trusts that "the period of philosophical lovers will probably begin and end with Frank Henley."

Mary Wollstonecraft's review in the *Analytical* is largely favourable. She finds the characters of Anna and Henley rather high-flown, and fears that "young people . . . might catch from the highly-wrought pictures a spice of romance, and even affectation, and attempt to stride on *stilts* before they

had learned to walk steadily." But as one would expect, she recognises that
the work as a whole is far from being immoral:

> It is calculated to strengthen despairing virtue, to give fresh energy
> to the cause of humanity, to repress the pride and insolence of birth,
> and to show that true nobility which can alone proceed from the
> head and the heart.

She notes too that the story "carries the reader along, and makes him pa-
tiently swallow not a few improbabilities." In the *Monthly* William Enfield
attempts to balance these two views, admitting but excusing the improbabilities: "To convict a writer of occasionally overstepping the bounds
of nature, if it be a reflection on his judgement, is at the same time a compliment to his talents." He thinks Anna a very romantic and unlikely
character, but praises that of Henley and finds much to admire in both,
commending their noble sentiments without fully discussing them. Like
Mary Wollstonecraft, he finds the story exciting.

   The *Monthly* and *Analytical* both give fair criticisms of *Anna St. Ives.*
This group of reviews provides a study in the art of synopsis: the summary
in the *Critical* makes the novel seem ridiculous and immoral; that in the
Monthly gently brings out the extravagance of Anna's behaviour; that in
the *Analytical* is wholly sympathetic.

   Anna St. Ives describes models of virtue: *Hugh Trevor* attacks existing
vices. Holcroft's hero, like Candide, is an idealistic young man compelled
to discard one by one his illusions about society. The novel also explores
the problem of what profession may be adopted by an honest man, and
vigorously attacks most of the professions. A loose, picaresque form is now
adopted; and the work is generally closer to human life than *Anna St. Ives,*
though rather overloaded with philosophy and satire. Holcroft draws
directly upon his own experience for some of the best parts of the narrative, and for the minor episode (quoted in chapter 1, above) in which
Wilmot turns reviewer.

   The first three volumes of *Hugh Trevor* appeared in 1794, and were
reviewed while Holcroft was in prison awaiting trial for high treason. The
British Critic naturally regretted that two such novelists as Holcroft and
Godwin had enlisted in "the opposition to revealed religion and to civil
society." The reviewer accuses Holcroft of ridiculing the institution of marriage, and also University discipline, without suggesting any substitute for
either.[49] He concludes that "the length of the tale . . . is the only chance it
has of not rendering its writer answerable for a great deal of mischief."
The *Critical* and *Monthly*, though not wholly favourable, were more
reasonable and appreciative. The *Critical* points out that *Hugh Trevor* is
negative in outlook: "that the world is full of misery and vice, we know but

too well; but what is the practical inference?" The only solution Holcroft
seems to offer is that of honest labour and stoic indepencence, which the
Critical apparently finds inadequate. The author's views, it declares, are
"wild and enthusiastic," but not dangerous, since "to truth there can be no
danger from discussion." The critic praises Holcroft's plot and characters
and his "strong satire against real vice and folly," though he thinks the
satire is "made too general for the sake of accommodating his depressing
and uncomfortable system." In the *Monthly,* Enfield again praises
Holcroft's talents:

> He appears to have conversed much with the world, and to have
> been a diligent and shrewd observer of manners. He possesses, also,
> a happy freedom and boldness of pencil, which enable him to
> draw his portraits, if not actually from the life, yet with all the
> effect of living manners; so that the reader cannot doubt that,
> in studying the characters exhibited by this writer, he is acquiring
> a knowledge of mankind.

He agrees with the *Critical* reviewer that the satire is too sweeping: "from
individual characters, even though drawn after the life, it would be unfair
to deduce an indiscriminate conclusion against any body of men. — Yet
Mr. Holcroft . . . has made the stigma general and universal." This remark
may be prudent, in view of the large number of professional men among
the *Monthly's* readers, but it is also sensible. On the whole Enfield is
pleased with the novel: "it would not, perhaps, be easy to find within the
same compass a greater variety of character, nor a more amusing description of incidents." But he disapproves of Holcroft's religious scepticism and
his hostility towards the law, and ends by describing *Hugh Trevor* as "a
performance which displays great abilities and very peculiar tenets."
Holcroft himself enjoyed Enfield's article, and wrote to Griffiths commending the way these volumes had been criticised.[50]

The second part of *Hugh Trevor* (vols. 4-6) was delayed by Holcroft's
imprisonment, and did not appear until 1797. Enfield once more gave a
thorough review, examining the novel carefully, blaming some improbabilities and excrescences, and praising some of the minor characters.
While he generally approves of Holcroft's moral reflections, he argues sensibly and at length against the idea that laws should be superseded by the
principle of benevolence. He also objects to the trite ending, and points out
that such an escape from difficulties is inconsistent with Holcroft's general
intentions in the novel. The *Critical* raises the same objection, commenting drily:

> A man may well relinquish the drudgery, absurdity, or wickedness (if
> the author pleases), of law, physic, and divinity, provided he can
> meet with a generous old gentleman who will enrich him at once.

(When Holcroft met elsewhere with this criticism of *Hugh Trevor,* he noted that it was "true; blamable."[51]) Otherwise this reviewer has little to say, observing merely that these volumes are little if at all inferior to the earlier ones. The *British Critic* did not review the second part of *Hugh Trevor* and, inexplicably, the *Analytical* did not review either part. Only the *Monthly* has a successful record in reviewing Holcroft's novels.

Godwin

The most powerful novel written during this period is probably *Things as They Are; or, The Adventures of Caleb Williams* (1794), by William Godwin. Fully to explain its power, however, seems no easier now than when it was first published. The book has three main phases: the story of the chivalrous Falkland and his rivalry with Tyrrel; Caleb's "fatal curiosity" about Tyrrel's death, and his ambiguous and tormented relationship with Falkland; and his flight, with Falkland in seemingly supernatural pursuit. In each phase Godwin shows great narrative and dramatic power and psychological insight, and by 1832 he himself was willing to account for the novel as a well imagined story. But in 1794 he had thought of it as having a wide political and social significance, as his original title and suppressed preface show; and some recent critics have found this kind of significance. As a literal description of "things as they were" in 1794, *Caleb Williams* is not much more accurate than one of Blake's Prophetic Books. Symbolically it has more force, not all of it of a political kind. Falkland embodies Godwin's mixed feelings about the spirit of aristocratic chivalry, the "chastity of honour, which felt a stain like a wound," whose passing Burke had deplored; Tyrrel is a simpler figure of brute power; and Caleb is in several senses Godwin's *alter ego*. It has been argued, indeed, that the whole novel is a "symbolical picture of Godwin himself in the act of writing *Political Justice*"; and the power with which its melodramatic story is charged has been traced to still deeper levels of personal fantasy.[52]

The *British Critic* acknowledged Godwin's ability, but concentrated on the subversive tendencies expected from the author of *Political Justice:*

> This piece is a striking example of the evil use which may be made of considerable talents, connected with such a degree of intrepidity as can inspire the author with resolution to attack religion, virtue, government, laws, and, above all, the desire (hitherto accounted laudable) of leaving a good name to posterity.

The *Critical* ranked *Caleb Williams* far above most novels, declaring that "in the construction and conduct of the narrative" Godwin surpasses even Fielding, Smollett, and Fanny Burney. Less perceptively, this reviewer describes the plot as centering on the enmity of Falkland and Tyrrel, which is true only of the first volume; indeed, he makes no mention of Caleb, and represents Falkland as the central figure of the book. The *Critical* also wishes that religious principles had been more strongly advocated; recommends the deletion of some "political reflections"; and suggests that the title might as well have been *Things as They Have ever Been*. The *Analytical* reviewer admits to being puzzled:

> He has no tale of rational love, no marked instance of personal attachment, no fondly anxious parent, or child devoted to filial duty . . . ; but by the exertion of genius, which is indeed astonishing, he rivets our attention to a minute dissection of the characters, feelings, and emotions, of three insulated men, in a great measure confined to their own individual ease and comforts.

This does define an important part of Godwin's originality. The critic does not, however, entirely admire it, pointing out that though love and friendship may be excluded from Godwin's theory of social justice they are fit themes for the novelist. (Godwin was, in fact, to explore these themes later, but he had no reason to do so in *Caleb Williams*.) The *Analytical* reviewer also points out, more justly, that the story is too extraordinary for any general moral to be drawn from it, though he concedes the truth of Godwin's remarks on particular topics.

The only really satisfactory review of *Caleb Williams* is Enfield's excellent article in the *Monthly*. After some introductory remarks placing the work as a novel of purpose, Enfield appreciates the figure of Falkland:

> This visionary character is drawn with uncommon strength of conception and energy of language. The reader, while he respects and adores the virtues of Falkland, feels infinite regret that his mad passion for reputation should suppress every feeling of humanity, and become the source of unspeakable misery to himself, and of the most tragical calamity to others.

He describes Caleb's story in a way that shows he has fully experienced its power, in particular Godwin's use of concrete detail: the adventures, sufferings, and contrivances, Enfield observes, are "related with an interesting particularity that evidently shows the hand of a master." His summary of the political implications is less enthusiastic, and he remarks that the human animal must be tamed "before the old fences of law be broken down." But his general verdict is that *Caleb Williams*—"interesting but not gratifying to the feelings and the passions, and written in a style of laboured dignity rather than of easy familiarity"—combines philosophy with genius.

In April 1795 the *British Critic* returned to the attack by printing a long anonymous letter, methodically examining from a legal viewpoint the many instances of tyranny and injustice that occur in *Caleb Williams*. It is pointed out, for example, that for malicious damage such as Tyrrel inflicts upon his tenant Hawkins the customary methods of redress are both swift and cheap; that to break open the padlocks of a gate, as young Hawkins does, could not lead to criminal proceedings, certainly not to a charge of burglary; that after Miss Melvile's death Tyrrel would probably have been prosecuted; that no magistrate can summarily dismiss a case of homicide, as Falkland does, when the fact is witnessed and confessed; that Caleb could not have been kept in gaol indefinitely without being convicted, and would have been tried at the first assizes; and that Falkland could not have been retried for an offence of which he had previously been acquitted. The correspondent concludes that Godwin is very ignorant of the legal system he purports to be criticising.[53] In July 1795 the *British Critic* published a reply from Godwin that left most of the legal points unanswered. "I am far from a consummate lawyer," he wrote, adding loftily: "I do not bear that affection for the laws of my country which should lead me to study them farther than the pressure of immediate occasion may seem to demand." His main defence is that he had not been concerned to attack English laws, but "to expose the evils which arise out of the present system of civilized society." His second defence is that, whether or not such oppressive acts as Tyrrel's are illegal, they "are known to be perpetually practised with impunity." Doubtless some English squires were tyrannical and flouted the law; nevertheless, it may be felt that Godwin's adversary had the better of the exchange. As seen from the paradise of reason and benevolence adumbrated in *Political Justice*, "civilized society" was as near the nightmare world of *Caleb Williams* as made no difference, and the exact state of its laws did not matter. From a more ordinary point of view the difference was considerable, and the *British Critic* was within its rights in pointing this out.

The story of *St. Leon, a Tale of the Sixteenth Century* (1799) suggests a romance rather than a novel: its hero acquires both the *Elixir Vitae* and the Philosopher's Stone. Yet Godwin succeeds to a remarkable degree in making the thoughts and feelings of his narrator convincing, and at times — as when St. Leon tries in vain to use his wealth for the benefit of an ungrateful populace — seems again to have identified himself with his hero. *St. Leon* is less powerful than *Caleb Williams*, is too long, and comes at last to a halt rather than an end; but it remains one of the best works of fiction of this period, and deserves the high praise that Shelley more than once gave it.[54]

The *British Critic* predictably disliked the work. Some of the reviewer's comments are accurate, as when he remarks that "it has nothing of the sixteenth century but dates and names," and shows that here as in *Caleb Williams* Godwin uses the theme of unjust persecution; but elsewhere he is wildly unfair. Thus he inaccurately describes one passage (vol. 1, chap. 3, pp. 81-82 in the 1800 edition) as "an elaborate panegyric on prostitution," and omits to point out that one of the most prominent themes of the book is the praise of domestic pleasures and virtues. In condemning Godwin's atheism and supposed immorality he makes no distinction between Godwin's opinions and those of his characters; and his foregone conclusion is that *St. Leon* does its author no credit "as a philosopher, an author, or a man." The *Critical* notice is more favourable, but contains little specific criticism. "That a writer so romantic in his ideas as Mr. Godwin should make these delusions the foundation of a romance, is not a matter for astonishment," he writes ambiguously; he finds the work unnecessarily distressing, but admits the value of its moral. In the *Monthly*, Christopher Moody takes the opposite view. In a discussion of the value of romances and novels as vehicles for instruction, he declares that though the writer is at liberty to invent cases to support his theories, they must be as close to real life as possible. As for Godwin's fantasy,

> is it a mode of instruction which such a philosopher ought to select? Is truth obliged to invoke the aid of the wildest fictions; and will it be said that virtue and contentment are best taught in the school of romance?

Moody admits that Godwin's is an extremely interesting tale,

> yet why imagine incredible situations and absolute impossibilities, in order to work on our feelings, passions, and convictions? Might we not as well imagine men who could fly, or live under water like fish, or support life without eating and drinking? Of what use can such idle imaginations be to man in the actual state of his existence?

Good and meaningful romances might of course be written on all the themes Moody ridicules; he seems here to be invoking not only the prejudice of the Enlightenment against romance, but the old Puritan hostility to the element of "feigning" in all art. In other respects his review is fair and even favourable: he disagrees with some of Godwin's opinions but also quotes examples of his "just observation and acute remark." Though too unimaginative to be satisfactory, this review is still the best of the three.

Mary Hays

Mary Hays[55] declared herself a disciple of Godwin in her *Letters and Essays* (1793), and in her novels she discusses advanced opinions learned from Godwin and Mary Wollstonecraft. She too was a reviewer: according to A. F. Wedd, George Dyer introduced her into the *Critical* in 1795, and a letter written by Mary Wollstonecraft in 1797 shows that she sometimes contributed to the *Analytical*.[56] The literary quality of her novels is not high, but their reception is of interest here since they deal with the question of the status of women. *The Memoirs of Emma Courtney* (1796) describes a girl who candidly avows her love for a man and unsuccessfully woos him. Through her story the cause of women's equality and social freedom is championed with courage, though sometimes without humor — as when Emma sends the man of her choice a letter discussing under six heads the objections she thinks he may have to her proposals. In her preface Mary Hays declares that Emma is to be taken as a warning, not an example; but the novel consistently presents her as a noble figure.

Reviews were mixed, but on the whole less hostile than might have been expected. The *Critical* gives a brief synopsis, a quotation, and some sensible platitudes: "we do not hold up Emma Courtney as a character for general imitation, any more than, we presume, the authoress herself would. . . . Strong sensibilities require more than ordinary management." The *Analytical* takes the Preface at its face value, and praises Mary Hays for showing the danger of indulging the passions. Some accurate criticisms are made of the plot:

> If it were natural, with such strong emotions, at first to avow the passion, it was certainly much otherwise to tease him with her neglected love; and, after the appeal to his passions had proved ineffectual, to attack his principles, and argue, on the ground of utility, that it was incumbent on him to return the attachment.

But despite these and other objections the reviewer is pleased with *Emma Courtney,* which he describes as "the vehicle of much good sense and liberal principle." The *British Critic* admits that Mary Hays has "respectable talents," but refuses to recommend her novel. Ignoring the disclaimer in the Preface, this reviewer condemns Emma and her "philosophy," states inaccurately that she offers to be Harley's mistress, and advises the author to widen the circle of her reading and acquaintance. In the *Monthly,* William Taylor more generously gives her credit for tackling a serious problem:

> viz. whether it be prudent in minds of a superior mould . . . to exempt themselves from the common delicacies or hypocrisies of life . . . or patiently to submit to the incumbent mountains of circumstance, without one volcanic effort to shatter the oppressive load into ruin.

He sympathises with Emma, and seems to regret that she should be presented only as a cautionary figure. Despite some interesting remarks and an avowed admiration for Mary Hays's intellectual powers, Taylor attempts little criticism; thus he quotes Emma's famous letter to Harley in full but without comment. The *Analytical* gives the only satisfactory review in this group.

The Victim of Prejudice (1799) depicts a girl who is intelligent, brave, and honest, but the daughter of a murderer and a prostitute. Thus the gentleman who falls in love with her feels unable to marry her, and instead rapes her. The novel tells of her unsuccessful attempts to overcome the stigma of unchastity. Besides protesting against false standards of "purity," Mary Hays bestows blame with a heavy hand upon the English law and the male sex. The *Analytical* found the story "pathetic and instructive," and complimented the author on a "mind apt at moral description, fertile in sentiment, and considerably skilled in the science of the feelings." Nevertheless, most of this review consists of adverse criticism. The most important objection is that many of the heroine's misfortunes are irrelevant to the moral design of the work:

> If we have understood her rightly, this was, to exhibit the impropriety of the means used to ensure female chastity, and to expose the inconsistency of man, in expecting from women a virtue which he so grossly neglects himself. The connexion between the moral of the story before us, and the enforcement of this doctrine, we confess we do not clearly perceive; and many of the incidents, so far from being at all illustrative of the doctrine, thus professed to be the great purport of the story, have scarcely any connexion with each other.

This critic also finds that the heroine is too easily ravished, and that her ravisher is loaded with more guilt than he appears to deserve.

The *Critical* gives a good review from a conservative moral and social viewpoint. The reviewer fears that Mary Hays's undoubted talents are being used in a manner harmful to society:

> An author collects a series of severe and unmerited misfortunes; and, under the form of a novel, represents them as originating from opinions and habits commonly adopted in the world from a sense of their utility and decorum. . . . The superficial head and the susceptible heart are confounded and led astray: society is contemplated with disgust, as a state of artificial depravity; and the salutary institutions of human intercourse are despised and violated by that rising generation, from which they ought to receive the profoundest reverence and the most ardent support! . . . It is not the ability or the intention of Miss Hays that we dispute: it is the accuracy of her judgement. The Victim of Prejudice is a tale of considerable interest; it has many passages which, for warmth and vigour of pathos and composition, are scarcely inferior to the effusions of Rousseau; but it also exhibits that splenetic irritability which, by distorting decorum into prejudice, and custom into tyranny, tends to excite

and to nourish the contagious and consuming fever of perverted sensibility.

Applying this general criticism to the story of the heroine's mother, the reviewer asks:

> Is the law to be represented as completing the "triumph of injustice" because it punishes a murder committed in the uproar of a brothel? Do our municipal institutions afford no redress for the seductive or forcible violation of female chastity . . . ? A reform of manners cannot be promoted by indiscriminate imputations on society and the laws.

In the *Monthly*, Christopher Moody agrees that such misfortunes are hardly evidence of tyranny; but his grasp of the doctrines of *The Victim of Prejudice* is not firm.

> By the novels which issue from this school, love, which is a transient passion, is to be complimented, in all cases, at the expence of the regulations and institutions of society; and a respect for virtue and decorum is to be classed in the list of vulgar prejudices.

Of course this is a travesty of Mary Hays's ideals and of the aims of contemporary feminists. Moody (a clergyman) makes his own views very clear: though the heroine is lovely, amiable, and innocent, Pelham is right not to marry her, and had he done so he would have had cause to blush in later years when his children enquired about their mother's history. "According to the fixed laws of nature, we suffer from the vices of our parents; and this, with every wise man, will be a very strong motive to virtue." Moody's sentimental pity for the victim of nature's laws seems worthless when joined to such moral obtuseness. The other two reviews are satisfactory, though written from very different points of view.

On the whole the Reviews were unsympathetic towards the reforming or revolutionary novel of purpose. Of the 28 notices discussed in these sections, only six[57] express sympathy with the ideas put forward in these novels; ten of the others show hostility, while twelve preserve an appearance of neutrality. The *Monthly*, which at the beginning of the period was markedly liberal in tone, later became more cautious; the *Critical* gave no support to these advanced ideas, although for most of our period it pursued Foxite policies; the *British Critic* was emphatically and undiscriminatingly conservative. The *English* contributes only one article here. After 1792, when *Man as He Is* won praise from the *Monthly* and *English,* the only Review to write encouragingly about the content of these novels was the *Analytical*.

The reviewing of these works is not of a high standard: only eleven of the 28 notices can be called satisfactory. This is more often owing to the prevailing atmosphere of caution than to overt bigotry. Only six of the unsuccessful reviews seem vitiated by prejudice, four of these appearing in the *British Critic*.[58] A more common fault is for the reviewer to give inadequate criticism, or none at all; most of the *Critical* notices suffer from this defect. Enfield of the *Monthly* deserves credit for his appreciative reviews of *Caleb Williams* and *Anna St. Ives,* written in 1794 during the treason trials; but in 1797 Enfield died, to be replaced by the far less competent Moody. The *Analytical* has the best record, supplying four of the good reviews and only two poor ones. Though radical in its policies, the *Analytical* nearly always offers intelligent adverse criticism; the conscientious Dissenters and advanced thinkers who wrote for this journal were not the persons to sink minor differences in the face of a common enemy. The *British Critic* awards no praise but that of "misapplied talents" to any of these novels.

Seven Other Novels

Apart from the development of the romance and the novel of purpose, these fifteen years saw much creative activity in other forms of prose fiction. *Zeluco, A Simple Story* and *Castle Rackrent* are accomplished and original works; *Sir Roger de Clarendon* is an essay in the very recent genre of the historical novel; *Henry* is a spirited imitation of Fielding, and *Rosamund Gray* a talented exercise in sensibility. To these novels I have added *Camilla,* a less interesting work but one whose author enjoyed unique prestige. These seven works provide a fair mixed sample of the better novels with which the reviewers were confronted.

Zeluco (1789) was Dr. John Moore's first novel, though he had achieved some reputation with his *Medical Sketches* and two travel books; its authorship was an open secret. The central theme of this work is the education and adult progress of a villain. Moore analyses Zeluco's thoughts and feelings with unusual minuteness, intending him as a cautionary example; unluckily for this purpose, the character acquires something of the fascination of the Byronic hero. The first part of the narrative moves briskly, though it slows down when Laura and her family are introduced in chapter 26. The novel also contains several lively debates in the manner of Bage, and some brief comic interludes.

The *Monthly* and *Analytical* were very favourable; the *English* (to which Moore had been, possibly still was, a contributor[59]) assigned *Zeluco* "a middle rank between the bad and the excellent," while the *Critical* found it inferior to Moore's earlier works. Several objections were made to the plan of the novel. Mary Wollstonecraft, in the *Analytical,* doubted whether Moore had succeeded in the difficult task of making a villain interesting; the *Critical* implied that the task should never have been attempted, and that in making the vicious Lovelace a charmer even Richardson had erred. The *English* makes a more cogent criticism:

> we have too much reasoning, and too little acting; it is the reasoning too of the author, and not of the personages of the story, which keeps them too long out of sight, and gives a languor to the performance. This fault he has copied from Crebillon, and some other French novelists of repute, who have never done with anatomising the feelings and motives of their characters; leaving nothing to be discovered by the actions of those characters, nor by the discernment of the reader.

The *Critical* likewise remarked that Moore had taken more pains to enforce his moral than to keep his story alive. But Dr. John Gillies, in the *Monthly,* approved of Moore's design: he admires Moore's accurate observation of "those inward pangs of sorrow, remorse, and terror, which a vicious conduct never fails to produce," and suggests that the novel may be read as "a series of moral essays, connected by one entertaining and instructive story." Mary Wollstonecraft also praises the rendering of Zeluco's "anxious restless hours," and thinks that Moore has managed to keep the main design of the novel in view.

Gillies commended Moore's "true and original humour," and Mary Wollstonecraft chose for her extract the comic duel between the two enraged Scots, Buchanan and Targe (chapter 65). Both these critics also praised Moore's characters, though Mary Wollstonecraft finds some of them "overcharged or rather caricatured." The *English* pronounces Moore to be "a man of good sense, who is well acquainted with the world"; Gillies agrees that the author has read the book of life with attention and profit, and Mary Wollstonecraft gives special praise to his sound and reasonable morality. On the whole Moore had no reason to be displeased with the reception of his first and best novel. The *Monthly* gave the best review, but both the *English* and the *Analytical* dealt with the work satisfactorily; the *Critical* alone gave a somewhat perfunctory notice.

The method of *A Simple Story* (1791), by Elizabeth Inchbald, is very different from that of *Zeluco.* The author writes with economy, rarely obtrudes herself, and conveys most of her points through dialogue and restrained gesture. These virtues, learned in the theatre, were rare in the novels of this period. The first two volumes of *A Simple Story* describe the developing relationship between Dorriforth and his ward, Miss Milner, and their marriage; the story then moves forward seventeen years, and the remaining two volumes centre round Dorriforth (now Lord Elmwood) and his daughter Matilda. Some attempt is made to contrast, in the persons of the two heroines, the effects of a good and bad education. Nevertheless, *A Simple Story* is not a novel of purpose: it is a novel of sentiment, but closer to real life and more delicate in its effects than most of its kind.[60]

This work was received with the commendation it deserved. The *Monthly* and *Critical* give very similar notices: both praise the interesting narrative, the well-drawn characters, and the "elegant simplicity" of the whole; both object to the lapse of time in the middle of the novel, though they allow that some degree of unity is preserved through the character of Dorriforth; both criticise the hasty method of removing difficulties at the close. On this point the *Critical* is particularly severe: "Never was an impatience to conclude more manifest than in this novel." (We may note in passing that *A Simple Story* was published by the Robinsons, who were part-proprietors of the *Critical,* so that by conventional accounts this notice should have been a simple puff.) The best appreciation of Elizabeth Inchbald's technique was given by George Griffiths in the *Monthly:*

> The secret charm, that gives a grace to the whole, is the art with which Mrs. Inchbald has made her work completely dramatic. The business is, in a great measure, carried on in dialogue. In dialogue the characters unfold themselves. Their motions, their looks, their attitudes, discover the inward temper. The sentiments are the workings of the speaker's mind; and . . . while they lay open the heart, they prepare the incidents, and give spirit and energy to the work.[61]

The *Analytical* review may well be by Mary Wollstonecraft, whose signature is the next to appear in that journal.[62] This critic praises the dramatic plan of the work, its simple plot, the well-discriminated characters developed by "little individual traits," and the lively conversations. But objections very much in Mary Wollstonecraft's manner are raised to the moral of the work. The contrast between mother and daughter is not, in the opinion of this critic, drawn forcefully enough to display the real effects of good or bad education:

> It were to be wished, in fact, . . . that the faults of the vain, giddy miss Milner had not been softened, or rather gracefully withdrawn from notice by the glare of such splendid, yet fallacious virtues as flow from sensibility. And to have rendered the contrast more useful still, her daughter should have possessed greater dignity of mind. Educated in adversity she should have learned (to prove that a cultivated mind is a real advantage) how to bear, nay, rise above her misfortunes, instead of suffering her health to be undermined by the trials of her patience, which ought to have strengthened her understanding. . . . We alluded to the absurd fashion that prevails of making

the heroine of a novel boast of a delicate constitution; and the still more ridiculous and deleterious custom of spinning the most picturesque scenes out of fevers, swoons and tears.

Though this reviewer carries rather too far his (or her) plans for remodelling the novel, there is obvious truth in these criticisms, which pay Mrs. Inchbald the compliment of taking her work and her professed moral design seriously. The *Analytical* review complements rather than contradicts the others, and none of the three is less than adequate.

The historical novel has its beginnings in *Longsword* (1762) and *The Recess* (1783-86). In the 1790s it was extremely popular. "By 1790 the flyleaves of novels . . . are full of advertisements of Legendary Tales, Old English Tales, Historical Stories and Historical Romances."[63] So far, however, the reviewers had regarded this genre with suspicion. Nothing had yet been achieved of much literary value, and it was feared that young readers would be confused by the mixture of fiction and (often inaccurate) fact. One of the most popular examples was Clara Reeve's *The Old English Baron* (1777); this work was well above the average in quality, but received short and not wholly favourable notices.[64]

Clare Reeve's second historical novel, *Memoirs of Sir Roger de Clarendon* (1793), has a more definite background than her first: passages of Froissart are introduced, and Sir Roger himself is presented as a natural son of the Black Prince. The Preface announces the author's purpose of combating the "levelling tendency" of the age, and the novel itself compares the men of the fourteenth century very favourably with their descendants. The story is improbable without being very exciting—J.M.S.Tompkins notes that "it makes few concessions to the trifling human demand for entertainment, and is wholly unlike the Gothic Romances in the middle of which it appeared"[65]—and the chief interest of the work lies in its comparatively sober treatment of historical material, rare before Scott.

The reviewers of 1793 showed more interest in the genre than those of 1777, and awarded *Sir Roger* main articles whose average length was five pages. Only the *British Critic* raised the old objection to "the prevailing and fashionable fault, of blending truth with fable"; and James Bannister, in the *Monthly*, prefaced his article by a long disquisition on the origins and advantages of this kind of writing:

> The feudal system . . . was founded on generosity and gratitude, supported by valour, embellished by courtesy, and refined by that delicate and disinterested attachment subsisting between the sexes, which alone deserves the name of love. It is therefore reasonable to suppose that the representation of the manners of such a period in society must be highly pleasing to a well informed mind. — The chaste and amiable pictures of female virtue, the glorious ach-

ievements of heroes, with those sudden changes of fortune which the times of chivalry afforded, cannot but sensibly affect the heart, and call forth our noblest affections.

The old romances, Bannister admits, were often absurd; but the novels which superseded them were no less so, and frequently immoral as well. Thus "many serious persons" had decided that tales of chivalry, if suitably refined, were less pernicious than tales of modern life. The *Critical* reviewer has some thoughtful remarks on the difficulty of introducing history that will be new and interesting but true, and suggests that "the manners of the times," if well portrayed, would be more interesting than "a record of historical personages." The critics also recognised Clara Reeve's moral purpose: the *Critical* found "the sentiments (those excepted which tend to give a false gloss to rank or antiquity) favourable to virtue," and the *Monthly* praised her "laudable zeal for the interests of virtue, and a just abhorrence of vice." Had *Sir Roger* been reviewed in the Catalogues the reviewers would have been content to award these certificates of morality; but in the main review sections they were more exacting. "Morality alone, though among the best things, cannot support a novel," observed the *British Critic,* and the other journals agreed. Reluctantly, apologetically, they found the novel dull. "We must confess there is a want of interest which renders the general effect but feeble," wrote the *Critical*; the *Monthly* was "sorry to observe that the subject and detail of her history are tedious, that the manners are for the most part insipid, and that the characters are generally uninteresting." Clare Reeve's rather unselective use of historical information was a chief source of complaint: "as for the historical extracts, and Master Clement Woodville's register of the Knights of the Garter," implored the *British Critic*, "gentle ladies—beware of reading them on a winter's evening too near the candle—strong soporifics should be taken in a safer situation." The *Critical* likewise found such matters "for history too trivial, and for romance too dull."

All three reviews are satisfactory, but the one in the *British Critic* is much the liveliest. Sprightly and facetious, decorated with allusions and quotations, this article gives us a foretaste of both the good and bad qualities of the *Edinburgh Review.* The writer has read *Sir Roger* and has much to say about it, but seems at times more interested in displaying his own wit than in doing justice to the author. The other reviewers are generally more sympathetic and also show more interest in the genre.

Henry (1795), Richard Cumberland's second novel, is an avowed imitation of Fielding and an unusually good one. The work is divided into books, each prefaced by a discursive essay; the hero makes his way through most of the plot without the assistance of parents, and resists the overtures of women both attractive and unattractive. The scenes of temptation are rather numerous, but have a pleasant human quality that raises them above the usual level of the genre;[66] and in some passages of grotesque humour Cumberland shows real originality. The reviews were unusually long (averaging seven pages) and largely favourable. The *Critical* found *Henry* to be "enriched with humour, variety, and character"; the *British Critic* discovered "abundant marks of the author's well-known genius"; Holcroft "frequently both laughed and shed tears" while reading the novel for the *Monthly;* Mary Wollstonecraft declared it "a masterpiece" and "the mature production of ingenuity, taste, and experience." After enumerating the devices of romance which Cumberland has dispensed with — forests, caves, castles, ghosts, "gothic knights," and so on — Mary Wollstonecraft comments: "If the reader be disposed to ask how all these *unpardonable defects* are supplied, we answer in one word, by exhibiting real men and women, and describing real life and manners."

The temptation scenes caused the critics some concern. "We know not whether Mr. Cumberland means to gratify the taste of the men, by representing his women as made of such melting materials," wrote the *Critical;* "but we hope at least the ladies will view with a proper indigna- tion any attempts to degrade the female character, by depriving it of its most essential charm." Holcroft, a stern moralist, has much to say on the same point, and the *British Critic* raises similar objections (Mary Wollstonecraft does not). But the preponderantly favourable verdict shows that admiration for a talented follower of Fielding outweighed prudish considerations. The *Monthly* and *British Critic* give thorough reviews; the *Critical* gives short comments and long quotations. The *Analytical* account is satisfactory, even though one cannot be quite sure that Mary Wollstonecraft has appreciated Cumberland's humorous intentions: she describes Henry as a picture of "steady consistency and manly vigour." Her review suggests that this novel won favour partly by contrast with the Gothic romances among which it appeared.

Evelina (1778) and *Cecilia* (1782), notable achievements in themselves, had appeared when the English novel was at a low ebb; and the critics of the 1790s invariably mention Fanny Burney with respect, even classing her with the great novelists of the mid-century. *Camilla* (1796) was published by subscription at a time when the standard of the better novels had im- proved, and criticism was more exacting.[67] Though Jane Austen was fond of this work, it is usually held to mark a decline in Fanny Burney's art. Compared with the earlier novels, it lacks imaginative vitality; it is over- burdened with doctrine; the moral it enforces is severe and prudish; its hero, according to Joyce Hemlow, is one of the two greatest prigs in English literature; its prose is often heavy and stilted, and the whole is much too long. Despite his regard for this author, Horace Walpole needed some time to recover from a reading of "deplorable *Camilla*"; Ernest Baker describes it roundly as "a rambling, dull, and amateurish performance."[68]

The reviewers were anxious to do justice to the occasion, and gave *Camilla* reviews averaging five pages in length. Though respectful, they were evidently disappointed in the novel; but it is a fault of most notices that this disappointment is not fully or firmly enough expressed. Mary Wollstonecraft, in the earliest review, notes a decline in Fanny Burney's power, but her criticism is very general:

> As a whole, we are in justice bound to say, that we think it inferiour to the first-fruits of her talents, though we boldly assert, that Camilla contains parts superiour to anything she has yet produced.

The *English* reviewer likewise finds that *Camilla* falls short of his expectations, though his slight article contains more praise than blame. The *Critical* describes the work as "an admirable picture of modern life," but its review consists largely of quotation; and the *British Critic* gives a preponderantly favourable, but very general, account.

The review that gives most detailed comment, both favourable and adverse, is William Enfield's in the *Monthly*. His judicious article is all the more creditable, both to reviewer and Review, in that Fanny Burney's father, Dr. Charles Burney, was known to be intensely anxious for the success of his daughter's work; and Burney was a contributor to the *Monthly* and a fairly close friend of Griffiths.[69] Enfield discusses the general merits of *Camilla,* implying that its strength lies in characterisation and in "scenes of life and manners" rather than in an exciting story, and then summarises the plot. His comments on this are apt, and not overwhelmingly favourable; indeed, he anticipates that readers will find the work dull in places:

> Possibly, on a general review of the principal story, the reader may think it not quite natural that a young man like Edgar, entirely and tenderly devoted to a generous passion, should give himself up to the direction of his tutor; whose personal disappointments had rendered him harsh, distrustful, and severe, in his judgment of female characters. Edgar's mistakes might, perhaps, more properly have proceeded from that extreme sensibility which naturally produces suspicion and jealousy; and the whole character of Dr. Marchmont might have been spared. We think also, that Camilla's conduct is not always quite consistent with her natural good sense and the openness of her temper; and that she too frequently acts contrary to Edgar's advice, and, on some occasions, towards the close of the work, does not treat him with sufficient frankness. The adventures of Eugenia . . . form an interesting under-part of the story. The meeting with the beautiful idiot, as contrived by Eugenia's father, furnishes an admirable lesson on beauty; and the picture of idiocy is a striking one: but we are not sure that it is sufficiently distinct from that of madness. The whole plot is, perhaps, drawn out to too great a length: some of the

adventures, particularly at Southampton, might have been omitted with advantage; and Camilla's ramble (not to say her whole acquaintance) with Mrs. Mitten is unnatural. If, however, in the course of this long work, the reader should occasionally experience some degree of lassitude, and be disposed to think the writer tedious, he ought to recollect that *aliquando bonus dormitat Homerus.*

Enfield warmly praises Fanny Burney's power of characterisation, especially through dialogue: "we particularly admire the happy facility with which she gives to each person a language of his own, and preserves it uniformly throughout the work." His favourite characters are Sir Hugh Tyrold and Dr. Orkborne. Before leaving *Camilla,* Enfield devotes a whole page to instances of inaccuracy, obscurity, or affectation in the style. To this article Griffiths himself added two paragraphs, one pointing out a few more improbabilities in the plot, the other bringing the piece to a close on a note of praise for the moral.

Enfield was a courteous reviewer, and on this occasion he was probably well aware of the need to be tactful. His praise is generous, and his adverse criticisms ("not quite natural" . . . "not quite consistent") are phrased with studied moderation. Yet this makes them all the more damaging, as though much more might have been said by one less perfectly polite. His review certainly angered Dr. Burney and disappointed his daughter; though Fanny later became reconciled to it, and profited by Enfield's criticism in her revisions.[70]

Despite one or two scenes of terror bordering on the Gothic (which were removed in later versions),[71] Camilla belongs firmly to the tradition of the "natural" novel, which in 1796 was a point in its favour. The *British Critic* goes out of its way to condemn the extravagances that other writers have "imported from the regions of fairy-tale"; for this reviewer, *Camilla* exemplifies "the more reasonable modern novel" that should by now have superseded the unreasonable romance. Enfield praises Fanny Burney for keeping to her own way of writing, and disapproves of "that taste for the marvellous and the terrible" which the romance gratifies. The *Critical,* too, makes clear its preference for the traditional type of novel. Such comments as these anticipate the reception of *The Italian* in the following year. Though the moral theme of *Camilla* is not made the chief consideration, both the *Monthly* and the *British Critic* praise the long sermonising letter sent to his daughter by Mr. Tyrold; the *Critical* gives it in full.

Everything seems to have worked in favour of *Camilla* except the experience of reading it: its author's prestige, her faithfulness to traditional forms of fiction, the earnest and unexceptionable morality of her work, and whatever influence her father could bring to bear. Yet the novel was greeted with politeness rather than enthusiasm. The reviewers did not mistake the design for the achievement; and it is perhaps not surprising that, awed by the author's reputation, or perhaps simply stupefied by her book, most of them failed to articulate their disappointment.

The critics disapproved of the cult of terror, but against that of sensibility they made no serious protest. Two obvious imitations of Henry Mackenzie's work appeared within our limits—the anonymous *Wanley Penson* (1791) and Mary Robinson's *Walsingham* (1797)—and both were favourably reviewed.[72] Reviewers, like other readers, found cause for self-congratulation in their receptiveness to such works: the *Critical* reviewer remarks complacently that *Wanley Penson* "will not be generally interesting, nor often called for by the readers of circulating libraries." The only objection to the cult was its link, through Rousseau, with the French Revolution. Gillray's cartoon in the *Antijacobin Review* for July 1798 includes the figure of Sensibility, wearing a Phrygian cap, weeping over a dead bird and trampling upon a crowned and severed head; and in December of that year the *British Critic* remarked à *propos* of *Walsingham* that "A little sympathy bestowed here [i.e., on the French aristocrats] would have been quite as natural as that which is lavished upon a *snow-drop*."

Charles Lamb's *Rosamund Gray* (1798), however, is not open to objections of this kind: it teaches the virtue of resignation. Lamb makes his highly conventional story the channel of free-flowing feelings, some personal and deep-felt, others with obvious literary antecedents. The critical paragraphs are short enough to be given in full:

> The simplicity, delicacy, and tenderness of this little volume set criticism at defiance, and appeal at once to the heart: while the pure benevolence that pervades it, commands our reverence for its author. If unassuming goodness, amiable piety, modesty, gentleness, sweetness, will disarm the fastidious, and soften the morose, Rosamund Gray and old blind Margaret can have nothing to fear. The writer's tale, manner, style, are all appropriate, and all his own—they breathe, like his Rosamund, "a certain charm—a grace without a name."   *(Analytical)*

> This little tale reminded us strongly of Mackenzie's style; and the imitation, we think, equals the original. The story is perhaps too simple: but it is so related as to invite a frequent perusal; and it abounds with passages which the reader will wish to remember, and which he will be the better for remembering. The genius and feeling with which it is written, will appear in our extract.   *(Critical)*

> In the perusal of this pathetic and interesting story, the reader, who has a mind capable of enjoying rational and moral sentiment, will find much gratification. Mr. Lamb has here proved himself skilful in touching the nicest feelings of the heart, and in affording great pleasure to the imagination, by exhibiting events and situations which, in the

hands of a writer less conversant with the springs and energies of the
moral sense, would have made a very *"sorry figure."*

(Christopher Moody in the *Monthly*)

The quotations given by the *Analytical* and *Critical* both include the
description of Allan Clare's benevolent visits to hospitals and lazar-houses;
the *Critical* adds the passage on "old friendships."[73] Clearly all three
reviewers felt the sensitiveness and the skill of Lamb's writing and were
almost too ready to succumb to the pathos of his tale. The *Analytical* seems
here to abandon the language of criticism; the other two notices are adequate to the occasion.

Castle Rackrent (1800) is quite unlike any other novel of its time. It is
usually remembered as the first regional novel: Scott and Turgenev have
testified that Maria Edgeworth's writing inspired them to attempt for
Scotland and Russia respectively what she had done for Ireland. The
Irishness of the work is not, however, its most interesting quality. With
great skill the author puts her tale into the mouth of a servant, "honest
Thady," who provides her with a constant source of gentle irony. Since
elaborate flights of psychology and morality are beyond Thady's powers,
all the observation, wit, and human sympathy of the work are conveyed
through the eccentric behaviour and racy speech of its characters, moving
within a concise and lively narrative.

The anonymous first edition found two appreciative critics, though their
enthusiasm was confined to the Catalogues. The *Monthly* wrote:

We most heartily offer our best thanks to the unknown author of these
unusually pleasing pages, which we have closed with much regret. They
are written with singular humour and spirit; and it is seldom indeed that
we meet with such flowers in our walks in the rugged and thorny paths of
literature, through which we are often obliged to explore our weary way.

The reviewer regrets that the "peculiar and singular cast" of the novel
makes it impossible for him to detach a specimen, but is convinced that the
admirable pictures of Irish life are authentic. The *British Critic* describes
Castle Rackrent as "a very pleasant, good-humoured, and successful
representation of the eccentricities of our Irish neighbours"; the reviewer
particularly admires the character of Thady, and the author's success in
"hitting off" the Irish idiom. Within the limits of the Catalogues the
reviewers could hardly have been more appreciative, and there seems no
reason to think, with Ernest Baker, that they were "nonplussed" by this
novel.[74] But of course *Castle Rackrent* should have been given full-length
reviews. As with the *Critical* account of *Hermsprong,* the work seems to
have been assigned to the Catalogues without adequate appraisal; possibly

Griffiths and Nares were misled by the title into thinking that here was yet another Gothic romance. Despite the critics' enthusiasm, neither notice is long enough to be really satisfactory.

Zeluco, A Simple Story, Sir Roger de Clarendon, Henry, and *Rosamund Gray* were on the whole well reviewed; *Camilla* was overpraised, and *Castle Rackrent* less fully treated than it deserved. Fifteen of the twenty-four notices discussed in this section may be considered satisfactory pieces of reviewing: of these the *Monthly* contributed six, the *Critical* and *Analytical* three each, the *British Critic* two, and the *English* one. These reviews express individual judgements rather than critical trends; nevertheless, those of *Sir Roger* provide some evidence of increasing respect for the historical novel, those of *Camilla* and *Henry* show a tendency to praise the traditional type of novel at the expense of the Gothic romance, and those of *Henry* and *Sir Roger* show (in opposite ways) that "morality" was not always the paramount concern of the reviewers.

Despite the difficulties mentioned at the beginning of this chapter, the reviewers may be said to have dealt fairly successfully with the novels of the period. Starting from adverse prepossessions, they developed a tolerance for the Gothic romance that reached its zenith about 1794; they appreciated the most important work of Charlotte Smith and Ann Radcliffe, but resisted the vogue for cruder and more violent tales of terror. Their reviews of novels of purpose often seem inhibited by caution, but even these include some good articles, and they noticed the merit of most of the minor successes here sampled which elude these categories. By far the greater number of the eighty-eight reviews here examined (i.e., excluding reviews discussed as background) make a genuine attempt at criticism, and fifty of them may be called satisfactory. It is unfortunate that less than justice was done to two of the best and most original novels appearing within these limits — *Caleb Williams* and *Castle Rackrent.*

The *Monthly, Critical,* and *Analytical* all have more successful than unsuccessful notices, with the *Monthly* in the lead (17:9). The *Monthly* was well served by William Enfield and the *Analytical* by Mary Wollstonecraft, though her criticism is occasionally too moralistic. The *English* and *British Critic* provide smaller samples, but in each case the unsatisfactory reviews slightly outnumber the satisfactory ones. The average total length of articles in the *Critical* and *British Critic* is over 2,000 words, and in the other journals between 1,400 and 1,700. But the *Monthly* gives the most criticism (on average 850 words), followed by the *British Critic* (725), *Critical* (600), *English* (450), and *Analytical* (300). Badcock's description of his rivals as "Transcribers, not Critics" still has some point when applied to the *Critical* and *Analytical,* which give long reviews containing a high proportion of summary and quotation. The *Monthly* is the only journal to give the larger part of its space to criticism (an average of 850 words out of nearly 1,500).

Though the reviewers were interested in the "moral tendency" of novels, it does not determine their criticism to anything like the extent suggested by Ernest Baker in the passage quoted near the beginning of this chapter. When novelists themselves announce their moral objectives — as in *Camilla* and *A Simple Story* — critics are obviously right to discuss whether or not these have been fulfilled. Sometimes the comments prompted by morality are outweighed by other considerations, as in the reviews of *Sir Roger de Clarendon*. Occasionally, as with *The Monk,* a moral limiting judgement seems reasonable. When such cases, together with perfunctory compliments and brief clearance certificates, have been set aside, we are left with only eight reviews[75] in which moral prepossessions seem to distort the final judgement. Political prejudice vitiates several reviews in the *British Critic* but not in other journals, where reviewers were either more conscientious or more cautious. So far as we can tell, personal influence has not caused bias in any of these articles, and Enfield's review of *Camilla* shows clearly how such influence could be resisted.

Robert D. Mayo has written that despite their generally conservative canons the eighteenth-century reviewers, "when faced with real talent, . . . often allowed the novel to be what it was intended to be"; he adds that "as time went on they tended increasingly to outgrow the rules." J. M. S. Tompkins finds that "they were glad to get anything tolerably good, . . . and on the whole dealt out rough justice."[76] Despite some failures, the present study confirms these favourable impressions.

4

The Reviewing of Political
and Religious Writings

At present . . . I see nothing to expect but either the horrors of civil commotions, or the *dead calm of terror,* produced by inquisitorial oppression. We must not, however, suffer ourselves to be deterred from speaking the truth, with temper and moderation, as honest and prudent citizens. The sentiments we inculcate, and the language we hold, ought not to give offence; and I think we may safely persevere in maintaining, to the fullest extent, the doctrine of *Reform.*

William Enfield to Ralph Griffiths, December 1792, Bodleian MS. Adds. C.89, ff. 66^v - 67^r. Griffiths endorsed the sheet: "A good letter."

Politics and the Reviews

The eighteenth-century Reviews inevitably influenced the general opinions of the country gentlemen, clergymen, merchants, professional men, and book-club subscribers who read them. As the foregoing quotation shows, the *Monthly* reviewers took this influence seriously; and at different times the *Critical, Analytical,* and *British Critic* assumed quite openly the role of journals of opinion. This role was not easy to combine with that of the encyclopaedic journal of record, nor did the Review pattern established by the *Monthly* lend itself well to this purpose. The technique, later perfected by the *Edinburgh,* of using the book under review as a peg on which to hang a long political or philosophical essay was still undeveloped, though Samuel Johnson accused the *Critical* of something very like it.[1] Only a small proportion of the publications these Reviews undertook to summarise and evaluate were works of controversy; and current affairs often came to them "through the polluted medium of party-violence in a despicable pamphlet, which may deserve the most ignominious corner of the Catalogue."[2] Partly to overcome these restrictions, first the *English,* later all other Reviews except the *Monthly* issued regular supplements on "Public Affairs," in which editorial policy was more freely and sometimes more strongly expressed than in the reviews. Even so, these supplements appeared only two or three times a year; and in dealing with current affairs editors never quite forgot that they were supposed to be creating a permanent and dignified record. For these reasons ephemeral topics were left to the nimbler newspaper writers and pamphleteers, or dealt with briefly in the Catalogues. But on great questions such as electoral reform, the Test Acts, or the slave trade the Reviews were expected to take some stand, and "consistency" was as much valued in these matters as in literary judgements. None of these journals addressed itself particularly to the working men in the book clubs, and though the current affairs supplements are often fairly popular in style the Reviews were written very largely for, as they were written by, the more educated members of the middle classes.

The changing currents of English opinion in the decade following the French Revolution have often been described. Most men rejoiced to hear of the Tennis Court Oath and hoped for a peaceful triumph of constitutional over arbitrary government. The storming of the Bastille, long a symbol of oppression, was also approved. These events, and the spectacle of Frenchmen redesigning their society, gave new inspiration to overlapping groups of English reformers: Whigs resentful of exclusion from office and the supposed encroachments of royal power; Dissenters seeking full civil rights; Parliamentary reformers wishing to abolish rotten boroughs and enfranchise new towns; theorists disposed to test the whole social and political framework by the criteria of reason and utility, or natural rights. But the violence at Versailles on 5 and 6 October 1789 made many men uneasy, and in 1790 conservative opinion was dismayed by the confiscation of Church property, the abolition of the aristocracy, and other sweeping measures of the National Assembly. Burke's *Reflections* (November 1790) gave this body of opinion a voice and a doctrine, and predicted that the French experiment would end in bloodshed and tyranny. In the literary debate that followed Burke's opponents seemed to have the best of the argument, and a hardening of opinion on the part of the government was met by a mounting agitation for reform. But the tide began to turn against the reformers in the summer of 1791, when the flight to Varennes revealed the plight of Louis XVI and made nonsense of the French attempt to construct a constitutional monarchy. After a year's lull came events that alienated still more English sympathisers and showed Burke a true prophet: the attack on the Tuileries (August 1792), the prison massacres (September 1792), the decree offering aid to revolutionaries in other countries (November 1792), the trial and execution (21 January 1793) of Louis XVI, the declaration of war on England and Holland (1 February 1793). In England a genuine revulsion against French excesses, felt at many levels of society, was fostered and exploited by a government determined to prevent revolution and fearful that any discussion of reform might lead in that direction. The milestones of this reaction are the destruction by a mob of Priestley's library and laboratory (July 1791), the proclamations against sedition (1792), the forming of loyalist associations, the Treason Trials (1793-94) and the suppression of popular political societies. In Parliament most Whigs came to see that the French Revolution could not be interpreted in terms appropriate to 1688; and by May 1794 the more conservative half of the party had rallied to the defence of the country, and of property, by coalescing with the ministry. By 1798, when Brune's invasion of Switzerland disillusioned most of the remaining supporters of revolutionary France, the Foxite Opposition was ineffective and unpopular and the cause of reform had largely gone underground. It was in this changing climate of opinion that what Professor Cobban calls "perhaps the last real discussion of the fundamentals of politics in this country"[3] took place.

The *Monthly* entered the Revolutionary period with an excellent reputation for "consistency," for over the past forty years Ralph Griffiths had maintained the principles of "an Old *Whig,* and a consistent *Protestant*" more steadily than most political parties. During the American war he had supported the colonists, not only by his editorial policy, but by providing a "post office" for their intelligence agents, and his honorary LL.D. from the University of Philadelphia had been awarded partly in recognition of these services.[4] There were Churchmen as well as Dissenters on his staff, but in controversy the *Monthly* expressed the views of moderate Dissent; and for the last twenty years of the eighteenth century its favourite causes were

Parliamentary reform and the repeal of the Test Laws. The *Monthly* was far from being a party organ, and there is no firm evidence of any link between this Review and Whig politicians before 1794. But it is an interesting coincidence that from 1784 or 1785 until some time in the early 1790s the main Whig propaganda organisation had its headquarters in the same building as the *Monthly*—at no. 42 Pall Mall, premises of the bookseller Thomas Becket. This organisation had begun as a literary club, the "Esto Perpetua," whose members collaborated in writing pamphlets and newspaper articles on the Opposition side. By 1788 it had developed into an important establishment financed out of Whig party funds; and Becket, who had formerly been Griffiths' partner and still distributed the *Monthly,* rented rooms and provided several other services to this group.[5] The *Monthly*'s reviewing of pamphlets thrown up by the Regency crisis of 1788-89 was noticeably more favourable to Fox than that of the *Critical.*[6]

As might be expected, the *Monthly* sympathised strongly with the French Revolution; and in the battle of books which followed the appearance of Burke's *Reflections* it gave the highest honours to James Mackintosh, author of *Vindiciae Gallicae* (1791).[7] (Four years later Mackintosh himself became a *Monthly* reviewer, his enthusiasm for the Revolution now much abated.) One of the most active and able political reviewers at this period was Thomas Pearne, a Unitarian Fellow of Peterhouse;[8] other contributors were Thomas Holcroft and John Wolcot ("Peter Pindar"). In January 1793 Griffiths was alarmed to learn that the Attorney-General was considering a prosecution on account of a review of *Principles of Government,* a book by Robert Nares, editor-designate of the *British Critic.* The review was by Pearne and had declared, amongst other things, that a nation may "dismiss or controul its king, whenever it thinks fit." Nothing came of this threat, though such reviews offended conservatives, who in the same year tried "to prevent the continuance of the M.R." in a circulating library at Yarmouth.[9] In January 1794 Griffiths provided a platform for the Foxites by publishing the first of more than sixty reviews on political subjects by Sheridan. By this time the Whig party was disintegrating, the propaganda establishment at Becket's had almost certainly ceased to function, and Sheridan (who had been a prominent member of the "Esto Perpetua") was looking for new channels for Foxite opinion. Before the end of the year, however, Griffiths had decided that though the Foxites were the most honest politicians they were not the wisest.[10] The *Critical* was now taking a strong Opposition line, and Griffiths intended to steer the *Monthly* on a more moderate course; by the beginning of 1796 he had notified contributors of a "new code" for dealing with political subjects, causing at least one reviewer, Dr. William Enfield, to "sigh over the *departed spirit* of British Liberty."[11] Possibly Holcroft

and Wolcot refused to work within this code, for their contributions ceased
early in the same year. In September 1796 Griffiths achieved a "friendly
separation" from Sheridan, whose verbose reviews had needed a good deal
of condensing and rewriting;[12] and from then on the *Monthly* took the
discreetest of Opposition lines, lamenting rather than opposing the war
and the frustration of all hopes of reform.

The *Critical* had been known for most of its existence as a "Tory"
Review, and reached the year 1789 with this reputation intact, though by
this time its dealings with reformers and Dissenters were very courteous
and moderate.[13] To the French Revolution this Review responded at first
with benevolent approval, changing in a few months to scepticism about
the doings of the National Assembly and fear of mob rule. In 1790 the
Critical was the only Review to take Burke's part, giving a very favourable
account of his *Speech on the Army Estimates* in April and his *Reflections*
in November. So far the *Critical* had taken the line of moderate conservative opinion. But with the beginning of a second series of this Review in
1791, a transformation of policy began to be visible; and by 1793 the
Critical was opposing Pitt and the war, and advocating reform, as strongly
as the Foxites. Following the *English,* the *Critical* now produced a regular
supplement on "Public Affairs," which it promised would be written
"without the violence, the illiberality of party, neither dictated by a bigot-
ted attachment to old forms nor an impetuous fondness for every innovation." The disparagement of "attachment to old forms" shows a movement
away from the views of Burke, and when the first of the supplements appeared it revealed a strong reforming bias:

> A great revolution seems of late to have taken place in the state of
> politics in this country. A third party has arisen, and is gradually though
> silently encreasing, which pretends to regard both ancient and modern
> whigs and tories as mere aristocratic divisions; who, under the stale
> pretext of public good have only sought to gratify their own avarice and
> ambition, while the interests of the nation at large have been neglected
> and despised. It is rumoured that the first decisive appearance of this
> party, which aspires to the name of the National, will take place in an
> invitation to all subjects, who pay a direct tax of 5s. a year, or upwards,
> and have no vote for members of parliament, to meet in their respective
> towns and counties, and appoint deputies to consider of the mode of
> redress. In England it is computed that out of five millions, about three
> hundred thousand vote; and in Scotland it is certain that out of a million
> and a half, there do not vote upwards of three thousand.
> A new spirit of examination, of reform, of political liberty, and
> frugality, seems to have arisen in most countries; and we shall applaud
> those moderate governments which wisely yield somewhat to the public
> wish. When the tempest arises, it is safer to be a willow than an oak.[14]

The first of these paragraphs might have been written by Horne Tooke, who in 1792 described the parties as "two factions who had been long contending, and still continue to contend, for the plunder and patronage of the country."[15] (The desirability of a national association for reform was also urged by the *Analytical*; see p. 194.) The same supplement includes a brisk attack on Pitt's handling of the Nootka Sound affair. Many readers must have been antagonised by this reversal of policy, yet until the *British Critic* began publication in 1793 they had no Tory Review to turn to as an alternative; and for two years the *Critical* tried by discreet tactics to keep up an appearance of consistency and lose as few of its old readers as possible. Notices of books are rarely as outspoken as the above-quoted supplement: some hint the new policy, some are evasive, others bear signs of editorial adjustment, and still others seem to have been written by survivors of the old regime.[16] Frequent claims are made for impartiality and moderation, Paine and Burke becoming the stock examples of extreme opinion in either direction. Once the *British Critic* had appeared on the scene it was no longer worth while to bid for conservative-minded readers, and from 1793 onwards the *Critical* took a fiercer line against the ministry and in favour of reform than the *Monthly*. From this year too the *Critical* gives more specific support to the Parliamentary Opposition, despite earlier remarks about "ancient and modern whigs," and the supplements give great prominence to the speeches of Fox and Grey.

The mechanics of this transformation are obscure;[17] but two figures who must have played important parts are the bookseller George Robinson and the Rev. Dr. George Gregory. Robinson had acquired a share in the *Critical* about 1774; since then his publishing business had grown much larger, and he had come to specialise in books by reformers and radicals.[18] In this period of acute controversy he must have felt the unwisdom of owning a Review in one camp to attack his publications in the other. He seems never to have edited the *Critical*, but would probably have been able to make sure that it was edited by someone who agreed with his views; and to supervise the metamorphosis of the *Critical* he apparently chose Gregory, who was editing the Review by 1793 and had probably been doing so for some time.[19] Gregory was a latitudinarian Churchman whose associates were Dissenters and reforming Whigs. Simultaneously with the *Critical* he was editing the Foxite *New Annual Register* in opposition to the *Annual Register* of Burke, which would have made it easy for him to write the *Critical* supplements. He may have been in touch with Opposition politicians, though we have no direct proof of this.[20] By 1801 his views or allegiances had changed, for his obituary relates that during Addington's administration Gregory "had the address" to bring over the *New Annual Register* to the Government side. But his connection with the *Critical* probably ceased before May 1799, for by that time the editorship seems to have passed to Samuel Hamilton, a grandson of one of the founders of the

Review. The *Critical* remained loyal to its new principles until it changed hands in 1805, after a fire had caused the bankruptcy of both Hamilton and the Robinsons.

The most radical of the Reviews was certainly the *Analytical*, owned and edited by the Unitarian bookseller Joseph Johnson. Johnson was the publisher and friend of many learned or literary Dissenters, including Priestley, Lindsey, John Aikin, Mrs. Barbauld, Erasmus Darwin, Richard Lovell Edgeworth and his daughter Maria, Thomas Beddoes, and Humphry Davy; and a number of *Analytical* reviewers were recruited from this network.[21] Overlapping this system was the "remarkable coterie of Jacobins" with whom Johnson was on dining terms. These included Thomas Christie, who first projected the Review and contributed to its early numbers; Mary Wollstonecraft, an industrious contributor; John Horne Tooke, Godwin, and Paine.[22] It is not surprising that the *Analytical* became known as "a principal repository of sentiments most favourable to rational liberty, both in politics and religion."[23] But these sentiments were not always fully explicit, and might be conveyed through the tone and manner of a summary rather than paragraphs of criticism. Though a friend to radicals, Johnson was cautious: in 1791 he transferred *Rights of Man* to another bookseller after copies had been printed, and perhaps sold, with his name, and in the same year either he or the author withdrew Blake's *French Revolution* from publication when it was already in proof.[24] The "analytical plan" suited Johnson's prudence as well as Christie's ideas about how reviewing should be done.

By 1798, however, Johnson had made himself sufficiently obnoxious for the Government to welcome a chance to prosecute. On 17 July he was convicted, despite a defence by Erskine, of selling a supposedly seditious pamphlet, Gilbert Wakefield's *Reply to the Bishop of Llandaff.*[25] (Paine's publisher, Jordan, was convicted of the same offence.) On 15 November, after four months on bail, Johnson was committed to the King's Bench Prison while the Lord Chief Justice examined evidence as to his character — including a recent number of the *Analytical Review.* On 12 February 1799 he was sentenced to a further six months' imprisonment and a fine of fifty pounds. His prison term seems to have been spent in expensive lodgings within the Rules; but away from his shop he could not continue to manage the *Analytical,* which had already suffered a blow from the death of Mary Wollstonecraft. By the beginning of 1799 Johnson had transferred it to another proprietor — perhaps Anthony Robinson, the radical sugar-baker derided in the *Antijacobin Review,* who had been contributing political articles since 1797.[26] For another six months the *Analytical* continued to appear as "Printed for the Editor." Henry Crabb Robinson, who had recently become a contributor, wrote to his brother on 4 February 1799:

I have to recommend to you & with more than ordinary Solicitude the new Analytical Review. The gross trimming & apostacy of the Monthly & the vast inconsistency & inequality of the Critical throws upon the New Review almost all the Burthen of supporting on principle & with firmness the great principles of Liberty & Truth which are cast now more than ever in the shade. *I know the principal Conductors & can assure you it is their Determination to make a vigourous & bold stand agt the Encroachmts of Toryism and Timidity which are apparent in the most popular Works of the kind.*[27]   [H.C.R.'s italics]

But by June these efforts had failed and the *Analytical* ceased publication. The *Antijacobin Review* claimed credit for giving its deathblow,[28] and published a cartoon (reproduced on the endpapers of the present volume) in which a figure representing the *Analytical* is shown as "fallen never to rise again."

Three years before the *Analytical* expired it had absorbed by a merger what remained of the *English Review*.[29] This journal had been in existence since 1783, and was the first of these Reviews to imitate the *Annual Register* by issuing regular supplements on "National Affairs." These were written by Dr. William Thomson, a leading spirit in the Review, and aimed at attracting as wide a range of opinion as possible. In 1783 Thomson had published a facetious romance[30] in which Fox was reproached for his coalition with North; but Thomson himself was attached to no political party. One of his favourite causes was the defence of Warren Hastings, whom he championed in a series of articles in the *English* and in an *Appeal to the People of England* (1788). During the early years of the *English* Godwin and Holcroft were contributors, Holcroft specialising in the theatre sections;[31] but the presence on the staff of two stout Tories—John Whitaker and Richard Polwhele[32]—shows that the *English* was no radical organ. For the French Revolution Thomson's supplements at first showed great enthusiasm, and though this subsequently became modified the *English* always showed more sympathy for the French than the *British Critic,* or the *Critical* of 1790. In the early 1790s the *English* also supported reform and even approved of *Rights of Man;* but by 1795 it was calling Paine a "pestilent fellow." A notable contributor to this Review was Dr. John Moore, whose disenchantment with the French Revolution sprang from the experience of living in Paris during the attack on the Tuileries and the prison massacres; another was John Gurney, junior counsel under Erskine in the treason trials of 1794.[33] In November 1793 John Murray I, the founder and joint-editor of the *English,* died, and Thomson became owner, editor, and chief contributor. These combined roles proved too much even for his well-attested energies, and after two and a half years he and some of his colleagues joined the staff of the *Analytical,* where Thomson continued to write the political supplements. Long before its demise the *English* had resigned all claim to "consistency" on controversial topics, which must have hastened its failure.

In the latter part of 1791, when all four Reviews were siding with the reformers and Dissenters, a group of Anglican clergymen[34] came together under the leadership of William Jones of Nayland to discuss means of

> preventing the corruption, which prevails among scholars, and persons of the higher orders of life, from evil *principles,* and what may be called *a monopoly of the press.*[35]

Constituting themselves a "Society for the Reformation of Principles," they issued on 1 January 1792 a statement declaring the need for (amongst other things) a new Review. Their call was answered by two clergymen of a more worldly stamp who subsequently became joint editors and part-owners of the *British Critic:* Robert Nares, chaplain to the Duke of York and author of two anti-reforming pamphlets, and William Beloe. Pitt's ministry seems to have encouraged the project at least to the extent of helping with initial expenses, for Nares received £50 from the secret-service money in March 1792 and a further £50 one year later.[36] In June 1792 a prospectus appeared inviting subscriptions and contributions; but it was not until May 1793 that the *British Critic* made its appearance. These lengthy preparations had not gone unnoticed. "The Clergy are going to attack us," wrote Pearne of the *Monthly* to his editor in September 1792:

> Well! I do not say: *"nous les mangerons tous";* but I say let them come; and let them see if they can light up afresh the fires of Birmingham with their *war-hoop* of "Church and King." We fear them not. Our device is, *Dieu et mon droit;* and our *cri-de-guerre* is *Vive la liberté!* A little opposition will do us good.[37]

After reading the first number another *Monthly* reviewer wrote shrewdly to Griffiths:

> They are at present rather too mild; our greatest security in the competition would arise from their being so violent, that all but violent people would be disgusted.[38]

Though firmly Tory, the *British Critic,* like the Reviews it was founded to oppose, dealt in gentlemanly controversy: "violence" of matter or manner was for newspapers, pamphlets, handbills, and the *Antijacobin Review.* Its main strength continued to be supplied by scholarly Anglican clergymen, some of whom supported the cause by reviewing without fees.[39] By 1795 William Jones, though disappointed in the theological tone of the *British Critic,* thought it was coping well with "such subjects as befit the Crown and Anchor":

They have had the good effect of lessening the sale of the Monthly Review to the value of 1000 copies a month, which is a circumstance worth all the trouble I took in giving birth to the undertaking.[40]

Even after the founding of the *British Critic* and the demise of the *English* there remained three radical or reforming Reviews against one Tory journal, which disquieted some minds. In a shilling pamphlet called *An Oblique View of the Grand Conspiracy against Social Order*, published anonymously in 1798, one Thomas Atkinson declared

that all these Reviews are in one interest; and *artfully arranged* to further one and the same cause, that the Analytical, for instance, is ingeniously calculated to influence men of a *sanguine temperament*, by dealing in bold sarcastic assertions, while the Monthly is addressed to men of more *reasoning*, and less *hasty minds*, and that the Critical *affects* to differ from these in *religious principles*, merely to adminster the same political figments with greater success, to men, whom they know to be prejudiced against Unitarians.

In the *Monthly*, Atkinson admitted, "many excellent sentiments" were to be found; but "this abominable Review" the *Analytical* existed only to propagate "a destructive set of principles by which the venerable constitution of our ancestors, was intended to be gradually subverted." But help was on the way, for in the same year the *Antijacobin Review and Magazine* (1798-1821) was founded. Though its articles have generally been excluded from this study, the *Antijacobin Review* deserves mention as a political phenomenon and an example of what the other Reviews, however partisan, were not. This monthly periodical began to appear in July 1798, soon after the *Anti-Jacobin* — the brilliant weekly to which Canning and Ellis had contributed — ceased publication. The *Antijacobin Review* was a distinct and different concern, though a few contributions left over from the *Anti-Jacobin* may have been passed on for its use.[41] It was edited and to a considerable extent written by "John Gifford," alias John Richards Green, the disreputable author of several ministerial pamphlets who was eventually to be rewarded by the post of a London police magistrate.[42] Other contributors were John Bowles and John Taylor, both "Treasury hirelings"; John Reeves, a leading government propagandist and informer and the organiser of the loyalist associations; Robert Bisset, the Rev. William Heath, and a number of other zealous or ambitious clergymen, some of whom also wrote for the *British Critic*.[43] Only the first section of each number provided "Original Criticism"; this was followed by "The Reviewers Reviewed," in which Gifford carried out his promise "to *review* the *Monthly*, *criticise* the *Critical*, and *analyse* the *Analytical*." Next came a "Miscellanies" section containing articles on such topics as "The Progress of Jacobinism" or "Quakers Detected."

It is hard to say which ingredient in the mixture supplied by the *Anti-jacobin Review* is most disagreeable: the hysteria of the zealots, the brutality of the hacks (very noticeable, of course, in their treatment of Mary Wollstonecraft), or the ubiquitous nonsense — like Gifford's description of Wordsworth and Coleridge going abroad to absorb the "abominable principles" of German philosophy.[44] Dealing largely in moral indignation, these reviewers were far from ethical in their own practices, as the marked file in the British Museum reveals. Books by contributors were not only blatantly puffed, they were on occasion reviewed anonymously by the authors themselves — a practice not detected in any other Review in this period. Thus Dr. A. F. M. Willich reviewed his own *Lectures on Diet,* and the emigré A. F. B. de Moleville gave three admiring instalments to his own *Annals of the French Revolution.*[45] In the "Reviewers Reviewed" section the Rev. Thomas Wright and the Rev. Richard Polwhele, still writing anonymously and with different degrees of indignation, defended their own works from the aspersions of the *Critical Review.*[46] (It is Polwhele, a shameless self-advertiser, who introduces a two-and-a-half page extract from his own *History of Devon,* with complimentary acknowledgements, into his review of Gilpin's *Observations on the Western Parts.*[47]) In the correspondence section a letter on the Income Tax, signed "Impartial," proves to be the work of the Treasury hack John Bowles; while "A Friend to Episcopacy" turns out to be yet another of the reviewers — John Skinner, Bishop of Aberdeen![48] Almost the only thing of value to appear in the *Antijacobin Review* was the splendid series of cartoons by Gillray.[49]

The above summary does no more than indicate the orientation and main development of each Review. To explore the attitude of even one of them to all the controversies and political groupings of the period would be a major task, especially since several shades of opinion were represented in each journal: even in the comparatively consistent *Monthly* Griffiths did not always succeed in harmonising the political reviews of men as different as Pearne, Holcroft, Moody, and Sheridan. What clearly emerges is how strongly the Dissenters and other reforming groups were posted in the literary world. In 1791 all four Reviews were upholding reform, the French Revolution, and the abolition of the slave trade; it is not surprising that these views seemed normative to men like Coleridge, who grew up into this period. It is also clear that a strong body of middle-class liberal opinion already existed to support these Reviews. Even when the *British Critic* had drawn the more conservative readers away from the *Monthly* and *Critical,* these journals flourished for many years; and the *Analytical* survived through six years of anti-Jacobin fever, to be destroyed at last by Johnson's imprisonment. Government resources were employed against these Reviews in the prosecution of Johnson and Robinson, and in the setting-up of the *British Critic* and *Antijacobin Review;* but there is no evidence that any of the reforming Reviews were subsidised out of Opposition funds. Though the *Monthly* was in touch with the Foxites through Sheridan, I am certain that Griffiths neither needed a subsidy nor would have compromised the independence of his journal by accepting one. The *Analytical* was too radical to attract Whig support, and the *English* too inconsistent. It is less certain that Robinson and Gregory received no financial aid from the Foxites during the dangerous period when they were changing the politics of the *Critical.* For performing almost the reverse change in the *New Annual Register* ten years later, Gregory is said to have been rewarded with the living of West Ham.[50] But Robinson, a wealthy publisher, would probably have been willing to lose money on the *Critical* during a transition from which he stood ultimately to benefit. And unless the *Critical* emerged from the transition with a substantial readership, it would hardly have been worth while either for the politicians or for Robinson himself to support it. Its sale in 1797 is in fact estimated at 3,500 copies, equal to the *British Critic* and second only to the *Monthly;*[51] since its price was the same as theirs, there is no need to suppose that it was anything but independent.

Many letters to Griffiths from Enfield and Pearne show them to have been sincere and intelligent believers in the policy of their journal. The same is patently true of the *Analytical* reviewers, and of men like Dyer in the *Critical* and Partridge[52] in the *British Critic.* The best reviews discussed in this chapter, and many others which have been omitted, show the qualities that make controversy in this period something more than a propaganda war between conflicting interest-groups: a belief in free enquiry, intellectual integrity, and a zealous pursuit of truth. Such reviews more than compensate for the productions of party hacks, time-servers, and bigots.

Price's *Discourse on the Love of our Country*

"The history of the French Revolution in England begins with a sermon and ends with a poem."[53] In a meeting-house in the Old Jewry on 4 November 1789, Dr. Richard Price reminded the Revolution Society of their interpretation of the events of 1688: as an affirmation of the right of peoples to choose their own governors, to cashier them for misconduct, and to frame a government for themselves. In defining the scope of rational patriotism Price touched on several national grievances, including the Test Laws and the need for Parliamentary reform; and in his peroration he gave ardent, unqualified praise to the greater revolution taking place in France. As *A Discourse on the Love of our Country* (1789),[54] his sermon quickly went through several editions, and was taken as a text or pretext for the *Reflections* of Burke.

The only real question for the reviewers was how far to approve of Price's uncompromising political statements. In the *Analytical* the *Discourse* was warmly approved by Mary Wollstonecraft, who had been a member of Price's Unitarian congregation at Newington Green:

> This sermon breathes the animated sentiments of ardent virtue . . . many passages occur which are truly eloquent — the heart speaks to the heart in an unequivocal language, and the understanding, not bewildered by sophistical arguments, assents, without an effort, to such obvious truths.

She does not discuss the political implications of the *Discourse*, but quotes approvingly some of its strongest passages — that beginning "Why are the nations of the world so patient under despotism?", that describing unequal Parliamentary representation, and the peroration from "What an eventful period is this!"

Christopher Moody, in the *Monthly*, was also largely favourable: "We do not hesitate in expressing our general approbation of those sentiments of freedom and benevolence, which glow in the pages before us." Himself an Anglican clergyman, Moody comments with warm approval on Price's treatment of the Test Laws and agrees with his proposal (advanced in its day) to extend complete toleration to Catholics. The only part of the *Discourse* that he dislikes is Price's treatment of the person and office of George III:

> His loyalty appears offered to the abstract idea of *the majesty of the people*, while he may be thought deficient in proper respect to the great personage who possesses and displays it. That blunt, unceremonious address, which Dr. P. would have recommended on a late joyful occasion [the king's recovery from madness; Price had been disgusted by the "adulation" offered at that time] would have justly offended Majesty, without answering one good purpose. Is it requisite, or is it even decent, in every approach to the throne with a congratulatory address, to inform the king, in plain English, that he is only the servant of the people? . . . Dr. Price, indeed, makes a bad figure as a courtier.

Like Mary Wollstonecraft, Moody quotes Price's peroration with its "spirited and affecting reflections on the FRENCH REVOLUTION."

The *Critical* pronounces no judgement on the sermon as a whole, but makes several criticisms of detail. The reviewer disagrees with Price's statement that "universal benevolence," or the love of mankind, should be preferred to other affections: it is impossible to know what will be best for mankind, and "neither reason nor religion can warrant our doing a certain injury to our own country, from an opinion that an accidental good may be derived by this means to another." Here he anticipates Burke, as also when he points out that the notion that the king is the people's servant finds no support in English history or law:

> If in these passages he gives abstract, speculative propositions, which, like the social contract, never were or can be reduced to practice, we would not oppose them. But if he means to apply them to our own country, it is necessary to observe, that they convey false ideas, and may probably have a dangerous tendency.

The general tone of this review is one of respectful disagreement. The *English* avoids committing itself, by equivocation of which the following is typical:

> On the subject of *liberty* it is impossible not to admire the honest zeal of this well-meaning preacher. It is, however, in many respects by far the most exceptionable part of the work; but as it has been taken notice of by more than one writer whose performance will come before us, we shall suspend what we have to say on the subject at present.

More is said about Price's character than his *Discourse,* though even on this subject the *English* remains ambiguous: "in such characters we are to look for failings in the extreme of their virtues."

To the fourth edition of the *Discourse* (1790) Price added a short preface defending himself from some of the charges made in Burke's *Reflections.* Contrary to its usual practice with new editions, the *Critical* reviewed this publication at some length, taking a stronger line against Price:

> attached as we are, by principle, to the present establishment in church and state, the innovations of pretended patriots we consider as dangerous, and oppose as fatal.

The reviewer tries to forestall the charge that this is inconsistent with sympathy previously expressed by the *Critical* for the French Revolution:

> On the subject . . . we early engaged, and we hailed the progress of liberty with as much heartfelt applause as any member of the Revolution Society. We pronounced the first steps to be cool, deliberate, and judicious. We still think so, and the horrors of the first moments were the evils to be unavoidably encountered in the way to a more perfect and more permanent good. But to the destruction of despotism insult need not have been added; and those who had consented to resign their power, should have preserved their lives secure from even the suspicion of danger.

These remarks must refer to the march on Versailles and subsequent in-cidents; yet these had taken place in October 1789, almost four months before the *Critical* review of the original edition of Price's *Discourse* had appeared. This reviewer also notes that the National Assembly have spent the intervening time in idle speculations, and have seemed earnest only in seizing the executive power. For these reasons the *Critical* reviewers have ceased to praise the Revolution and have applauded Burke's *Reflections*. Price claims in his new Preface that he has never approved of the Versailles incidents, yet, the reviewer notes, he has never explicitly condemned them; and even now he does not seem to think the French have been barbarous, unmanly, or unjust.

Within their limits, both the *Monthly* notice and the first *Critical* notice are satisfactory. The second *Critical* notice is a palinode rather than a review, and its attempts to show consistency are unconvincing. Mary Wollstonecraft's article is sympathetic but uncritical, and too emotive to be an adequate response to Price's sermon — a work of powerful logic as well as of passion. The *English* review is worthless.

Burke's *Reflections*

Edmund Burke's *Reflections on the Revolution in France* (1790) com-prises a forceful though unmethodical attack on the French Revolution, a hymn of praise to the existing order of things in England, and an essay in political philosophy. About the French Revolution Burke was ill-informed and biased, treating it for the most part as an imposture practised on fools by knaves; but his grasp of the dangers of unsettled government and mob violence enabled him accurately to predict its course. His praise of the established order in England shows an equal and opposite bias, dignifying even the unreformed electoral system. His underlying view of politics has to be pieced together from scattered statements and implications. Burke em-phasised, not men's perfectibility, but their limitations; he saw only rashness and impiety in their attempt to destroy social forms that had evolved through centuries under the guidance of Providence. Behind his insistence on the need for cautious, inductive methods in politics, as against the mechanical application of abstract principles, lay his vision of the state as a complex historical growth serving complex needs. If these deeper insights were not understood by most of his contemporaries, the cause lay partly in Burke's rhetorical style — more effective when declaim-ing against crimes and errors than when sorting out ideas. His imaginative flights often seemed, and sometimes were, an escape from rational con-troversy:

He can parade his arguments with masterly generalship, where they are strong. He can escape from an untenable position into a splendid declamation. He can sap the most impregnable conviction by pathos, and put to flight a host of syllogisms with a sneer. Absolved from the laws of vulgar method, he can advance a groupe of magnificent horrors to make a breach in our hearts, through which the most undisciplined rabble of arguments may enter in triumph.[55]

The *Reflections* were reviewed promptly and at length, but of the four notices that appeared only one was favourable. Not unnaturally, the critics concentrated on Burke's treatment of the state of things in England and France, and from this point of view they would have preferred something more methodical and factual. The *Monthly, English,* and *Analytical* condemned Burke's exaggerated conservatism, and had no difficulty in showing fallacies and inconsistencies in his writing; the friendly *Critical* reviewer showed little discretion in his praise. The brilliance of Burke's style was recognised, but all four reviewers found it unsuitable for a political essay: its limitations were well demonstrated in the *Monthly* by Pearne, who noted that "panegyric and invective are perpetually substituted for argument." The *Critical* used an almost exactly similar phrase, while the *Analytical* declared that Burke "loses himself in a wilderness of words and figures." The *English* even accused him of "bold falsity" and "artful misrepresentation," but the other Reviews recognised his sincerity: the *Analytical* called him "the dupe of his imagination or his passions," and the *Critical* found that Burke's tenderness, humanity, and gallantry had led him from the cool path of argument.

   Thomas Pearne of Peterhouse, a good classical scholar, turned his training to account in the only thorough appraisal of Burke's style:

It is declamatory, diffuse and desultory. An idea, originally started for the purpose of illustration, is often pursued so far, that it misleads more than it illustrates. . . . Both in the whole, and in the subordinate parts, there is a great want of compactness. We rarely see any regular beginning, middle, or end. The characteristic feature of its diction, of its sentiments, and of its arguments, is amplification. The language possesses much more of the periphrastic verbosity of Cicero, than of his neatness, of his correctness, or of his elegance; much more of the warmth and vehemence of Demosthenes, than of his force and energy. . . . His reasoning is of that species, which is calculated to affect, rather by the accumulation and combined force of a number of arguments, each of which appears light, and airy, and refined, in itself, than by the strength and solidity of any single and independent proposition.

Pearne admires Burke's effective satire and his command of metaphor, but also notes a superfluity of epithets, a weakness for paradox, and a profusion of ornament. A long "guided tour" through the *Reflections* now begins. At first Pearne makes substantial criticisms, showing himself quite capable of grappling with Burke on fundamental issues. Price had unwisely described George III as "almost the only lawful King in the world, because the only one who owes his crown to the choice of his people"; Burke replied by an elaborate demonstration that the kings of England succeed by hereditary right and not by popular election; Pearne dismisses this as irrelevant and glosses "lawful" as meaning "in obedience to the free, voluntary, and enlightened will of his subjects," expressed in their choice of William III in 1688 and their acquiescence in the Protestant succession ever since. Following Locke as against Burke, Pearne argues that social rights are ultimately derived from certain inalienable "natural" rights:

> We think the ground of *ancient usage* is full as dangerous as, and perhaps less tenable than, that of *divine right*. If natural rights were to be destroyed, as false and fictitious, we apprehend that social, municipal, rights would all fall to the earth for want of support.

Like Price, Pearne interprets the Revolution of 1688 as an occasion when natural rights were reasserted. His ironical comments on the misapplied pathos of Burke's descriptions of the Versailles incidents and of Marie Antoinette anticipate the famous comment of Paine; and he finds Burke's praise of the old chivalrous ideals "overwrought, and extravagantly bespangled." As the "tour" progressess, Pearne's extracts grow longer and his criticisms shorter. He continues to make good points, however, as when he describes Burke's panegyric upon the Established Church as "a mere encomium on religion." On Burke's account of the National Assembly at work Pearne comments, aptly enough, that "every evil is studiously brought forward and magnified, while every good is concealed. On this plan of criticizing, nothing can ever stand the test." Summing up, Pearne praises Burke's benevolence and good intentions, and concludes that "Mr. Burke's character stands much higher as a worthy man, and as an eloquent writer, than as a sound reasoner." This review shows exceptional ability to follow Burke closely, to disagree reasonably, and to evaluate his style.[56]

The *Critical* implies that by their excesses the revolutionaries have forfeited all claim to sympathy:

> our neighbours have shown that a revolution may be effected by the coolest, the wisest, and best-conducted plans, and afterwards followed by the wildest, the cruellest, and most inconsiderate.

Despite some prejudice, "declamation occasionally too florid, and resentment a little too acrimonious," the reviewer finds the *Reflections* the most able, eloquent, and interesting political work to appear for many years. But the review that follows this judgement is badly proportioned, too much space being given to Burke's thrusts at the Revolution Society and the Society for Constitutional Information; and the comments made show more willingness to agree than discernment. Thus "great force of argument and depth of constitutional knowledge" is found in Burke's discussion of George III's hereditary title, which Pearne had sensibly dismissed as obvious and irrelevant. Burke is said to have examined "the boasted rights of man" with great accuracy, and his ill-informed account of the work of the National Assembly receives special praise. Burke's style is also admired — and here the reviewer's vagueness may be contrasted with the precision of Pearne:

> The language, in general that of mild expostulation, flows with an even tenour, and in so soft a stream, that while we seem occasionally to look for variety, the wish subsides in the admiration of the elegance with which each sentence is usually finished.

In conclusion, the *Critical* prophesies that the *Reflections* will endure as a model of elegant composition and pathetic description, "containing the most judicious political principles, and a very accurate examination of one part of the British constitution."

The *English,* conversely to the *Critical,* offers little but disagreement. The reviewer makes some of the same points as Pearne, but shows neither Pearne's fairness nor his willingness to discuss fundamentals. His favourite method is that of ironical paraphrase:

> Mr. Burke considers next the general state of the old government. His principal arguments in its favour are, that it was not so despotic as that of Persia; that fewer people were sent to the Bastile than in former reigns; and, what is more to the purpose, that the population and quantity of specie were increasing.

This may be effective political journalism, but it is poor criticism. The reviewer has read Burke with attention, however, and shows him to be wrong on several points of fact concerning the new French electoral system. In conclusion he praises Burke's style, but points out that it is one which conceals rather than expresses the truth: the reader

> will find himself charmed with every period, and rather anxious to get on to the next, than closely examine the truth, or perhaps even the meaning of the last; he will be led from one region of the fairy world to another; he will fancy himself *convinced,* and at the same time wonder how he could be convinced.

The *Analytical* was the only review not to adopt the "guided tour" method for the *Reflections:* an excellent and almost completely impartial

summary is followed by a series of reasoned objections, a much shorter
series of points of agreement, and a final paragraph of evaluation. Some of
the critic's objections are valid and important, as when he points out that
Burke's argument that liberty and good government should be claimed on
grounds of prescription and inheritance rather than on those of reason — a
"monstrous and extraordinary doctrine" — not only cuts off hope of future
improvement, but destroys the foundations of present benefits:

> On what principle, we would ask, were these franchises *originally*
> grounded . . . but on the simple dictate of common sense, the maxim
> "that government was instituted for the *good* of the governed?"

Reasonable criticisms are also made of Burke's "extravagant idolatry of
ancestry and rank" and his "florid declamations in favor of the times of
chivalry." Less reasonable are the accusations that Burke is trying "to
render the French king dissatisfied with his present situation," and encouraging Marie Antoinette to commit suicide. The conclusion is predict-
able:

> The imagination of Mr. Burke is more vigorous and excursive than
> that of any modern writer. His mind is well stored with various
> literature, and there is scarcely a science to which he is not able to
> appeal for matter of illustration. His style is splendid. . . . With
> all these accomplishments, as a speaker Mr. Burke is scarcely attended
> to; as a writer, his works will probably never attain to permanent
> popularity. . . . The truth is, that brilliant as are Mr. Burke's abilities,
> they are untempered with . . . judgement.

Tongue, in fact, with a garnish of brains.[57] Though this reviewer was
wrong about the judgement of posterity, his sensible criticisms outweigh
his errors.

Generally speaking, the reviewers saw and deplored the exaggerations of
Burke's conservatism without noticing the valuable insights that went with
it. Within this almost inevitable limitation the *Monthly* gave an excellent
review and the *Analytical* a satisfactory one. The latter review showed that
"analysis" followed by criticism could provide good results. Burke's style
was generally admired, but with reservations — a response that corresponds
more closely with one's experience of reading the *Reflections* than purely
laudatory accounts.

Paine's *Rights of Man*

Part 1 (1791) of *Rights of Man*, by Thomas Paine, gives an optimistic
account of the French Revolution and the work of the National Assembly,

drawing attention to those revolutionary ideals which Burke had largely ignored. Paine also meets Burke's conservative philosophy with an exposition of individualist theory, derived ultimately from Locke, to the effect that the State is for the people and not the people for the State; and he sharply criticises the injustice and inefficiency of those ancient institutions which Burke venerates. As an example of what men can achieve when freed from prejudice and superstition, he points to the constitution of the United States. Paine wrote in simple, vivid language: "No one since him or before him has stated the plain democratic case against monarchy and aristocracy with half his spirit and force."[58]

Rights of Man aroused strong partisan feelings among the reviewers, the *Critical* attacking both parts as they came out, the *English* and *Analytical* defending them. The *Critical* treated Part 1 with unintelligent contempt:

> With all our care, we have scarcely found, in the present Answer, one atom of that useful quality, Common Sense, which, if our author ever possessed, he seems to have exhausted it in the production of his favourite first-born.

A few of the less important passages are quoted and ridiculed, and the reader is warned against "the evils arising from such inflammatory publications." The *Analytical,* in a wholly favourable review, compares the methods of the two opponents as writers: Burke, a conscious stylist, "delights the imagination by the beauty of his metaphors," while Paine, "plain but forcible," appeals to the judgement by "the native vigour of his arguments." A summary of the work follows, showing agreement with Paine on all important points: Paine's ridicule of Burke is said to be very successful, and his defence of natural rights very able. His sketch of the French Revolution is given special praise, as tracing its causes "with the acuteness and perspicacity of a Tacitus." On the whole, *Rights of Man* "is one of the most curious, original, and interesting publications, which the singular vicissitudes of modern politics have produced."

In the *Monthly* Pearne awarded praise and blame in roughly equal proportions. He finds the strong light of Paine's common sense admirable for showing up the absurdity of some of Burke's notions, and quotes with approval several passages of this kind, including Paine's attack on religious establishments.[59] But he thinks Paine out of his depth in his own theorising:

> When he attempts to reason scientifically, on the first principles of government; on the rights which men retain, and on those which they give up, when they enter into society; on the *unity* of man, as he affectedly calls it; . . . he reasons very superficially. He contends that we have no constitution, in this country; because it cannot be produced, and quoted, article by article, from some visible, legal

record! He might just as well contend that there was no common law in this country, because it is a *lex non scripta.*

Pearne prefers Paine's account of the French Revolution to the rest of the book. As for style,

> the less his friends say of it, the better: but our duty obliges us to say, that it is desultory, uncouth, and inelegant. His wit is coarse, and sometimes disgraced by wretched puns; and his language, though energetic, is awkward, ungrammatical, and often debased by vulgar phraseology.

This way of writing, Pearne remarks, will do little to allay Burke's fears of an imminent return of barbarism.

The *English* reviewer, who is likely to have been Dr. William Thomson,[60] gave Paine exaggerated praise both as a historian and as a political philosopher. Some abuse is likewise bestowed on Burke; and the whole review, with its violent tone and irresponsible generalisations, resembles a parody in the *Anti-Jacobin:*

> Everything worth notice in Mr. Burke's volume is answered with a readiness and strength of judgement that shows a writer above the trifling trammels of prejudice, precedent, or artificial rights. By tracing things to their origin, he saves himself the trouble of disputing all Mr. Burke's idle positions. . . . The expensive burthens of a court are finely pourtrayed, and the *old governments,* as they are called, are advised to be ready in admitting every melioration, in order to protract, as long as possible, that overthrow which time and the gradual unfolding of the human intellect must ultimately produce.

By February 1792, when Part 2 of *Rights of Man* went to press, at least 40,000 copies of Part I had been sold,[61] and the reviewers paid Part 2 prompt attention. In this part Paine develops his ideas still farther, "combining principle and practice." Though his first chapter still expounds the individualist view of government as a necessary evil, to be restricted to a minimum, his fifth chapter considers government as an instrument of social justice. Among the many measures suggested are maternity benefits, family allowances, old-age pensions, and free compulsory education, all to be financed in part by a graduated income tax. Thus Paine outruns his theoretical premises and those of almost every other reformer of his period, looking ahead towards a measure of socialism. Confronted with this highly original work the *Monthly* continued to be fairly objective, and the *Critical* to be hostile; but the approval of the *Analytical* was less open, and that of the *English* more qualified, than in the previous year. (Seven weeks after these reviews had appeared, the proclamation against seditious writings was issued, together with a summons against Paine; and in the following

year Thomas Muir was sentenced to fourteen years' transportation on an
indictment based on evidence of his having recommended Paine's works.)

Pearne opens his review in the *Monthly* by mildly ridiculing the vanity
with which Paine boasts, in the Preface to Part 2, of the sale of Part 1 and
of his other achievements. His verdict on the early, theoretical chapters of
the book was the same as on Part 1:

> Here we often listen to him with pleasure, because he often speaks
> much to the purpose: not indeed when he attempts to argue
> scientifically or profoundly, . . . but when he exposes prejudice,
> either in practice or opinion, and shews its absurdity by some new
> and unexpected resemblance or comparison, or by some uncommon
> and forcible description; — and at this, Mr. Paine generally aims.

Among the examples Pearne gives of this kind of success is Paine's comparison of the king's function in government to that of a sacred goose. He
dismisses Paine's schemes of financial reform and social welfare as "crude,
and indigested." The work is said to lack unity and coherence, and though
Paine's grammar has improved his style is still found "harsh, rude, and in-
elegant."

The *Critical,* which in April 1791 had called Paine "an object of detestation," evidently realises that it has dismissed *Rights of Man* too hastily:

> If we had thought it possible that the virulence of party, the disap-
> pointment of soaring ambition, or the rage of innovation could, for
> a moment, have contributed to bestow a temporary celebrity on
> ignorance and absurdity, blended with the low vulgarity of col-
> loquial errors, and boldly depending on insignificance for safety,
> we should have taken some pains to have pointed out the numerous
> errors both in the facts and reasoning of the "Rights of Man."

But these errors remain undefined: instead of justifying his verdict the
reviewer continues in the vein of scornful abuse. His one genuine point is
that in distinguishing sharply between society and the State, Paine
underestimates the importance of government as a precondition of any
social intercourse.

The *Analytical* professes to leave the reader free to form his own judgement:

> Wert thou pleased with the first part? Thou wilt be delighted with
> the second. Didst thou say of the former, such a work deserves no
> other confutation than that of criminal justice?[62] Thou wilt say
> of this, this only way to answer it is to hang the author.

This show of impartiality is not very thorough. The reviewer first summarises the work in sympathetic terms and then makes some general com-

ments, almost all of which are favourable. Paine's style is said to be popular without being vulgar: "Mr. Paine, we acknowledge, does not abound with so many flowers as Mr. Burke; but we think he hath as many beauties, and fewer blemishes." Without pronouncing on the question of whether England has a constitution, the reviewer declares that what is *called* the constitution certainly needs reform. He strongly agrees with Paine on the excessive expense of present government, and on the need for reform of the electoral system:

> As to our representation, to talk of it is to trifle. It is not sufficient to say, our representation is partial: when all the circumstances . . . are taken into consideration, it is not speaking at random to say the people of England are not represented at all. . . . If a national association were formed, and justice requires that it should be formed, every real evil might find a remedy.

The practical reforms outlined by Paine are discussed and in general praised. The reviewer notes his striking self-confidence, and, while professedly leaving readers to decide for themselves how far this is justified, gives a strong hint that at least "this is no common man; this is the poor man's friend."

The *English* is more judicial than in its earlier review, and makes reasonable criticisms of several of Paine's opinions. Thus the reviewer agrees with the *Critical* that government is more fundamentally necessary to society than Paine, in his early chapters, seems to think. He points out too that not all human wrongdoing can be set down to the influence of kings:

> Common reflection might have taught a writer of less penetration that the most simple form of government is monarchy; that of course it must be adopted in an unlimited state in the early stages of society; that in this period it is not the dispositions of princes only, but of subjects also, frequently to interrupt the peace of their neighbours . . . . Thus what he attributes to a faulty government, may, in a great measure, be ascribed to the temper of the times, and the subsequent improvement, to the gradual unfolding of the human intellect.

Paine's view of history is, indeed, drastically foreshortened. With his main ideas the critic expresses neither agreement nor disagreement; but he pronounces that the work "unites boldness of design with accuracy of reasoning and minuteness of detail," and adds:

> Political subjects on a broad scale are now the reigning topics everywhere; and bold as Mr. Paine's reasonings at first seemed, the world appears every day better reconciled to them.

This group of reviews is noteworthy as showing Paine's public reputation standing generally high before being obscured by the "black legend" of propagandists, or driven underground.[63] Yet unqualified approval of *Rights of Man* reveals a better partisan than a critic. On this view both *Analytical* notices (published by the original publisher of *Rights of Man*) are unsatisfactory, though the summaries they contain are excellent. The first *English* review is unsatisfactory for the same reason; the second contains enough fair criticism to pass for a reasonable review. The *Critical* reviews are too largely abusive. Pearne alone, in the *Monthly*, produced two balanced articles: sympathetic but scrupulous, he sees Paine's weaknesses and a good part of his strength, his intelligence and his conceit. No critic of 1792 can be blamed for rejecting Paine's vision of a socialist society, especially since this vision is contradicted by Paine's own individualism. Otherwise, Pearne's only serious limitation is not to have realised that for a popular work the style and method of *Rights of Man* could hardly have been more effective. A cultivated classical scholar, he deplores what he considers Paine's coarseness; but "the success of *Rights of Man* with ordinary people sprang from the fact that it dealt with political problems clearly, in their own language, and without classical erudition or embellishment."[64]

Mary Wollstonecraft's *Rights of Woman*

A Vindication of the Rights of Woman (1792) is not a political work but, as the *Analytical* reviewer perceived, "an elaborate *treatise* of *female education*." Mary Wollstonecraft's main thesis is that instead of being brought up in an artificial state of ignorance and helplessness, women should be given the same opportunities as men to develop their mental and physical powers. Only once[65] does she hint, with a plea for indulgence in what will seem a ridiculous idea, that one day they may even be allowed a voice in the government of their country. Among the particular possibilities she discusses are "equality of opportunity in work and the professions, . . . co-education, sex education, state schools, the provision of playgrounds for exercise, equality in custody of the children of a marriage and the father's responsibility in the case of illegitimate children."[66] The work is not methodically arranged, and has no particular graces of style; but it deserves the respect it has always received from feminists by reason of its shrewd, original thought — often astonishingly emancipated — and its ardent and generous spirit.

Of the three reviews *Rights of Woman* received, one was wholly favourable, one preponderantly favourable, and one decidedly hostile. The first of these, in the *Analytical,* might have been expected to show bias in favour of a regular contributor, and it is likely enough that it was reviewed by another member of the radical circle that met at Johnson's. However, the fault of this review is not undue praise but a lack of specific criticism. For the most part it summarises *Rights of Woman* in neutral terms, giving plenty of quotation. The few comments made in the course of the summary are favourable, special praise going to Mary Wollstonecraft's treatment of conventional female education as a source of ignorance and superstition: "We cannot sufficiently commend the good sense and intelligence of this section." Some attempt at evaluation is made at the end of each of the two instalments of this review. In the first, *Rights of Woman* is described as a "singular, and, on the whole, excellent production," and the importance of its subject is emphasised:

> The lesser wits will probably affect to make themselves merry at the title and apparent object of this publication; but we have no doubt if even her contemporaries should fail to do her justice, posterity will compensate the defect; and have no hesitation in declaring, that if the bulk of the great truths which this publication contains were reduced to practice, the nation would be better, wiser, and happier, than it is upon the wretched, trifling, useless and absurd system of education which is now prevalent.

The second instalment ends by recommending the work to readers of all classes: even those who do not agree with female suffrage or co-education "will find some benefit from her pointed observations on the maintenance of pernicious prejudices, and from her judicious thoughts on the different branches and objects of education." Mary Wollstonecraft's style is said to be "strong and impressive." Though generally appreciative, this article does not include enough real discussion to count as a satisfactory review.

The *Critical* review combines political conservatism with traditional satire of bluestockings. *Rights of Woman* is said effectually to demonstrate the absurdity of "the boasted rights of man" upon which it is founded. Mary Wollstonecraft cannot have been pleased by this reviewer's mode of address, though she may have felt that it proved much of her case:

> in truth, dear young lady, for by the appellation sometimes prefixed to your name we must suppose you to be young, endeavour to attain "the weak elegance of mind," the "sweet docility of manners," "the exquisite sensibility," the former ornaments of your sex; we are certain you will be more pleasing, and we dare pronounce that you will be infinitely happier.

Sentences are taken at random from the work and treated with sarcasm and ridicule. Much of the article is on familiar lines, as when the critic enquires who will do the women's work once they have been emancipated, fearing that the female Plato will find it unsuitable to "the dignity of her virtue" to dress the child, and descend to the disgusting offices of a nurse; the new Archimedes will measure the shirts by means of the altitude taken by a quadrant.

(Mary Wollstonecraft had in fact disavowed the idea that women should throw off family duties; her case is rather that an educated woman will perform them better.[67]) The author is accused of "alluding a little too freely to the communication of the sexes," and her distinction between true and false modesty is rejected on grounds of "morality." Faults of grammar and expression are also dwelt upon. The review ends with a list of the book's defects: it is "weak, desultory and trifling," marred by "the indelicacy of her ideas and expressions," and written in language "flowing and flowery; but weak, diffuse, and confused." Mary Wollstonecraft is consigned "at least to oblivion: her best friends can never wish that her work should be remembered."

As so often, the *Monthly* supplies the fairest and most satisfactory review. A middle-aged male, Dr. William Enfield, shows there a grasp of the essential issues, a willingness to discuss them reasonably, and a capacity for judicious evaluation. Enfield insists that it is in men's best interests — encumbered as they are by prejudices and by stultifying institutions — to give all new opinions a fair hearing. He states the main principles of *Rights of Woman* very accurately: "that, except in affairs of love, sexual distinctions ought to be disregarded, and women be considered in the light of rational creatures"; and that the degradation of the female character "springs entirely from the want of a due cultivation of the rational powers." Well-chosen quotations cover the main ideas of the book. Enfield's tone is courteous and sympathetic, nor is he offended by Mary Wollstonecraft's outspokenness; agreeing with her distinction between true and false modesty, he adds:

> This subject is still farther pursued, with a degree of freedom which may perhaps be thought singular in a female, but with a philosophical air of dignity and gravity, which precludes every idea of indecorum, and almost prohibits . . . a smile.

His conclusions, though neither daring nor profound, show that he has kept his head. He finds that *Rights of Woman* shows "great energy of intellect, vigour of fancy, and command of language . . . and suggests many reflections, which well deserve the attention of the public." He allows that some of its theses may be fanciful or romantic, that women might not perhaps be improved by taking part in politics, that chivalrous attentions do not really degrade the female character, and that differences of sex will be ignored only by a society of angels:

Notwithstanding all this, however, we entirely agree with the fair writer, that both the condition and character of women are capable of great improvement; and that by means of a more rational plan of female education . . . women might be rendered at once more agreeable, more respectable, and more happy in every station of life. Both men and women should certainly, in the first place regard themselves, and should be treated by each other, as human beings.

Such a review, seen in conjunction with the outraged conventionality of the *Critical,* deserves respect.

Godwin's *Political Justice*

William Godwin, unlike Burke, believed that political and social institutions should be founded on principles. *An Enquiry Concerning Political Justice* (1793) is an attempt to outline the ideal society whose arrangements would be wholly determined by considerations of general morality. That such a society presupposes ideal human beings does not deter Godwin, since he also differs from Burke by his emphasis on man's rationality and ultimate perfectibility.[68] His system, though widely eclectic, owes most perhaps to the traditions of Rational Dissent;[69] in it all rights, both of men and of governments, are subordinated to the claims of virtue as interpreted by reason, and the liberty chiefly valued is that of conscience. If *Political Justice* now seems a self-consistent system invalidated by false assumptions about human nature, it should be remembered that these assumptions were shared by many of the best minds of Godwin's day. The book appeared early in 1793, when the sedition trials were already under way in Scotland; shortly afterwards, in May, came the conviction of John Frost, the first English victim of the drive against sedition.[70] In spite of its high price[71] and academic style and method, *Political Justice* became widely known, and its influence on the thought of Wordsworth, Coleridge, Hazlitt, and (above all) Shelley has often been described.[72]

The *Monthly* and *Analytical* gave Godwin's work muted and qualified approval. The *Critical* began by treating it with respect, but ended on a much less favourable note. The *British Critic* ridiculed the work, while the *English* gave it no real review.

In the *Monthly*, *Political Justice* was reviewed by Thomas Holcroft, a friend and ally of Godwin's who agreed with most of his opinions and had helped to stimulate the writing of the book.[73] Hazlitt relates that Griffiths was alarmed by Godwin's theories and persuaded Holcroft not to review the work too favourably;[74] and his account of it is certainly more reserved than we might expect. The first instalment is favourable, but written in very general terms: Holcroft finds the book eminently worthy of attention "from the freedom of its inquiry, the grandeur of its views, and the fortitude of its principles." He emphasises that Godwin is no Jacobin, but advocates peaceful and gradual reform. A tour through the work then begins, Holcroft pointing out the "originality and force" of some of Godwin's arguments but disclaiming complete agreement: "Knowledge is not yet arrived at that degree of certainty, which is requisite for any two men to think alike on all subjects." The second article opens with this announcement:

> The farther we proceed in our examination of this bold and original work, the more we are convinced that it is proper, at this particular period, to present our readers with as clear an analysis of its contents as the nature of our publication will allow, rather than to obtrude any decided opinion of our own. The minds of men are at present so agitated, and their principles are unfortunately so opposite, that we think it *our duty* thus to limit ourselves, and to suffer each reader to draw his own conclusions.

It is unlikely that Holcroft ever considered such restraint to be his duty to the public, but he may have thought it due to Griffiths. His second and third articles turn out to contain more long extracts than "analysis." While withholding his own judgement, however, Holcroft earnestly recommends the reading of *Political Justice* "as a labour worthy of all inquiring minds"; and he ends by praising Godwin's intentions:

> whether the author's opinions prove to be truths . . . or the visions of an over-zealous mind . . . it is certain that his intentions are friendly to man. The tone of virtue is uniform, and predominates throughout the work; so that the reader, who may take offence at the writer's doctrines, cannot but applaud his motives.

The *Critical* also reviewed *Political Justice* in three instalments and began by giving it first place in the April number, declaring that "the public are under considerable obligations to the very ingenious author of this elaborate treatise." The tone of this article is favourable in spite of disagreements with Godwin. One valid criticism made is that Godwin expects too much of government, which, being human, must always be imperfect;[75] another is that "the doctrine of necessity . . . destroys at one blow all the moral attributes of God, and the responsibility of man."[76] In the second instalment (July) the reviewer maintains his cordial tone while disagreeing with Godwin on the main point discussed, his preference for republican government. The critic's own preference is apparently for the English system, checked by *"the controuling influence of public opinion."* With the third instalment (October) the tone has become much sharper: the reviewer, who had evidently not been reading ahead or making intelligent inferences, is now shocked to come upon Godwin's arguments for disestablishing the Church, equalising property, and abolishing marriage. He thereupon defends these institutions, and even the laws penalising Dissenters:

> To us nothing is more clear, than that the man who occupies a superior office in the state, should not be hostile to the religion of the state. How far the obligation ought to descend in the scale of subordinate offices, is another question, and must in all cases be regulated by the particular expediency of the times.

Godwin is advised to expunge his treatment of marriage "and many other disgraceful eccentricities," while his "extraordinary reasonings concerning the prolongation of human life" are found "totally inconsistent with the scheme of Providence in every thing that respects this world." The critic finally pronounces *Political Justice* a singular, unequal work:

> The mind of the author is evidently warped by the false philosophy of the times, and, however *free* he may fancy himself, writes more in fetters than any author we have lately perused. Where he disengages himself from these prejudices . . . we frequently discern the efforts of a vigorous mind, and have generally to admire his ingenuity, even where we cannot applaud his judgment. . . . The work . . . contains some valuable matter, but with much alloy of error and absurdity.

This is not a case of favourable opinions muffled for prudential reasons, as in the *Monthly,* but of disagreement present from the beginning and mounting irresistibly into disapproval. Some of the adverse criticisms might have been made by any moderate reformer; they resemble those of Godwin's old landlord and tutor, the Rev. Samuel Newton.[77] But the defence of the Test Laws shows that Godwin's critic was one of the more conservative-minded of the *Critical* reviewers in this transitional period — certainly the wrong man to have been sent *Political Justice* if the editor hoped for a favourable review. Given such opinions, what is surprising is the cordiality with which the review begins. Possibly a hint had been dropped that this was a notable work and published, moreover, by the Robinsons, who were part-proprietors of the *Critical.* If so, the reviewer deserves some credit for making such adverse comments, and the editor for publishing them. Some of these comments are apt enough, but the review is too piecemeal in its judgements to count as satisfactory.

The bulk of the *Analytical* review is taken up by a long and careful summary of Godwin's book. In his introductory sentences the reviewer approves of Godwin's purpose, which he sees is to consider government primarily in relation to morality:

> Where the constitution of a state, and the administration of it's government are repugnant to the principles of wisdom and equity, *there* it is impossible for virtue to exist in any considerable degree. . . . We deem it therefore our duty to encourage every attempt . . . to illustrate the principles of sound and rational morality, and to establish the theory of a wise and equitable government.

He closes his review by a paragraph of criticism which, though accurate as far as it goes, is too general to be very helpful:

> For our part, . . . among several extravagant and Utopian ideas, we have found much close reasoning, judicious argument, and profound thought. If his ardent enthusiasm in favour of truth and liberty, with a sanguine anticipation of the perfection of human nature, have betrayed Mr. G. into a few extraordinary and chimerical positions, though we may be disposed to smile at their singularity and extravagance, we can scarce censure the principle in which they originate. His morality is bold and imperious: if in any instance it be either impracticable or inconsistent, it seems to be in his doctrine of sincerity.

Godwin is blamed for some oblique remarks against the custom of public worship and belief in life after death, and is urged to "come forward into the open field of discussion and argument. . . . Contemptuous insinuations, without argument, are impertinent and illiberal." The plan, execution, and style of *Political Justice* are praised in general terms, and Godwin is said to possess "considerable talents, a clear intellect, and an ardent mind in the pursuit of truth."

The *British Critic* made Godwin's work the pretext for an entertaining essay on the theme of "this enlightened age." Modern Europeans flatter themselves on their understanding of the scientific method, and yet outside the natural sciences their thinking is remarkably superficial,

> since it has been found, it seems, that a casual thought upon an abstruse subject decides it better than a profound enquiry; and that wisdom and knowledge come, to *enlightened ages,* like Sir Andrew Aguecheek's reading and writing, *by nature.*

Unlike most of the specious philosophers of the age, Godwin has talents:

> A weak man cannot produce a long work of connected subtilty and argument. It is the property of a very different state of mind to take for granted one or two extravagant absurdities, and then to reason justly and correctly from them, as though they were truths.

The first of Godwin's fundamental absurdities is "the omnipotence of truth." The reviewer finds that this often-used phrase has little meaning, since by Godwin's own definition truth is nothing more than "the perceived agreement or disagreement of the terms of a proposition." Godwin has used this notion to replace God, because "nothing can be carried on, by any system-maker, without the intervention of some omnipotence." The second absurd notion is human perfectibility: "and thus solidly is it concluded, that because men can invent speaking and writing, they can, by their own powers, make themselves immortal!" The third is the mechanical nature of thought: the reviewer maliciously quotes Godwin's account of how the most powerful impression irresistibly drives out its competitors from the sensorium, and is driven out by others in its turn, with the comment: "Is it not credible that this new teacher should have written thus?" The fourth is the doctrine of necessity, "which doctrine of course annihilates all merit and demerit." Several of Godwin's arguments on particular points are unsympathetically paraphrased; for example,

> Property is overturned in the following manner: No man has a right to any thing but because he wants it, and if one man can be proved to want a thing more than another man, it is his of course. Thus falls property.

Political Justice, in fact, is in itself a refutation of any pretensions the age may have to enlightenment, "for alas! it must appear, to sober reason, a very foolish age." The book provides the *reductio ad absurdum* of the speculations of Helvétius, d'Holbach, Rousseau, and "some English writers of equal extravagance." The reviewer "takes leave of it finally, careless whether he shall ever view it again; certainly neither wishing or expecting to behold another like it." In the derisive method of this as of some other articles, the *British Critic* anticipates the *Edinburgh Review.*

The *English* did not notice the first edition of *Political Justice,* but began a review of the second edition (1796) which consisted almost entirely of quotation. A continuation of this review was promised, but did not appear, though it was another five months before the *English* expired.

None of these reviews can really be called satisfactory. The *Monthly* and *Analytical* make gestures in the right direction, but give little specific criticism; the *Critical* makes some good as well as some superficial points, but is not very coherent; the *British Critic* supplies an entertaining essay rather than a review. Oddly enough, this last journal gives a better idea of the structure of the work and of Godwin's deductive method of reasoning than the more sympathetic journals which reviewed it in several instalments.

Since the next four sets of articles deal with religious publications, mention should be made of the religious affinities of the Reviews, which are very much in harmony with their politics. The *British Critic* had escaped

coming under the influence of a group of High Church Hutchinsonians at
the time of its founding,[78] and may be said to follow a middle-of-the-road
Anglicanism. (Later it was to adopt a distinctively High Church policy,
and in its last phase it became an organ of the Oxford Movement.) The
Monthly, the *Critical* (after about 1793), and the *Analytical* represent different degrees of what was proudly called "Rational Dissent," by contrast
with the supposed irrationality of the Methodists and Evangelicals (who as
yet had no Review). Their assumptions are well illustrated by a letter from
Enfield to Griffiths of March 1796, arising out of his review of *Christian
Philosophy,* by Vicesimus Knox:

> On this subject the state of public opinion is altering very fast,
> and will soon render the business of reviewing this class of publications
> very difficult and delicate; but we cannot be wrong in keeping our
> defenders of the faith close to the point of rational argument and
> historical evidence; for if once this ground is abandoned, it is all
> *up* with Christianity; and, if it ought to be abandoned, as Dr. Kn.
> plainly enough intimates, in the name of common sense *be* it so:
> but let us not have in its stead a bastard kind of Christianity,
> fit only for the region of Moorfields.[79]

Unitarians of various kinds were writing in all three Reviews, but the Socinian followers of Priestley were strongest in the *Analytical;* in the *Monthly*
and *Critical* latitudinarian Churchmen were also at work. After 1793 the
Critical shows, in its own words, "a strong tendency to convert a religious
question into an antiministerial engine."[80] It will be seen that in the
Review press the Socinian moonlight is much more in evidence than the
Methodist stove.[81]

Paine's *Age of Reason*

Among thinkers of the Enlightenment it was, of course, common to look
to "nature" rather than to the Bible or to any church for a simple and satisfying revelation of God's existence and his purposes. A philosophical interpretation of Newton's *Principia* had been publicised by Voltaire in France,
and by Martin and Ferguson in England;[82] and in the first part of *The Age
of Reason* (Paris, 1794) Paine expounds a rational Deism based on New-
tonian philosophy, acknowledging his debt to Martin and Ferguson.[83] Few
of his arguments were new, but they were delivered in a popular and aggressive style such as no English writer on the subject had yet employed.
Paine himself was by this time a hero to a minority, an "object of detestation" to many more. It is not surprising that no review of this work was
predominantly favourable, though some praise was bestowed on Paine's
misapplied talents. But the book proved hard to criticise. When Paine

pointed out inconsistencies and seeming absurdities in the Bible, and
declared that to him all this was not revelation but hearsay, he was saying
what many men knew but would have preferred not to be put so crudely:
that the age of faith had passed, and that no sure means of upholding
Christianity without an appeal to faith had been found.

All five reviewers mentioned the inadequacy of Paine's learning; but
with the exception of the *British Critic* they took his objections to orthodox
Christianity seriously, though pointing out that such objections had often
been raised by Rational Dissenters. The *English* argued that revelation is
necessary to compel men's belief, as heaven and hell are necessary to influence their conduct:

> from his theory it must follow, that we have no certainty, either
> that we shall exist hereafter, or that our future existence will be
> happy or miserable, according to the part we have acted here.
> Thus the *practical* influence of religious belief is completely an-
> nihilated, and there remains only the metaphysical proposition,
> "that there is a God."

The reviewer suggests that Paine has published this book "to make his
peace with the ruling party [in France], by meeting them at the first point
where they and he could agree"; and, fearing the effects of Paine's specious
arguments on the young and ignorant, he recommends a volume of essays
published by Johnson as a useful antidote. The *Analytical* recognises that
Paine is a powerful and popular writer, and that "it is in vain to expect,
that either contemptuous silence, or coercive prohibition, will prevent the
work from being read." Nothing can be lost, the critic declares, by free enquiry and discussion, and if *The Age of Reason* contains any new ideas
they should be considered. But after methodically summarising the work
he makes several unfavourable criticisms: Paine does not give proper examples and authorities, and despite his intelligence fails to deal adequately
with the subject of revelation because of his lack of erudition. Some "striking proofs of literary deficiency" are produced, such as Paine's use of the
term *New Testament* in the sense of *new will.* When the reviewer comes to
more central issues—the doctrines of the Fall, the Atonement, and the
Trinity—he seems willing to meet Paine half-way:

> Mr. P. can scarcely be so ignorant of the state of religious opinions,
> as not to know, that a large body of christians regard these, and
> many other doctrines commonly called christian, as excrescences,
> which those who are desirous of preserving the main trunk must
> hasten to lop off.

This far-from-inflammatory review, written from a Unitarian standpoint,
was made the text or pretext for a *Letter to the Analytical Reviewers . . .*

by a True Briton (Southampton, 1794), in which the reviewers are complimented for their "talents," but condemned for their "false bias" and
seditious practice.

The most favourable review of the four, however, is by Christopher
Moody in the *Monthly*. He too argues in favour of free religious controversy, pointing out that the attacks of earlier Deists have benefited Christianity:

> To them we owe many learned writings on the side of Revelation,
> and its purification from the chaff, the dust, and the cobwebs,
> which during the dark ages, became blended with it. All may not yet
> be swept away; and Mr. P.'s *Age of Reason*, though it does not
> boast of any deep and erudite investigation, being nevertheless the
> fruit of a mind capable of conceiving objections with force, may
> lead . . . to such an examination as may assist in separating divine
> truth from human error.

Moody finds much to object to in Paine's work: Paine's discussion of the
possibility of a future life is "evasive and unsatisfactory," and his method of
dealing with the Bible is "pert" and irreverent. Paine's main arguments are
here bypassed, and it is left to others to refute various cavils that are
"founded in ignorance." Nevertheless, since the work is not atheistical it is
said to have no bad "tendency"; and Moody concludes by speculating that
if Paine had not previously been required to believe too much, he would
now be a Christian. Moody's tolerant sentiments are praiseworthy, but he
cannot be said to have extended a very cordial welcome to this new
labourer in the vineyard.

The *Critical* found *The Age of Reason* "a bold, keen, undisguised, and
popular, but slight, and ill-sustained attack upon Christianity." Though
hostile, the reviewer does not belittle the work:

> It bears . . . marks of a strong mind, and an original turn of
> thinking; as also much shrewdness of remark, and keenness of sarcasm,
> not expressed in the ambiguous phrase and studied innuendos of a
> Gibbon, but with that bluntness which has rendered him so successful
> in saying forcible things in a popular way. — It likewise shews great
> self-sufficiency, not a few gross mistakes, and an utter deficiency in
> that sound learning and knowledge of history, necessary to render
> him competent to the subject.

He attempts to meet Paine's point that revelation is not valid at second
hand by arguing that historical evidence of revelation "is a mode of proof
equally adapted as mathematical evidence, to convince beings made as we
are." Here he is really agreeing with Paine, who does not deny that
historical evidence may be valid but insists that it is not the same as revelation.[84] His other criticisms are of very minor points: thus he dwells on the

absurdity of Paine's suggestion that the doctrine of Redemption may have been invented to encourage the sale of pardons and indulgences as though this were an important part of Paine's case, whereas this is only an unwise conjecture made in passing. He rebukes Paine for disparaging the value of a classical education, and for boasting of his own miscellaneous accomplishments. Yet on the credit side he, like Moody, points out that Paine is a firm believer in a God, and as such may be a good apostle in France though a heretic in his own country. The critic quotes "some passages full of noble ideas of the Divine Being," and pays handsome tribute to "the native strength and acumen of [Paine's] mind, and the genuine vigour of his original conceptions."

The *British Critic* uses the last adjective with a difference:

> Tom is an original writer, certainly, and his objections to Christianity are such in general, as not many would have committed to writing, had they even floated in their brains; others, indeed, are trite; but they are all such as cannot weigh for a moment with any who have read or thought.

In view of "the perfect emptiness of this paltry pamphlet," the critic is surprised that any educated man should have answered it.[85] Several of Paine's opinions are briefly paraphrased, and usually misrepresented, to show his ignorance and impudence, and the book is pronounced "neither worth answering nor prohibiting; were it not that a mere jest against religion, however empty, has a bad effect upon ignorant minds."

Paine wrote Part 2 of *The Age of Reason* (1795) as a reply to critics who objected that he had dismissed the Scriptures without specific examination. In it he criticises the books of the Bible in turn from various points of view. Though some of his comments are acute,[86] the essay as a whole is a failure, since Paine was ill-qualified for textual criticism and paid little attention to the work of previous scholars. Thus he delivered himself into the hands of his enemies, and the *Monthly* and *Critical* at least took full advantage of their opportunity. It was particularly unfortunate that in the Preface to this work, and elsewhere, Paine should have boasted rather naively of his achievements.

The *Analytical* was offended by Paine's conceit:

> Without deigning to give a distant rejoinder to his respondents, . . . he tells his antagonists, that they must return to their work, and spin their cobweb over again, the first being brushed away by accident. This is arrogant language; and much more of the same kind will be found in the course of the work.

Paine's handling of "persons and writings, which, being commonly held sacred, ought at least to be treated with decent respect," is declared to be scurrilous. But the reviewer's faith in free controversy remains unshaken:

All this, however, does not invalidate Mr. P.'s claim to attention from the public, when he condescends to argue; or [*sic*] does it lessen our obligation, as literary purveyors, to report faithfully the substance of his objections. Truth can only be discovered by unrestrained research and free discussion.

After summarising the work he again points out that many of Paine's objections have been raised by earlier Deists, and answered by "a numerous train of able defenders." Readers unversed in these controversies are urged to suspend judgement on Paine's work until they have heard the other side of the question.

The first three pages of the *English* review are transcribed from Paine's preface. The reviewer then declares that his criticisms of Part 1 will also apply to Part 2, and refuses to give any further quotations or comments, "being unwilling to administer to the *sensus ridiculi* of those who like to laugh at any thing they may think calculated to puzzle the doctor of divinity." Paine is called a "pestilent fellow," and the "review" ends with a few clumsy generalisations on the need for preserving religion.

Moody confesses himself tempted by Paine's vanity "to violate the decorum appertaining to true criticism":

In this second part, Mr. P. seems to consider all believers in revelation as a herd of fools; and himself as a clear-sighted individual, capable at one glance of detecting all the cheats and fallacies, by which men through a succession of ages have been deluded and led astray.

He refutes in detail several of Paine's "rash and impotent attacks on the scripture." In one case quotations are given in Hebrew, but English transliterations are supplied "that the common reader may see how unfounded are the objections of these sagacious writers, and with what hesitation their statements ought to be admitted."[87] Though willing to admit rational criticism of the Bible, Moody stands firm on the principle of revelation:

There are some books which future Christians will most probably consent to expunge from the canon of scripture, and in those which will be retained there may be some errors and interpolations: but the great cause of revealed religion will never be destroyed by the accident of a scholium, or marginal note, being by mistake transferred into the text, nor by the illiberal strictures of half-informed deists.

Moody quotes with approval a passage in which Paine draws from the creation itself reasons for believing in immortality; otherwise the review consists of severe and well-reasoned condemnation.

The *Critical* admits that it is most important to distinguish what has been authentically revealed from other material, and that parts of the

Bible found "absolutely contrary to pure morality, or well-formed notions of the supreme being" should be rejected. Before accusing those who wrote the scriptures of "enthusiasm" or of deliberate fraud, however, we must be very certain of our grounds. Such criticism demands patience and scholarship: we must not throw the book aside at the first appearance of an objection, nor require kinds of proof which the case will not admit. Paine shows no such care, scholarship, or patience. He boasts of his destructive labours, and compares himself to a woodsman and the books of the Bible to trees beneath his axe: "this is not the temper of mind fit for a searcher after truth." The work is full of ridicule, bombast, and puerility. Paine's objections are those every scholar is familiar with, yet, since he is a popular writer and his work may impress weak minds, it is necessary to deal with them once more. No one supposes that all the Psalms are by David, or all the Pentateuch by Moses, but the greater part of these books may still be regarded as authentic. On the book of Joshua Paine's remarks are trite; on Judges they are superficial; on Ruth they are ribald. "Who ever said that the book of Ruth was the word of God?" Paine does not know what is meant by the phrase. The Bible is a collection of extremely varied writings:

> To call every word in this miscellany the word of God, is absurd; but we maintain, that in this miscellany we meet with many things which really did proceed from God; and on that question Mr. Paine may justly be called upon to lay the stress of his arguments, instead of diverting to things really of no consequence.

Paine's attempt to date the Book of Genesis is so feeble that "we are almost tempted to fling the work from us, lest our readers should think that we are wasting too much time on a publication of no importance, and trifling with their feelings." His ignorance is shown by his remarks on the names of the constellations; his lack of taste by his account of the Book of Isaiah.[88] He often indulges in profane language or indiscriminate abuse, particularly in dealing with the New Testament. His work would have been dismissed with contempt had it not been likely to make an impression on the uneducated. As it is, the reviewer hopes that some answer will appear which, "at the same time that it is satisfactory to the learned, shall be written in a popular style, and promote the cause of truth in the mind of every unprejudiced and dispassionate reader." This very full review, written from the point of view of a by no means fundamentalist Christian, is the fairest and best of the four.

   Part 1 of *The Age of Reason* raises such large issues that to have written a good review in 1794 would have required quite unusual intelligence and objectivity. It cannot be said that any reviewer displayed these qualities, though the *Critical* deserves credit for its balanced view of Paine's merits as a writer. Part 2 required to be read with fair-mindedness and some scholarship, which were supplied by the *Monthly* and *Critical.* Reviews of both parts in the other journals are either inadequate or prejudiced. But in spite of these shortcomings the critical reaction to *The Age of Reason* was generally rather different, and more intelligent, than a recent account of Paine and his age would lead us to expect. Audrey Williamson writes:

> the outrage with which his examination was greeted sprang from the almost total acceptance of the entire Bible as the Word of God, his Revelation, among churchmen and their followers in Paine's own time and later.[89]

Clearly the *Monthly, Critical,* and *Analytical* reviewers did not regard the Bible as totally inspired, and had no objection in principle to criticism of the scriptural canon. But they sharply condemned Paine's rash method of settling questions, his ignorance of Bible scholarship, his cocksure tone, and the flippancy with which he treated matters that most Englishmen of the day felt to be sacred. They believed in free enquiry and controversy, but also in decent manners. They recognised too Paine's popularising genius, and feared his work would intoxicate and mislead readers who did not know enough about theological controversy to evaluate it. For all these views they had reasonable justification.

Paley's *Evidences of Christianity*

William Paley's *View of the Evidences of Christianity* (1794), a methodical survey of the historical grounds for belief in the main Christian doctrines, was intended as an answer to the Deists who had preceded Paine. "Paley represented the consummation of the apologetic and evidential studies of the epoch with singular clarity and force,"[90] and his work remained required reading for theological students for more than half a century. His rational views, cool tone, and carefully undenominational appeal represent the farthest lengths to which latitudinarianism could go towards a compromise with Rational Dissent: too far, indeed, for some Evangelicals, who found in Paley no "open avowal of scriptural truth, as exemplified in the surrender of the soul to God, and the preponderating influence of eternity."[91] His approach nevertheless pleased the reviewers. The *Monthly, English, Analytical,* and *British Critic* received the *Evidences* very favourably, while the *Critical,* apparently willing to wound, was unable to strike at the work itself. The *Monthly* and *Analytical* gave special praise to Paley's non-sectarian treatment, and the *Monthly* commended his broad-minded attitude towards problems of scriptural evidence. The *English* and the *British Critic* did not stress these latitudinarian aspects of the work, and sounded a more militant note in their challenge to "doubters and Deists."

The *English* suggests that Paley and other Churchmen have given the Deists undue publicity by replying to their works; nevertheless, the *Evidences* is

> a seasonable antidote to the contagion of a frivolous, immoral, and wild philosophy, the tenets of which have no better aim or end, than to violate the most sacred obligations, and, by introducing barbarism, to disband society. . . . In this age of anarchy and libertinism they are the friends and patrons of the human kind, who with a charitable zeal contend earnestly for the faith once delivered to the saints.

Though the reviewer does give two instances in which Paley follows his authorities too uncritically, the greater part of this notice may be described in Pearne's phrase—"a mere encomium on religion."

The *Analytical* gave its usual long, careful summary, prefaced and concluded by favourable comments. In his opening paragraph the reviewer declares that "in the present awakened and agitated state of society" men need to be given the means of forming their own opinions about the many controversies, and continues:

> Though so many valuable works have been written in proof of the divine authority of the christian religion, there is still room for other elementary treatises on the subject; and we have no hesitation in saying . . . that no popular view of the evidences of christianity has hitherto been given, at once so judicious in the selection and arrangement of materials, so happy in illustration, and so well supported by citations, as that which now comes under our consideration.

After his summary the reviewer notes that the perspicuity of the *Evidences* makes it suitable for general readers, and that students will find it useful as a methodical arrangement of well-chosen materials. Finally, he points out with special approval "that this work is drawn up on so broad and liberal a plan, that christians of all sects may with equal satisfaction acknowledge their obligations to the author as an able pleader in the common cause."

In November 1794 the *British Critic* noted with satisfaction that the book was already in a second edition. Religion is gaining ground again, the reviewer believes, and the *Evidences* "cannot fail to be a powerful instrument, towards procuring so desirable an effect." The summary which follows is interspersed with ardent praise (unlike that of the *Analytical*, which had been in neutral terms):

> The reader who casts an attentive eye over these contents will easily see how much matter for conclusive argument they comprehend, and in how lucid an order the arguments are digested. When we

add . . . that they are all treated with that clearness and acuteness of distinction, for which Mr. Paley is so eminent, much more will not be wanting to excite his curiosity.

Of one textual suggestion the reviewer remarks "This is the observation of a master." He raises only one small point of disagreement, and his conclusion is triumphant:

> We think the author has very happily executed what he professes to have been his design. . . . To this book . . . let the doubter or the Deist have recourse; and when he has satisfied himself, as here abundantly he may, of the irrefragable evidence of the whole, let him carefully consider the sacred books themselves, and adopt as doctrines whatever he finds there delivered.

The *Monthly* reviewer, William Enfield, agreed with the *Analytical* that there was room for such a book as Paley's. Scholarly works and popular tracts had appeared,

> but a succinct treatise was still wanted, which should contain all the essential proofs of the divine origin of the Christian religion, digested into a connected train of reasoning; supported, where necessary, by references to antient writings; yet brought within such a moderate compass, and expressed in such easy language, as to render it fit for general reading.

Paley has provided "the most complete summary of the evidences of Christianity that has ever appeared," and earned the thanks of all friends to religion. His reply to Hume's argument against miracles is "particularly successful,"[92] and is quoted in full. A brief outline of the *Evidences* follows, with an occasional note of praise—thus "the argument from the rapid and successful propagation of Christianity is stated very accurately, and, perhaps we may add, more forcibly than by any former writer." Like the *Analytical* reviewer, Enfield commends Paley's tact in avoiding sectarian issues, and also pays tribute to his moderation:

> In the answer to objections, we are equally pleased with the author's candour and liberality in conceding many discrepancies in the different gospel histories; in admitting that many of the quotations from the Old Testament, found in the New, are nothing more than accommodations; in allowing, with certain limitations, the fallibility of the apostolic judgement; and in fairly owning that Christianity is not answerable for the circumstantial truth of each separate passage of the Old Testament, for the genuineness of every book, nor for the information, fidelity, and judgement, of every writer in it.

The *Critical* review opens with a gibe at Paley's recent preferments:[93]

The reputation which archdeacon Paley had acquired by his former publications, and the merit in particular of his *Horae Paulinae*, have not only secured for the work before us a very favourable reception, but something more substantial to the author. In this instance at least, —whatever may have been said of the backwardness of the episcopal bench in encouraging amongst the clergy those who by their writings do honour to their profession, —there can be no imputation of neglect; on the contrary, the emoluments which have been showered upon the present occasion will fully justify the language of the proverb, that *it cannot rain, but what it pours.* May Mr. Paley long live to enjoy what he so amply possesses!

A summary follows in which some crumbs of faint praise are awarded: thus "many pointed and judicious remarks" are found among Paley's replies to popular objections, but it is suggested that in future editions this section will need to be much enlarged. Few criticisms are made even of this unsatisfactory kind; and the reviewer grudgingly concludes that the *Evidences,* "considered as intended for general use, must be allowed to possess a high degree of merit."

None of the reviews of Paley's *Evidences* is written from a point of view that makes for important adverse criticism, and more interesting articles than any of these might have been written by Paine, or by Wilberforce. But fair and accurate accounts are supplied by the *Monthly* and the *Analytical,* both of which indicate Paley's non-sectarian treatment and his skilful popularisation of scholarship. These points are missed by the *English* and the *British Critic,* while the *Critical* review seems marred by prejudice—perhaps personal, perhaps a result of the developing radical element in the Review. The best account of Archdeacon Paley's book is given by Dr. Enfield, Dissenting minister at the Octagon Chapel, Norwich.

Wilberforce's *Practical View*

"No book, since the publication of the 'Serious Call,' had exerted so wide and deep an influence as the 'Practical View.' " In his writings as in his life William Wilberforce provides a notable contrast with Paley: his views of Christianity may have been narrower, but he held them with all the fervour and other-worldliness that the Archdeacon seemed to lack. Compared with any of Paley's writings, *A Practical View of the Prevailing Religious System of Professed Christians, in the Higher and Middle Classes in this Country, Contrasted with Real Christianity* (1797) is less rational, but perhaps fundamentally more reasonable. "Wilberforce was no theologian; he was simply a good man who read his New Testament in a guileless spirit, and expostulated affectionately with those who, professing to take that book as their standard, were living lives plainly repugnant to its principles."[94] Within a few months of publication 7,500 copies of the *Practical View* had been sold, and it eventually passed through more than fifty editions.[95] This success owed little to the Reviews, for only one of the four notices it received was even predominantly favourable. The *Monthly, Critical,* and *Analytical* voiced the kind of criticism we should expect from Rational Dissent; and even the *British Critic,* though eager to praise the book, condemned its "fanatical interpretations of the doctrines of Grace, and Divine Influence"—views that strong Evangelicals like Wilberforce shared with the Methodists. When contrasted with the favourable reception of Paley's *Evidences* this group of articles very clearly shows the reviewers' preference for rationality and moderation, their mistrust of anything resembling "enthusiasm."

The *Analytical* opens a decidedly unfavourable review by regretting that it should be possible to deduce so many contradictory doctrines from the Scriptures. Most Englishmen are certainly not Christians in the sense in which Wilberforce proposes to use the word:

> They are, we will suppose, amiable in their dispositions, and regular in their manners; they lead sober, honest, and useful lives, and pray devoutly on Sunday. . . . But all this, says Mr. W., is no more than may be found in many a deist, mussulman, or hindoo . . . he comes forward in this publication, to instruct and warn his ignorant and thoughtless countrymen . . . that they are strangers to real *vital* christianity; and consequently, with all their morality, are in the broad road to perdition.

The analysis of the *Practical View* that follows is, for once, interspersed with comments, most of them in the same ironical vein: "Thus does this theological statesman prudently contrive to unite the revival of vital christianity with the preservation and security of church and state." The reviewer agrees with Wilberforce that the anomaly of an Established Church, most of whose members disagree with its professed doctrines, will not much longer be tolerated; but he hints at "a speedy termination of this incongruity, very different from the revival of vital christianity." Wilberforce's language, he thinks, shows not only the warmth of genuine piety and benevolence but also an over-confident dogmatism, which is not likely to impress any one but the Methodists. Unbelievers will be confirmed in their view that Scriptures from which such doctrines are drawn cannot be of divine origin; Unitarians will plead "that the Bible, critically examined, and rationally commented upon, neither teaches the peculiar doctrines, nor enjoins the peculiar character, which Mr. W. supposes"; and the cool and candid Anglican will resist teaching which makes religon so much a matter of the emotions ("affections"), and reserves heaven for one class of Christians. "The work, on account of the high station and respectable character of the author, may excite a transient attention, but we are much mistaken, if it will not be soon thrown by and forgotten." This sharp review won the approval of Johnson's Unitarian connection,[96] whom Wilberforce had placed firmly outside the Christian pale.

The *Critical* was even less favourable. Like the *Analytical* it deplored Wilberforce's tendency to emphasise doctrine rather than behaviour, and emotion rather than reason; his insistence on human depravity and the need for "looking unto Jesus" met particular criticism.

> Our Saviour is the bright example for our conduct. We are to follow it to the utmost of our power in every instance, in his love, his rational and enlarged piety, in his prudence, wisdom, sobriety, in all the virtues of his character, which are seen in every page of the gospel. But this *looking unto Jesus* must be distinguished from the false raptures of a nun looking unto the crucifix.

The reviewer points out that Wilberforce has not discriminated among the different classes of Unitarians, some of whom believe most of the doctrines he preaches, but has secured the favour of the Anglicans "by many a direct or oblique hint against their enemies the Unitarians, Socinians, Democrates, Jacobins." An ironical reference is made to "those ornaments of the bench," the bishops. Wilberforce's politics are given rather disproportionate attention, and the critic champions the cause of revolutionary France in a way that was becoming uncommon in 1797:

> Zealous as our author is to rescue his friend the minister from the sarcasm of a newspaper writer, the representatives of the French nation meet with no quarter; and they are said, "as a body, to have withdrawn their allegiance from the majesty of heaven." Much as we may be inclined to censure a variety of acts perpetrated by both parties on the continent in the late unhappy contest, we cannot but consider every attempt to make our enemies appear more odious [than they are] peculiarly unjustifiable in one who pretends to greater sanctity, and a firmer attachment to Christianity, than his neighbours. So far from having withdrawn this allegiance, the representatives of the nation itself express it in their constitutional acts, which begin in the most solemn manner, in the following words. *"Le peuple français proclame en présence de l'Etre Suprême la déclaration suivante des droits et des devoirs de l'homme et du citoyen."*

While noting Wilberforce's political prejudices and his zeal "for the established order of things in church and state," the reviewer endorses his condemnation of corruption among the upper classes.

William Enfield, in the *Monthly*, gives Wilberforce full credit for sincerity and good intentions; but he too objects to *devotionalism*—the characteristic of "Puritans, Nonconformists, Independents, Methodists, &c." He praises the work of Wesley and Whitefield, and admits that

Methodism has had great success among the poor: "but success is in no case a proof of truth, and least of all where the passions of the vulgar are the instruments of operation." If religion is to keep its authority, Enfield concludes, it must rest on an appeal to reason and not to the passions. Here too the political note is sounded:

> We admire Mr. W.'s zeal for clearing the reputation of his *friend* [Pitt] from aspersion; and we are only sorry that he has not been able to add an assurance, that he is lately become one of Mr. W.'s *real Christians;* as this might have afforded the public some encouragement to hope that a change of religious principles might lead to a change in political conduct: but, perhaps, even in this hope we might presume too far; for we have seen that even Mr. W., whose real Christianity cannot be doubted, has not scrupled to give his parliamentary support to a war which it might be difficult to reconcile, on any system, to Christian principles.

(In fact Wilberforce had "scrupled" to the extent of speaking against the war in December 1794; it was a grievance to Foxites that he had not continued his opposition.)

The *British Critic* hailed the *Practical View* as "one of the most impressive books, on the subject of religion, that have appeared within our memory," and hoped it would prove a "providential instrument" in assisting England to preserve her faith through the present upheaval in opinions. The reviewer himself wishes to subordinate all other considerations to this purpose:

> Differing from the author in a few points, which we shall mention in their proper place, we agree entirely with him as to the necessity . . . for awakening many nominal believers to a recollection of the most important doctrines of Christianity, and to an active and heart-felt sense of religion.

He finds that the criticisms already made of the book — that it is too severe, and inclined to "enthusiasm" — show the truth of its main thesis:

> Mr. W. may be connected with a sect; of this we are not anxious to enquire. — But of his book, by far the greater part, is sound and genuine Christianity; and would as such be received, were not his readers more anxious to invent excuses for their own indifference, than to derive the proper advantage from a work of real piety.

The summary that follows includes plenty of praise: parts of the *Practical View* are said to rise "to a degree of sublimity." Less evangelical in his opinions than Wilberforce, the reviewer makes every attempt to meet him half-way; thus his "scripture doctrines" are quoted in full, with the comment:

That these doctrines ought to excite in us the strongest sense of our dangerous state without redemption, and the warmest affection and gratitude to the author of our hopes, is the clearest of all positions.

Wilberforce's argument that the emotions should not be excluded from religion is said to be very able and useful, and his discussion of "the prevailing error, that useful lives, and amiable tempers, may safely be substituted for the religious principle" is found valuable and convincing. His attack upon upper-class morals, which the *Critical* had singled out for approval, is here passed over in vague terms. In his conclusion the reviewer touches on the "points of difference" which he has already mentioned:

It cannot be denied, that . . . he shows, in some parts, a bias towards a sect, which, by its fanatical interpretations of the doctrines of Grace, and Divine Influence, has thrown the greatest discredit upon the genuine tenets respecting these subjects. He palliates . . . the vulgarity and violence of uninstructed and ignorant teachers, whose interference is, in all respects, dangerous and pernicious: and seems to take his notions of [Anglican] ministers rather from the reviling of those sectaries than from the fact.

Wilberforce is also too severe upon the English public schools, and upon theatres: "His arguments apply rather to the abuse than to the existence of theatrical entertainments." But the reviewer refuses to dwell on the faults of this work:

The general tendency of the book, as we have said, is excellent; and we will not hazard the possibility of lessening its effect by any objections which we might find it possible, on a minute examination, to throw out.

Of this group of reviews, that in the *Analytical* is the best, despite its hostile point of view. The *Critical* review includes much of doubtful relevance, but also a thoughtful consideration of two of Wilberforce's main themes. That in the *British Critic* deserves praise for a fairly specific treatment, and though this reviewer ingenuously announces that he will turn a blind eye to the book's faults, it will have been seen that he does not altogether do so. The *Monthly* review begins well, but Enfield does not develop his criticisms or apply them closely to the work. It would be difficult to guess from reading these criticisms of Wilberforce how greatly Evangelicism was to transform both the Established and the Dissenting Churches during the next forty years.

Malthus's *Essay on Population*

Godwin and Condorcet had envisaged a future society in which all wants would be provided for, and crime and poverty unknown.[97] In his *Essay on the Principle of Population* (1798), Malthus pointed out that in such a society the population would increase by geometrical progression until it outran the means of subsistence — a prediction which does not now seem at all fantastic. He suggested that crime and poverty were necessary checks upon population, underwritten in a mysterious way by Providence, which had created in man a less rational, less perfectible being than Godwin had supposed. Discussing England's particular problems, Malthus assumed in the first version of his *Essay* that she would be able to import little food, so that any large increase of population would soon lead to famine and pestilence. He concluded that poor relief should be kept to a minimum, since it encouraged the poor to have more children than it would eventually be possible to feed. Clear, forceful, and by no means inhumane in its intentions, the *Essay* created a widespread conviction that any attempt to remove the sufferings of the poor must be worse than futile, and led to the harsh provisions of the Poor Law Amendment Act of 1834.

The "rights of man" championed by the reforming Reviews of the 1790s were political and religious rights, as conceived, usually, by a middle-class Dissenter; not the economic and social rights of the working classes. This is well illustrated by their reception of Malthus's *Essay*. The most favourable review appeared in the intellectually radical *Analytical Review* and was written by Anthony Robinson, a prosperous Unitarian sugar-refiner.[98] The *Monthly* reviewer, a rising young lawyer named Thomas Wallace, also found himself in agreement with Malthus's main theories. Strangely enough, the conservative *British Critic* treated Malthus with as much scorn as it would have bestowed on a follower of Godwin. Only the *Critical*, in the single satisfactory review, takes Malthus seriously but finds him too pessimistic in the short term. All four critics scorned the notion of human or social perfectibility; none made the suggestion that England might solve her problems for a time by importing food; none (to their credit) offered the solution of "moral restraint."

The two earlier notices praised Malthus's *Essay* and accepted his conclusions. Robinson begins by mildly ridiculing "the pleasing dreams of Condorcet and Godwin" concerning man's perfectibility, and twice refers to the revolutionary philosophers as "the family of visionaries." He welcomes Malthus's book:

We are glad to see a refutation of the new philosophy, if it, indeed, merit the name of philosophy, and more especially by such a man, by a man inclined to admit whatever is admissible in it's favour, and to embrace with eagerness whatever promises benefit to mankind.

Malthus, he declares, is the first writer to attempt a refutation of Godwin's fundamental principle, and has succeeded so well that no others will need to follow him. A summary of the *Essay* follows, interspersed with favourable comments. Robinson finds it astonishing that Godwin did not take the increase of population into account when he prophesied that men would be able to live by the produce of half an hour's daily labour. Malthus's estimates are indeed too conservative: "Our author gives his opponent every advantage, and bottoms his calculations upon indisputable data." Robinson also points out that Malthus has inadvertently provided the best defence of prostitution ever written, but does not explore this avenue of thought. In conclusion, he praises the *Essay* as an able treatment of an important subject:

> The view it gives us of human life is not the most flattering; neither is it such as affords any pleasure to the author, who appears to feel warmly for the interests of humanity. But, if it be a true view, we must submit to the painful necessity of receiving it.

In the *Monthly* Wallace likewise treats "the new philosophy" with scorn, and represents Malthus as one willing to test the "fantastic speculations" of Godwin and Condorcet by the light of reason. After stating the main principles of the *Essay* he summarises its arguments in terms implying assent ("He proves that . . . ," "Having established that . . . ," etc.). He nevertheless disagrees with some of the metaphysical speculations Malthus included in this edition, and seems hesitant in passing final judgement on "this ingenious and respectable writer."

The *Critical* pointed out that Malthus had underestimated the food available, and suggested emigration as an expedient when this should prove insufficient. More important, it raised the question of social justice and rejected, by implication, Malthus's *laissez-faire* view that any distress caused by food shortage must fall directly on the poor. If Malthus's theories are correct, the reviewer admits, they overthrow "the fanciful systems of Godwin and Condorcet," though these hardly require such elaborate confutation: but Malthus presents too pessimistic an account.

> We need not consider this argument till some evident inconvenience shall arise from excessive population in a given place, from a superabundance which cannot be remedied by the removal of a part of the number of the inhabitants to uncultivated districts.

However things may be in China, there is no material necessity for men to starve in England:

Servants, younger brothers, &c cannot marry, in the present situation
of things, without impairing in general their condition in life: but
that condition which they wish to preserve is less the result of a
well-organised society, than of a rich luxurious unnatural state.
In England, at present, those who absolutely want the necessaries of
life are not very numerous: a much greater proportion revel in
excess and wanton in superfluities.

Instead of inferring the uselessness of social reform, this reviewer points out
that the corn used to keep horses for luxury purposes would support many
thousand families. He rejects, too, the suggestion that the population principle expresses the moral order of the universe: "The evils at present attributed to population are not imputable to the nature of the thing itself,
but to man's neglect of the command for subduing the earth." The review
ends with some general praise of Malthus's style and method of argument.

The *British Critic* treated Malthus with less respect than any other
Review, finding him hardly less absurd than the perfectibilitarians whom
he opposes. He has greatly underestimated the food available now, not to
mention new sources that can easily be developed:

by giving up the use of fermented liquors, the land for bread-corn
would be doubled, or support fourteen millions: and, by a change
in the consumption of bread-corn for potatoes . . . the same land
could support forty-two millions.

(The economies that occur to the *British Critic* would chiefly affect the
labouring poor, whereas those suggested by the *Critical* would fall upon
the wealthy.) The critic supposes that Godwin's ideal society might support
itself for a generation at least beyond Godwin's calculations, were it not
that other factors would inevitably destroy it. Malthus's discussion of the
successive states of society (hunters, shepherds, cultivators) is found "long
and tedious"; his more detailed arguments against Godwin are said to show
misapplied ingenuity; and his metaphysical theories are unsympathetically
paraphrased. In conclusion the reviewer ironically quotes from *Comus:*
"How charming is *divine philosophy!*"

In 1798 the *Monthly* was still the most influential of the Reviews, and if
it had challenged Malthus's views some good might have been achieved.
Both this Review and the *Analytical* accepted his grim conclusions far too
easily. Possibly both Wallace and Robinson were influenced by the desire
to make it clear that they did not agree with the more imaginative speculations of Godwin. It is also possible that Wallace, a recent recruit to the
Monthly staff, was inclined to follow the lead given by Robinson a month
previously; and that Robinson looked the more favourably on Malthus's
Essay because it was one of Johnson's publications. The *British Critic* may
also have been influenced by the publisher's name in deciding that

Malthus was an unimportant crank. The *Critical,* though its final evaluation might have been more explicit, gave a good review and questioned
some of Malthus's most important assumptions.

These controversial works were on the whole less successfully reviewed
than poetry and novels. Of the 47 reviews dealt with in this chapter, only
seventeen can be considered satisfactory; and though this group may be
too small to be a valid sample, it seems fair that the Reviews should be
tried by their reception of the eleven most important works of their kind to
appear over a period of fourteen years. The proportion of successful
reviews becomes higher if we set aside the contribution of the *Analytical,*
which in most cases deliberately restricted its criticism to a minimum. In
the other journals about two notices out of five are satisfactory. Failure was
rarely due to underestimating the importance of the work reviewed, as is
shown by the length of these articles. The *Monthly, Critical, English,* and
British Critic give amongst them an average review of 4,000 words, of
which slightly more than half consists of quotation and straightforward
summary and the remainder of criticism; the average *Analytical* review is
nearly 6,000 words long, but gives only about 700 words of criticism. In
some cases the reviewer has simply been unable to achieve a clear and independent view of the book he is dealing with: this is true of most reviews
of *The Age of Reason* and the *Essay on Population,* and of the *Critical*
review of Burke's *Reflections.* In other cases he fails to criticise. Caution
muffled Holcroft's review of *Political Justice,* and perhaps other reviews.
Not unexpectedly, many reviews were marred by prejudice; and the
"guided tour" method produced several unsatisfactory articles.

The *Monthly* has the best record, being the only Review that can boast
more successes than failures and in which no article is unduly prejudiced.
Griffiths was especially well served by Enfield and Pearne. The *Critical*
comes next, with a standard of reviewing that improves as its political
transformation proceeds. The *Analytical* gives excellent summaries and
fair judgements, but the dearth of critical discussion must make this a
disappointing journal for anyone who has been attracted by Audrey
Williamson's description of it as "a kind of eighteenth-century *New
Statesman.*"[99] The *English* performs poorly, and the four reviews included
from the *British Critic* do not suggest high standards in this field. Of the
works reviewed, Paley's *Evidences* received the warmest, Paine's *Age of
Reason* the coldest welcome, though Burke's *Reflections* and Wilberforce's
Practical View were also given a generally cool reception.

It is natural for us to feel that the classics of the Revolutionary period
should have been more adequately appreciated; but this may be to
underestimate the gap between the thinking even of politically literate
middle-class readers and reviewers, and the conceptions of Burke, Paine,

Godwin, and Mary Wollstonecraft. Moreover, the battle of the books was no academic matter but part of a social and political conflict whose pattern was continually changing, whose outcome was uncertain, and in which all Englishmen were involved. Burke's *Reflections* was in 1790 a blow against the movement for Parliamentary reform; *Rights of Man* a threat to the English social order. Perhaps, after all, we should be surprised at the number of cases in which critics did not follow the path of prejudice but gave fair-minded and intelligent reviews. These journals certainly provided an important forum for "the debate on the French Revolution," and in any future collection of documents their articles might well be represented — some to illustrate the stock responses of the period, but others as genuine contributions to the debate.

Robert Nares, editor and part-owner of the *British Critic*
(Engraved by S. Freeman from the painting by J. Hoppner)

Thomas Holcroft, contributor to the *English* and *Monthly*
(Portrait by John Opie)

Dr. John Moore, *English* reviewer
(Drawing by George Dance, 1794)

Joseph Johnson, owner and editor of the *Analytical Review*
(Portrait, artist unknown, in the possession of
Mr. Christopher Mercier)

Mary Wollstonecraft, *Analytical* reviewer
(Portrait by John Opie)

William Taylor, contributor to the *Monthly* and *Critical*
(Engraved by J. Thomson, from an unidentified
portrait, for Robberds's *Memoir of Taylor,* 1843)

Dr. Charles Burney, contributor to the *Monthly* and *Critical*
(Drawing by George Dance, 1794)

5

The Reviewing of a History and a Biography

If History, then, can delight while it exhibits a distant view of human life, at once obscured by the remoteness of the scene, confused by the multiplicity of objects, and scarcely perceptible from the light and rapid pencil with which its outline is traced, how grateful must be the pleasure imparted by particular biography; which, placing the object of contemplation at the proper distance for distinct vision, enables the mind to observe its minutest parts, to trace its most delicate features, and to catch the symmetry and beauty of the whole.

Thomas Wallace in the *Monthly Review* 30 (November 1799): 241

As the introduction to this study shows, the Reviews of this period were, on the whole, less concerned to pronounce upon works of creative literature than to record the achievements of scholarship and science. Their longest and most painstaking articles dealt, not with new poems and plays, but with the latest volumes of the *Philosophical Transactions* or *Archaeologia*;

with Twining's translation of Aristotle or the *Asiatic Researches* of Sir William Jones. Bruce's *Travels to Discover the Source of the Nile* were reviewed at a length of more than eighty pages, both in the *Monthly* and the *Critical;* Southey's *Joan of Arc,* which was given longer reviews than any other poem of this period, received one-tenth of that space. To assess their performance in these different fields would of course be impossible within the limits of this or any other single book. But the appearance, within three years of each other, of the greatest work of history and the greatest biography in the English language allows us to observe the critics on two full-dress occasions.

Though history was fashionable as a polite form of instruction suitable for women as well as men, the achievements of the eighteenth century in this field had been comparatively small. Scholarship such as Robertson's was quite exceptional; and the only other British historian Gibbon could acknowledge as a master was Hume, admired for his clear, sometimes ironical style and for his congenial scepticism rather than for depth of research.[1] Interest in biography had been growing throughout the century, and collections of anecdotes and letters were popular, but few full-length lives of any note had appeared. On every count, therefore, the reviewers should have given emphatic welcome to these masterpieces of scholarship and literary art.

Gibbon's *History of the Decline and Fall of the Roman Empire* (1776-88) would be remarkable if only for the vast quantity of fact it contains. Most of these facts had previously been gathered by Petavius, Tillemont, and others, though Gibbon was careful wherever possible to investigate their primary sources, and the accuracy with which he did this has won praise from scholars of all periods.[2] But by unifying the results of their labours Gibbon fulfilled the aim, cherished since the Renaissance, of building a solid bridge between the ancient and modern worlds.[3] If modern scholars can point out errors, it is largely due to the discovery of fresh material and of new methods of historical criticism.

Gibbon interprets these facts through a consistent, intelligent, and wholly secular view of history. His work describes the struggles of human civilisation—the *summum bonum*—against both internal and external enemies. His conception of civilisation includes just and efficient administration, civil liberty, religious toleration, and progress in the sciences and arts: he measures the achievement of the emperors, not only by the firmness of their frontiers, but by the extent to which they realised these ideals. He sees Christianity as a disruptive force, and records its progress with an irony sharpened by personal distaste. Yet he does not represent it as the sole or even the chief cause of Rome's decline—a phenomenon for which he does not pretend to give a simple explanation. Instead, he suggests a plurality of causes, including the decay of military strength, the exhaustion of the oppressed provinces, the strength of Rome's enemies, the incompetence of many emperors, and the sheer size of the territory that she hoped to control.

In writing the *Decline and Fall* Gibbon evolved a new and appropriate style. Most of his sentences are moderate in length, simply constructed, and immediately intelligible; at the same time, the dignity of his language and the careful balance of his rhythms create a splendour matching that of his theme. At moments the splendour becomes obtrusive, and clarity is sacrificed for the sake of a rhythmical antithesis. The occasional use of French and Latin idioms (such as "actual" for "present") is also annoying. But these are small faults in a style that can be both witty and grand, that conveys both fact and nuance, and that carries the reader triumphantly through a work of great length.

The first instalment of Gibbon's history was published in 1776. Both the *Monthly* and the *Critical* showed a sense of its importance: both praised Gibbon's diligence and accuracy and admired his style. The *Critical* accepted without demur the controversial fifteenth and sixteenth chapters, in which Gibbon examined the "secondary causes" for the success of the Christian church; William Rose in the *Monthly*, however, foresaw that objections would be raised, though he himself appears to reserve judgement. The next two volumes appeared in 1781, when the Reviews again praised Gibbon's qualities as a historian and also as a prose writer, though both criticised his use of French and Latin idioms. Rose, who had reviewed several of the churchmen's attacks on Gibbon,[4] now took a firmer line against his scepticism; the *Critical* found nothing objectionable in the volumes. But it was not until 1788, when volumes 4, 5, and 6 of the *Decline and Fall* were published, that the critics were obliged to pronounce a final verdict.

By far the most successful appreciation appeared in the *Monthly*, where William Rose had given place to John Gillies—an acquaintance of Gibbon's and a historian and classical scholar of some note, whose *History of Ancient Greece* had been published two years before.[5] Gillies described the *Decline and Fall* as "such a monument of historical industry, enlightened by criticism, and adorned with taste, as hath seldom been produced by the labours of one man, in any age or country." The *Critical* also rose adequately to the occasion, the reviewer expressing feelings of awe:

> He has erected a monument to his fame, which will probably be as durable as the English language; and if empire, as has been predicted, shall travel westward, he may, after intestine wars, and another period of barbarian darkness, be rescued from oblivion, and received by a very distant age, as another Livy, unexpectedly recovered, and proportionally prized; as an author who could render the dark annals of a rude age interesting, and add a lustre even to the classical elegance of the most refined aera.

The *Analytical* refers to the *Decline and Fall* as "this great work," but is more articulate about its defects than its merits; and the criticism that follows its customary "analysis" is wholly negative. In the *English* Gibbon's work fell to be reviewed by John Whitaker, another acquaintance of Gibbon's and the author of a *History of Manchester* — but also a choleric and extremely conservative churchman.[6] Whitaker delivered a furious attack upon the *Decline and Fall,* pronouncing it

> only an elegant frost-piece, the production of a night; which glitters to the eye, plays upon the fancy, and captivates the judgment for a short period; but dissolves in the frailty of its fine materials, and fades away into air, as soon as the sun begins to shine upon it.

The factual content of the *Decline and Fall* is justly appreciated by Gillies:

> The value of the *materials* can only be estimated by those who have explored the rubbish of the middle ages, a period of a thousand years, between the taking of Rome and the conquest of Constantinople; and which, though it produced a total revolution in the affairs of the world, has not been illustrated by a single writer deserving the title of a classic. The desire of giving full satisfaction to the public has induced Mr. Gibbon to read such books as no other consideration could probably have prevailed on him to open. The catalogue of the works which he has perused or consulted, would fill a moderate volume.

The *Critical* defends Gibbon from the attacks of "some forward critics" who have accused him of inaccuracy:

> We have not been inattentive to the marginal notes; and, though we were unable, and perhaps unwilling, to raise a volume on the super-structure of his own laborious quotations, we have occasionally referred to the original authors, where they were within our reach, or where, from our former studies, we suspected him to be mistaken. In researches of this kind we have detected some errors, but they are few and unimportant: we have found the force of many passages given with singular conciseness and success.

The *Analytical* points out two small factual errors, but makes no general pronouncement on the accuracy of Gibbon's work. Whitaker, however, examines many of his references and finds many mistakes. A few of these are important, and Whitaker is justified in declaring that Tacitus is no authority for the state of Germany in the reign of Decius. Many more are trivial: a slight error in the placing of the Praetorian camp, a rendering of *rubinorum linea* as "a ruby" instead of as "a string of rubies," and similar matters are absurdly magnified. Many of the faults Whitaker finds are imaginary. His conclusion is uncompromising: "There is no dependence to be made, we apprehend, upon any one reference, or even any one citation, in it."

From the death of Heraclius to the Latin conquest Gibbon departs from chronological order to give a series of separate sketches, first of the internal history of Byzantium, next of the progress of each of her enemies. Gillies entirely approves of this method:

> [Gibbon] has considered it as his duty not only to relate events, but to explain their causes; and in explaining those causes, he has been chiefly attentive to their mutual connexion and dependence. For this reason, there is sometimes an obscurity in the narrative, which, for the most part, vanishes on a second perusal; and a learned reader will readily comprehend the difficulty of arranging, with lucid order, such a variety of matter, collected from sources the most remote; and instead of reproaching Mr. G. with obscurities of this kind, which sometimes occur, will rather admire his dexterity in allowing them to occur so seldom.

The *Critical* tentatively suggests that the sections which are not strictly part of Roman history might have been made shorter: "At present, for many succeeding chapters, a careless reader would think that the historian treated of everything except what related to Rome or to Constantinople." The *Analytical* makes a similar criticism, though allowing that perhaps "the variety of his materials would scarcely admit of a different arrangement." Whitaker makes no such allowances:

> This is surely a most strange and absurd disposition, of the parts of his history. . . . Mr. Gibbon has robbed the domestic and foreign history, of all their reciprocal connexion. . . . He has ranged them in a number of parallel lines, that never meet.

Gibbon also introduces general topics, which seem irrelevant until we remember that his subject is not merely an empire, but a civilisation: thus chapter 44 contains a history of Roman jurisprudence to the time of Justinian, followed by an analysis of that emperor's Institutes. Gillies describes this section, which has earned high praise from lawyers,[7] as a "masterly review":

> The chapter in which these subjects are treated, appears to us the most important in the whole work, and peculiarly adapted to serve as an alluring and luminous introduction to the study of the civil law. . . . When we consider that, in one short chapter, Mr. G. has clearly and fully illustrated a subject, "which has exhausted so many learned lives, and filled the walls of so many spacious libraries," we cannot help admiring the abilities as well as the industry of the historian who, in the course of a few months, could attain a comp-

rehensive knowledge of a science with which he was formerly un-
acquainted, and explain its principles with such perspicuity and beauty,
as will encourage and facilitate its study in all succeeding ages.

The *Critical* admires the "great precision" of Gibbon's treatment, and the
Analytical praises his "clear and interesting view" of the subject. Whitaker
finds the section both dull and irrelevant:

> The chapter is long and tiresome, from the ample nature of the
> subject, and from the necessary dryness of the disquisition. Yet
> it has much learning, much good sense, and more *parade* of both.
> But nothing can subdue the native barrenness of such a field as this.
> And, if any thing could, what has a disquisition on *all* the laws of
> *all* the Romans, to do with a history of the decline and fall of the
> empire? . . . A treatise on the domestic life of the Romans; a
> dissertation on the buttons, the strings, and the latchets of their
> military dress . . . would have been almost as proper for the history,
> as such a disquisition upon their laws.

Similarly Gillies gives warm praise to Gibbon's account, in chapter 66, of
the revival of Greek learning in Europe; the *Analytical* also praises it;
Whitaker alone condemns it as irrelevant. Gibbon's frequent departures
from the strict limits of his title never fail to provoke Whitaker's indignation, and in his summary he complains that "Two thirds of the whole . . .
are quite foreign to it."

Perhaps Gibbon's most obvious talent is for producing a clear and en-
thralling narrative from chaotic materials. The *Critical* recognises this
gift:

> In the conduct of the narrative, our author is often singularly
> happy in seizing those striking characteristic circumstances, those
> peculiar traits of character and situation, which render the facts
> clear, interesting, and impressive; in this Mr. Gibbon seems to have
> no equal.

The *Analytical* makes the same point:

> With singular felicity he seizes on all the most interesting facts and
> situations, and these he embellishes with the utmost luxuriance of fancy,
> and elegance of style.

Whitaker, who has found the battles of Nushirvan and Belisarius "dull and
drawling," pronounces Gibbon an inept narrator:

> He has not that happy power within him, to grasp "the important"
> points of the history; to seize peculiarly "the most important"; to detach

them from the rubbish of littleness and insignificance; and to make them the constituent parts of his history.

All four critics objected to Gibbon's disrespectful treatment of Christianity. Both the *Monthly* and the *Critical* regret that an otherwise objective history is disfigured by anticlerical prejudice, and Gillies sees this as the one serious fault of the work:

> Clear, comprehensive, and impartial, on every other subject, in all that concerns Christianity he discovers the bitterness of an adversary, alternately employing the sophistry of the sceptic, or the sneer of the satirist. . . . Yet, in justice to him, we must acknowledge that he seldom loses an opportunity of extolling the amiable system of morality inculcated in the Gospel.

The *Critical* takes a similar view:

> The opposers of Christianity are treated with a lenity, at least suspicious, and often obviously partial; nor, in the various disputes of ecclesiastics, can we find one instance of respect to those who zealously support the cause of religion, without being followed by a sneer levelled at the subject and the contenders.

Neither of these Reviews dwells upon this aspect of Gibbon's work. The *Analytical* pays it more attention, and gives more examples of Gibbon's innuendoes; the reviewer suggests that Gibbon is not deeply read in the Scriptures or in the works of the Protestant reformers, and comments:

> The illiberal reflections indiscriminately lavished on all who differ in sentiment from the author, indeed on all who seem to be actuated by any religious principles, except the Mahometan, are certainly beneath "a philosophical historian."

Whitaker, who became a reviewer "from a desire of serving the cause of religion,"[8] suspects that Gibbon became a historian from the opposite motive:

> Mr. Gibbon comes forward with all the rancour of an renegado, against Christianity. He tramples upon it at first, with the cloven-foot of Heathenism. He dungs upon it at last, from the dirty tail of Mahometanism. And literary absurdity, however glaring, even practical profligacy, however flaming, are both lost for a moment in the sense of this volcanick eruption of antichristian impiety.

The occasional ribaldry of the *Decline and Fall* was also offensive to the feelings of the period. Gillies complained that Gibbon's pages were disgraced by "ludicrous and obscene notes," and the *Critical* agreed that his trifling jests and impure allusions were unsuitable to the dignity of history. This reviewer anticipated the plan of Bowdler's edition by suggesting that "a careful hand might root up the weeds without injury to the crop." The *Analytical* made the obvious connection between Gibbon's "indecent allusions or anecdotes" and his infidelity: "they lead to the most unfavourable suspicions of his morals, and consequently will, in the eyes of sober persons, scarcely recommend that philosophy, which he seems to think so desirable a substitute for the Christian system of ethics." Whitaker's attack was even more personal:

> In his preface to these volumes Mr. Gibbon very truly informs us, that he is "now descending into the vale of years"; and the volumes themselves assure us, that he is descending with all the gross lasciviousness of unblushing youth about him. How full must be the fountain of impurity in the heart, when the stream is foaming and frothing so much through the page?

Whitaker apparently thinks the work beyond editorial redemption, for "obscenity stains it through its very substance."

The most intelligent appreciation of Gibbon's style came from Gillies, who gave this subject almost three pages. After praising Gibbon's merits as a writer, he considers the charges brought against him of artificiality and obscurity:

> That it [Gibbon's style] is *artificial,* no one will deny, who knows that grammar is an *art,* that rhetoric is an *art,* and that composition, particularly the historical, is a very complicated *art,* requiring the knowledge of these, and many other requisites. But that Mr. Gibbon's style is *artificial* to a degree beyond what the genius of the English language admits, is a position that we cannot allow.

Gillies finds it simpler in structure, but richer in imagery, than the prose of the Elizabethans; and more suitable for history, because more majestic, than that of Addison. He admits that Gibbon is sometimes obscure: his love of variety leads him into unnecessary circumlocutions, and his studied elegance takes him too far away from common English. But these are small faults. "A writer, ambitious always to please, must sometimes offend; and the ungrateful reader forgets ten obligations, and remembers one disappointment." The *Critical* allows that Gibbon's style is "brilliant, harmonious, and dignified," but dwells at some length on its defects:

> The style is not a natural one: affectation is often seen in its perverted arrangement, and foreign idioms occasionally assume the place of the more natural and nervous phraseology of the English language. With

the usual obscurity of Tacitus, Mr. Gibbon has not the collected force of his words, or the precision of his short, but expressive sentences. The difficulty arises from the arrangement, from the periphrasis, with which the harmonious sentence is frequently rounded, and sometimes from the reflections on a fact preceding the account of the fact itself.

The *Analytical* is rather more severe:

The uniform stateliness of his diction sometimes imparts to his narrative a degree of obscurity, unless he descends to the expedient of a note to explain the minuter circumstances. His style is, indeed, on the whole, much too artificial: and this gives a degree of monotony to his periods, which extends, we had almost said, to the turn of his thoughts.

This reviewer later describes Gibbon's style as "affected and meretricious." Whitaker naturally concentrates on its defects:

It is often just, elegant, and manly; but it is often also stiff, affected, and latinised, carrying the poor air of a translation, and forming harsh and unclassical combinations of words. The harshness is that of one of Johnson's dissertations, utterly incompatible with the native ease and the familiar dignity of historical composition.

It is fair to add that some of his examples, such as Gibbon's reference to the silkworm's chrysalis as its "golden tomb," are aptly chosen.

In a note to draft E of his *Memoirs*, written probably in 1791, Gibbon remarked: "I have never seen, in any literary review, a tolerable account of my History."[9] This seems ungrateful. Whitaker apart, the reviewers of 1788 recognised Gibbon's mastery of fact, admired his narrative method, and appreciated his incidental treatment of important general topics. They were somewhat more critical of his style and of the arrangement of materials in his last two volumes, and condemned with different degrees of emphasis his hostility to Christianity and his occasional ribaldry. The *Analytical* reviewer made good minor criticisms but was unable, or unwilling in view of the recently proclaimed plan of that journal, to evaluate the work as a whole. The *Monthly* and *Critical* have good records in the reviewing of Gibbon. Each gave a fair account of the first volume of the *Decline and Fall* in 1776, when the pamphlet war generated by the famous fifteenth and sixteenth chapters was still raging; each did justice to the subsequent volumes, and each gave a satisfactory final review, though the *Critical* fell short of the *Monthly* in exactness of appreciation. Miss J. E. Norton suggests that most eighteenth-century reviewing of Gibbon was courteous and fair-minded, contrasting it in these respects with contemporary pamphlets and with the ferocious reviewing (particularly in the *Quarterly*) of the nineteenth century.[10] So far as the *Monthly, Critical,* and

Analytical are concerned, her picture is a true one. The exception is Whitaker's review in the *English,* which reaches back in spirit to the attacks of Chelsum and Davis. To condemn the *Decline and Fall,* despite its scholarship, on religious or moral grounds might have been justifiable; to attempt a total demolition of the scholarship itself was futile, as most of Gibbon's opponents had already seen. Whitaker was blinded by zeal, and perhaps by some form of vanity or self-intoxication. Nevertheless, his vigorous polemic and industrious fault-finding impressed some contemporaries. His editor rewarded him well, and Lord Lansdowne (formerly Lord Shelburne) encouraged him to reprint the review in book form.[11] Sixty years later Macaulay glanced into the work and dismissed it as "pointless spite, with here and there a just remark."[12] But it has been useful to at least one modern scholar as a storehouse of illustrations of Gibbon's failings.[13]

Samuel Johnson was in many ways more at odds with his age — though it has sometimes been named after him — than Gibbon. Deeply conservative, pessimistic, full of private prejudices and eccentricities as well as antiquated loyalties and superstitions, his personality is not easy to reconcile with one's idea of the Enlightenment, and might have been expected to alienate the Dissenters and Foxites who in 1791 were so powerful in the Reviews. The *Monthly* critics, whom Johnson had called "Christians with as little christianity as may be," had in fact given generous recognition to his achievements;[14] but they were not above laying comic stress on the foibles, the *quaintness* of his character. These aspects, of course, emerge prominently under the high magnification of Boswell's biography.

Boswell had no precedent either for the scale of his long-planned *Life* or for his copious use of original materials. In printing numerous letters he follows the example of Gray's biographer, Mason; but to these he adds countless conversations transcribed (with improvements) from his journals, filling up chronological gaps with table talk and anecdotes gathered from Johnson's other friends. By this means, though the narrative of Johnson's life is almost lost to view, his mind and personality are conveyed with unrivalled success. "The conception of biography which had been seeking expression in scores of Lives, Memoirs, collections of anecdotes, and published correspondence, found its complete illustration in the *Life of Johnson.*"[15] Yet there has been a perennial temptation for readers to underrate Boswell's art, the skill with which he develops the drama of Johnson's life even when it becomes comedy at his own expense, and to think of him as a naive tattler. Of this tendency Macaulay's essay in the *Edinburgh Review* provides a brilliant example.[16]

In *The Journal of a Tour to the Hebrides* (1785) the critics were given a foretaste of Boswell's methods. All found the work amusing, but were surprised that Boswell should have recorded so many trivial absurdities. Thus the *English Review* complains of his "blind and undistinguishing admiration," and regrets the publication of Johnson's "follies and whims, his weaknesses, his vices." The review ends: "On the whole, this is a very entertaining journal; but it does by no means tend to exalt the fame either of its subject, or of its author." This criticism is typical, and none of the Reviews shows a really adequate recognition of Boswell's gifts.

When *The Life of Johnson* (1791) appeared, however, the *Monthly* published a very favourable review written by Griffiths himself. Though the tone of his article is light and conveys a sense of enjoyment, Griffiths sees that the work is valuable as well as entertaining: he describes it as "an almost inexhaustible store of wonderfully varied materials." The *Critical* reviewer, who may have been George Steevens,[17] takes a different view, and the spirit of his notice is shown in the opening sentences:

> The Life of Johnson extended to two quarto volumes! If he had been employed in conquering or in emancipating a kingdom . . . we could scarcely have expected his labours to have filled one half of the space.

The *Analytical* pronounces: "Of Mr. Boswell's work much can be said in commendation, but the best that can be said is, that it is impossible to read it without being very much entertained." No other commendation is given, though several defects are pointed out. The *English* review is by far the shortest and, though favourable, it does not sufficiently distinguish the *Life* from other amusing compilations:

> The variety of anecdotes, the notoriety of persons, and, above all, the airy garrulity of the narrative, will effectually recommend these volumes to volatile and desultory readers; and we own we should not envy, in the gravest student, that fastidiousness which should disdain the entertainment here provided for him.

The critics paid more attention to Johnson than to his biographer, and were quite as ready as more recent commentators to discuss early influences on his character. The *Critical* supposes that he absorbed in his childhood certain Calvinistic doctrines which "gave an irritability to his mind on these subjects." The *English* puts forward the same hypothesis in more detail:

> His mother was remarkable for rigid devotion; hence that peculiar turn in the son, whether weakness or piety, in consequence of which his understanding was appalled, and fell prostrate before certain objects. But this requires explanation; all devout mothers do not make pious children. Disgust is most frequently the fruit of their well-intended, but imprudent zeal: it began to appear even in Johnson. A boy in good

health and spirits flies from the irksome lesson with the greater alacrity
to his sports and companions. . . . Johnson was cut off from this re-
source; he partook but little of the sports of children; the imperfection of
his sight disqualified him for such enjoyments, to which the melancholy
he inherited from his father doubtless contributed.

These Reviews agree that Johnson showed signs of mental unbalance; thus
the *English* points out that his exaggerated fear of death and his involun-
tary physical gestures "indicate a condition of mind harassed by tortures to
which men of sound intellect are strangers." The *Analytical* attempts to
explain Johnson's overbearing disposition: "His temper had at first been
soured by disappointment and penury, and his petulance was afterwards
cherished by universal flattery and submission."

This reviewer also deplores Johnson's political and religious prejudices:

> Bigotted as to a particular system of politics, he appears obstinately to
> have closed his eyes against the light of truth; and so far from seeking in-
> formation on that subject, studiously resisted it. In divinity too we have
> to regret that his researches were limited. He was well acquainted with
> the general evidences of Christianity, but he does not appear to have
> read his bible with a critical eye, nor to have interested himself at all
> concerning the elucidation of obscure or difficult passages.

The *Critical* suggests that in politics Johnson was inconsistent, since despite
his Jacobite sentiments he accepted George III's pension—surely a factitious criticism in 1791—and that in religion his views were unreasonable:

> He . . . saw an avenging jealous God, ready to take advantage of every
> idle word, and every inconsiderate action; he sees the Almighty in a
> different light from what he is represented in the purer page of the
> Gospel.

Griffiths does not refer to Johnson's religious opinions, and on the subject
of politics contents himself with mildly teasing Boswell. Quoting the well-
known passage in which Johnson declares that when governmental abuse is
enormous nature will assert her rights, and Boswell voices ardent
approval,[18] he comments:

> Bravely said, Mr. B.!—and now, who are they who pronounced our
> biographer a flaming Tory? Sir, you are as good a Whig as most, and, it
> may be, a better than many of them: —as such, Brother PATRIOT!
> your Reviewer greets you well!

The *English* does not join issue on these topics.

Each of the Reviews quotes Johnson's famous letter to Chesterfield.

Griffiths describes it as "justly-admired," and the *Analytical* calls it "the noblest lesson to both authors and patrons that stands upon record in the annals of literature." The *Critical,* however, finds that it "owes its chief fame to the great curiosity excited by its being so long withheld."

In summing up Johnson's character, Griffiths declares that his virtues far outweighed his notorious failings:

> On the whole, we cannot but consider the great ORIGINAL as really a wonderful and highly estimable character! As for the inelegance of his person, and the general boisterousness of his manner, when not in his pleasant moods and softer moments, —these are, comparatively, in our opinion, circumstances of so little account, that we shall conclude with repeating what was once admirably said of him, by the late Dr. Horne . . .: "To reject wisdom, because the person of him who communicates it is uncouth, and his manners are inelegant; —what is it, but to throw away a pine-apple, and assign for a reason, the roughness of its coat?"

The *Critical* pays tribute to Johnson's vigorous mind, but makes several complaints against his harsh manners and hints that his reputation was inflated:

> The numerous instances which he has recorded of Johnson's unreasonable severity, his uncandid churlishness, and deficiency in scientific knowledge, as well as of taste, render the anecdotes unpleasing; nor can we pardon those who swelled the importance of one man, estimable and able in many respects, till he became dictator in subjects which he could neither feel, understand, nor judge of.

And 'on subjects of taste," according to this reviewer, "his decisions were almost constantly mistaken ones." The *Analytical* takes a more charitable view of Johnson's character:

> With these defects [conversational tyranny and a gloomy outlook] there was not however a virtue of which Dr. Johnson was not in principle possessed. —He was humane, charitable, affectionate and generous. His most intemperate sallies were the effects of an irritable habit; he offended only to repent.

This critic declares that, though biased in politics and religion, Johnson had no rival as a moralist. The *English* describes Johnson ambiguously as "a striking phenomenon in the moral and intellectual world."

Griffiths has more to say of Boswell than the other reviewers, and gives him handsome praise. Boswell, he points out, was well qualified for his undertaking, not only as Johnson's intimate friend, but as a man of letters and a man of the world, and has completed his design with patient and persevering attention. The *Critical* not only represents Boswell as a servile and infatuated attendant, but suggests that he "hung on Johnson's lips" for the sake of the biography he planned to write. Such praise as this review awards Boswell is condescending:

> Lively, flippant, occasionally intelligent, and always entertaining, we can laugh with him or at him with equal ease. He is nearer our level: we never leave him but in good humour, and even sometimes, in his greatest excentricities, we are compelled to own, that we "could have better spared a better man."

The *Analytical* objects to Boswell's vanity and snobbery:

> His narrative is generally too prolix, and his egotisms too fre- quent. —There is scarcely a person of note with whom our biographer does not claim either relationship or intimate acquaintance. There is also too general an adulation of the *great* observable in this work, nor is there a discrimination of character, such as to distinguish the man who has risen by chance and by his vices, from him whose eminence is the consequence of merit and abilities.

This reviewer also complains of Boswell's indiscretion in publishing certain anecdotes. The *English* is more indulgent:

> Mr. Boswell's remarks are of a very diversified nature; sometimes acute, frequently sensible, now and then whimsical, and not uncommonly marked by that species of absurdity which provokes a good-natured smile, though, in the present performance, "the pride of his heart" never transports him from a successful imitation of the cow to imitate the ass. . . .[19] Mr. Boswell's vanity is never offensive.

The most careful discussion of Boswell's biographical method is given by Griffiths.

> With respect to the peculiar mode and fashion in which this work has been cast, something may be said for it, and something against it. An objector may say, that in the formal garb, and with all the minutiae of conversation, the progress of the reader . . . can never be rapid; and that as tastes vary, many particulars will appear [frivolous, dull or uninstructive]. On the other hand, an approver will contend, that where the biographer has for his subject the life and sentiments of so eminent an instructor of mankind as SAMUEL JOHNSON . . . there can be no just exception taken against the number and variety of the objects ex- hibited. He will ask, "What conversation could have passed, where so great a genius presided, at which every man of learning and taste would not wish to have been present, or, at least, to have it faithfully reported to him?" —To the reporter, would he not say, "Give us *all*; suppress nothing; lest in rejecting that which, in your estimation, may seem to be of inferior value, you unwarily throw away gold with the dross."

Griffiths shows himself to be an "approver," highly appreciative of the advantages of Boswell's ample treatment:

> Perhaps it will be observed, that it is improper to style this work a *resemblance* of Johnson, for that it is THE MAN himself; that here we have the sage, the philosopher, the moralist, the warm friend, the improving companion, in all his humours, whether grave or mellow; whether pensive in his study, oppressed with "morbid melancholy" in his chamber, or enlivened at the social board; —whether musing in the rural scene, wherever friendship invited him, —debating in the Urban portico of Bolt-court, or philosophizing in the academic walks of Fleet-street. In these situations, we view him in his mind's undress; not studiously arrayed for public observation; not designed to catch the applause of the admiring world!—All is natural, spontaneous, and unreserved.

He also discusses the different kinds of materials used by Boswell—reported conversations, letters, and anecdotes—and suggests that the conversations have the most value and interest. The *Critical,* of course, is an "objector," and contrasts the pomp of Boswell's Introduction with the triviality of much of his subject matter:

> He has discovered that Johnson perhaps prostituted his venial pen, to praise a king, whom he *then* disliked [,] in one year, rather than another, or that his sonorous roll was particularly conspicuous at the Mitre, on a Saturday rather than a Monday. . . . A slight reflection might have told Mr. Boswell that to boast of such accuracy was a greater weakness than the attempt to attain it.

The *Analytical* reviewer apparently does not think Boswell's biographical methods worthy of any comment. The *English* is favourable, but too general in its criticisms: Boswell's narrative is described as engagingly fluent, his use of original letters enlivening and characteristic, and the work "every where equally amusing." Yet this reviewer has one lively simile: "A book of more variety we never remember to have perused; it is like a place of public resort. You are sure to meet some of your acquaintance."

Among these critics, only the veteran editor of the *Monthly* shows real appreciation of Boswell's achievement. The review in the *Critical* seems inspired by malice towards both Johnson and his biographer. The *Analytical* gives a fair summary of Johnson's character and attainments from the point of view of a Rational Dissenter, but says nothing of importance about the *Life.* The *English* reviewer seems to have enjoyed the work without becoming fully aware of its originality and value.

Whether these reviews were favourable or otherwise, their length shows that the critics of the *Decline and Fall* and the *Life of Johnson* recognised the importance of these occasions. Reviews of the final instalment of Gibbon's work average 73 pages; to the complete work the *Monthly* and *Critical* gave 95 and 112 pages respectively, twice the space they had bestowed upon another admired work, Robertson's *History of America*. Reviews of Boswell's *Life* in the *Monthly, Critical,* and *Analytical* average 31 pages, which may be compared with the average of 24 pages given by the same Reviews to Roscoe's *Life of Lorenzo de Medici.* The *English* was niggardly of space on this occasion, but even this Review gave ten pages. In view of Gibbon's treatment of Christianity and of Boswell's highly original method, it is to the credit of the critics that only two reviews were marred by prejudice — the industrious but hopelessly warped review of Gibbon in the *English,* and the sneering account of Boswell in the *Critical.* On the other hand, only three reviews may be counted as satisfactory performances — the two *Monthly* reviews and the *Critical* review of Gibbon. The *Analytical* gives good summaries of both works but, in accordance with its recently-announced plan, offers little criticism. The *English* review of Boswell is favourable but inadequate.

"Upon the Whole Matter"

Looking back over this survey, we can form some reasonably well-based conclusions about the performance of these Reviews in the fields of literature and controversy. They dealt fairly successfully with the most important poetry and fiction appearing in this period, less well with political and religious works. The importance of Gibbon's *Decline and Fall* was better understood than the originality of Boswell's *Life of Johnson*. On the 255 articles discussed, 121 may be called satisfactory pieces of reviewing. A success rate of 48% is far from ideal, but it is very much better than conventional accounts of these Reviews would lead one to expect; and I doubt whether it is surpassed by the *Edinburgh* and *Quarterly* in their dealings with the work of the Romantics. This degree of success becomes remarkable when we remember that summary and quotation were still in some quarters preferred to criticism, and that one of these five Reviews was in theory devoted to the publication of "analyses."

The *Monthly* has the best record of reviewing, over half its notices being satisfactory; the *Critical* is not far behind, and the *British Critic, Analytical,* and *English* follow in that order. Whatever the merit of the *English* in the previous decade, it had declined by the 1790s, with only nine good reviews out of twenty-eight. The *Monthly* is less successful in dealing with poetry than with other kinds of literature; Griffiths was not, perhaps, deeply interested in his "poetical department," which in 1782 Badcock had found to be "very generally disliked."[1] The *Critical* is fairly successful with poetry and novels, less so with political and religious works (owing partly to its own shifting policies). The *Analytical* is sometimes hampered by the restrictions of its plan, but has some good reviews of novels as well as excellent summaries of controversial works. The *British Critic* is more successful with poetry than in other fields.

Little evidence has been found for the much-repeated statement that these journals existed to advertise the wares of the booksellers who owned them. *Critical* reviews of books published by the Robinsons[2] are sometimes favourable, of course, but not more so than reviews in other journals; the *Critical* review of *Udolpho* gives the best account of the disappointments of the Gothic genre, and that of *Anna St. Ives* is decidedly hostile. Johnson published Coleridge's *Fears in Solitude* and Mary Hay's *Victim of Prejudice;* the *Analytical* review of this poem is not exceptionally favourable, and that of the novel consists mainly of adverse criticism. Political bias inevitably influenced reviewing, and personal relationships played some part (though not, as far as these works go, a harmful part) in a few reviews of poetry. Enfield's review of *Camilla,* by the daughter of another *Monthly* reviewer, is certainly no puff; his reviews of Holcroft's novels are balanced and obviously sincere: and the *Analytical* could hardly have have said less than it did in favour of *Rights of Woman.* On the whole the Reviews seem to have achieved a creditable standard of impartiality, as their editors must have wished.

In the end everything depended on the skill and conscientiousness of individual reviewers. Griffiths was lucky to have the services of Aikin, Enfield, and Pearne; Johnson, of Mary Wollstonecraft. Contributors adapted themselves in different ways to the demands of comprehensive reviewing. Southey, once he had settled down, got through large numbers of books by giving short judgements and long extracts. *"Criticism,"* says Swift ironically, "contrary to all other Faculties of the Intellect, is ever held the truest and best, when it is the very *first* Result of the *Critick's* Mind"; and it is doubtful whether many second thoughts of Southey's found their way into the *Critical.* This sharpshooting technique may have been a more important cause of his inadequate review of *Lyrical Ballads* than any obtuseness on his part, or grudge against Coleridge. Yet Enfield and Mary Wollstonecraft, working under similar pressure, wrote pages of well-considered criticism. Reviewers like Dr. Burney, who had no great need of the money, took on fewer books and wrote more leisurely articles.

If Jeffrey and his friends had not broken with the tradition of comprehensive reviewing, others would have done so, and the advantages of the new form of Review have been acknowledged in chapter 1. Southey lived to earn much larger fees each quarter by reviewing one or two selected books; and one wishes that Enfield and Mary Wollstonecraft (both of whom died in 1797) could have provided for themselves without dealing with scores of inferior works — what Enfield valiantly called "my share of the Trash." Freed from this burden, the new reviewers were able to pursue their ideas through long essays that were sometimes valuable, usually entertaining. Yet for many years some readers preferred the older type of

Review: the *Critical* survived until 1817, the *Monthly* for much longer. One reason may be that these readers still wanted to learn about as many new books as possible; another, that the famous quarterlies were not always quick to spot new talent. Last, despite the brilliance of Jeffrey, Macaulay, and Carlyle, some tastes must still have preferred the sobriety and attempted objectivity of journals in which a reviewer "was expected to make the author, and not himself, the most prominent object of attention."[3]

Appendix A:
References to
Review Articles

In this list the works reviewed are arranged alphabetically by author or editor, and are followed in each case by the reviews in order of appearance. An asterisk precedes articles which have been counted as satisfactory pieces of reviewing. The writers of most *Monthly* articles before 1815 have been identified by Benjamin Christie Nangle in *The Monthly Review: First Series* (Oxford, 1934) and *The Monthly Review: Second Series* (Oxford, 1955). These attributions rest on the marked set kept by Ralph Griffiths, later by his son and successor George Griffiths, which is now in the Bodleian Library. Ralph Wardle has shown that in the *Analytical* Mary Wollstonecraft used the signatures "M", "W", and "T" ("Mary Wollstonecraft, *Analytical* Reviewer," *PMLA* 62 [1947]: 1000-1009). Articles thus signed have been positively, and a few belonging to groups ending with these signatures tentatively, attributed to her. Evidence for all other identifications of reviewers is given in the notes where their articles are discussed.

Abbreviations

AR: Analytical Review (First Series unless otherwise indicated); *BC: British Critic* (First Series); *CR: Critical Review* (Second Series unless otherwise indicated); *ER: English Review; MR: Monthly Review* (Second Series unless otherwise indicated).

ANDERSON, ROBERT, ed. *The Works of the British Poets: with Prefaces, Biographical and Critical* (13 vols., Edinburgh and London, 1792-95). *BC* 4 (July 1794): 41-44; 6 (February 1796): 172-84. *MR* 26 (August 1798): 386-97; 27 (September 1798): 9-23, by Samuel Rose. *CR* 25 (January 1799): 40-50, by Robert Southey.

[BAGE, ROBERT.] *Man as He Is. A Novel* (4 vols., 1792). *ER* 20 (December 1792): 437-43. *MR* 10 (March 1793): 297-302, by Thomas Holcroft. *AR* 24 (October 1796): 398-403, ? by Mary Wollstonecraft.

[BAGE, ROBERT.] *Hermsprong; or, Man as He Is Not. A Novel . . . by the Author of 'Man as He Is'* (3 vols., 1796). *MR* 21 (September 1796): 21-24, by William Taylor. *AR* 24 (December 1796): 608-9, by Mary Wollstonecraft. *CR* 23 (June 1798): 234.

BLOOMFIELD, ROBERT. *The Farmer's Boy: a Rural Poem* [ed. by Capel Lofft] (1800). *CR* 29 (May 1800): 66-75, by Robert Southey. *BC* 15 (June 1800): 601-8. *MR* 33 (September 1800): 50-56, by Ollyet Woodhouse.

BLOOMFIELD, ROBERT. *Rural Tales, Ballads and Songs* (1802). *BC* 19 (April 1802): 338-43. *CR* 35 (May 1802): 67-75, by Robert Southey. *MR* 42 (October 1803): 215-17.

BOSWELL, JAMES. *The Journal of a Tour to the Hebrides, with Samuel Johnson, LL.D.* (1785). *CR*, ser. 1, 60 (November 1785): 337-45. *ER* 6 (November 1785): 369-78. *MR*, ser. 1, 74 (April 1786): 277-82. (Discussed as background only.)

BOSWELL, JAMES. *The Life of Samuel Johnson, LL.D. . . .* (2 vols., 1791). *CR* 2 (July 1791): 333-40; 3 (November 1791): 254-68; 4 (March 1792): 257-68. *ER* 18 (July, August 1791) 1-8, 137-40. *AR* 10 (July 1791 and Appendix): 241-50, 481-89; 11 (December 1791): 361-76. *MR* 7 (January, February 1792): 1-9, 189-98; 8 (May 1792): 71-82, by Ralph Griffiths.

BRITISH ALBUM. *The British Album, containing the Poems of Della Crusca, Anna Matilda, Arley, Benedict, The Bard, &c.* (2 vols., 1790). *MR* 3 (October 1790): 213-16, by Christopher Moody.

BURKE, EDMUND. *Reflections on the Revolution in France, and on the Proceedings in Certain Societies in London Relative to that Event. In a Letter intended to have been Sent to a Gentleman in Paris* (1790). *MR* 3 (November, December 1790): 313-26, 438-65, by Thomas Pearne. *CR*, ser. 1, 70 (November 1790): 517-30. *ER* 16 (November, December 1790): 371-81, 449-60; 17 (January 1791): 24-32. *AR* 8 (November 1790): 295-307.

BURNS, ROBERT. *Poems, chiefly in the Scottish Dialect* (Kilmarnock, 1786). *MR*, ser. 1, 75 (December 1786): 439-48, by James Anderson. *ER* 9 (February 1787): 89-93, probably by John Moore. *CR*, ser. 1, 63 (May 1787): 387-88.

BURNS, ROBERT. *The Works . . . with an Account of his Life, and a Criticism on his Writings. To which are affixed some Observations on the Character and Condition of the Scottish Peasantry.* [ed. by James Currie] (4 vols., Liverpool, 1800). *CR* 29 (August 1800): 401-9; 30 (September, November 1800): 44-55, 300-311. *BC* 16 (October 1800): 367-79; 17 (April 1801): 416-22. *MR* 34 (March, April 1801): 278-86, 374-84, by Samuel Rose.

CAMPBELL, THOMAS. *The Pleasures of Hope: with Other Poems* (Edinburgh, 1799). *AR*, n.s., 1 (June 1799): 622-23. *BC* 14 (July 1799): 21-26. *MR* 29 (August 1799): 422-26, by Alexander Hamilton. *CR* 27 (October 1799): 158-62.

COLERIDGE, SAMUEL TAYLOR [and SOUTHEY, ROBERT]. *The Fall of Robespierre. An Historic Drama* (Cambridge, 1794). *CR* 12 (November 1794): 260-62, probably by George Dyer. *AR* 20 (Appendix, September-December 1794): 480-81, ? by John Aikin. *BC* 5 (May 1795): 539-40.

COLERIDGE, SAMUEL TAYLOR. *Poems on Various Subjects* (1796). *BC* 7 (May 1976): 549-50. *MR* 20 (June 1796): 194-99, by John Aikin. *CR* 17 (June 1796): 209-12, probably by George Dyer. *AR* 23 (June 1796): 610-12. *ER* 28 (August 1796): 172-75.

COLERIDGE, SAMUEL TAYLOR. *Ode on the Departing Year* (Bristol, 1796). *MR* 22 (March 1797): 342-43, by John Aikin. *CR* 20 (July 1797): 343-44.

COLERIDGE, SAMUEL TAYLOR. *Fears in Solitude, written in 1798, during the Alarm of an Invasion. To which are added, France, an Ode; and Frost at Midnight* (1798). *AR* 28 (December 1798): 590-92, ? by Anna Laetitia Barbauld. *MR* 29 (May 1799): 43-47, by Christopher Moody. *BC* 13 (June 1799): 662-63. *CR* 26 (August 1799): 472-75, ? by Robert Southey.

[COWLEY, HANNAH.] *The Poetry of Anna Matilda.* (2 vols., 1788). *ER* 12 (August 1788): 99-100. *MR*, ser. 1, 80 (January 1789): 63-67, by Christopher Moody.

[CUMBERLAND, RICHARD.] *Henry, by the Author of Arundel* (4 vols., 1795). *CR* 13 (April 1795): 444-53. *AR* 21 (May 1795): 511-16, by Mary Wollstonecraft. *BC* 5 (May 1795): 478-87. *MR* 17 (June 1795): 133-38, by Thomas Holcroft.

[D'ARBLAY, FRANCES.] *Camilla: or, A Picture of Youth. By the Author of Evelina and Cecilia* (5 vols., 1796). *AR* 24 (July 1796): 142-48, by Mary Wollstonecraft. *ER* 28 (August 1796): 178-80. *CR* 18 (September 1796): 26-40. *MR* 21 (October 1796): 156-63, by William Enfield (the last two paragraphs added by Ralph Griffiths). *BC* 8 (November 1796): 527-36.

[EDGEWORTH, MARIA.] *Castle Rackrent, an Hibernian Tale. Taken from Facts, and from the Manners of the Irish Squires, before the Year 1782* (1800). *MR* 32 (May 1800): 91-92. *BC* 16 (November 1800): 555.

[ELLIS, GEORGE, ed.] *Specimens of the Early English Poets* (1790). *MR* 1 (April 1790): 449-50. *AR* 7 (May 1790): 42, signed "Z." *CR*, ser. 1, 70 (July 1790): 95-96. *ER* 19 (January 1792): 22-26.

ELLIS, GEORGE, ed. *Specimens of the Early English Poets. To which is Prefixed an Historical Sketch of the Rise and Progress of the English Poetry and Language* (3 vols., 1801). *CR* 33 (September 1801): 44-47, by Robert Southey. *BC* 19 (March, June 1802): 217-24, 615-23. *MR* 42 (October 1803): 154-57, by John Ferriar.

FOX, JOSEPH. *Santa-Maria; or, The Mysterious Pregnancy* (1797). *AR* 25 (May 1797): 524. *MR* 23 (June 1797): 210-11, by Arthur Aikin. *CR* 22 (January 1798): 113-14. *BC* 12 (August 1798): 183-84. (These Catalogue notices are discussed as background and not counted in the evaluation of the Reviews, though the *CR* notice is distinctly good.)

GIBBON, EDWARD. *The History of the Decline and Fall of the Roman Empire*. Vol. 1 (1776). *CR*, ser. 1, 41 (February, March, April 1776): 114-22, 169-78, 264-71. *MR*, ser. 1, 54 (March, May 1776): 188-95, 388-93; 55 (July 1776): 41-50, by William Rose. Vols. 2-3 (1781). *MR*, ser. 1, 64 (March, April, June 1781): 223-24, 357-67, 442-53; 65 (July 1781): 29-37; 66 (June 1782): 459-63, by William Rose. *CR*, ser. 1, 51 (March, April, May, June 1781): 161-69, 249-57, 342-51, 416-26. (These early reviews are discussed as background.) Vols. 4-6 (1788). *MR*, ser. 1, 78 (June 1788): 468-72; 79 (July, August, September 1788): 12-20, 121-33, 221-37, by John Gillies. *AR* 1 (June, August 1788): 129-45, 428-51; 2 (October 1788): 129-52. *CR*, ser. 1, 66 (July, August, October, December 1788): 35-44, 102-10, 257-67, 425-33; 67 (February, March 1789): 95-105, 175-82. *ER* 12 (October, November, December 1788): 241-54, 321-37, 407-24; 13 (January, February, March, April, May, June 1789): 1-16, 85-93, 169-82, 241-56, 332-41, 401-14; 14 (July 1789): 9-22, by John Whitaker.

[GIFFORD, WILLIAM.] *The Baviad, a Paraphrastic Imitation of the First Satire of Persius* (1791). *CR* 4 (February 1792): 193-96. *MR* 8 (May 1792): 93-96, by Christopher Moody. *ER* 19 (May 1792): 349-53.

[GIFFORD, WILLIAM.] *The Maeviad, by the Author of The Baviad* (1795). *BC* 6 (August 1795): 130-33. *MR* 18 (December 1795): 418-20, by Christopher Moody. *CR* 20 (August 1797): 458-59.

GODWIN, WILLIAM. *An Enquiry concerning Political Justice, and its Influence on General Virtue and Happiness* (2 vols., 1793). *MR* 10 (March, April 1793): 311-20, 435-45; 11 (June 1793): 187-96, by Thomas Holcroft. *CR* 7 (April 1793): 361-72; 8 (July 1793): 290-96; 9 (October 1793): 149-54. *AR* 16 (June, August 1793): 121-30, 388-404, signed "Y." *BC* 1 (July 1793): 307-18. *ER* 27 (February 1796): 138-43 (an incomplete review of the 2d ed.).

GODWIN, WILLIAM. *Things as They Are; or The Adventures of Caleb Williams* (3 vols., 1794). *CR* 11 (July 1794): 290-96. *BC* 4 (July 1794): 70-71. *MR* 15 (October 1794): 145-49, by William Enfield. *AR* 21 (February 1795): 166-75, signed "X."

GODWIN, WILLIAM. *St. Leon: a Tale of the Sixteenth Century* (4 vols., 1799). *CR* 28 (January 1800): 40-48. *BC* 15 (January 1800): 47-52. *MR* 33 (September 1800): 23-29, by Christopher Moody.

GROSSE, CARL. *The Dagger. Translated from the German of Grosse* (1795). *CR* 16 (January 1796): 116. *ER* 27 (January 1796): 77. *MR* 19 (February 1796): 207. *BC* 8 (August 1796): 180-81. (These reviews are discussed as background.)

GROSSE, CARL. *The Genius: or, The Mysterious Adventures of Don Carlos de Grandez. Translated from the German by Joseph Trapp* (2 vols., 1796). *CR* 18 (November 1796): 342. *MR* 22 (January 1797): 93. *AR* 25 (April 1797): 443-44. (Discussed as background.)

GROSSE, CARL. *Horrid Mysteries. A Story from the German of the Marquis of Grosse. Translated by P. Will* (2 vols., 1796). [An abridgement of *Der Genius*.] *CR* 21 (December 1797): 473. (Discussed as background.)

HAYS, MARY. *Memoirs of Emma Courtney* (2 vols., 1796). *CR* 19 (January 1797): 109-11. *AR* 25 (February 1797): 174-78, signed "L.M.S." *BC* 9 (March 1797): 314-15. *MR* 22 (April 1797): 443-49, by William Taylor.

HAYS, MARY. *The Victim of Prejudice* (2 vols., 1799). *AR, n.s., 1 (March 1799): 326-29. *CR 26 (August 1799): 450-52. MR 21 (January 1800): 82, by Christopher Moody.

HOLCROFT, THOMAS. *Anna St. Ives: a Novel* (2 vols., 1792). CR 4 (April 1792): 460-61. *AR 13 (May 1792): 72-76, by Mary Wollstonecraft. *MR 8 (June 1792): 151-55, by William Enfield.

HOLCROFT, THOMAS. *The Adventures of Hugh Trevor*. Vols. 1-3 (1794). BC 4 (July 1794): 71. *MR 15 (October 1794): 149-53, by William Enfield. *CR 13 (February 1795): 139-43. Vols. 4-6 (1797). *MR 23 (July 1797): 281-87, by William Enfield. CR 21 (October 1797): 189-95.

INCHBALD, ELIZABETH. *A Simple Story* (4 vols., 1791). *CR 1 (February 1791): 207-13. *MR 4 (April 1791): 434-38, by George Griffiths. *AR 10 (May 1791): 101-3, ? by Mary Wollstonecraft.

KRAMER, CARL GOTTLOB. *Herman of Unna: a Series of Adventures of the Fifteenth Century, in which the Proceedings of the Secret Tribunal . . . are Delineated* (3 vols., 1794). MR 15 (September 1794): 21-28, by William Taylor. CR 14 (May 1795): 68-79. (Discussed as background.)

LAMB, CHARLES. *A Tale of Rosamund Gray and Old Blind Margaret* (1798). AR, n.s., 1 (February 1799): 208-9. *CR 25 (April 1799): 472-73. *MR 32 (August 1800): 447, by Christopher Moody.

LANDOR, WALTER SAVAGE. *The Poems of Walter Savage Landor. (Latine scribendi defensio)* (1795). *AR 22 (August 1795): 152-57. *BC 6 (September 1795): 302-3. MR 21 (November 1796): 253-55, by James Bannister.* CR 19 (April 1797): 403-5.

[LANDOR, WALTER SAVAGE.] *Gebir: a Poem in Seven Books* (Warwick, 1798). *CR 27 (September 1799): 29-39, by Robert Southey. MR 31 (February 1800): 206-8, by John Ferriar. BC 15 (February 1800): 190.

[LANDOR, WALTER SAVAGE.] *Poetry. By the Author of Gebir* (1802). BC 20 (October 1802): 432-33. CR 38 (June 1803): 235-36.

[LEWIS, MATTHEW GREGORY.] *The Monk: a Romance, by M•G.L.* (1796). BC 7 (June 1796): 677. *AR 24 (October 1796): 403-4, ? by Henry Fuseli. *CR 19 (August 1797): 194-200, by S.T. Coleridge. MR 23 (August 1797): 451, by William Taylor.

[MALTHUS, THOMAS ROBERT.] *An Essay on the Principle of Population, as it affects the Future Improvement of Society, with Remarks on the Speculations of Mr. Godwin, M. Condorcet, and other Writers* (1798). AR 28 (August 1798): 119-25, by Anthony Robinson. MR 27 (September 1798): 1-9, by Thomas Wallace. *CR 25 (January 1799): 56-58. BC 17 (March 1801): 278-82.

[MERRY, ROBERT.] *Diversity, a Poem. By Della Crusca* (1788). AR 3 (January 1789): 70-71, by Mary Wollstonecraft. CR, ser. 1, 67 (February 1789): 129-30. *ER 13 (April 1789): 283-88. MR, ser. 1, 80 (June 1789): 529-32, by Christopher Moody.

MERRY, ROBERT. *The Laurel of Liberty, a Poem* (1790). *AR 8 (Appendix, September-December 1790): 548-50, ? by Mary Wollstonecraft. *MR 4 (January 1791): 56-62, by Thomas Pearne. CR 1 (January 1791): 70-73. *ER 20 (July 1792): 26-32.

[MOORE, JOHN.] *Zeluco. Various Views of Human Nature, taken from Life* *and Manners, Foreign and Domestic* (2 vols., 1789).* *MR*, ser. 1, 80 (June 1789): 511-15, by John Gillies. *CR*, ser. 1, 67 (Appendix, January-June 1789): 505-6. **ER* 14 (September 1789): 216-22. **AR* 5 (September 1789): 98-103, by Mary Wollstonecraft.

MOORE, THOMAS, trans. *Odes of Anacreon, translated into English Verse with Notes* (1800). **CR* 30 (October 1800): 202-8. *MR* 35 (August 1801): 404-9, by Charles Burney. **BC* 20 (July 1802): 27-32. *Edinburgh Review* 2 (July 1803): 462-76 (review of the 3d ed.).

[MOORE, THOMAS.] *The Poetical Works of the Late Thomas Little* (1801). *CR* 34 (February 1802): 200-205. *MR* 39 (October 1802): 174-79, by John Ferriar. *BC* 18 (November 1802): 540-41.

PAINE, THOMAS. *Rights of Man; being an Answer to Mr. Burke's Attack on the French Revolution* (1791). *CR* 1 (March 1791): 337-41. *AR* 9 (March 1791): 312-20. **MR* 5 (May 1791): 81-93, by Thomas Pearne. *ER* 17 (May 1791): 363-65, ? by William Thomson.

PAINE, THOMAS. *Rights of Man. Part the Second. Combining Principle and Practice* (1792). **MR* 7 (March 1792): 317-24, by Thomas Pearne. *CR* 4 (March 1792): 297-305. *AR* 12 (March 1792): 287-304, signed "Z." **ER* 19 (April 1792): 266-75, ? by William Thomson.

PAINE, THOMAS. *The Age of Reason; being an Investigation of True and Fabulous Theology* (Paris, 1794). *ER* 23 (May 1794): 351-55. *AR* 19 (June 1794): 159-65. *MR* 14 (August 1794): 393-97, by Christopher Moody. **CR* 12 (September 1794): 77-82. *BC* 4 (October 1794): 438.

PAINE, THOMAS. *The Age of Reason. Part the Second. Being an Investigation of True and Fabulous Theology* (Paris and London, 1795). *AR* 22 (November 1795): 498-505. *ER* 26 (December 1795): 453-56. **MR* 19 (February 1796): 157-61, by Christopher Moody. **CR* 16 (March 1796): 312-19.

PALEY, WILLIAM. *A View of the Evidences of Christianity* (1794). *ER* 23 (June 1794): 421-28. **AR* 20 (September, October 1794): 28-39, 185-96. *BC* 4 (November 1794): 487-97. **MR* 17 (August 1795): 404-10, by William Enfield. *CR* 14 (August 1795): 371-80.

The Poety of the World. Vols. 1-2 (1788). *ER* 12 (August 1788): 126-36. *MR*, ser. 1, 79 (November 1788): 449-52, by Christopher Moody. *CR*, ser. 1, 66 (Appendix, July-December 1788): 534-36. Vols. 3-4 (1791). *MR* 6 (September 1791): 21-24, by Christopher Moody.

PRICE, RICHARD. *A Discourse on the Love of our Country, delivered on Nov. 4, 1789, at the Meeting-House in the Old Jewry, to the Society for Commemorating the Revolution in Great Britain . . .* (1789). *AR* 5 (December 1789): 471-75, by Mary Wollstonecraft. **MR* 1 (January 1790): 114-17, by Christopher Moody. **CR*, ser. 1, 69 (January 1790): 68-75. *ER* 15 (July 1790): 440-42. Review of the 4th ed. (1790): *CR*, ser. 1, 70 (December 1790): 683-85.

[RADCLIFFE, ANN.] *The Castles of Athlin and Dunbayne. A Highland Story* (1789). *CR*, ser. 1, 68 (September 1789): 251. **MR*, ser. 1, 81 (December 1789): 563, by Andrew Becket.

[RADCLIFFE, ANN.] *A Sicilian Romance* (2 vols., 1790). *MR* 3 (September 1790): 91, by William Enfield. **CR* 1 (March 1791): 350.

[RADCLIFFE, ANN.] *The Romance of the Forest; interspersed with some Pieces of Poetry. By the Authoress of A Sicilian Romance* (3 vols., 1791; Mrs. Radcliffe's name appeared on the title-page of the second and subsequent editions). *CR* 4 (April 1792): 458-60. *MR* 8 (May 1792): 82-86, by William Enfield. *ER* 20 (November 1792): 352-53.

RADCLIFFE, ANN. *The Mysteries of Udolpho, a Romance; interspersed with some Pieces of Poetry* (4 vols., 1794). *ER* 23 (June 1794): 464-68. *AR* 19 (July 1794): 140-45, by George Dyer. *CR* 11 (August 1794): 361-72. *BC* 4 (August 1794): 110-21. *MR* 15 (November 1794): 278-83, by William Enfield.

RADCLIFFE, ANN. *The Italian, or The Confessional of the Black Penitents. A Romance* (3 vols., 1797). *MR* 22 (March 1797): 282-84, by Arthur Aikin. *AR* 25 (May 1797): 516-20, by Mary Wollstonecraft. *BC* 10 (September 1797): 266-70. *CR* 23 (June 1798): 166-69, by S.T. Coleridge.

REEVE, CLARA. *Memories of Sir Roger de Clarendon, the Natural Son of Edward Prince of Wales, commonly called the Black Prince; with Anecdotes of many other Eminent Persons of the Fourteenth Century* (3 vols., 1793). *BC* 2 (December 1793): 383-88. *CR* 10 (March 1794): 280-87. *MR* 14 (June 1794): 152-55, by James Bannister.

[ROGERS, SAMUEL.] *The Pleasures of Memory, a Poem, in Two Parts. By the Author of "An Ode to Superstition and some other Poems"* (1792; acknowledged by Rogers in the 5th ed., 1793). *CR* 4 (April 1792): 398-402. *AR* 12 (Appendix, January-April 1792): 515-16, ? by Mary Wollstonecraft. *MR* 8 (June 1792): 121-24, by William Enfield. *ER* 22 (December 1793): 411-15.

SCHILLER, J. C. FRIEDRICH. *The Ghost-Seer; or Apparitionist. An interesting Fragment, found among the Papers of Count O*****, from the German of Schiller* [trans. D. Boileau] (1795). *BC* 6 (August 1795): 188-89. *MR* 18 (November 1795): 346-47, by William Taylor. (These reviews discussed as background only.)

SCOTT, WALTER, ed. *Minstrelsy of the Scottish Border: consisting of Historical and Romantic Ballads, collected in the Southern Counties of Scotland; with a Few of Modern Date, founded upon Local Tradition* (2 vols., Kelso, 1802; a 3d vol. added to the 2d ed., Edinburgh, 1803). *BC* 19 (June 1802): 570-76; 23 (January 1804): 36-43, by George Ellis. *MR* 42 (September 1803): 21-33; 45 (October 1804): 126-34, by Lockhart Muirhead. *CR* 39 (November 1803): 250-59, ? by William Taylor.

SMART, CHRISTOPHER. *The Poems of the Late Christopher Smart. . . . To which is prefixed an Account of his Life and Writings* [ed. and intro. Christopher Hunter] (2 vols., Reading, 1791). *MR* 7 (January 1792): 36-43, by Charles Burney. *AR* 12 (February 1792): 153-59. *ER* 19 (May 1792): 372-76; 20 (August 1792): 114-17.

SMITH, CHARLOTTE. *Emmeline, the Orphan of the Castle* (4 vols., 1788). *ER* 12 (July 1788): 26-27. *AR* 1 (July 1788): 327-33, by Mary Wollstonecraft. *CR*, ser. 1, 65 (Appendix, January-June 1788): 530-32. *MR*, ser. 1, 79 (September 1788): 241-44, by Andrew Becket.

SMITH, CHARLOTTE. *Ethelinde; or, The Recluse of the Lake* (4 vols., 1789). *AR* 5 (December 1789): 484-86. *MR* 2 (June 1790): 161-65, by Andrew Becket. *CR* 3 (September 1791): 57-61.

SMITH, CHARLOTTE. *Celestina. A Novel* (4 vols., 1791). *AR 10 (August 1791): 409-15, by Mary Wollstonecraft. ER 18 (October 1791): 259-61. *MR 6 (November 1791): 286-91, by William Enfield. *CR 3 (November 1791): 318-23.

SMITH, CHARLOTTE. *Desmond, a Novel* (3 vols., 1792). AR 13 (August 1792): 428-35. CR 6 (September 1792): 99-105. MR 9 (December 1792): 406-13, by William Enfield. ER 20 (September 1792): 176-79. (Not discussed in text.)

SMITH, CHARLOTTE. *The Old Manor House. A Novel* (4 vols., 1793). ER 21 (April 1793): 264-70. *CR 8 (May 1793): 44-54. *AR 16 (May 1793): 60-63, signed "D.M."—? John Aikin. *MR 11 (June 1793): 150-53, by William Enfield. *BC 1 (June 1793): 148-50.

SMITH, CHARLOTTE. *The Banished Man. A Novel* (4 vols., 1794). AR 20 (November 1794): 254-55. BC 4 (December 1794): 621-23. MR 16 (February 1795): 133-35, by William Enfield. CR 13 (March 1795): 275-78. (Reviews of this novel and of those by Charlotte Smith which follow have not been fully discussed or evaluated.)

SMITH, CHARLOTTE. *Montalbert. A Novel* (3 vols., 1795). AR 22 (July 1795): 59-60. MR 19 (January 1796): 87-88, by Arthur Aikin. BC 7 (February 1796): 127-29. CR 20 (August 1797): 469.

SMITH, CHARLOTTE. *Marchmont, a Novel* (4 vols., 1796). CR 19 (March 1797): 256-60. MR 22 (April 1797): 468, by Arthur Aikin. AR 25 (May 1797): 523.

SMITH, CHARLOTTE. *The Young Philosopher: a Novel* (4 vols., 1798). AR 28 (July 1798): 73-77. CR 24 (September 1798): 77-84. MR 28 (March 1799): 346-47, by Samuel Rose and Thomas Wallace.

SMITH, CHARLOTTE. *The Letters of a Solitary Wanderer* (3 vols., 1801). CR 32 (May 1801): 35-42. MR 35 (August 1801): 332.

SOUTHEY, ROBERT, and LOVELL, ROBERT. *Poems: containing The Retrospect, Odes, Elegies, Sonnets, etc.* (Bath, 1795). AR 21 (February 1795): 179-83. ER 25 (March, May 1795): 230-32, 389-93. CR 13 (April 1795): 420-21. MR 17 (July 1795): 354-56, by Thomas Holcroft. BC 6 (August 1795): 185-87. (Reviews of this volume and of *Joan of Arc* have not been fully discussed or evaluated.)

SOUTHEY, ROBERT [and COLERIDGE, SAMUEL TAYLOR]. *Joan of Arc, an Epic Poem* (Bristol, 1796). AR 23 (February 1796): 170-77, ? by John Aikin. MR 19 (April 1796): 361-68, by John Aikin. CR 17 (June 1796): 182-92. BC 8 (October 1796): 393-96.

SOUTHEY, ROBERT. *Joan of Arc. The Second Edition* (2 vols., 1798). CR 23 (June 1798): 196-200. MR 28 (January 1799): 57-62, by John Aikin. AR, n. s., 1 (April 1799): 403-6.

SOUTHEY, ROBERT. *Poems* (Bristol and London, 1797). AR 25 (January 1797): 36-40. *MR 22 (March 1797): 297-302, by John Aikin. CR 19 (March 1797): 304-7. BC 10 (July 1797): 75.

SOUTHEY, ROBERT. *Poems* (2 vols., Bristol, 1799; an expanded version of the *Poems* of 1797). AR, n.s., 1 (April 1799): 403-6. CR 26 (July 1799): 161-64. *MR 31 (March 1800): 261-67, by John Ferriar.

[SOUTHEY, ROBERT, ed. and contrib.] *The Annual Anthology.* Vol. 1, (Bristol, 1799). *BC* 14 (November 1799): 478-82. *CR* 28 (January 1800): 82-89. *MR* 31 (April 1800): 352-63, by John Ferriar. Vol. 2 (Bristol, 1800). *BC* 16 (October 1800): 403-5. *MR* 33 (December 1800): 364-66, by John Ferriar. *CR* 30 (December 1800): 426-31.

SOUTHEY, ROBERT. *Thalaba the Destroyer. (A Metrical Romance)* (2 vols., 1801). *BC* 18 (September 1801): 309-10. *Edinburgh Review* 1 (October 1802): 63-83, by Francis Jeffrey. *MR* 39 (November 1802): 240-51, by Francis Jeffrey. *CR* 39 (December 1803): 369-79, by William Taylor.

WARTON, THOMAS. *The Poems on Various Subjects of Thomas Warton . . . now first Collected* (1791). *AR* 11 (December 1791): 211-12. *MR* 10 (March 1793): 271-78, by Charles Burney. *CR* 10 (January 1794): 20-25.

WILBERFORCE, WILLIAM. *A Practical View of the Prevailing Religious System of Professed Christians, in the Higher and Middle Classes in this Country, contrasted with Real Christianity* (1797). *AR* 25 (May 1797): 503-11. *CR* 20 (June 1797): 164-68. *MR* 23 (July 1797): 241-48, by William Enfield. *BC* 10 (September 1797): 294-303.

WOLLSTONECRAFT, MARY. *A Vindication of the Rights of Woman: with Strictures on Political and Moral Subjects.* Vol. 1 (all published, 1792). *AR* 12 (March 1792): 241-49; 13 (Appendix, May-August 1792): 481-89, signed "D." *CR* 4 (April 1792); 389-98; 5 (May 1792): 132-41. *MR* 8 (June 1792): 198-209, by William Enfield.

WORDSWORTH, WILLIAM. *An Evening Walk. An Epistle, in Verse; addressed to a Young Lady; from the Lakes of the North of England* (1793). *AR* 15 (March 1793): 294-97. *CR* 8 (July 1793): 347-48. *MR* 12 (October 1793): 216-18, by Thomas Holcroft. *ER* 22 (November 1793): 388.

WORDSWORTH, WILLIAM. *Descriptive Sketches, in Verse, taken during a Pedestrian Tour in the . . . Alps* (1793). *CR* 8 (August 1793): 472-74. *MR, ER,* and *AR* reviewed this poem together with *An Evening Walk* (above).

[WORDSWORTH, WILLIAM, and COLERIDGE, SAMUEL TAYLOR.] *Lyrical Ballads, with a few other Poems* (Bristol, subsequently London, 1798). *CR* 24 (October 1798): 197-204, by Robert Southey. *AR* 28 (December 1798): 583-87. *MR* 29 (June 1799): 202-10, by Charles Burney. *BC* 14 (October 1799): 364-69, attributed to Francis Wrangham. *Antijacobin Review and Magazine* 5 (April 1800): 434, by William Heath.

WORDSWORTH, WILLIAM [and COLERIDGE, SAMUEL TAYLOR.] *Lyrical Ballads, with other Poems* (2 vols., 1800; pub. January 1801). *BC* 17 (February 1801): 125-31, by John Stoddart. *MR* 38 (June 1802): 209 (brief announcement only; ? by Christopher Moody).

Appendix B: Four Reviewers

Brief sketches follow of four of the less famous reviewers whose work is discussed in this study. Taken together, they form a reasonable sample with which to answer the question "What kind of men wrote these articles?" Three of them illustrate how closely knit and how active was the Dissenting network which controlled the major Reviews between 1791 and 1793. Yet differences of outlook and temperament are as obvious as similarities of background, and were more important when literary reviews were being written. Details about articles contributed to the *Monthly* are taken from *The Monthly Review: First Series* and *The Monthly Review: Second Series* (Oxford, 1934, 1955), by B. C. Nangle, who first identified Ferriar as a *Monthly* reviewer.

JOHN AIKIN, M.D. (1747-1822), was an intensely active man with wide interests. He received part of his education at Warrington Academy, where his father, the Rev. John Aikin, D.D., was a tutor. Later he studied medicine under various masters, with periods at London and Edinburgh, and gained his doctorate at Leyden in 1784. He then practised at Yarmouth until 1792, when his practice dwindled after he had alienated important townsfolk by writing pamphlets against the Test and Corporation Acts. After six years of medical and literary activity at London, ill health caused him to move again to Stoke Newington, where he spent most of his time writing until disabled by a stroke in 1817. Twenty-nine "principal works" are listed by his daughter Lucy in her *Memoir of John Aikin*; among these are *Essays on Song-Writing* (1772), *Evenings at Home* (6 vols., 1792-96; a work for children written with his sister, Mrs. Barbauld), *Letters from a Father to his Son* (1793-1800), *General Biography* (10 vols., 4to, 1799-1815; Aikin edited this work and wrote nearly half the articles), and *Annals of the Reign of George III* (1816). Aikin was active in setting up the *Monthly Magazine,* published by Richard Phillips, which he edited from its beginning in 1796 until 1806 and for which he wrote many articles; William Enfield and William Taylor were also contributors. A volume of poems by Aikin appeared in 1791.

Griffiths recruited several reviewers from Warrington Academy: John Seddon was writing for the *Monthly* as early as 1762, and Aikin's father and his own close friend Enfield had both been contributors. Aikin reviewed medical books for the *Monthly* from 1776 to 1784, and then put in a second spell of service during his London residence, reviewing medical, political, literary, and miscellaneous works. Between 1793 and 1799 he wrote well over a hundred main articles for the *Monthly,* besides Catalogue paragraphs. Johnson, his friend and publisher, would almost inevitably have asked him to contribute to the *Analytical,* and Aikin is listed as an *Analytical* reviewer by William West (*Aldine Magazine* [1839], p. 37). In April 1796 Coleridge told Cottle that Aikin "was the person who reviewed Joan of Arc in the Analytical Review" (*Collected Letters,* 1: 201). There is some possibility of confusion with a review of *Joan* that Aikin wrote for the *Monthly* (but would not yet have appeared). The review that was published in the *Analytical* (23: 170-77) is one of a group of articles on poetry and drama, the last of which is signed "D.M." If Coleridge's information was correct, this is likely to be Aikin's signature, standing perhaps for "Doctor of Medicine." This signature appears more than two hundred times in the *Analytical* between 1790 and 1798. Occasional variations (D.M.S., D.M.D., D.M.N.) may indicate reviews by other members of Aikin's literary family (see chap. 2, n. 76).

Aikin was forward-looking in both his political and literary ideas. His letter on "The Rights of the Poor" (*Gentleman's Magazine,*1788, no. 1, pp. 40-41; reprinted in Lucy Aikin's *Memoir,* 1: 123-28) gives an almost Marxian account of the alienation of workers' labour. But like other liberals, he was disheartened by the course of the French Revolution and rise of Napoleon; and by 1802 he had been "cured of all theoretical ideas of reform" (*Memoir,* 1: 247). In literature he was an ardent admirer of Cowper, of whom he wrote: "This masculine vigor of vernacular diction . . . by no means precludes . . . the highest degree of grace and elegance when those qualities are congenial with the subject" (*Memoir,* 2: 190-91). He also enjoyed the "eccentricity and genius" of Browne's *Religio Medici* as early as 1775, when Browne was unfashionable and almost unknown. Coleridge and Southey were each indebted to this intelligent and receptive critic for several encouraging reviews. But Aikin believed that "nothing is such an obstacle to the production of *excellence,* as the power of producing what is *pretty good* with ease and rapidity" (*Memoir,* 2: 279). When reviewing Southey's *Poems* of 1797 he tried to convey this point, and if the hint had been taken, Southey might have been spared much harsher criticism from other quarters.

(See Lucy Aikin, *Memoir of John Aikin, M.D.*, 2 vols. [1823]; *D.N.B.* A portrait of Aikin is reproduced above.)

WILLIAM ENFIELD, LL.D. (1741-97), was born of poor parents at Sudbury in Suffolk. Helped by a local Dissenting minister, at the age of seventeen he became a pupil on the Presbyterian Fund at Daventry Academy, where he completed the five-year course. After serving for some years as minister to a Liverpool congregation, he was in 1770 invited to Warrington Academy to become resident warden and tutor in the *belles-lettres.* While at Warrington he published more than a dozen miscellaneous works, among them *The Speaker* (1774) — a collection of pieces for recitation prefaced by an "Essay on Elocution." This work was widely used in schools and often reprinted. In 1774 Enfield received the degree of LL.D. from the University of Edinburgh. Warrington Academy was at this time suffering from a lack of funds and other handicaps, and in 1783 it was closed. Enfield remained in Warrington for two years as a private tutor and minister to the Cairo Street congregation; then in 1785 he accepted an invitation to the Octagon Chapel, Norwich. For a time he continued to take private pupils as boarders: among these were Thomas Denman (later Lord Chief Justice) and Edward Maltby (later Bishop of Durham). His most ambitious publication was a translation from the Latin of Brucker's *History of Philosophy* (2 vols., 4to, 1791). He contributed to the *Monthly Magazine,* whose editor, John Aikin, had been his friend since Warrington days; and at the time of his unexpected death from illness in 1797 he was looking forward to a long period of co-operation with Aikin in the *General Biography.*

As a reviewer Enfield was probably recommended to Griffiths by the elder Aikin, and he contributed to the *Monthly* from 1774 until the year of his death. In twenty-three years he wrote nearly five hundred main articles and innumerable paragraphs for the Catalogue. The subjects he dealt with were various and included politics, philosophy, and religion. He also reviewed novels, and though he did this well it was often with reluctance. "I have no objection to lounging now and then an hour in Lane's shop," he wrote to Griffiths in October 1795, "but to be shut up for several days together in his warehouse is to an old man an irksome confinement" (Bodl., MS. Adds. C.89, f. 93). Nevertheless, when reviewing Charlotte Smith's *Celestina* he paid generous tribute to the possibilities of the novel as a genre (*Monthly Review*, 6: 287).

Enfield's publisher was Johnson, and when the *Analytical* began publication in 1788 Enfield assured Griffiths that he had no part in it; "and will have none, as long as you have occasion for me at your Board" (Bodl. MS. Adds. C.89, f. 53). Yet by 1791 Enfield was reviewing for both journals, as a surviving letter to Johnson makes clear (Brit. Mus. Montagu d.12, f. 297). Enfield was never very comfortably off, and it is only too likely that he took on this extra work chiefly for the sake of payment. How much reviewing he did for the *Analytical* is hard to estimate, for none of the reviews mentioned in the letter appeared with a signature; but it seems that he had received from Johnson a substantial "parcel."

Enfield was a Unitarian of the kind the eighteenth century called "Socinian." He regretted the differences between the churches, and hoped for a comprehension until the conflicts of the 1790s made this impossible. The "Speculative Society" he founded at Norwich included equal numbers of Anglican and Nonconformist clergy. All who knew him recall his amiable character, and his reviews give a strong impression of kindliness as well as of clear-headed judgement. Aikin thought it was Enfield's "peculiar talent to arrange and express other men's ideas to the greatest advantage"; this talent at least found full scope in the contemporary mode of reviewing.

(See John Aikin's "Biographical Account of the Late Rev. Dr. Enfield," prefixed to a posthumous selection of his *Sermons on Practical Subjects* [1798] and reprinted in vol. 1 of Lucy Aikin's *Memoir of Dr. John Aikin;* MSS cited; *D.N.B.* A silhouette portrait of Enfield is reproduced above.)

JOHN FERRIAR, M.D. (1761-1815), pioneer in public health, was the son of a minister living near Jedburgh. In 1781 he graduated M.D. at Edinburgh, and after practising for a few years at Stockton-on-Tees removed to Manchester. "On 8 Oct. 1789 he was appointed to the post of a physician of the Manchester Infirmary. An epidemic fever in the town was the means of drawing public notice to the wretched condition of the dwellings of the working classes, and led Ferriar to take an active and important part in causing the local authorities to pay more attention to the sanitary laws. He urged especially the establishment of baths, the shortening of the protracted hours of labour of the factory children, and the closing or cleansing of insanitary dwellings. He was a principal worker in connection with the Manchester board of health, and with the establishment of fever-wards at Stockport" (*D.N.B.*). Ferriar's *Medical Histories and Reflections* (1792-98) include valuable discussions of sanitary matters. His most important literary publication was *Illustrations of Sterne* (1798), which traces Sterne's borrowings from Rabelais, Robert Burton, and other authors. Ferriar was an active member of the Manchester Literary and Philosophical Society, and an exponent of Parliamentary reform. He remained at Manchester until his death.

Ferriar's reviews began to appear in the *Monthly* in April 1799, shortly after Aikin's retirement. Since his interests likewise embraced both medicine and literature, it seems obvious that he was taken on as a replacement, and it is quite possible that Aikin recommended Ferriar to Griffiths and acted as intermediary. There is no record of contact between the two men, but they would have had common friends in Manchester and Warrington; Ferriar may have been one of the Mancunians who gave Aikin help with his *Description of the Country . . . Round Manchester* (1795). From Aikin Ferriar took over the reviewing of Southey's poems, with effects seen in the present study. Time increased his dislike for Southey's work, and he attacked *Madoc* both in the *Monthly* (48: 113-22) and in the edition of his "Bibliomania" appended to the 1812 reprint of *Illustrations of Sterne* ("MADOC'S mass conceals its veins of lead," 2: 202).

Both Ferriar's reviews and his original writings express a much more conservative outlook than Aikin's. J. H. Alexander describes his early reviewing as a "crusade against the Germans, childish simplicity, medieval barbarism, immorality, and romance, and in defence of late neoclassical orthodoxy." Certainly his approval of seventeenth-century authors was highly selective; and he disliked Taylor's "Lenora"—

> Here Bürger's muse, with ghostly terrors pale,
> Runs 'hurry-skurry' through her nurs'ry tale

("Knaster," quoted from the 1798 *Illustrations* by J. W. Robberds, *Memoir of William Taylor* [1843], 1: 273)—with all it stood for. He thought "genius" (a term sometimes used too readily and loosely by Aikin) was simply "the power of doing best, what many endeavour to do well" (*Illustrations* [1812], 2: 180). His own best poem, "The Bibliomania," is a successful exercise in the style of Pope's Horatian epistles. He reviewed for the *Monthly* until the year of his death, writing more than 150 main articles. Alexander finds that his conservatism, if not actually a virtue, is redeemed by the consistency of his attack and by his lively style.

(See *D.N.B.* and sources there cited; J. H. Alexander, *Two Studies in Romantic Reviewing* [Salzburg, 1976], 1: 90-96. For information about Ferriar's medical work see also Edward M. Brockbank, *John Ferriar; William Osler* [Heinemann Medical Books, 1950]. A Portrait of Ferriar is reproduced above.)

WILLIAM TAYLOR (1756-1836) employed his considerable talents and learning almost entirely in writing for periodicals. His father was a wealthy textile manufacturer of Norwich, and a Unitarian. After five years at the Suffolk boarding-school kept by Mr. and Mrs. Barbauld, Taylor was sent abroad in 1779 to learn modern languages. He mastered German during a year's residence at Detmold, developed a passion for the literature, travelled in several parts of Germany, and met Goethe at Weimar. In 1782 Taylor returned to Norwich, where he declined to enter his father's business and spent the rest of his life in literary pursuits. In later years his circumstances were restricted by the collapse of family investments. He translated much German literature into English, including poems by

Bürger, Lessing's *Nathan der Weise,* Goethe's *Iphigenie auf Tauris,* and some of Wieland's prose dialogues. His was the earliest and most important English version of Bürger's "Lenore" — a ballad, according to J. G. Robertson, that "has exerted a more widespread influence than perhaps any other short poem in the literature of the world," and "helped materially to call the Romantic movement in Europe to life" (*A History of German Literature* [1959], pp. 259-60). Taylor's "Lenora" was written in 1790, appeared in the *Monthly Magazine* for March 1796, and proved a direct source of inspiration to both Coleridge and Scott. To the *Monthly Magazine* Taylor contributed 764 articles between 1796 and 1824. He also wrote for the *Monthly Review,* the *Critical Review,* Arthur Aikin's *Annual Review,* Flower's *Cambridge Intelligencer,* and other periodicals. But the major work that a life dedicated to literature might have been expected to produce never took shape. Taylor's *Historic Survey of German Poetry* (3 vols., 1828-30) was little more than a chronological arrangement of his articles and translations, badly dated by the time it appeared. It has value chiefly as a record of Taylor's opinions, and of his efforts over forty years to make German literature better known.

Taylor was introduced into the *Monthly Review* by his friend and fellow-townsman William Enfield in 1793, and gave invaluable service in the Appendixes dealing with foreign literature. But his writing had certain peculiarities — he enjoyed neologisms, and would write "body-spirit" instead of *esprit de corps* — and in 1799 these led to a collision with George Griffiths, who was in the process of taking over the editorship from his father. Taylor thereupon withdrew from the *Monthly* for ten years. His friend Southey introduced him into the *Critical,* to which he contributed from December 1803 until November 1804 and again in 1809. He then became a *Monthly* reviewer once more until 1824. His own marked volumes showed a total of 550 reviews written for the *Monthly* (200 between 1793 and 1799) and more than sixty for the *Critical.* In his *Memoir* Robberds lists these articles and gives extracts from relevant correspondence; the letters he prints from Ralph Griffiths and his son are almost the only ones that survive of the many thousands that must have been written.

Alexander calls Taylor "the most striking of all the reviewers during the nineties." He admits that Taylor can be dull or undiscriminating, but finds among his virtues "a gift for capturing the essence of an author's work in . . . brief sketches which in their semi-impressionistic quality anticipate those of Hazlitt," and "an ability, akin to Goldsmith's, to place a work in its total literary context." Even in short notices like that of *Herman of Unna* (above, chap. 3) Taylor liked to relate the book under review to general principles or wider themes. Perhaps for this reason, Hazlitt credited him with introducing "the style of philosophical criticism, which has been the boast of the Edinburgh Review," into the *Monthly* "about the year 1796." I do not know how Hazlitt identified Taylor's articles. By middle life Taylor was a Deist, or perhaps an agnostic; and despite his interest in the *Sturm und Drang,* he remained in some ways a characteristic figure of the Enlightenment. Carlyle went so far as to call him "a natural-born English Philistine," meaning apparently that his turn of mind was materialist and utilitarian. By then two generations of English Romantics had made some of Taylor's writing look obsolete: but his reviews and translations had helped to bring those generations into being.

(See J. W. Robberds, *A Memoir of the Life and Writings of the late William Taylor of Norwich* [2 vols., 1843]; Carlyle's *Edinburgh* review of Taylor's *Historic Survey,* reprinted in the Centenary Edition of Carlyle's *Works* [1896-99], 27: 333-70; J. H. Alexander, *Two Studies in Romantic Reviewing,* 1: 42-46; *D.N.B.* George Borrow gives a reminiscential sketch of Taylor in *Lavengro* [1851], chap. 23. A portrait is reproduced above.)

Notes

Chapter 1: The Reviews

1.   See Edward A. Bloom, " 'Labors of the Learned': Neoclassic Book-reviewing Aims and Techniques," *Studies in Philology* 54 (1957): 537-63. My summary account of reviewing before 1749 is largely indebted to this article and to Walter Graham. *English Literary Periodicals* (New York and London, 1930; reprinted 1966), pp. 22-26, 196-208.

2.   See Lewis M. Knapp, "Ralph Griffiths, Author and Publisher, 1746-1750," *The Library*, ser. 4, 20 (1939): 197-213.

3.   The famous controversy over Pope's *Essay on Man* (attacked by Crousaz in *The Present State of the Republic of Letters;* defended by Warburton in *The History of the Works of the Learned*) is hardly an exception, since the poem was treated as a work of doctrine.

4.   In his preliminary Advertisement Griffiths promised only "to give a compendious account of those productions of the press, as they come out, that are worth notice." But in the third number he announced: "We propose, for the future, to register all the new Things in general, without exception to any, on account of their lowness of rank, or price" (ser. 1, 1: 238). A section consisting of very brief notices, some only transcripts of the title-pages, followed this announcement. This feature was repeated in two more numbers and then dropped until December 1750, when it was revived under the heading "Monthly Catalogue," with rather longer notices (ser. 1, 4: 156).

5.   *Monthly Review,* ser. 1, 2 (1750): 260.

6.   E.g., Dr. John Hill's crushing review of *The Natural History of Barbados,* by Griffith Hughes (ser. 1, 3 [July 1750]: 197-206); Dr. James Kirkpatrick's respectful but searching review of *Medical Principles and Cautions,* by Theophilus Lobb (ser. 1, 5 [December 1751]: 498-508). See also Cleland's review of *Amelia* (ser. 1, 5 [December 1751]: 510-15; reprinted in *Henry Fielding: The Critical Heritage,* ed. R. Paulson and T. Lockwood [1969], pp. 304-9). Some opportunities were missed. Gray's *Elegy in a Country Churchyard* was greeted with the sentence: "This excellent little piece is much read, and so much admired by every body, that to say

261

more of it, would be superfluous" (ser. 1, 4 [February 1751]: 309). None the less, Walter Graham's statement that "for more than thirty years of its career, the *Monthly* made little advance over its predecessors in the critical nature of its contents" (p. 209) is quite misleading. For a more just view see Bloom, "Labors of the Learned," p. 557.

7.   Griffiths began by printing 1,000 copies; in 1752 he printed 1,250; in 1756, 2,250; in 1760, 2,500; in 1768, 3,000; in 1776, 3,500. See Lewis M. Knapp, "Griffiths's *Monthly Review* as Printed by Strahan," *Notes & Queries* 203 (1958): 216-17.

8.   See B. C. Nangle, *The Monthly Review, First Series, 1749-1789: Indexes of Contributors and Articles* (Oxford, 1934), p. viii.

9.   See J. H. Plumb, "The Public, Literature, and the Arts in the Eighteenth Century," in *The Triumph of Culture: Eighteenth-Century Perspectives,* ed. Paul Fritz and David Williams (Toronto, 1972), pp. 27-48.

10.   These were the Dissenting schoolmaster William Rose; John Cleland, author of *Memoirs of a Woman of Pleasure (Fanny Hill)*; and John Ward, who soon afterwards became vice-president of the Royal Society. See the first volume of Griffiths's marked set of the Review in the Bodleian Library, and Nangle, *Monthly Review, First Series.* Similarly, Smollett began the *Critical Review* with only four helpers, one of whom had been a linen-draper's assistant and another of whom held a Chair of Greek at Cambridge. See Derek Roper, "Smollett's 'Four Gentlemen,' " *Review of English Studies,* n.s., 10 (1959): 38-44.

11.   See B. C. Nangle, *The Monthly Review, Second Series, 1790-1815: Indexes of Contributors and Articles* (Oxford, 1955), pp. 1-75.

12.   Griffiths signed himself thus in 1793 when writing to a reviewer who had resigned over political and religious differences (Bodl. MS. Adds. C.89, f. 287^v). An essay paper called *The Old Whig: or, the Consistent Protestant* was produced between 1735 and 1738 by the Dissenting divine Samuel Chandler and others.

13.   For Hamilton and his descendants, see John Nichols, *Literary Anecdotes of the Eighteenth Century* (1812-15), 3: 398-400.

14.   See Jacob Zeitlin, "Southey's Contributions to the *Critical Review,*" *Notes & Queries,* ser. 12, 4 (1918): 35-36, 66-67, 94-96, 122-25; also *New Letters of Robert Southey,* ed. Kenneth Curry (New York and London, 1965), vol. 1, passim.

15.   See Nichols, *Anecdotes,* 3: 121; 8: 662. Hamilton acknowledged Steevens as "his right Hand" in 1782 (Bodl. MS. Adds. C.90, f. 92^r), and Arthur Murphy placed Steevens "at the head of your society" in an address to the *Critical* reviewers in 1786 (Murphy's *Works,* vol. 7, Preface).

16.   Lamb's friend George Dyer refers to Gregory as editor in connection with Dyer's own contributions of that period. See Dyer, *Privileges of the University of Cambridge* (1824), 2: [206].

17.   Discussing his recent labours, Good wrote to Nathan Drake in January 1803: "I have edited the Critical Review, besides writing several of its most elaborate articles." Only four of the articles have been identified. Good also wrote for the *Analytical.* See Olinthus Gregory, *Memoirs of . . . the late John Mason Good, M.D.* (1828), pp. 80-81.

18.   "For a short time the Critical Review, with but little success, was under his superintendance" (*Gentleman's Magazine,* 1826, no. 1, p. 472). The period is not specified. Contemporaries associated Pinkerton with the *Critical* from 1795 until 1806: see *Letters of Joseph Ritson* (1833), 2: 67-68, 75; Richard Polwhele, *Biographical Sketches in Cornwall* (Truro, 1831), 3: 130; Thomas Constable, *Archibald Constable and his Literary Correspondents* (Edinburgh, 1873), 1: 359.

19. See Roger Lonsdale, "Dr. Burney and the *Monthly Review*," *Review of English Studies*, n.s., 14 (1963): 347-48; also idem, *Dr. Charles Burney* (Oxford, 1965), pp. 108-10, 121-24, 178-80, 311-12. Though only one review can be identified as Burney's, he was closely connected with the *Critical* between 1771 and 1785, and was probably a regular contributor.

20. See David V. Erdman, "Immoral Acts of a Library Cormorant: The Extent of Coleridge's Contributions to the *Critical Review*," *Bulletin of the New York Public Library* 63 (1959): 433-54, 515-30, 575-87; Derek Roper, "Coleridge and the *Critical Review*," *Modern Language Review* 55 (1960): 11-16.

21. See [Parr,] *Remarks on the Statement of Dr. Charles Combe* (1795), pp. 37-38; William Field, *Memoirs of . . . the Rev. Samuel Parr, LL.D.* (1828), 1: 332-33.

22. See J. W. Robberds, *Memoir of . . . the late William Taylor of Norwich* (1843), 2: 25-41, 306-7, where sixty-seven articles are identified.

23. See Derek Roper, "The Politics of the *Critical Review*, 1756-1817," *Durham University Journal*, n.s., 22 (1961): 117-22.

24. For the founding of the *English Review* see Samuel Smiles, *A Publisher and his Friends: Memoir and Correspondence of John Murray* (1891), 1: 12; Robert Kerr, *Memoirs of the Life . . . of William Smellie* (Edinburgh, 1811), 2: 1; Nichols, *Anecdotes*, 3: 731.

25. See *Annual Biography and Obituary* 2 (1818): 101-2.

26. See William Wallace Currie, *Memoir of James Currie, M.D., F.R.S.* (1831),1: 237. The only review identified is of Erasmus Darwin's *Zoönomia*. Currie was a distinguished physician, later a leading opponent of the slave trade and the first editor of Burns. See R.D. Thornton, *James Currie: The Entire Stranger and Robert Burns* (Edinburgh and London, 1963).

27. "My principal employment was now [1784] writing for the 'English Review' . . . at two guineas a sheet" (Godwin's MS memoir of his own life written in 1800, quoted by C. Kegan Paul, *William Godwin, his Friends and Contemporaries* [1876], 1: 20).

28. See *Monthly Mirror* 8 (1799): 326; Elbridge Colby, *A Bibliography of Thomas Holcroft* (New York, 1922), p. 40. Holcroft probably reviewed printed plays in the early numbers as well as writing the "Theatre" sections.

29. Murray's advertisement in the *Whitehall Evening Post* for 18-20 January 1785 mentions "J. O. Justamond, F.R.S., Surgeon to the Westminster Hospital" as one of the writers of the *English Review*. Justamond was connected with the Review world by marriage, having married a sister of Paul Henry Maty, editor of the *New Review* (1782-86). See Nichols, *Literary Anecdotes*, 3: 257-59.

30. Smiles, *A Publisher*, 1: 12. Moore was a physician, the author of *Zeluco* (1789) and other novels, and of *A Journal . . . during a Residence in France* (1793-94).

31. Nichols, *Literary Anecdotes*, 3: 731; Smiles, *A Publisher*, 1: 12; see also Polwhele, *Biographical Sketches*, 3: 68, 91 ff. Whitaker was a topographer and antiquarian, best known for his *History of Manchester* (1771-75).

32. Smiles, *A Publisher*, 1: 23-25.

33. Ibid. p. 28; *Annual Biography and Obituary* 2 (1817): 101-2.

34. For Christie see *D.N.B.* article by Richard Copley Christie; Alexander Chalmers, *General Biographical Dictionary* (1813), 9: 294-96; Nichols, *Anecdotes*,

9: 366-90; John G. Alger, *Englishmen in the French Revolution* (1889), pp. 78-79, 98; Claire Tomalin, *The Life and Death of Mary Wollstonecraft* (1974), passim.

35.   Christie's ideas are set forth at length in this prospectus, which was reprinted as a Preface to vol. 1 of the *Analytical Review*. For Christie's authorship, see Chalmers. He expounded the same views in a letter of January 1788 meant for publication in the *Gentleman's Magazine* (Nichols, *Literary Anecdotes*, 9: 384-85n.).

36.   See *Collected Letters of Samuel Taylor Coleridge*, ed. E. L. Griggs (Oxford, 1956-71), 1: 201; *Aldine Magazine* (1839), p. 37.

37.   See Currie, *Memoir of James Currie*, 1: 45-46.

38.   See John Knowles, *Life and Writings of Henry Fuseli* (1831), 1: 80-81, 383; Eudo C. Mason, *The Mind of Henry Fuseli* (1951), pp. 355-59.

39.   Geddes wrote the first article of the first number and contributed forty-five other articles, almost all on biblical criticism or ecclesiastical history. See John Mason Good, *Memoirs of . . . the Reverend Alexander Geddes, LL.D.* (1803), pp. 190-95. He broke with the *Analytical* in September 1793 to become a regular contributor to the *Monthly*.

40.   See *Love-Letters of Mary Hays*, ed. A. F. Wedd (1925), p. 240.

41.   See John Towill Rutt, *Life and Correspondence of Joseph Priestley* (1831), 2: 20. Toulmin seems to have used the signature "A.N." in both the *Analytical Review* and the *Theological Repository: see Monthly Repository* 10 (1815): 674n.

42.   See Ralph M. Wardle, "Mary Wollstonecraft, *Analytical* Reviewer," *PMLA* 62 (1947): 1000-1009; Derek Roper, "Mary Wollstonecraft's Reviews," *Notes & Queries* 203 (1958): 37-38.

43.   The signatures "P.P." and "G.G." are identified as Cowper's by Charles Ryskamp in his *William Cowper of the Inner Temple, Esq.* (Cambridge, 1959), pp. 246-52. Ten reviews of poetry appeared over these signatures between March 1789 and April 1790; another signed "P.P." appeared in March 1793.

44.   See Jane Worthington Smyser, "The Trial and Imprisonment of Joseph Johnson, Bookseller," *Bulletin of the New York Public Library* 77 (1974): 418-35.

45.   "When . . . for the unconscious offence of selling a few copies of a pamphlet of which he was not the publisher, and which was a reply to one of which he had sold a much larger number, the opportunity was taken of involving him in a prosecution that brought upon him the infliction of fine and imprisonment, it was by many considered as the ungenerous indulgence of a long-hoarded spleen against him on account of publications not liable to legal censure, though displeasing to Authority." John Aikin, "A Biographical Account of Joseph Johnson," *Gentleman's Magazine*, 1809, no. 2, p. 1167. For Johnson's career and associates see Leslie F. Chard II, "Joseph Johnson: Father of the Book Trade," *Bulletin of the New York Public Library* 79 (1975): 51-82.

46.   Henry Crabb Robinson wrote to his brother Thomas on 4 February 1799 recommending "the new Analytical Review," adding that "No Bookseller has any Connection with the Work; nor any of the *trading literati*" (typed transcript of correspondence in Dr. Williams's Library, vol. 1, no. 106, p. 2).

47.   Henry Crabb Robinson describes his namesake as "zealous in support" of the *Analytical* in February 1799 (ibid., no. 108, p. 2). Anthony Robinson was a prosperous sugar refiner and may have given financial help, as well as the reviews of political works which he contributed from 1797 onwards. See his obituary by

"H.C.R." (Henry Crabb Robinson), *Monthly Repository*, n.s., 1 (1827): 288-93, esp. 290.

48. See his correspondence, vol. 1, no. 125, p. 2.

49. See *No. I. A Proposal for the Reformation of Principles* (1 January 1792). This circular and *No. II. A Sequel to the Proposal* (11 June 1792) are bound up with some copies of vol. 1 of the *British Critic,* e.g. that in the Bodleian Library. For accounts of the Society and the founding of the *British Critic* see Nichols, *Literary Anecdotes,* 9: 95; John Britton, *Autobiography* (part 1, 1850), p. 260n.; James Allan Park, *Memoir of William Stevens* (1859), pp. 119-20.

50. "Payments of £50 in March 1792 and March 1793 to the Rev. Robert Nares were probably for pamphlet or newspaper work" (Arthur Aspinall, *Politics and the Press c. 1780-1850* [1949], p. 166). It seems very likely that these sums were paid to help with the expenses of launching the Review. Nares's personal reward came in his many subsequent preferments.

51. Nichols, *Literary Anecdotes,* 9: 95n. Nares's share in the *British Critic* was of considerable value when he sold it in 1813: see John Nichols and John Bowyer Nichols, *Literary Illustrations of the Eighteenth Century* (1817-58), 7: 614. For a selection of Nares's editorial correspondence see ibid., 7: 588-619.

52. See Nangle, *Monthly Review, Second Series,* p. 17.

53. "Dr. White is the reviewer of publications in Hebrew and subjects of oriental literature in 'the British Critic' " *(Public Characters of 1798-99,* 2d. ed. [1799], p. 259). See also Nangle, *Monthly Review, First Series* and *Monthly Review, Second Series.* White was Regius Professor of Hebrew at Oxford 1804-14; "both as a theologian and as a critic he was ultra-conservative" *(D.N.B.).*

54. Richard Polwhele, *Biographical Sketches in Cornwall* (Truro, 1831), 3: 113-14. After 1796 Whitaker accepted payment, but at a lower rate than Nares had offered (ibid., pp. 120-21).

55. Nichols, *Illustrations,* 7: 637.

56. Ibid., 6: 532.

57. Ibid., 7: 670.

58. Ibid., 7: 589-606.

59. Nichols, *Literary Anecdotes,* 9: 129; Polwhele, *Biographical Sketches,* 3: 100.

60. Both Maurice and Rennell are named as reviewers in the *British Critic* by "Peter Pindar" (John Wolcot) in *Tristia; or, the Sorrows of Peter* (1806): see "Elegy to Mr. Sheridan," stanzas 7-9. Maurice was closely connected with Nares and Beloe, and Rennell's son became editor of the *British Critic* soon after he graduated from Cambridge in 1811.

61. "Some admirable critiques in the early volumes of this work, together with the spirit of opposition among a larger portion of the people to the principles it was intended to counteract, procured for it an established sale and reputation" (John Mason Good, Olinthus Gregory, and Newton Bosworth, *Pantologia: A New Cyclopaedia* [1813], vol. 3, s.v. "Criticism").

62. *Encyclopaedia of Literary and Typographical Anecdote* (1842), p. 795.

63. See above, n. 7.

64. Quoted by A. S. Collins in *The Profession of Letters . . . 1780-1832* (1928), p. 29.

65. See Timperley (n. 62 above).

66. See John Clive, *Scotch Reviewers: The Edinburgh Review, 1802-1815* (Cambridge, Mass., 1957), pp. 30-31, 133. The circulation of the *Edinburgh* went on rising steeply for another ten years, reaching 13,000 in 1814 (ibid., p. 134).

67. See John O. Hayden, *The Romantic Reviewers, 1802-1824* (1969), p. 64.

68. See *Sale Catalogues of Eminent Persons*, gen. ed. A. N. L. Munby (1971-), for Beckford (3: 456), Blair (7: 195, 214), Day (2: 187,191), Dodd (5: 384), Hastings (8: 265), Hayley (2: 88), Hollis (8: 8,48), Southey (9: 122,182), Sterne (5: 307), and Wilkes (8: 108,159). For Gibbon see Geoffrey Keynes, *The Library of Edward Gibbon* (1940), p. 201; for Parr, *Bibliotheca Parriana* [by Henry Bohn] (1827), pp. 274-82; for Walpole, *Horace Walpole's Correspondence,* ed. W. S. Lewis et al., 15 (New Haven, Conn., and London, 1951): 238-39. Parr's annotated volumes of the *Critical* are now in the library of University College, London. Besides the substantial runs here referred to, sale catalogues include many short runs of volumes and "parcels" of monthly numbers; e.g., Hayley owned the *Monthly* and *Critical* for 1782-86, and Gibbon the *Analytical* for 1788-89.

69. On my shelves are some volumes of the *Monthly* with the bookplates of the Earl of Guilford (heir to the celebrated Lord North); of Captain Sir Edwyn Stanhope, Bt., R.N.; and of P. Small Keir, Esq., of Kindrogan. Another *Monthly* subscriber was Lord Kinnaird (probably Charles, eighth baron, 1780-1826), whose volumes are now owned by the Queen's University, Belfast. A thirteen-year run of the *Critical* from 1795 was included in Byron's first sale of furniture from Newstead *(Sale Catalogues,* 1: 211). Richard Pryce of Gunley, Montgomeryshire, subscribed to the *Critical* (volumes now in Birmingham University Library); the Houstouns of Johnstone, a Renfrewshire family, to the *English* (volumes now in Edinburgh University Library); and Lady Newdigate (probably Hester, second wife of Sir Roger Newdigate, Bt., 1719-1806) to the *British Critic* (volumes now owned by University College, London).

70. John Douglas (1721-1807), Bishop of Salisbury, owned many volumes of the *Critical,* now in the Bodleian Library. Edward Maltby (1770-1859), Bishop of Durham, bequeathed his volumes of the *British Critic* to the University of Durham. The first six volumes of the *British Critic* were sold from the library of an unnamed clergyman in 1837 *(Sale Catalogues,* 4: 219). Thomas Pearne, a Fellow of Peterhouse, owned a complete set of the *Monthly* in 1790 (Bodleian MS. Adds. C.89, f. 292v).

71. Medical subscribers included the surgeon James Kenion (*Monthly* volumes in the Leeds Library, of which Kenion was first president); John Coakley Lettsom, M.D., F.R.S., the Quaker philanthropist and medical reformer (*Critical* volumes in my possession); and John White, M.D. (*Monthly* volumes now owned by the Queen's College, Dundee).

72. Volumes of the *Monthly* that belonged to James Tobin, Bristol merchant and friend of Coleridge, are now owned by Bristol Public Libraries. The dates (1772-94) of the *Monthly* volumes sold from the library of Samuel Rogers suggest that they were collected by his father, Thomas Rogers, a Dissenting banker of Stoke Newington *(Sale Catalogues,* 2: 248).

73. Letter to Jeffrey of 29 November 1804, quoted by Clive, *Scotch Reviewers,* p. 136.

74. Unless otherwise noted, these volumes still belong to the universities and colleges named.

75.   Exeter College volumes now owned by Manchester College, Oxford; Coward College volumes by the Victoria Art Gallery and Municipal Libraries, Bath.

76.   Volumes now in London University Library.

77.   The present whereabouts of volumes formerly owned by this society is unknown; the latest record I have been able to trace is William S. Ward, *Index and Finding-List of Serials Published in the British Isles, 1789-1832* (Lexington, Ky., 1953).

78.   Volumes owned by the Writers to the Signet now in the Central Public Library, Edinburgh; those owned by Lincoln's Inn now in Cambridge University Library.

79.   Volumes still owned by this library.

80.   Volumes now in Worcester City Library.

81.   Volumes now owned by Bristol Public Libraries.

82.   This library now forms part of the Harris Library, Preston.

83.   William Enfield reports having access to the *Monthly* and its indexes at the Norwich Public Library (Bodleian MS. Adds. C.89, f.71^v). Some volumes now in my possession formerly belonged to the Halifax Circulating Library.

84.   Gloucester volumes now in Gloucester City Library; Hull volumes now in the University Library at Oregon, Eugene.

85.   Volumes now owned by Liverpool City Libraries.

86.   See Ward, *Index and Finding-List*. Volumes of the *Monthly* and *Critical* formerly owned by this society are now in Sheffield University Library; of the *Analytical*, in the Bodleian Library.

87.   Volumes still owned by the Society.

88.   Volumes now in Liverpool University Library.

89.   See Frank Beckwith, "The Eighteenth-century Proprietary Library in England," *Journal of Documentation* 3 (1947): 84-85.

90.   Paul Kaufman, "A Bookseller's Record of Eighteenth-century Book Clubs," *The Library*, ser. 5, 15 (1960): 282-84.

91.   "Country Book-clubs Fifty Years Ago," *Gentleman's Magazine*, 1852, no. 1, p. 572.

92.   *Antijacobin Review* 1 (1798): 475; writer identified from marked volumes in the British Library.

93.   *The Correspondence of William Cowper*, ed. Thomas Wright (1904), 1: 484.

94.   J. M. Thompson, *The French Revolution* (Oxford, 1943, reprinted 1951), p. 111. For Griffiths's efforts in 1764 to increase subscriptions in the American colonies see Elizabeth E. Kent, *Goldsmith and his Booksellers* (Ithaca, N.Y., 1933), p. 13. A well-reviewed book might quickly be reprinted in America: see Southey's 1837 Preface to *Joan of Arc*. For Mann see *Horace Walpole's Correspondence*, ed. W. S. Lewis et al., 22 (New Haven, Conn., and London, 1960): 36, 49.

95.   See for example Wordsworth's letter about Southey's review of *Lyrical Ballads*, quoted below, chap. 2, n. 99; also Joseph Cottle, *Reminiscences of Coleridge and Southey* (1847), p. 259. For Southey see J.W. Robberds, *Memoir of . . . William Taylor* (1843), 1: 462.

96.   See Richard Polwhele, *Traditions and Recollections* (1826), 1: 149-53; 2:

364-69 and passim. See also *The Life of Thomas Holcroft*, ed. Elbridge Colby (1925), 1: 259.

97.   *Boswell's Life of Johnson*, 3: 32, 44.

98.   See Herbert A. Wichelns, "Burke's *Essay on the Sublime* and its Reviewers," - *Journal of English and Germanic Philology* 21 (1922): 645-61.

99.   *Remarks on the Statement of Dr. Charles Combe, by an Occasional Writer in the British Critic* (1795), pp. 37-38; reprinted with minor changes in William Field's *Memoirs of . . . Samuel Parr* (1828), pp. 333-34. For Parr's contributions to the *Monthly*, *Critical*, and *British Critic*, see *Remarks*, pp. 36-37; Field, pp. 332-33; Nichols, *Illustrations*, 7: 609. For his collection of Reviews see above, p. 24.

100.   Robberds, 1: 300, 387. Cf. Taylor's comments of 14 November 1801: "Reviewing is very favourable to reading with observation: it forms the style; it accustoms to selection; it impresses a thousand facts and opinions which would else be skimmed over; it necessitates the profounder investigation of a thousand minutenesses which it is proper to search into; above all, it generates a habit of literary application" (ibid, p. 381). See also *New Letters of Robert Southey*, ed. Kenneth Curry (1965), 1: 258.

101.   *Pantologia* (1813), vol. 3, s.v. "Criticism."

102.   *Blackwood's Edinburgh Magazine* 14 (July 1823): 81-82. Here Maginn and Wilson draw a generally favourable comparison of the *Monthly* to the *Edinburgh* and *Quarterly*. I owe this reference to Mr. Michael Munday.

103.   Oliver Elton, *A Survey of English Literature, 1780-1830* (1912, reprinted 1920), 1: 387.

104.   A. R. D. Elliott in *The Cambridge History of English Literature*, 12 (1915): 141.

105.   A. S. Collins, *The Profession of Letters . . . 1780-1832* (1928), pp. 101, 203-4.

106.   John Wain, ed. *Contemporary Reviews of Romantic Poetry* (1953), pp. 13-14. As the century ebbed the *Critical* was anything but Tory.

107.   Clive, *Scotch Reviewers*, p. 32.

108.   Edgar Johnson, *Sir Walter Scott: The Great Unknown* (1970), 1: 215.

109.   E.g., by George McLean Harper in *William Wordsworth* (1916, rev. 1929), p. 297. After giving a distorted summary of the *Monthly* review of *Lyrical Ballads* (1798), Harper writes: "This article, like almost everything else published in *The Monthly Review* in the last decade of the eighteenth century, indicates the general alertness to detect and crush all manifestations of the 'levelling' spirit." It is hard to guess whence this misconception about the *Monthly* has been derived: its liberal politics led to the threat of a government prosecution in 1793.

110.   Prospectus of the *Critical Review*, published on 30 December 1755 in the *Public Advertiser;* reprinted by Lewis M. Knapp in *Tobias Smollett* (Princeton, N.J., 1949), pp. 171-72.

111.   *Critical Review* 7 (1759): 151. Forster makes much use of this attack in his *Life of Goldsmith* (1848), pp. 79-81.

112.   Thus, he describes the *British Critic* as a continuation of the *Critical Review;* but it was founded twenty-five years before the *Critical* ceased publication, and the two journals took opposite sides on almost every question.

113.   *Life of Goldsmith*, pp. 79-81 and elsewhere.

114.   Nangle, *Monthly Review, First Series,* pp. v-vi.

115.   See "Francis Jeffrey," in *Three Studies in Literature* (New York, 1899), pp. 46-51. Apart from Forster, Gates's only source is J. W. Robberds's *Memoir of William Taylor* (1843), a few quotations from which are interpreted to suit Forster's melodramatic conceptions.

116.   With Clive's "scores of hacks and penny-a-liners" cf. Gates's "drudges and penny-a-liners", "an indefinite number of penny-a-liners", etc. Gates uses the phrase *penny-a-liners* four times; it belongs properly to newspaper journalism.

117.   *Poor Kit Smart* (1961), p. 52; passim for treatment of the Reviews.

118.   George Saintsbury, *A History of English Criticism* (1911, reprinted 1955), pp. 229-30; Jacob Zeitlin, "Southey's Contributions to the *Critical Review*," *Notes & Queries,* ser. 12, 4 (1918): 35; William Haller, *The Early Life of Robert Southey* (New York, 1917), p. 276.

119.   Six of the twenty or so writers who contributed to the *Monthly* in 1756 and 1757 were or became Fellows of the Royal Society. See Nangle, *Monthly Review, First Series,* pp. 1-47 for the contributors and periods of service. To compare the *Monthly* and *Critical* staffs at this time is to appreciate the impudence of Smollett's attacks.

120.   *Monthly Review,* ser. 1, 2 (1749): 431-32. For the fullest account of the publication of *Memoirs of a Woman of Pleasure* (brought out by Griffiths's brother Fenton) and of the much-expurgated version, *Memoirs of Fanny Hill,* see William H. Epstein, *John Cleland: Images of a Life* (New York and London, 1974), chap. 5. See also C. H. Timperley, *Dictionary of Printers and Printing* (1839), p. 763; Lewis M. Knapp, "Ralph Griffiths, Author and Publisher," *The Library,* ser. 4, 20 (1939): 212-13. It is not true that Griffiths commended *Fanny Hill* "as a rival of *Tom Jones*"; his article is almost wholly concerned with the charge of immorality, and he cites *Tom Jones* as another work condemned on those grounds (in France) on hearsay.

121.   See R. W. Seitz, "Goldsmith's *Lives of the Fathers,*" *Modern Philology* 26 (1929): 304. The reviews consist largely of summaries, which Goldsmith was well placed to write; but they also include some favourable comment, and it is obviously unsatisfactory that this should have been paid for by Newbery.

122.   See above, pp. 21-23. It is not known whether Griffiths's principal assistants originally owned shares in the *Monthly*; the bookseller Becket sold out his sixteenth share to Griffiths in 1777 for ?250 (Bodl. MS. Adds. C.89, receipt bound in after f.14). The *Critical* seems to have been begun under a joint-ownership scheme in which some at least of the contributors took part, thus giving some substance to its claim to be written "by a Society of Gentlemen." I conjecture that the original shareholders were Smollett, Armstrong (see Knapp, *Tobias Smollett,* p. 174), Francklin, the printer Archibald Hamilton I, and the bookseller Baldwin, whose name appears on the title page of the first two volumes. An interesting scheme of ownership was set out by Gilbert Stuart in 1774 when projecting an *Edinburgh Review*: a share each was to be given to Gillies as the Edinburgh manager, Creech as Edinburgh publisher, Murray as London publisher and Smellie as printer; the remaining two shares were to go to "the conductor," i.e. Stuart. Murray approved the scheme in general, and though it was eventually dropped, its main lines may well have been followed when Murray, Gillies, Stuart, and others founded the *English Review* seven years later. See Robert Kerr, *Memoirs of . . . William Smellie* (Edinburgh, 1811), 1: 427-36.

123.   Two traits emphasised by John Aikin are Johnson's "honourable principles of

dealing" and his "decided aversion to all arts of puffing and parade" (*Gentleman's Magazine*, 1809, no. 2, p. 1167). His dealings with Cowper and with Mary Wollstonecraft are well known.

124.   In 1789 all current Review numbers cost one shilling; but by 1791 the *Monthly, Critical,* and *Analytical* had all raised their price to ls. 6d., and by 1800 the *Monthly, Critical,* and *British Critic* each cost two shillings. The *Monthly* and *Critical* published appendixes three times a year at the same price as the monthly numbers, making the annual cost in 1800 thirty shillings, plus the cost of binding three volumes. Readers who changed over to the *Edinburgh* made a considerable saving, for though numbers cost five shillings each they appeared only quarterly; and there were no appendixes.

125.   The publishers of all these Reviews are named on their title-pages, except that the *Critical* is shown only as "Printed for A. [S.] Hamilton." But advertisements for the *Critical* regularly show Robinson as one of the proprietors; see *St. James's Chronicle,* 31 January - 2 February 1775; 30 January - 1 February 1781; 29 January 1 February 1791; 30 May - 1 June 1793. Robinson's name may also have appeared on the paper covers of the monthly numbers.

126.   It may be that where books were published by several firms jointly, not all were named. I have not investigated this possible source of abuse.

127.   "John Gifford," himself an extremely unscrupulous writer and editor, attacks the *Critical Review* in 1797 as "GEORGE ROBINSON'S MONTHLY ADVERTISER." (See "A Rod for the Backs of the Critics . . . by Humphrey Hedgehog," prefixed to the English edition of *A Bone to Gnaw, for the Democrats,* by "Peter Porcupine", i.e. William Cobbett.) This attack was quoted with approval in Gifford's own *Antijacobin Review* 1 (1798): 346. Three months later the *Antijacobin Review* was indignant at the harsh treatment given by the *Critical* to one of Robinson's own publications, Jonathan Boucher's *View of the Causes and Consequences of the American Revolution* (1797); see ibid, pp. 675-78 and *Critical Review* 23 (1798): 189-96. Boucher was a violent Tory and was himself a contributor to the *Antijacobin Review.* As this example suggests, political influences on reviewing cut across commercial ones and were far more important. Alexander Chalmers, who knew Robinson well, emphasises his "natural aversion to every thing little, mean, and partaking of subterfuge and undue artifice" (*Gentleman's Magazine*, 1801, no. 1, 579).

128.   In 1777 the *Monthly* must already have been a commercial property worth £4,000 (see above, n. 122). At that date it could be printed for about a penny (exclusive of distribution costs and payments to reviewers) and sold for a shilling. See Knapp, "Griffiths's *Monthly Review* as printed by Strahan," *Notes and Queries* 203 (1958); 216-17, and below, n. 147.

129.   "Before the year 1780, he [Robinson] had the largest wholesale trade that was ever carried on by an individual" (*Gentleman's Magazine*, 1801, no. 2, p. 579). For the role of the wholesale bookseller see Samuel Johnson's well-known letter to Nathan Wetherell, printed in *Boswell's Life of Johnson,* ed. G. B. Hill, rev. L. F. Powell (Oxford, 1934-50), 2: 424-26.

130.   *Letters of Sir Walter Scott,* ed. H. J. C. Grierson (1932-37), 2: 128.

131.   Ibid., p. 129.

132.   *The Watchman,* ed. Lewis Patton (Princeton, N.J., and London, 1970), p. 15.

133.   *Boswell's Life of Johnson,* 5: 274, 550.

134.   See above, n. 19. Burney's usual reviewer was Samuel Crisp; on one occasion, Thomas Twining.

135.   For Ellis's and Taylor's reviews see chap. 2. Taylor also reviewed Southey's translation of *Amadis de Gaul,* but refused to deal with his projected *History of Portugal* because he was "not up to criticising it properly"; see Robberds, *Memoir of William Taylor,* 1: 462, 464; 2: 27n. For Polwhele's reviews see his *Traditions and Recollections,* 1: 251, 281-82; 2: 497-9.

136.   Eudo C. Mason, *The Mind of Henry Fuseli* (1951), pp. 32, 354. According to Mason, Fuseli was not over-scrupulous about abusing his position as an *Analytical* reviewer thirty years later: "one of his practices was to review books containing references to himself, and quote the passages in which his name occurred, especially if the reference was a complimentary one." He also reviewed his own translation of *Archives of Etymology* (1795) by his brother, John Gaspard Fuessli (Mason, *Mind of Fuseli,* pp. 358-59).

137.   Hayden, *The Romantic Reviewers, 1802-1824* (1969), p. 258; *Letters of Sir Walter Scott,* 4: 318-19; *Quarterly Review* 16 (January 1817): 430-80.

138.   See *Letters of William and Dorothy Wordsworth, 1806-1811,* ed. E. de Selincourt, rev. Mary Moorman (Oxford, 1969), pp. 155, 173. Edmund Blunden has denied the gossip about Le Grice, which probably originated in a remark thrown out by Coleridge, confidently elaborated by Southey (see e.g. *New Letters,* 1: 465) and received by Woodsworth as fact. For Anna Seward see her *Letters* (Edinburgh, 1811), 5: 295-96. The *Critical* review of *Gebir* was by Southey.

139.   Robberds, *Memoir of Taylor,* 1: 353; cf. account of Ferriar in Appendix B.

140.   Roger Lonsdale, *Dr. Charles Burney* (Oxford, 1965), pp. 209, 344-46. The review of Burney's *General History of Music* was apparently attributed to Jackson because it criticised (*inter alia*) one of Burney's footnotes, which took issue with a publication by Jackson.

141.   Nangle, *Monthly Review, First Series,* pp. ix-x.

142.   "Dr. Burney and the *Monthly Review,*" *Review of English Studies,* n.s., 14 (1963): 350-51.

143.   Ibid., p. 350; cf. Nangle, *Monthly Review, First Series,* pp. ix-x.

144.   Robberds, *Memoir of Taylor,* 1: 122-25.

145.   *Two Studies in Romantic Reviewing* (Salzburg, 1976), 1: 81; Alexander's rather brief discussion of "puffing" occupies pp. 78-82.

146.   For this review see chap. 2; see also Alexander's comments, *Two Studies,* 1: 142-45.

147.   See above, n. 50; no other payments are recorded. The *British Critic* must have been a profitable concern in 1812 despite the competition of the *Edinburgh* and *Quarterly,* for when Nares retired from the editorship he "could not afford to give away a property of so much value" as his share in the Review (Nichols, *Illustrations,* 7: 614).

148.   Technology was not adequately covered, and probably could not be by means of a Review; though in 1795 the *English* began a scientific section and changed its title to *The English Review of Literature, Science, Discoveries, Inventions, and Practical Controversies and Contests.* I suspect that some reviews of scientific publications in the *Analytical* were written by the inventor William Nicholson, who in 1797 founded the *Journal of Natural Philosophy, Chemistry, and*

the Arts. (See typescript of Henry Crabb Robinson's Diary in Dr. Williams's Library, MS. 5146, 2: 56-57.)

149.   There is evidence of the reprinting both of separate numbers and of complete volumes. Most early numbers of the *Monthly* now in the Leeds Library bear the words "The Second Edition" on the first page, under the title; those for November and December 1750 have "The Third Edition"; my own copy of the first number of the Second Series (January 1790) has "*Second Edition.*" Probably the separate numbers were reissued only during the first few months after publication, in some cases from standing type. But "human labour was cheap, and it was not worth while to lock up capital either by keeping type standing or by printing large editions requiring a heavy outlay on paper" (R. W. Chapman, "Authors and Booksellers," in *Johnson's England,* ed. A. S. Turberville [Oxford, 1933], 2: 329). The Leeds Library copy of vol. 4 of the *Monthly's* First Series has on the title page "The Second Edition" and the date 1759; my copy of vol. 65 has "*NEW EDITION, M,DCCC,IX*": these volumes were therefore reissued eight and twenty-eight years respectively after their first appearance. In January 1810 the *Monthly* announced that "all deficient numbers" had been reprinted and that "a few complete setts, from 1749 to the present time" were available (61: 112). Reprints were not always identical. In the British Museum (formerly George III's) copy of vol. 17 of the *Critical Review,* a passage in Dyer's review of Coleridge's *Poems on Various Subjects* reads as follows: "The liberty too taken by Mr. Coleridge of coining words, and the impetuosity of a most powerful imagination, hurry him sometimes into what his readers will call bombast" (p. 211). In the copies owned by London University Library, Sheffield University Library, and myself, the last three words become "may think exceptionable language." Though it is impossible to be certain which reading is the earlier, Coleridge had lately joined the reviewing staff of the *Critical,* and it may be that "bombast" was softened by editorial discretion. The "bombast" reading has kindly been confirmed for me by Mr. J. R. de J. Jackson, who follows it in his "Critical Heritage" volume.

150.   J. Green to Ralph Griffiths, Bodl. MS. Adds. C.89, f. 126r.

151.   Charles Knight gives the average number of books (excluding "pamphlets") published annually between 1750 and 1756 as 93; between 1792 and 1802 as 372 (*Shadows of the Old Booksellers*) [1865], p. 313).Robert D. Mayo estimates that in 1788 "the number of new books had increased by at least fifty per cent since 1769. The *Monthly* and *Critical* now noticed about 750 books annually, instead of five hundred and had augmented the number of their major reviews in about the same proportion" (*The English Novel in the Magazines, 1740-1815* [Evanston, Ill., and London, 1962], p. 204).

152.   J. H. Alexander finds that in the period 1800-1802 the *Monthly, Critical, British Critic,* and *Antijacobin Review* dealt with a total of 814 "literary" works, but that no Review came near to dealing with them all: the *Critical* had the highest score with 452. See "Literary Reviewing in Five British Periodicals, 1800-1808," Oxford D.Phil. thesis 1968, pp. 55-56; see also Mayo's estimates given in the preceding note.

153.   Bodl. MS. Adds. C.89, f. 75r.

154.   Ibid., f. 93.

155.   *Collected Letters of Samuel Taylor Coleridge,* ed. E. L. Griggs (Oxford, 1956-71), 1: 318 (16 March 1797).

156.   *New Letters of Robert Southey,* ed. Kenneth Curry (New York and London, 1965), 1: 157 (24 December 1797).

157.   Ibid., p. 308 (from a letter in dog-Latin to Bedford, 10 February 1803). "I have God only knows how many books to review! big books, middle-sized books, little books, books of every kind, which must all be killed off without delay."

158.   "It brought me from 50 to 100£ yearly, a very acceptable addition to my very straitened income" (ibid., p. 523).

159.   See e.g. Bodl. MS. Adds. C.89, f. 80^v. Enfield suggests on one occasion that an article should be promoted to "the upper House" (ibid., f.99^r).

160.   Southey's *Joan of Arc* took the leading place in the *Monthly* for April 1796 (19: 361-68); Ann Radcliffe's *Mysteries of Udolpho* in the *Critical* for August 1794 (11: 361-72).

161.   In the *Analytical* the short notices were not put into a separate section; each number was arranged by subject, and within each subject the short notices followed the long ones.

162.   The regular rate for the *Monthly* was two guineas, rising to three or four for special services (see Percival Stockdale, *Memoirs*, 2: 57-8; Robberds, *Memoir of Taylor*, 1: 130-32; Bodl. MS. Adds. C.89, f. 369^r). The *Critical* paid Stockdale two guineas in 1770, but paid Southey three guineas from 1797 to 1804 (*New Letters*, 1: 523). The *English* paid two guineas both to Godwin (see above, n. 27) and to Whitaker (see Richard Polwhele, *Biographical Sketches*, 3: 113). Later the *British Critic* offered Whitaker four guineas (ibid., pp. 113, 120).

163.   *The Adventures of Hugh Trevor*, 3 (1794): 184-85.

164.   See above, pp. 84-85.

165.   *The Watchman*, ed. Lewis Patton (Princeton, N.J., and London, 1970), p. 15 (1 March 1796).

166.   See John Clive, *Scotch Reviewers* (Cambridge, Mass., 1957), pp. 33-34; cf. A. S. Collins, *The Profession of Letters . . . 1780-1832* (1928), p. 209.

167.   See *New Letters of Southey*, 1: 524.

168.   See Polwhele, *Biographical Sketches*, 3: 113, 120-21.

169.   Quoted by Clive, *Scotch Reviewers*, p. 35.

170.   Ibid., pp. 32-33. The original scheme was for "all gentlemen, and no pay," and the publisher, Constable, was to absorb both risks and profits.

171.   See John O. Hayden, *The Romantic Reviewers, 1802-1824* (1969), pp. 270-98, and the "Critical Heritage" volumes for individual authors.

172.   See Hayden, *Romantic Reviewers*, p. 257.

173.   Ibid., p. 7.

174.   Robberds, *Memoir of Taylor*, 1: 126-7.

175.   *Monthly Review*, 34 (1802): 126; quoted by Clive in *Scotch Reviewers*, p. 39.

176.   "Dr. Shaw, we hope, will pardon us if, for the sake of the ladies and such of the gentlemen as love plain English, we again suggest that, in his future volumes, he should abstain from a few newly created or crabbed terms [footnote: Such as *tardity, torvity, sulcus, dimidiated, verincose* and *subverincose, comissure, decussations, latibulize, subpandiniform,* &c.], which disfigure the purity and terseness of his style."

177.   E.g., that of John Haygarth's *Letter to Dr. Percival on the Prevention of Infectious Fevers* (1801), in *Edinburgh Review* 1 (1802): 245-52; the final paragraph is very like that cited by Clive. Cf. also the article on W. Craven's *Discourses on the*

Jewish and Christian Dispensations (1802), in *Edinburgh Review* 2 (1803): 437-43.

178.   Nangle, *Monthly Review, Second Series*, p. 47.

179.   A page of criticism has been counted as 400 words, a page of quotation (set in slightly smaller type) as 500. The length of poetry reviews has been shown as though quoted lines of verse filled the printer's measure. Reviews of Ellis's *Specimens*, Anderson's *British Poets*, Scott's *Border Minstrelsy* and Burns's *Collected Works* have been excluded from the poetry tables, since they were dealt with on the scale accorded to scholarly publications. Short summarising passages have sometimes been allowed to count with the criticism when inextricably entwined.

180.   Comparisons are difficult to make because of the greater number of new publications and the very different pattern of journalism. But in an ordinary week, among periodicals combining literary pretensions with a fairly wide circulation, the *Observer* reviewed three novels in one article of fewer than 1,000 words (30 August 1970); *T.L.S.* reviewed five novels at an average length of 320 words, the longest review being 480 words (28 August 1970, p. 941); the *London Magazine* reviewed eleven volumes of verse at an average length of 420 words and five novels at an average length of 320 words (July-August 1970, 10: 154-90); *Encounter* discussed four works by John Fowles in an article of 1,500 words (August 1970, 35: 64-67). The previous number of *T.L.S.* to review new poetry dealt with four volumes in one article of 900 words (21 August 1970, p. 916).

181.   Comparison may be made with another modest volume published in the provinces, Philip Larkin's *The Less Deceived* (Hull, 1955). The *T.L.S.* recognised the "quite exceptional importance" of this book but reviewed it in fewer than 300 words (16 December 1955, p. 762). In the *London Magazine* Roy Fuller gave it 270 words plus two quotations (April 1956, 3: 84-88). In December 1956, when *The Less Deceived* was in its third edition, *Encounter* reviewed it together with four other volumes in an article of 2,400 words (7: 74-78).

182.   See *Boswell's Life of Johnson*, ed. G. B. Hill, rev. L. F. Powell (Oxford, 1934-50), 4: 214; also a letter of 1793 in Bodl. MS. Adds. C.89, f. 369[r]. Since extracts were set in smaller type the rate of payment per thousand words would in effect have been slightly lower, but not enough to affect the point here discussed.

183.   Bodl. MS. Adds. C.90, f. 7[v].

184.   Ibid., f. 45[r]. Extracts were not always copied out by hand, as Badcock implies, but were sometimes set up from the books under review; see letters of 1791 and 1793 in Bodl. MS. Adds. C.89, ff. 69, 299[r].

185.   Ibid., f. 294[r].

186.   Ibid., f. 97[v].

187.   *British Critic* 15 (1800): 48.

188.   *The Life and Correspondence of Robert Southey*, ed. Cuthbert Southey (1849-50), 2: 24. The review is discussed in chap. 2.

189.   *The Letters of Charles and Mary Anne Lamb*, ed. Edwin W. Marrs, Jr. (Ithaca and London, 1975-) 1: 143.

190.   Cf. Coleridge, *Biographia Literaria*, ed. J. Shawcross (1907), 1: 43-4; 2: 90-91.

191.   Bodl. MS. Adds. C.90, f. 100[v].

192.   *Boswell's Life of Johnson*, 4: 214-15.

193.   Robberds, *Memoir of Taylor*, 1: 384. Cf. *Biographia Literaria*, 2: 85 for the desirability of "written canons of criticism" in reviewing.

194. *A propos* of some unidentified speculations by Taylor in the *Monthly Review,* George Griffiths wrote: "I must beg you [*sic*] to advert to the difference between the 'Monthly Review' and a Magazine, as to the propriety of throwing out such adventurous conjectures. The Review ought to be always consistent; and one writer should not advance opinions on established points which he may deem just, but which others are not prepared to maintain, and may even be disposed to contradict; while in a Magazine there is no necessity for homogeneity, and each writer may *sport* what he pleases, without reference to other papers, past, present, or future" (Robberds, *Memoir of Taylor,* 2: 492).

195. For the importance attached to consistency see the previous note; see also MS. Adds. C.90, ff. 49^v, 71^v, 95^r; Robberds, *Memoir of Taylor,* 1: 135, 196, 492-93. That successive numbers of a Review should not contradict one another was not in itself an unreasonable doctrine, but could have a discouraging effect if pedantically applied, as in the above-quoted letter. Nineteenth-century practice seems to have allowed more freedom in matters not essential to the "character" of the Review.

196. These reviews are more fully discussed in chap. 2. Ian Jack notes that "since [the nineteenth-century reviewer] had a great deal of space at his disposal, he had every opportunity to summarize the book as well as developing his own views on the subject with which it dealt" (*English Literature 1815-1832* [Oxford, 1963], pp. 11-12). This sentence well illustrates the eventual reversal of eighteenth-century reviewing priorities.

197. Clive, *Scotch Reviewers,* p. 37.

198. "It was the task of the critic to judge poetry by its successful appeal to universal associations, but there was no reason at all why the critic himself should not follow his individual bent in his personal tastes. Thus there was no real contradiction in Jeffrey's shedding tears over Wordsworth's poems, and at the same time condemning and ridiculing him in the *Review*" (ibid., p. 160). To say the least, this use of a double standard gave Jeffrey great advantages when the *Edinburgh* was in need of "a little pointed criticism." See ibid., pp. 153-65, for a survey of the controversy about Jeffrey's attitude to the "Lake School" and some interesting new material.

199. For reviews of Wordsworth and for some of the hostile references to him see *Edinburgh Review* 1 (1802): 63-68; 11 (1807): 214-31 (on *Poems in Two Volumes*); 12 (1808): 132-37; 13 (1809): 276; 14 (1809): 1-3; 19 (1812): 373-75; 24 (1814): 1-30 (on *The Excursion—* "This will never do"); 25 (1815): 355-63 (on *The White Doe of Rylstone—* "the very worst poem we ever saw imprinted in a quarto volume"); 37 (1822): 449-56 (on *Memorials of a Tour*) "The Lake School of Poetry, we think, is now pretty nearly extinct"). For Coleridge see 2 (1803): 96; 12 (1808): 133; 27 (1816): 58-67 (on the *Christabel* volume— "the thing now before us, is utterly destitute of value. It exhibits from beginning to end not a ray of genius"); 27 (1816): 444-59 (on *The Statesman's Manual*); 28 (1817): 488-515 (on *Biographia Literaria*). J. R. de J. Jackson, who makes generous allowances for the problems of reviewers, comments that "the treatment of Coleridge's writing during this period [1816-17] is one of the sorriest performances in the history of reviewing" (*Coleridge: The Critical Heritage* [1970], p. 9, q.v. also for reprints of the Coleridge reviews).

200. The *Quarterly* published a favourable review of *The Excursion* in 1814 (12: 100-111) and a mixed review of *The White Doe* in 1815 (14: 201-25). To Coleridge it gave a favourable review of *Remorse* in 1814 (11: 177-90) and two ambiguous references in 1816 (15: 473; 16: 204). No attempt was made to defend Coleridge from the attacks of 1816 and 1817.

201.   *Quarterly Review* 19 (1818): 204-8 (on *Endymion;* the *Quarterly* ignored the 1820 volume); *Edinburgh Review*, 34 (1820): 203-13. Jeffrey's verdict on *Endymion*—"at least as full of genius as absurdity"—is defensible. The chief defect of his article is that it deals almost entirely with *Endymion*, called "by much the most considerable of [Keats's] poems." His only comment on the great 1820 volume, also supposedly under review, is to advise Keats not to go on with *Hyperion*. G. M. Matthews suggests that Jeffrey wrote a fairly favourable account of *Endymion*, "lost his nerve in the face of all the mockery," and then two years later made a superficial attempt to make his original draft do for both volumes (*Keats: the Critical Heritage* [1971], pp. 26-27). For discussions and reprints see, besides Matthews's volume, John O. Hayden, *The Romantic Reviewers, 1802-1824* (1969) and *Romantic Bards and British Reviewers* (1971); Theodore Redpath, *The Young Romantics and Critical Opinion, 1807-1824* (1973).

202.   *Quarterly Review* 14 (1815): 188-201 (by Scott); 24 (1821): 352-76 (by Whately). Both articles are reprinted in B.C. Southam, *Jane Austen: The Critical Heritage* (1968).

203.   *Quarterly Review* 21 (1819): 460-71 (on *Laon and Cythna* and *The Revolt of Islam*); *Quarterly Review* 26 (1821): 168-80 (on *Prometheus Unbound*); *Edinburgh Review* 40 (1824): 494-514 (a preponderantly unfavourable review by Hazlitt of the *Posthumous Poems*). Shelley's other publications, including *Alastor*, *Adonais* and *Hellas*, went unreviewed by these journals. For reprints see *Shelley: the Critical Heritage*, by James E. Barcus (1975).

204.   *Contemporary Reviews of Romantic Poetry*, ed. John Wain (1953), p. 35.

205.   *The Romantic Reviewers*, p. 257. Hayden singles out for praise the *British Critic*, the *Champion*, the *Eclectic Review*, the *Edinburgh Magazine*, and the *Monthly Review*. But in terms of circulation and influence these periodicals were very much overshadowed by the giant quarterlies. By 1818 both the *Edinburgh Review* and the *Quarterly Review* had circulations of about 13,000; whereas that of the *Champion* varied between 475 and 1,225, and the figures for the *Eclectic Review* and *Edinburgh Magazine* are estimated at 3,000 and "under 2,500." Ibid., pp. 27, 69 n. 4, 49, 61; Clive, *Scotch Reviewers*, p. 134. No contemporary estimate is known for the *Monthly Review* and *British Critic;* in 1797 their circulations are estimated at 5,000 and 3,500. *Blackwood's Magazine*, founded in 1817, soon achieved great notoriety and a circulation of 6,000. Hayden finds that *Blackwood's* is "without question the worst of the critical organs; it had a record of critical irresponsibility, political bias, and personal slander" (p. 258; cf. p. 61).

206.   As Hayden notes, the most complete reversal of opinion occurs in the *British Critic*; with the favourable reviews of *Lyrical Ballads* discussed in chapter 2 above, cf. *British Critic* 33 (1809): 298-99. Hayden describes the critical reception of Wordsworth's *Poems in Two Volumes* as "one of the most disgraceful in the annals of reviewing" (*Romantic Reviewers*, p. 81).

207.   William Hazlitt, *Table-Talk*, Essay 22, in *Complete Works*, ed. P. P. Howe (1930-34), 8: 216-17.

Chapter 2: The Reviewing of Poetry

1.   For some examples and a discussion see Edward Niles Hooker, "The Reviewers and the New Trends in Poetry, 1754-1770," *Modern Language Notes* 51 (1936):

207-14; idem, "The Reviewers and the New Criticism, 1754-1770," *Philological Quarterly* 13 (1934): 189-202.

2.   *Biographia Literaria,* ed. John Shawcross (1907), 1: 50-52. Though Coleridge begins by postulating "the omission of less than an hundred lines," he apparently goes on to describe the kind of reception that he feels unprejudiced readers would have given to the entire work. The injustice and irrelevance of the Review attacks is of course a main theme of the *Biographia.*

3.   See Joseph Warton, *Essay on the Writings and Genius of Pope* (1756), p. 202. For a good discussion of critical vocabulary in the Reviews see J. H. Alexander, *Two Studies in Romantic Reviewing* (Salzburg, 1976), 1: 55-75.

4.   See Earl Reeves Wasserman, "Elizabethan Poetry in the Eighteenth Century," *Illinois Studies in Language and Literature* 32 (1947): 7-291, esp. p. 239 et seq.; idem, "The Scholarly Origin of the Elizabethan Revival," ELH 4 (1937): 213-43.

5.   A set of Anderson was in Wordsworth's possession in 1800, when the second edition of *Lyrical Ballads* was being prepared; see Mary Moorman, *William Wordsworth* (1957-65), 1: 515. From it he "became first familiar with Chaucer," Drayton, Daniel, and other pre-Restoration poets.

6.   References to all reviews quoted or discussed in these chapters will be found in Appendix A.

7.   Identified by Jacob Zeitlin in "Southey's Contributions to the *Critical Review*," Notes & Queries, ser. 12, 4 (1918): 94-95. Southey later reworked and amplified this article to provide an introduction to his *Specimens of the Later English Poets* (1807).

8.   Including Wyatt, "My lute awake"; Surrey, "Give place, ye lovers here before"; several poems from *Astrophil and Stella;* Lyly, "Cupid and Campaspe"; Marlowe, "The Passionate Shepherd to his Mistress"; Ralegh, "The Nymph's Reply" and "The Soul's Errand"; Donne, "Go, and catch a falling star"; Beaumont and Fletcher, "Take, oh take those lips away"; Shirley, "Death's Final Conquest"; Lovelace, "To Lucasta, going to the Wars" and "To Althea, from Prison"; Suckling, "Why so pale and wan, fond lover?"; Herbert, "Life."

9.   See Zeitlin, "Southey's Contributions," pp. 122-23.

10.   *D.N.B.* (C. W. Sutton); see also Appendix B.

11.   *Border Minstrelsy,* 1: cxvi-cxvii; cf. Percy's apologetic Preface to his *Reliques.*

12.   In his edition of *The Letters of Sir Walter Scott* (1932-37), H. J. C. Grierson mentions a letter from Ellis to Scott of 29 May 1802 that tells of his reviewing Scott and Leyden in the *British Critic* (1: 185 n. 1). No biographer says exactly when the two men first met; they may not have done so till later. Scott had sent Ellis the first two volumes of *Border Minstrelsy* early in 1802, and on 5 March Ellis had written back: "I have been devouring them, not as a pig does a parcel of grains . . . , but as a schoolboy does a piece of gingerbread; nibbling a little bit here, and a little bit there" (John Gibson Lockhart, *Memoirs of Sir Walter Scott* [Edinburgh, 1837-38], 1: 344).

13.   The method, style, and opinions of this review are very much those of Taylor, though according to his biographer Taylor's first articles in this journal appeared a month later. Taylor certainly reviewed Scott's edition of *Sir Tristrem* in the following year. See J. W. Robberds, *Memoir of . . . William Taylor* (1843), 2: 25-26, 38.

14.   See for example Robert Brittain, ed., *Poems by Christopher Smart* (Princeton, N.J., 1950), pp. 44-45; Christopher Devlin, *Poor Kit Smart* (1961), passim; Sophia Blaydes, *Christopher Smart as a Poet of his Time* (The Hague,

1966), pp. 20-23. Reviews of *A Song to David* were much more favourable than these accounts suggest and should be read in full; see *Monthly Review*, ser. 1, 28 (1763): 320-21 and *Critical Review*, ser. 1, 15 (1763): 324. It is true that the reviewers had heard that Smart was mad and found signs of madness in the poem. That makes it all the more creditable for Langhorne in the *Monthly* to have declared it, not "greatly irregular," but "irregularly great." For the hostilities that developed later between Smart and the reviewers, Smart must bear some of the blame. It is surprising that Sophia Blaydes does not mention any of the reviews (discussed in the text) of the 1791 volume, either in her survey of Smart's reputation or her bibliography (*Christopher Smart*, pp. 23-24, 181-82).

15.   For Burney's "views on the essential nature of poetry . . . with their emphasis on unfettered genius" see Roger Lonsdale, "Dr. Burney and the *Monthly Review*," part 2, *Review of English Studies* 15 (1964): 32-36. Earlier in this article Lonsdale quotes from a letter of Griffiths to Burney, 31 December 1791, discussing the review of Smart. The passage begins: "You have not only well supported our Credit, as to critical Taste, but you have done honour to the *Moral* Character of the M. R. by your generous treatment of the Singular Mortal . . . ."

16.   See passages quoted by Moira Dearnley, *The Poetry of Christopher Smart* (1969), pp. xvii-xviii. Mrs. Dearnley, who does not recognise the origin of these passages, justly remarks: "we have to keep reminding ourselves that he is not writing about the *Song to David.*" Burney, of course, knew that poem.

17.   For Moore's connection with the *English Review* see Samuel Smiles, *A Publisher and his Friends* (1891), 1: 12. Moore's early interest in Burns marks him out as the likely reviewer of the Kilmarnock volume. He had been sent the book late in 1786 by Mrs. Dunlap, who seems also to have sent MSS of poems intended for the Edinburgh edition. She forwarded Moore's MS criticisms to Burns on 30 December 1786, and the two men began a correspondence. In 1787 Moore presented a copy of the Kilmarnock volume to Dr. Currie, Burns's first editor and biographer. See *The Letters of Robert Burns*, ed. J. De Lancey Ferguson (Oxford, 1931), 1: 68-70; R. D. Thornton, *James Currie, the Entire Stranger, and Robert Burns* (Edinburgh and London, 1963), pp. 259-60.

18.   *Selections from the Correspondence of Robert Bloomfield*, ed. W. H. Hart (1870), p. 40. I have removed the semicolon that Hart prints after "intellects."

19.   On 3 May 1802 Bloomfield told his brother George: "Southey wrote the article respecting 'The Farmer's Boy,' which appeared in the 'Critical'; and most likely will have the same task as to the '[Rural] Tales' " (ibid., p. 23). Bloomfield may have had the information from Southey himself, for the two men met at about this time: see *Life and Correspondence of . . . Robert Southey*, ed. Charles Cuthbert Southey (1849-50), 2: 190.

20.   Southey wrote to Coleridge on 4 August 1802: "I have reviewed [Bloomfield's] Poems with the express object of serving him; because if his fame keeps up to another volume, he will have made money enough to support him comfortably in the country" *(Life and Correspondence*, 2: 190-91). Bloomfield knew "almost for a certainty" that this article was by Southey (*Selections from the Correspondence*, ed. Hart, p. 28).

21.   Capel Lofft, who edited both these publications of Bloomfield's, suggests in a note to *Rural Tales* that two of the verse stories have qualities in common with Dryden (p. 34).

22.   A fifth edition (1,000 copies) of *The Pleasures of Memory* appeared the year after publication, and by 1816 more than 23,000 copies had been printed (P.W.

Clayden, *The Early Life of Samuel Rogers* [1887], pp. 213-17). *The Pleasures of Hope* reached its seventh large edition in 1803 (*Life and Letters of Thomas Campbell*, ed. William Beattie [1849], 1: 265, 435). See also the "triangular *Gradus ad Parnassum*" drawn by Byron in his journal for 24 November 1813.

23.　Clayden, *Early Life of Samuel Rogers*, p. 235.

24.　Ibid., p. 212.

25.　Ibid., pp. 68-70.

26.　Beattie, *Life of Campbell*, 1: 187.

27.　Ernest de Selincourt, "Classicism and Romanticism in the Poetry of Walter Savage Landor," *Bibliothek Warburg: Vorträge 1930-1931* (Leipzig, 1932), p. 235.

28.　"Postscript to Gebir" (written 1800, but never published by Landor), *Works of Walter Savage Landor*, ed. T. E. Welby and S. Wheeler (1927-36), 13: 352. It is clear from the context that this is the "commendation" of the Reviews.

29.　He praised it enthusiastically to Cottle, Bedford, Taylor, Davy, and Anna Seward; some of his remarks are brought together by Malcolm Elwin in *Landor: a Replevin* (1958), p. 82.

30.　*Collected Letters of Coleridge*, ed. E. L. Griggs (Oxford, 1956-71), 1: 573. For the account of this review given by Southey to Landor in 1809 see *The Life and Correspondence of Robert Southey*, ed. C.C. Southey (1849-50), 3: 230.

31.　Yet this Review was published by the Rivingtons, who were responsible for the London sale of *Gebir*. See Elwin, *Landor*, p. 66.

32.　Strangely enough, it was Ferriar who had reviewed Pybus's poem *The Sovereign* (1800) in the *Monthly*, 33 (1800): 378-80. The passage in Landor's "Postscript" has been misunderstood to mean that he thought Pybus had reviewed *Gebir* (John Forster, *Walter Savage Landor* [1869], 1: 128; R. H. Super, *Walter Savage Landor* [1954], p. 518 n. 17). In fact Landor mentions Pybus only as an example of the kind of poet the *Monthly* admired.

33.　*Landor* (1902), p. 37.

34.　See for example the *Edinburgh Review*, 2 (1803): 462-76, where the *Odes of Anacreon* are said to be "calculated for a bagnio"; ibid., 8 (1806): 456-65, where the popularity of Moore's *Epistles, Odes, and Other Poems* is said to be "owing almost entirely to the seduction of the subjects on which it is employed"; *London Magazine* 9 (1824): 424-27 (an essay by George Darley claiming that the chief characteristic of modern poetry is its sensuality, and attacking Moore with others).

35.　Preface to *Poems of Thomas Little*.

36.　See Thomas Medwin, *The Life of Percy Bysshe Shelley*, ed. H. Buxton Forman (1913), p. 257.

37.　Howard M. Jones, *The Harp that Once—A Chronicle of the Life of Thomas Moore* (New York, 1937), p. 53.

38.　Francis Fawkes's translation of *The Works of Anacreon* (1760) was reprinted in 1789 and included in Anderson's *British Poets*.

39.　This review is attributed to Southey by Jacob Zeitlin, on the rather slender grounds that Southey also thought the work immoral (*Notes & Queries*, ser. 12, 4 [1918]: 123).

40.　See Ferriar's *Illustrations of Sterne* (1798), chap. 2.

41.　The four lines from Wordsworth's *Evening Walk* quoted by Holcroft in the *Monthly Review* are very much in the Della Cruscan manner. These poets made frequent use of metrically convenient Shakespearean epithets such as "paly" (= pale) and "foamy." "Paly," condemned by Pearne in his review of *The Laurel of Liberty*, occurs in Wordsworth's *Evening Walk* (1793 text, l. 335) and Coleridge's "Lines: On an Autumnal Evening" (1793 text, l. 31). Cf. Wordsworth's use of "sombrous" and "foamy" (*Evening Walk*, ll. 72, 119, 139) and the neologisms quoted by Coleridge's early reviewers. Rogers was temporarily on the fringe of the group, and his much-anthologised "On a Tear" appeared in *The Poetry of the World* (1791); the *Monthly* reviewer, Moody, quoted it in full. Hazlitt calls *The Pleasures of Memory* "a more minute and inoffensive species of the Della Cruscan" kind of poetry, and regards Campbell's *Pleasures of Hope* as being "of the same school" ("On the Living Poets"). Hazlitt also describes a passage from Moore's *Lalla Rookh* as "the very perfection of Della Cruscan sentiment" ("Mr. T. Moore — Mr. Leigh Hunt"). The minor writers connected with this group were numerous, and though Wordsworth does not specify them, the Della Cruscans and their followers are clearly among the "many modern writers" whose phraseology he attacks in the Preface to *Lyrical Ballads*.

42.   According to Roy Benjamin Clark the Della Cruscans had ceased to function as a group before the *Baviad* appeared (*William Gifford* [New York, 1930], chap. 2).

43.   In his own set of the *Monthly Review* (now in the Bodleian Library) Griffiths has struck out the word "agreeably."

44.   On 11 December 1790 Pearne sent this review with others to Griffiths and wrote: "The two poets Geddes and Merry will not *thank* me for what I have said of them. It is well if the latter does not abuse me. And yet I have been, in my own opinion, very lenient; whatever he may think. Had it not been for the sake of *consistency*, I should not have given him the praise I have done. My conscience smites me when I read it, for being too partial. However, it is my wish always to lean to this side. In the present instance I could have no possible motive to censure, beyond what I saw in the poem itself, for I know nothing of the author but what the papers have told me; and they are all panegyric. As to his poetry, I never read a line of it before you sent this, which I took up prejudiced in its favour on account of the subject. But now, having gone through it, I am forced to say, in Mr. Merry's own words: 'Amidst the glitter nothing I descry.' . . . Surely the praise bestowed upon Mr. Merry in the papers must be *puff*, manufactured by himself or his friends. If so, it becomes the more necessary to hold the mirror up to him a little; both for his own sake, and for that of the public." On 4 January 1791 Pearne wrote again: "What you said of Merry's poem in your letter gave me pleasure. Whatever merit he can claim for the goodness of his intention, I was as ready to allow him as you can be. The subject prepossessed me in his favour. In addition to this, I was desirous of harmonising, as much as possible, with the critique of his former productions. It therefore gave me pleasure to hear that you had found, what I *wished* to find, in the poem; some good lines: and I shall be happy to see the expostulation with Burke made part of the article. I recollect I was in doubt myself whether I should introduce these lines, or those which I quoted about the Bastile . . . . As to any other alterations, there is not the smallest necessity to send the paper back. I give you full powers to change whatever you think fit; as, without the least hesitation, I am sure that I could trust your judgment and experience in matters that I should think of more importance than the present. When I dismissed this critique from my mind, I felt that I had acted more like a friend than like a rigid judge. Many faults which disgusted me in the reading I omitted to notice. And there was not a single passage which, *in my heart*, I thought above a very humble mediocrity. I cannot think, with

you, that he is the reigning favorite with the public; unless by the *public* we are to understand what Sterne says is to be understood by the word *world*, when he describes the midwife's fame as being celebrated throughout the world; i.e. a small circle of about a mile or two in circumference, including her own particular friends and acquaintance. To *this* public, I have no doubt, is owing all that we read in one or two papers about Mr. Merry's towering and unrivalled genius. The rogues betray the cheat by overdoing the matter. They beplaster and *begem* their hero too unmercifully. Mr. Merry's poem is of that kind, I admit, which will deceive those who do not search too nicely for a *meaning*. It sounds prettily; and is, in parts, very carefully and mystically wrapped up in the gaudy envelope of poetical patchery. But the discerning public cannot be imposed upon by this: especially as Mr. M. is not only not absolutely good, but, I think, not even comparatively so; for surely there are many of his contemporaries who are very far his superiors as poets." (Bodl. MS. Adds. C.89, ff. 294, 296-97.)

45. Clark, *William Gifford,* p. 72. Clark does not quote the review.

46. For reprints (not always accurate) or summaries of the Wordsworth reviews discussed here, see Elsie Smith, *An Estimate of William Wordsworth by his Contemporaries, 1793-1822* (Oxford, 1932). For some early Coleridge reviews see *Coleridge: the Critical Heritage,* ed. J. R. de J. Jackson (1970), and the apparatus to the *Collected Works* (Princeton, N. J., and London, 1970-). Some reviews of both poets are included in *Romantic Bards and British Reviewers,* ed. John O. Hayden (1971).

47. Bateson, *Wordsworth: a Re-Interpretation* (1954), p. 17.

48. William Smith Ward, "The Criticism of Poetry in British Periodicals, 1798-1820," Ph.D. diss., Duke University, 1943 (available on Microcard), p. 149.

49. See n. 41 to this chapter.

50. Holcroft was himself a poet, though better known for his novels and plays: he wrote *Elegies* (1777), *Human Happiness . . . a Poem* (1783), *Tales in Verse* (1806), a verse translation of Goethe's *Herman and Dorothea* (1801), and the libretti of several operas.

51. *The Letters of William and Dorothy Wordsworth: the Early Years,* ed. E. de Selincourt, rev. C. Shaver (Oxford, 1967), p. 120.

52. *Biographia Literaria,* ed. John Shawcross (1907), 1: 56.

53. Dyer's work for the *Critical* and *Analytical* at this period is acknowledged in his *Privileges of the University of Cambridge,* (2d ed. [1824] 2: [206]). Coleridge discovered at once that "Dyer . . . is a Reviewer." Dyer saw *The Fall of Robespierre* in MS and liked Act 1 "hugely," but later suggested alterations in Acts 2 and 3 (which were by Southey). He tried to persuade several London booksellers to publish it, and when it was finally brought out by Flower at Cambridge he undertook to dispose of fifty (later twenty-five) copies. After being so closely involved with *Robespierre* it is almost inevitable that he should have asked to review it, or "volunteered" an article. The *Critical* review shows inside information ("we have been informed, that the work before us was the production of a few hours exercise") and the same preference as Dyer for Act 1. See *Collected Letters of Coleridge,* ed. Griggs, 1: 97-101, 117; and below, nn. 57, 61.

54. For possible contacts with Aikin see *The Notebooks of Samuel Taylor Coleridge,* ed. Kathleen Coburn (1957-), 1: 174 (16) n.; for meetings with Mrs. Barbauld see *Collected Letters,* 1: 341n., 420. The reviews in the *Analytical* are discussed below, nn. 56, 76.

55.   See *Collected Letters*, 1: 201 and below, n. 77.

56.   The *Analytical* review of *Robespierre* is signed "D.M."; for evidence that this may be Aikin's signature, see Appendix B.

57.   Texts of or excerpts from these reviews are given in *Coleridge: the Critical Heritage*, pp. 24-29, and *Collected Works*, vol. 1 (1971), pp. 2, 23, 278-79. The single review given to *A Moral and Political Lecture* as a separate work appeared in the *Critical* for April 1795 (13: 455). It seems likely to have been written by Dyer, who had been offered "as many Copies as you may choose to give away" and had commented on the work by 10 March, when Coleridge wrote: "I did not expect, that you would have thought so well of my political lecture" (*Collected Letters*, 1: 152, 155).

58.   *Collected Letters*, 1: 197.

59.   *Biographia Literaria*, 1: 2.

60.   Coleridge said later that the sonnet "Not, Stanhope! with the Patriot's doubtful name" was a parody, and had been included in the volume without his consent because the "fool of a printer" wished to send a copy to Stanhope (Joseph Cottle, *Reminiscences of Coleridge and Southey* [1847], p. 111). This not entirely convincing claim is discussed by Carl R. Woodring in *Politics in the Poetry of Coleridge* (Madison, Wis., 1961), pp. 108-10.

61.   Lamb refers to the work Coleridge has on hand for the *Critical* in a letter of 9 June 1796. On 6 July, discussing the reception of *Poems on Various Subjects*, he wrote: "The Monthly Reviewers have made indeed a large article of it & done you justice. The Critical have in their wisdom selected not the very best specimens, & notice not, except as one name on the muster role, the 'Religious Musings.' I suspect Master Dyer to have been the writer of that article, as the Substance of it was the very remarks & the very language he used to me one day." The *Critical* comment on the metre of "Chatterton" agrees with Dyer's views, as reported by Lamb in 1798: "George could not comprehend how that could be poetry, which did not go upon ten feet, as George & his predecessors had taught it to do." (*The Letters of Charles and Mary Anne Lamb*, ed. Edwin W. Marrs, Jr. [Ithaca, N.Y., and London, 1975-], 1: 22, 41, 151.)

62.   For "will call bombast" some copies read "may think exceptionable language," probably a later softening by either Dyer or his editor; see n.149 to chap. 1.

63.   This review is not included in the "Critical Heritage" volume; Shawcross also seems to have overlooked it when he wrote that "the critic of the *Analytical Review* was apparently the only one who commented on the 'compound epithets' " (*Biographia Literaria*, 1: 204).

64.   *Collected Letters*, 1: 224. This and other passages make it hard to agree with J. R. de J. Jackson's description of Coleridge's attitude to the reviews as "good-humoured indifference" (*Coleridge: the Critical Heritage*, p. 3).

65.   *Collected Letters*, 1: 227.

66.   Ibid., 1: 207.

67.   See *Poetical Works*, ed. E. H. Coleridge (1912), 1: 112. Doubts about *unshudder'd* and *unaghasted* may have occurred to Coleridge and Dyer independently. But it is possible either that Coleridge himself drew Dyer's attention to the faults of this passage, or that by 5 May he had been given a foretaste of Dyer's criticism. The *English* reviewer was on the watch for false diction and could hardly have missed these examples, even if the *Critical* had not pointed them out.

68. Quoted in a brief review of the second edition in the *Critical*, 23 (1798): 266-68.

69. See *Collected Letters*, 1: 288-89.

70. Jackson is mistaken in attributing this review to Alexander Hamilton (*Coleridge: the Critical Heritage*, p. 39). Hamilton wrote the article that holds a corresponding place in the previous volume: see Nangle, *Monthly Review, Second Series*, p. 248, entries 5085, 5089.

71. "Marge" (l. 144) disappeared in a revision of 1797; "a bowed mind" (l. 6) was tamed to "a submitted mind" in 1803, but restored in 1834; "skirts" (l. 7) became "train" in *Sybilline Leaves*. See *Poetical Works*, 1: 160-68.

72. *Coleridge* (1953), p. 69.

73. Ibid., p. 78.

74. A phrase used by John Danby in comparing the structure of "Tintern Abbey" and "Frost at Midnight" (*The Simple Wordsworth* [1960], pp. 91-97).

75. Coleridge wrote in the Coleorton copy of the quarto edition: "Southey in a review made some (me judice) *unfounded* objections to this last Stanza — as if I had confounded moral with political Freedom" (quoted by Woodring, *Politics in the Poetry of Coleridge*, p. 185). The only Review that raised such objections was the *Critical*. Southey had been a regular contributor to that journal since the latter end of 1797; he had already reviewed *Lyrical Ballads*, and would therefore have been the likeliest person to be sent Coleridge's new poems. But it is possible that Coleridge inferred Southey's authorship from these same facts.

76. This conjecture is based on the signature of the article, "D.M.S." John Aikin's signature is likely to have been "D.M." (see Appendix B). A number of three-letter signatures beginning "D.M." appear in the *Analytical* in 1798, and my guess is that Aikin was getting help from his large literary family. "D.M.S." may then stand for "Doctor of Medicine's Sister" (Mrs. Barbauld), and "D.M.D." for "Doctor of Medicine's Daughter" (Lucy Aikin). Cf. the signatures of William Turner, who wrote in Johnson's *Theological Repository* as "Vigilius"; his son, who wrote in the *Analytical* and other periodicals as "V.F." (Vigilii Filius); and his grandson, who contributed to the *Monthly Repository* and other journals as "V.N." (Vigilii Nepos). See *Christian Reformer*, n.s., 10 (1854): 141; 15 (1859): 461.

77. The evidence is as follows. (1) Coleridge, who was in correspondence with Wrangham, told Cottle in 1796 that Wrangham wrote for the *British Critic* (*Collected Letters*, 1: 201). (2) Earlier reviews in that journal seem too brief to be by someone personally interested in Coleridge, but the notice of *Frost at Midnight* is very much what might be expected from "an admirer of me & a *pitier* of my principles." (3) The review of *Lyrical Ballads* that appeared in the *British Critic* four months later is the only one to name Coleridge as one of the authors.

78. When annotating the Coleorton copy (see above, n. 75), Coleridge gave this answer: "Surely the Object of the Stanza is to shew, that true political Freedom can only arise out of moral Freedom — what indeed is it but a Dilatation of those *golden* Lines of Milton —

> 'Licence they mean, when they cry — Liberty!
> For who loves that must first be wise & good.

79. *Coleridge*, p. 82.

80. E.g. *Oxford Companion to English Literature* (rev. 1967), p. 498.

81.   *Lectures on the English Poets*, no. 8: "On the Living Poets"; cf. "Mr. Jeffrey," in *The Spirit of the Age.*

82.   See T. M. Raysor, "The Establishment of Wordsworth's Reputation," *Journal of English and Germanic Philology* 54 (1955): 61-71.

83.   Ibid., p. 71; William Smith Ward, "Wordsworth, the 'Lake' Poets, and their Contemporary Magazine Critics," *Studies in Philology* 42 (1945): 87-8.

84.   For Southey's authorship see *New Letters of Robert Southey,* ed. Kenneth Curry (1965), 1: 176-77.

85.   Roger Lonsdale writes that Wordsworth "must eventually have read Burney's article and, since no other reviewer made the same point, it must have been in direct refutation of it that he devoted a large part of the famous Preface . . . to the argument that 'there neither is nor can be' any 'essential difference between the language of prose and metrical composition' " ("Dr. Burney and the *Monthly Review,*" pt. 2, *Review of English Studies* 15 [1964]: 35). I would not go so far as this, but it seems likely enough that Wordsworth read and noted the review.

86.   In *An Estimate of William Wordsworth* Elsie Smith attributes this review to Wrangham; for the evidence see n. 77 to this chapter.

87.   Coleridge makes the same criticism in *Biographia Literaria,* 2: 36.

88.   Lamb wrote to Southey on 8 November 1798: "If you wrote that review in 'Crit. Rev.,' I am sorry you are so sparing of praise to the 'Ancient Marinere;'—so far from calling it, as you do, with some wit, but more severity, 'A Dutch Attempt,' &c., I call it a right English attempt, and a successful one, to dethrone German sublimity." (*The Letters of Charles and Mary Anne Lamb,* ed. Edwin W. Marrs, Jr. [Ithaca, N.Y., and London, 1975-], 1:142.) In May 1798 Southey had paid a visit to William Taylor, *Monthly* reviewer and translator of Bürger's "Lenore" and other pieces of "German sublimity."

89.   See R. S. Woof, "John Stoddart, 'Michael' and *Lyrical Ballads,*" *Ariel* 1, no. 2 (April 1970): 7-22.

90.   Coleridge admitted to Southey in 1802 that the second half of Wordsworth's Preface was "obscure beyond any necessity" (*Collected Letters,* 2: 830).

91.   In Plate I of Hogarth's *Analysis of Beauty* (1753) a dancing-master, fully dressed, bewigged, and upright, is seen trying to correct the posture of a naked piece of classical sculpture, the Vatican Antinous.

92.   Hayden, *Romantic Reviewers, 1802-1824,* p. 79.

93.   See his review of Anderson's *British Poets,* quoted above, p. 52.

94.   Jack Simmons, *Southey* (1945), p. 77.

95.   See *New Letters,* 1: 158.

96.   Southey believed that the second of the "Nehemiah Higginbottom" sonnets, "To Simplicity," was meant in ridicule of himself. For Coleridge's denial see *Collected Letters,* 1: 358-59.

97.   *The Letters of Charles and Mary Anne Lamb,* 1: 142-43, 266. Lamb rebuked Southey for his choice of a specimen: "You have selected a passage fertile in unmeaning miracles, but have passed by fifty passages as miraculous as the miracles they celebrate. . . . But you allow some elaborate beauties—you should have extracted 'em."

98.   *New Letters,* 1: 176-77.

99.   Wordsworth wrote: "Southey's review I have seen. He knew that I published those poems for money and money alone. He knew that money was of importance

to me. If he could not conscientiously have spoken differently of the volume, he ought to have declined the task of reviewing it. The bulk of the poems he has described as destitute of merit. Am I recompensed for this by vague praises of my talents?" (To Cottle, 1799, in *Letters of William and Dorothy Wordsworth: The Early Years*, ed. E. de Selincourt, rev. C. L. Shaver [Oxford, 1967], pp. 267-68.) The dogmatic tone of Southey's adverse criticism is offensive, but it is difficult to accept Wordsworth's view that he was not entitled to write anything but a puff.

100. "Dr. Burney and the *Monthly Review,*" pt. 2, p. 36.

101. Like most articles published in the *Antijacobin Review,* the account of *Lyrical Ballads* (1798) published in April 1800 is of poor literary quality; but since it is wholly favourable it may serve as a political clearance certificate. "It has genius, taste, elegance, wit, and imagery of the most beautiful kind. 'The ancyent Marinere' is an admirable 'imitation of the style as well as the spirit of the elder poets.' 'The foster Mothers Tale' is pathetic, and pleasing in the extreme — 'Simon Lee the old Huntsman' — 'The idiot Boy,' and the Tale of 'Goody Blake, and Harry Gill' are all beautiful in their kind; indeed the whole volume convinces us that the author possesses a mind at once classic and accomplished, and we, with pleasure, recommend it to the notice of our readers as a production of no ordinary merit" (5: 434). The reviewer was William Heath.

102. References to these reviews are given in Appendix A.

103. For references see Appendix A. All reviews except that in the *British Critic* are reprinted by Lionel Madden in *Robert Southey: The Critical Heritage* (1972).

104. Preface of 1837 to *Joan of Arc,* in vol. 1 of Southey's *Poetical Works, Collected by Himself.*

105. For references see Appendix A.

106. See *New Letters,* 1: 128 for contact with Aikin by May 1797; ibid., 1: 157 for his engagement with the *Critical* shortly before 24 December 1797.

107. Madden reprints the *Monthly* review of *Poems* (1797), and the reviews of *Thalaba* in the *British Critic, Critical,* and *Edinburgh.* The *Edinburgh* review has often been reprinted.

108. George Ellis, who by 1802 was reviewing for the *British Critic* (see n. 12 to this chapter) had written for the *Anti-Jacobin.* "The Soldier's Friend" has been attributed to him, but claimed by Canning and Frere (*Poetry of the Anti-Jacobin,* ed. C. Edmonds [1890], p. 20).

109. See Mary Jacobus, "Southey's Debt to *Lyrical Ballads* (1798)," *Review of English Studies* 22 (1971): 20-36. Miss Jacobus concludes that Southey "borrowed from the very poems he attacked," and that "Southey's adaptations deliberately restore to poems from *Lyrical Ballads* the popular appeal which Wordsworth and Coleridge had ignored."

110. *New Letters,* 1: 196.

111. Cf. *Biographia Literaria,* 2: 62-63 n., where Coleridge applies this method to a passage from Wordsworth's "The Brothers."

112. *Cheap Repository Tracts* (1795-98) were published and in part written by Hannah More.

113. E.g. "The Bibliomania, an Epistle to Richard Heber, Esq.," included in Ferriar's *Illustrations of Sterne: with Other Essays and Verses* (2d ed., 1812).

114. See *Monthly Magazine* 8: 1052; Robberds, *Memoir of Taylor,* 1: 343.

115. This volume contained several poems by Coleridge, including "Lewti," "This

Lime-Tree Bower," political pieces reprinted from the *Morning Post,* and minor poems written in Germany. Only the political pieces caught the reviewers' attention: the *Monthly* and *Critical* praised "Recantation," and the *Monthly* found the "Ode to Georgiana, Duchess of Devonshire" to be "pleasing on the whole."

116.   See Burton R. Pollin, "Charles Lamb and Charles Lloyd as Jacobins and Anti-Jacobins," *Studies in Romanticism* 12 (1973): 633-47. Lloyd had voiced Godwinian sentiments on necessity and human perfectibility in the first poem of *Blank Verse,* and associated Lamb with these views in a footnote. Before *Blank Verse* appeared, however, Lloyd had published his anti-Godwinian novel *Edmund Oliver* (1798); and he succeeded in making a separate peace by means of his *Letter to the Antijacobin Reviewers* (Birmingham, 1799).

117.   See David V. Erdman and Paul M. Zall, "Coleridge and Jeffrey in Controversy," *Studies in Romanticism* 14 (1975): 75-83.

118.   *Antijacobin Review* 1: 365-76 ("The Anarchists"); 4: Preface (Wordsworth and Coleridge's trip abroad); 5: 334 (*Lyrical Ballads;* for review see n.101 above). For a summary sketch of the *Antijacobin Review* see chap. 4.

119.   Hayden, *Romantic Reviewers,* pp. 79, 296; *Critical Review,* 30: 185.

120.   *Anti-Jacobin* no. 30 (4 June 1798), introduction to "The Rovers."

121.   *Edinburgh Review* 1 (October 1802): 64.

122.   See Peter Cook, "Chronology of the 'Lake School' Argument: some Revisions," *Review of English Studies,* n.s., 28 (1977): 175-81. "Lake School" would in any case have been an inappropriate term for a group supposed to include Lamb. Southey did not settle at Greta Hall until 1803, and though Coleridge had deposited his family there in 1800 he himself was usually absent. The only real "Laker" in 1802 was Wordsworth.

123.   See John Clive, *Scotch Reviewers* (Cambridge, Mass., 1957), p. 157 n. 4.

124.   See Robberds, *Memoir of Taylor,* 2: 26, and references in foregoing letters. In January 1804 Taylor wrote to Southey "I shall be angry if [the editor] has omitted the sally against the Edinburgh reviewers . . . ." In March he wrote: "I want to hear if you are angry, — if the review of 'Thalaba' displeases you, or if you can bear that sort of amicable dissection, which may be compared to drawing teeth gratis." In May Southey wrote discussing the article, adding: " . . . how do these things of criticism depend upon private feeling! Compare the review of this one poem in the Critical and the British Critic!" Southey suspected that the *British Critic* reviewer was Sir Herbert Croft, with whom he had quarrelled; but he gives no evidence, and groundless conjectures of this kind were always being made. (Robberds, *Memoir of Taylor,* 1: 378, 381, 477, 484, 501-2.)

125.   See T. M. Raysor, "The Establishment of Wordsworth's Reputation," *Journal of English and Germanic Philology* 54 (1955): 61-71.

126.   A review of *Thalaba* in the *Monthly Magazine* (12: 581-83, supplement dated January 1802; reprinted by Madden) is of interest as the only one to approve of Southey's versificaton: " . . . those who delight in the narrative odes of Pindar, or the descriptive odes of Stolberg, will perceive that ages have sanctioned and nations have admired a similar structure of metre." The article may have been by John Aikin, Southey's well-wisher and the editor of the magazine.

127.   I.e. Anderson's *British Poets,* Ellis's *Specimens,* Scott's *Border Minstrelsy,* and Currie's *Burns.*

128.   The *British Critic* disparaged *Gebir,* although Rivingtons published that

Review and also sold *Gebir* in London. The *Critical* reviewed Coleridge's *Ode on the Departing Year* unfavourably when he was on its staff.

129.   These reviews are: Ellis on *Border Minstrelsy*, Burney on *Poems of Smart*, Southey on Bloomfield's *Rural Tales*, Dyer on *The Fall of Robespierre* and Coleridge's *Poems* of 1796, Aikin on Southey's *Poems* (1797), Stoddart on *Lyrical Ballads* (1800), and Taylor on *Thalaba*. The one review that may have been marred by personal considerations in Southey's on *Lyrical Ballads* (1798). The figures in the text should not, of course, be taken as a fair indication of the frequency of reviews by friends; in several cases it is only because of the friendship and printed correspondence that we can name the reviewer. Of the thirty-one *Monthly* articles here discussed whose authors can be identified, only two are known to have had any acquaintance with the author reviewed; and in one of these two cases the author reviewed (Smart) had been dead for twenty years.

130.   For both, see Appendix B.

Chapter 3: The Reviewing of Novels

1.   *Monthly Review* 2 (1790): 464; ibid., 4 (1791): 93.

2.   Ibid., 2 (1790): 465.

3.   The *Analytical* reviewed *The Hermit of Snowdon* in July 1789 (4: 351) and again in April 1790 (6: 466). The *English* reviewed *Man as He Is* in December 1792 (20: 437-43) and October 1796 (28: 382-84).

4.   Oxf. Bodl. MS. Adds. C.89, f. 93.

5.   Mayo, *The English Novel in the Magazines* (Evanston, Ill., and London, 1962), p. 201. Mayo gives an excellent survey of Review attitudes (pp. 190-208), and is one of the few scholars to give the Reviews recognition as "part of the encyclopedic movement in the eighteenth century" (pp. 190-91).

6.   *Monthly Review* 10 (1793): 297, introducing a review of *Man as He Is*.

7.   *Critical Review* 8 (1793): 44; *English Review* 12 (1788): 26; *British Critic* 5 (1795): 478.

8.   *Monthly Review*, ser. 1, 80 (1789): 443, 552; ser. 2, 3 (1790): 89, 475; *Critical Review*, ser. 1, 70 (1790): 97; ser. 2, 24 (1798): 77.

9.   Baker, *History of the English Novel* (1929-67), 5: 20-21.

10.   See *The Miscellaneous Prose Works of Sir Walter Scott* (1834-36), 4: 43-44 (letter quoted in Catherine Dorset's memoir of Charlotte Smith).

11.   This distinction seems first to have been made by Congreve in his preface to *Incognita . . . a Novel* (1692). See also Fielding's preface to *Joseph Andrews*, and prefatory chapters to books 4 and 8 of *Tom Jones*; Clara Reeve, *The Progress of Romance* (Colchester, 1785), esp. p. 111; Northrop Frye, *Anatomy of Criticism* (Princeton, N.J., 1957), pp. 304-7; Ioan Williams, ed. *Novel and Romance, 1700-1800: a Documentary Record* (1970).

12.   Logan Pearsall Smith, *Words and Idioms* (1925), p. 70.

13.   *Monthly Review* 9 (1792): 337.

14.   *Monthly Review,* ser. 1, 32 (1765): 97-99; *Critical Review,* ser. 1, 19 (1765): 50-51.

15.   Reviewed under its original title *The Champion of Virtue,* in *Monthly Review,* ser. 1, 58 (1778): 85; see also *Critical Review,* ser. 1, 44 (1777): 154 and 45 (1778): 315-16.

16.   *Monthly Review,* ser. 1, 68 (1783): 455; ibid., 75 (1786): 131-36; *Critical Review,* ser. 1, 55 (1783): 233-34.

17.   For this writer see Florence M. Hilbish, *Charlotte Smith: Poet and Novelist* (Philadelphia, 1941); also reprints of *Emmeline* (1971) and *The Old Manor House* (1969) in the Oxford English Novels series, with useful prefaces by Anne Henry Ehrenpreis.

18.   Vol. 1, chap. 5.

19.   E.g., of Mowbray Castle and its setting, vol. 1, chap. 6, and of the forest near Tylehurst, vol. 2, chap. 11. Picturesque description could still be thought "rather a novel way of writing": see William Gilpin, *Observations, relative chiefly to Picturesque Beauty, made in . . . the Highlands of Scotland* (1789), vol. 1, p.v.

20.   A reference to her popular *Elegiac Sonnets* (1784).

21.   Vol. 5, chap. 10.

22.   Vol. 1, chaps. 5 and 10.

23.   *British Critic* 4 (1794): 623 (on *The Banished Man*).

24.   She announces a policy of giving less description in *The Banished Man,* "Avis au Lecteur," vol. 2, pp. iv-v; cf. vol. 4, pp. 107-8.

25.   E.g. by Devendra P. Varma in *The Gothic Flame* (1957), who includes such novels as *Caleb Williams.*

26.   J. M. S. Tompkins, *The Popular Novel in England, 1770-1800* (1932), p. 258.

27.   Ibid., p. 255; see pp. 248-64 for a balanced appreciation of Ann Radcliffe's romances.

28.   See for example vol. 1, chap. 2, pp. 51-56 and vol. 2, chap. 11, pp. 94-95. In these and other such passages Julia "comes to life" in a way that Emily and Ellena never do.

29.   An unwitting tribute to Ann Radcliffe's skill in using literary sources, some of which are listed by Tompkins (pp. 375-77).

30.   "His countenance, which was stern, but calm, expressed the dark passion of revenge, but no symptom of pain; bodily pain, indeed, he had always despised, and had yielded only to the strong and terrible energies of the soul." (Vol. 2, chap. 6; see p. 270, and cf. p. 277, in the edition by Bonamy Dobrée in the Oxford English Novels series.)

31.   This review was formerly attributed to Coleridge; for the latest discussion of its authorship see my "Coleridge, Dyer, and *The Mysteries of Udolpho,*" *Notes & Queries* 217 (1972): 287-89. The *Critical* reviews of *Udolpho, The Italian,* and *The Monk* are reprinted by T. M. Raysor in *Coleridge's Miscellaneous Criticism* (Cambridge, Mass., 1936).

32.   See article cited above, n. 31.

33.   Scott gives this figure in his essay on Ann Radcliffe in *Lives of the Novelists*; he adds that £800 was paid for *The Italian.* See *Sir Walter Scott on Novelists and Fiction,* ed. Ioan Williams (1968), pp. 104, 106. At least one reader thought the

Critical review of *Udolpho* was not favourable enough (see Correspondence pages for November 1794, 12: 359-60).

34.   For a more favourable judgement see Frederick Garber's interesting introduction to the Oxford English Novels edition of *The Italian* (1968).

35.   For studies of the authorship of this and other reviews see David V. Erdman, "Immoral Acts of a Library Cormorant," *Bulletin of the New York Public Library* 63 (1959): 433-54, 515-30, 575-87, esp. 445n.; Derek Roper, "Coleridge and the *Critical Review*," *Modern Language Review* 55 (1960): 11-16.

36.   Tompkins, *Popular Novel*, p. 245.

37.   Edith Birkhead's pioneer work *The Tale of Terror* (1921) covers both classes, but distinguishes between the "Novel of Suspense" (as written by Ann Radcliffe) and the "Novel of Terror" (the German school).

38.   Varma, *The Gothic Flame*, p. 129.

39.   *The Monk* has been edited by Howard Anderson for the Oxford English Novels series (1973). Its critical reception has been discussed by André Parreaux in *The Publication of 'The Monk': a Literary Event* (Paris, 1960), esp. pp. 75-78. Parreaux's chapter includes material excluded from the present study (e.g. magazine articles), but is not entirely satisfactory in its treatment of the Reviews. The *Monthly* reviewer was not Sheridan (p. 76 n. 1), and it is not true that *The Monk* was not found immoral until the second edition identified the author as a member of Parliament (p. 87).

40.   Including "Alonzo the Brave," a horrific ballad rivalled in popularity only by Bürger's *Lenore;* interestingly, Taylor's translation of *Lenore* appeared in the *Monthly Magazine* for March 1796, the month in which *The Monk* appeared (Parreaux, p. 19).

41.   It is the second of four consecutive reviews of novels in the *Analytical,* the fourth of which is signed "M". Ralph M. Wardle would take the signature as applying to all the reviews in any such group, a view which needs modifying (see Wardle, "Mary Wollstonecraft, *Analytical* Reviewer," *PMLA* 62 [1947]: 1000-1009; Roper, "Mary Wollstonecraft's Reviews," *Notes & Queries* 203 [1958]: 37-38). The first article in this group deals with *Man as He Is* and may be by Mary, but is not distinctively hers (see discussion of this review in text). The coarsely genial manner of the *Monk* review suggests the hand of Fuseli. Rather strangely, Southey mentioned on 26 January 1797 that he hoped to review *The Monk* for the *Analytical,* apparently not having noticed that a review had appeared three months before. Nothing more is known of Southey's engagement to review for the *Analytical* "when in town" (*New Letters of Southey*, ed. Curry, 1: 119).

42.   See *New Letters of Southey*, ed. Curry, 1: 119; *Collected Letters of Coleridge*, ed. Griggs, 1: 318.

43.   *The Gothic Flame*, p. 178.

44.   See Allene Gregory, *The French Revolution and the English Novel* (New York, 1915); Gary Kelly, *The English Jacobin Novel, 1780-1805* (Oxford, 1976).

45.   *Monthly Review*, ser. 1, 24 (1761): 227.

46.   Gregory, *French Revolution and the English Novel*, p. 168.

47.   See *The Life of Thomas Holcroft, written by Himself*, ed. Elbridge Colby (1925), 1: xxiii, 2: 181; Colby, *A Bibliography of Thomas Holcroft* (New York, 1922), pp. 40, 66; Kelly, *English Jacobin Novel*, p. 114. For Holcroft's views, as expressed in articles for the *Monthly*, on "the nature and uses of the novel," see Kelly,

pp. 115-17. For reprints in the Oxford English Novels series see *Anna St. Ives*, ed. Peter Faulkner (1970) and *The Adventures of Hugh Trevor*, ed. Seamus Deane (1973).

48.   Cf. Kelly, *English Jacobin Novel*, p. 136.

49.   Holcroft does not, in fact, ridicule University discipline, but the contemporary lack of it (see vol. 1, chap. 14).

50.   Bodl. MS. Adds. C.89, f. 86^r.

51.   *Life of Holcroft*, ed. Colby, 2: 238.

52.   See David McCracken, ed. *Caleb Williams* (Oxford English Novels, 1970), for a good introduction, and for reprints of Godwin's preface (first published with the second edition, 1795), MS variants, and discussion of the composition of the novel (taken from his preface to *Fleetwood*, 1832). For other discussions and interpretations see Sir Leslie Stephen, "William Godwin's Novels," in *Studies of a Biographer*, 3 (1902): 119-54; P. N. Furbank, "Godwin's Novels," *Essays in Criticism* 5 (1955): 214-28; Rudolf F. Storch, "Metaphors of Private Guilt and Social Rebellion in Godwin's *Caleb Williams*," *ELH* 34 (1967): 188-207; Kelly, *English Jacobin Novel*, pp. 178-208; Raymond Williams, "The Fiction of Reform," *T.L.S.*, 25 March 1977, pp. 330-31.

53.   *British Critic* 5 (April 1795): 444-47; for Godwin's reply see ibid., 6 (July 1795): 94-95.

54.   Letters to Elizabeth Hitchener of 26 November 1811 and to Mary Shelley of 22 September 1818 (*The Letters of Percy Bysshe Shelley*, ed. Frederick L. Jones [Oxford, 1964], 1: 195, 2: 40).

55.   For this writer see J.M.S. Tompkins, "Mary Hays, Philosophess," in *The Polite Marriage* (Cambridge, 1938), pp. 150-90.

56.   See *The Love-Letters of Mary Hays*, ed. A. F. Wedd (1925), pp. 8, 240. The letters that presumably show her connection with the *Critical Review* are not among those published in this volume.

57.   The *Monthly*, *English*, and *Analytical* reviews of *Man as He Is*; the *Analytical* reviews of *Anna St. Ives*, *Emma Courtney*, and *The Victim of Prejudice*.

58.   I.e., all the *British Critic* reviews in this section. The other badly prejudiced reviews are the *Critical* review of *Anna St. Ives* and the *Monthly* review of *The Victim of Prejudice*.

59.   See above, chap. 1, n. 30.

60.   For further discussion see J. M. S. Tompkins's introduction to her edition of *A Simple Story* (Oxford English Novels, 1967); Tompkins, *Popular Novel in England*, pp. 349-53; William McKee, *Elizabeth Inchbald, Novelist* (Washington, D.C., 1935). See also Kelly, *Jacobin Novel in England*, pp. 64-93, though his classification of *A Simple Story* as a "Jacobin novel" is unpersuasive.

61.   A point made elsewhere by Maria Edgeworth; see Tompkins's introduction to *A Simple Story*, pp. vii-ix, where this passage from the *Monthly Review* is also quoted.

62.   See n. 41 to this chapter. Other *Analytical* reviewers might have made the same criticism, but without the note of irritability.

63.   Tompkins, *Popular Novel*, p. 238.

64.   See n. 14 to this chapter.

65.   *Popular Novel*, p. 231.

66.   E.g. vol. 1, chap. 10, pp. 292-98; vol. 2, chap. 7, pp. 268-73.

67.   See Tompkins, *Popular Novel*, pp. 172 ff.

68.   Hemlow, *The History of Fanny Burney* (Oxford, 1958), p. 255; *Horace Walpole's Correspondence*, ed. W. S. Lewis et al., 12 (New Haven, Conn., and London, 1944): 204; Baker, *History of the English Novel*, 5: 171. The other prig mentioned by Joyce Hemlow is Coelebs in Hannah More's *Coelebs in Search of a Wife* (1809).

69.   See Roger Lonsdale, "Dr. Burney and the *Monthly Review*," *Review of English Studies*, n.s., 14 (1963): 351. Some remarks made by Robinson led Burney to fear a harsh review in the *Critical*, and to counteract this he tried (unsuccessfully) to arrange that his son Charles should review *Camilla* in the *Monthly*.

70.   See *The Journals and Letters of Fanny Burney*, ed. Joyce Hemlow et al., 3 (Oxford, 1973): 221-29, 368; *Camilla*, ed. Edward A. Bloom (Oxford English Novels, 1972), pp. xxiii, xxv.

71.   See *Camilla*, ed. Bloom, pp. xvi, xxv.

72.   For *Wanley Penson* see *Analytical Review* 11 (1791): 215-17: *Critical Review* 4 (1792): 114-15; *Monthly Review* 7 (1792): 265-70. For *Walsingham* see *Monthly Review* 26 (1798): 441-44; *British Critic* 12 (1798): 610-12; *Critical Review* 22 (1798): 553-58.

73.   In *The Works of Charles and Mary Lamb*, ed. E. V. Lucas (1912), 1: 31-33.

74.   *History of the English Novel*, 5: 22.

75.   In six of these articles what seem misconceived objections are raised against sexual episodes, e.g. in the *Critical* review of *The Old Manor House*. In addition we have Mary Wollstonecraft's view that "fantastic scenes" like those in *Emmeline* may demoralise the young reader, and the *Critical* complaint that in *Caleb Williams* Godwin misses a good chance to enforce religious principles.

76.   Mayo, *English Novel in the Magazines*, p. 199; Tompkins, *Popular Novel*, p. 17.

Chapter 4: The Reviewing of Political and Religious Writings

1.   "The Critical Reviewers, I believe, often review without reading the books through; but lay hold of a topick, and write chiefly from their own minds. The Monthly Reviewers are duller men, and are glad to read the books through." *Boswell's Life of Johnson*, under date 10 April 1776 (3: 32).

2.   Advertisement to *Critical Review* 1 (1791), explaining the advantages of the new supplements.

3.   *The Debate on the French Revolution 1789-1800*, ed. Alfred Cobban, 2d ed. (1960), p. 31. This book has an excellent introduction and selection of documents. See also G. S. Veitch, *The Genesis of Parliamentary Reform* (1913; repr. with intro. by Ian Christie, 1965); Philip Anthony Brown, *The French Revolution in English History* (1918); Arthur Lincoln, *Some Political and Social Ideas of English Dissent, 1763-1800* (Cambridge, 1938); F. O'Gorman, *The Whig Party and The French Revolution* (1967); L. G. Mitchell, *Charles James Fox and the Disintegration of the Whig Party, 1782-1794* (Oxford, 1971).

4. Nangle, *Monthly Review: Second Series*, pp. 3-4.

5. See Donald E. Ginter, "The Financing of the Whig Party Organization, 1783-1793," *American Historical Review* 71 (1966): 433-39.

6. *Monthly Review*, ser. 1, 79 (December 1788): 549-54; ibid, 80 (January 1789): 77-81. Cf. *Critical Review*, ser. 1, 66 (December 1788): 492-99; ibid, 67 (January 1789): 71-75.

7. *Monthly Review* 5 (June 1791): 205-14 (review by Pearne).

8. He was one of the lay Fellows exempted by the Foundation from the requirement of taking orders. For information about Pearne see Nangle, *Monthly Review: Second Series*, pp. 52-53.

9. *Monthly Review* 9 (October 1792): 135-46; Bodleian MS. Adds. C.89, ff. 68, 307-8, 71-72.

10. The obvious inference from Enfield's letter of 7 January 1795, which ends: "I have scarcely a line left for politics — else, I should controvert your opinion on the distribution of *wisdom* and *honesty* among the parties" (Bodleian MS. Adds. C.89, f. 86^V). Enfield was less inclined to prudent counsels than Griffiths, being at this time only fifty-three years old as opposed to Griffiths's seventy-four.

11. Bodl. MS. Adds. C.89, f. 94.

12. Nangle, *Monthly Review, Second Series*, pp. 62-64, q.v. for Sheridan's connection with the *Monthly*. Sheridan's articles continued appearing until July 1797, but these later reviews were of works already in hand.

13. See, for example, the reviews of pamphlets called forth by Fox's motion for the repeal of the Test and Corporation Acts in 1790, *Critical Review*, ser. 1, 69 (March 1790): 338-51. It is curious that these articles were held up until the motion had been defeated. They speak favourably of most Dissenters but condemn the "republican" opinions of a minority, and suggest that the repeal should be postponed until the political situation is less alarming.

14. *Critical Review* 1 (1791): 583. The previous quotation is from the Advertisement to this volume.

15. Alexander Stephens, *Memoirs of John Horne Tooke* (1813), 2: 102-3.

16. Compare, for example, the different assumptions behind the hostile review of Robert Merry's *Laurel of Liberty* and the respectful review of Priestley's *Letters to Burke*, both in the *Critical* for January 1791 (1: 70-73, 75-82). In April 1792 a cautious passage seems to have been inserted into an enthusiastic account of *Mirabeau's Speeches*, breaking the thread of a discussion of his extempore style (4: 435-36). The *Critical* was slow to adopt Foxite views on the Test Laws, which it defended as late as October 1793.

17. For a more detailed discussion see Derek Roper, "The Politics of the *Critical Review*, 1756-1817," *Durham University Journal*, n.s., 22 (1961): 117-22.

18. The *Critical* was advertised until 2 February 1773 as "Printed for A. Hamilton"; from 2 February 1775 as "Printed for A. Hamilton, and G. Robinson" (*St. James's Chronicle*). Robinson was concerned in several radical newspapers and periodicals from 1785 onwards (the *Political Herald, Patriot, Courier*, and *Telegraph*); published Holcroft's novels and Godwin's *Political Justice*; and was fined in 1793 for selling *Rights of Man* (C. H. Timperley, *Encyclopaedia of Literary and Typographical Anecdote* [1842], p. 781). For an account of Robinson (ca. 1755-1801) see *Gentleman's Magazine*, 1801, no. 1, pp. 578-80.

19. For Gregory (1754-1808) see *D.N.B.* and *Gentleman's Magazine*, 1808, no. 1, pp. 277, 386-87. Gregory's editorship of the *Critical* rests on the authority of the Unitarian writer George Dyer, whom he recruited as a reviewer; see Dyer's

Privileges of the University of Cambridge (1824), 2: 206, and for comment D. V. Erdman, "Immoral Acts of a Library Cormorant," pt. 1, *Bulletin of the New York Public Library* 63 (1959): 433-48, esp. n. 17. Erdman suggests that the "quiet revolution . . . bringing in Gregory as conductor" of the *Critical* took place after the outbreak of war in 1793. As will have been seen, the change in politics (which could not be brought about overnight) had begun two years earlier; my conjecture about Gregory is that he reviewed for the *Critical* during the 1780s and became editor when the new series began in 1791. A largely self-educated man from Liverpool, Gregory had been leading an active literary life in London since 1782. As early as 1784 he had offered to "speak to the conductor" of a Review about a job for Gilbert Wakefield (*Memoirs of the Life of Gilbert Wakefield, written by Himself* [1804], 1: 510-11). The Advertisement to series 2, vol. 1 of the *Critical* announces that "of its first Conductors none remain," which must mean that Archibald Hamilton I (now seventy years old) had retired. And it was on 4 January 1792 that Wakefield wrote to Gregory on Dyer's behalf "to see, if he can procure any Employment in the Reviews &c " (Dr. Williams's Library MS. 12.45, f. 121).

20. Gregory may have been patronised by Lord Lansdowne, to whom he dedicated a *Life of Chatterton* in 1789; this would explain a fulsome and seemingly pointless compliment paid to Lansdowne in the supplement to the *Critical* for January-April 1793 (7: 581). Lansdowne supported Parliamentary reform, and in 1792 suggested to George III measures for breaking up the old party system (John Norris, *Shelburne and Reform* [1963], p. 278).

21. Aikin apparently became a regular contributor; so did Joshua Toulmin, William Turner, and William Enfield, all Dissenting ministers (Toulmin and Turner had contributed to Priestley's *Theological Repository*, also published by Johnson); Beddoes was invited to contribute, but it is not known whether he did so.

22. For Johnson and his radical friends see D. V. Erdman, *Blake: Prophet Against Empire*, rev. ed. (Princeton, N. J., 1969), pp. 153 ff.; Claire Tomalin, *The Life and Death of Mary Wollstonecraft* (1974), chap.6; Leslie F. Chard II, "Joseph Johnson: Father of the Book Trade," *Bulletin of the New York Public Library* 79 (1975): 51-82. Mrs. Tomalin is particularly informative about Christie (passim). Mary Wollstonecraft reviewed from 1788 until she went abroad in 1792, and then for another year after her return in 1796. For her articles see Ralph M. Wardle, "Mary Wollstonecraft, *Analytical* Reviewer, *PMLA* 62 (1947): 1000-1009; Derek Roper, "Mary Wollstonecraft's Reviews," *Notes & Queries* 203 (1958): 37-38.

23. *Monthly Magazine* 28 (1801): 682.

24. The title-page of Johnson's edition of *Rights of Man* is reproduced by Audrey Williamson in *Thomas Paine: His Life, Work and Times* (1973), p. 5. For differing interpretations of Johnson's failure to publish Blake's *French Revolution* see Erdman, *Blake*, p. 152 n. 10; J. Bronowski, *William Blake and the Age of Revolution* (1972), pp. 70-85.

25. For the best account of these proceedings see Jane Worthington Smyser, "The Trial and Imprisonment of Joseph Johnson, Bookseller," *Bulletin of the New York Public Library* 77 (1974): 418-35, which corrects earlier versions.

26. See *Monthly Repository*, n.s., 1 (1827): 290 (obituary by Henry Crabb Robinson); also transcripts of Henry Crabb Robinson's correspondence in Dr. Williams's Library, vol. 1, nos. 99, 108.

27. Robinson, Correspondence, no. 99.

28. Prefatory Address in vol. 1 (July-December 1798). Either the volume was very late in appearing or the claim was premature. The cartoon is dated 1 February 1799, and probably appeared with the January number.

29.   See Richard Polwhele, *Biographical Sketches in Cornwall* (Truro, 1831), 3: 127-28, 134.

30.   *The Man in the Moon; or Travels into the Lunar Regions, by the Man of the People* (pub. anonymously). For Thomson see *D.N.B.* and *Annual Biography and Obituary for 1817.*

31.   C. Kegan Paul, *William Godwin: His Friends and Contemporaries* (1876), 1: 20; Elbridge Colby, *A Bibliography of Thomas Holcroft* (New York, 1922), p. 40.

32.   For Whitaker's review of Gibbon see Polwhele, *Biographical Sketches,* 3: 60n., 88-91; it is discussed in chap. 5 of this book.

33.   For Moore see p. 22, n. 30 and p. 63. For Gurney see *D.N.B.* and *The Mirror of Literature* 28 (1841): 282-83.

34.   Some members of this group listed by Edward Churton (*Memoir of Joshua Watson* [1861], 1: 27-30) are Thomas Calverley, Nathan Wetherell, Samuel Glasse, and John Pankhurst.

35.   *A Proposal for a Reformation of Principles* (pub. anonymously 1 January 1792). This leaflet and its sequel, the prospectus of the *British Critic,* are bound up with vol. 1 of some sets of the Review, e.g. that in the Bodleian Library.

36.   Arthur Aspinall, *Politics and the Press, c. 1780-1850* (1949), p. 166.

37.   Bodleian MS. Adds. C.89, f. 304.

38.   Ibid., f. 75 (from William Enfield).

39.   See Whitaker's letter of 20 December 1796 in Polwhele, *Biographical Sketches,* 3: 114; also n. 52, below.

40.   John Freeman, *Life of the Rev. William Kirby* (1852), pp. 42-43.

41.   See John Taylor, *Records of my Life* (1832), 2: 279.

42.   See *D.N.B.*; Aspinall, pp. 47, 176n. "John Gifford" is not to be confused with William Gifford, editor of the *Anti-Jacobin* and the *Quarterly Review.*

43.   For Bowles and Taylor see Aspinall, pp. 83, 163-66, 176n. During the early 1790s Taylor was usually allowed £3 a week out of the secret-service money; Bowles, £100 a year. For Robert Bisset see *D.N.B.* (Leslie Stephen, in his article on Gifford, wrongly gives "Andrew Bisset" as the *Antijacobin* reviewer). For Heath see Taylor, *Records of my Life.* The clergymen included Whitaker, Polwhele, Henry George Glasse, George Gleig, John Skinner, Samuel Henshall, and Jonathan Boucher. The names of all these contributors appear in the marked copies of vols. 1-6 in the British Library.

44.   Preface to vol. 4 (September-December 1799).

45.   Vols. 4 (November 1799): 299-304 and 5 (January-March 1800): 48-56, 162-72, 277-86.

46.   Vols. 3 (August 1799): 480-83 and 6 (May 1800): 103-4.

47.   Vol. 5 (March 1800): 260-63.

48.   Vols. 2 (April 1799) and 5 (January 1800).

49.   Scientific and philosophical articles contributed by James Mill from 1802 have been found of interest: see Alexander Bain, *James Mill* (1882), pp. 37-48, 62-63.

50.   *Gentleman's Magazine,* 1808, no. 1, p. 277. If Lansdowne was still Gregory's patron in the early 1790s, finance could have come from that quarter: see n. 20 to this chapter.

51.   C. H. Timperley, *Encyclopaedia of Literary and Typographical Anecdote* (1842), p. 795. The source of these figures is not given.

52. For Samuel Partridge, a former Fellow of Magdalen who reviewed for the *British Critic* without payment as a means of propagating "his very sound principles in Church and State," see *Gentleman's Magazine*, 1817, no. 2, pp. 186, 198.

53. H. N. Brailsford, *Shelley, Godwin and their Circle* (Home University Library, 1945), p. 7.

54. Reprinted in *A Miscellany of Tracts and Pamphlets*, ed. A. C. Ward (World's Classics, 1927).

55. James Mackintosh, *Vindiciae Gallicae* (1791), p. vii.

56. Several of Pearne's letters to Griffiths may be read in Oxf. Bodl. MS. Adds. C.89; they show him an intelligent, honourable, and humane person. Though consistently supporting Reform in England and the Revolution in France, he deplores the crimes to which the Revolution led: "They have cast a stain upon a noble cause, which it will not easily wipe out," he writes on 12 September 1792 (f. 303^v). On 11 December 1790 he discusses his review of Burke's *Reflections:* "Whatever your readers may think of your account of Burke's 'piece of poetry,' they will never complain, if you insert all that I here send you, that you have not given them enough of it. And yet, to shorten it, I have cut out many good things of the author's, & several observations of my own that I originally intended to put in" (f. 294).

57. Goldsmith, "Retaliation," l. 6.

58. Brailsford, *Shelley, Godwin and their Circle*, p. 69.

59. *Rights of Man*, pt. 1 (1791), pp. 74-78.

60. Though not yet the editor, Thomson was already a major contributor to the *English Review*; and since he wrote the Appendixes on political affairs it is likely that he wrote other important political articles. He is known to have been "dazzled" for a time by enthusiasm for the French Revolution. The phrase about "the gradual unfolding of the human intellect," used in both reviews of *Rights of Man*, resembles Thomson's favourite phrase about "the progress of manners" (*Annual Biography and Obituary*; John Taylor, *Records of my Life* [1832], 2: 405-6).

61. See *Rights of Man*, pt. 2 (1792), preface, p. x.

62. A reference to Burke's *Appeal from the New to the Old Whigs* (1791), p. 95: ". . . if such writings shall be thought to deserve any other than the refutation of criminal justice."

63. For his reputation see Audrey Williamson, *Thomas Paine: his Life, Work and Times* (1973), chap. 22.

64. Williamson, *Thomas Paine*, p. 143.

65. "I may excite laughter, by dropping an hint, which I mean to pursue, some future time, for I really think that women ought to have representatives, instead of being arbitrarily governed without having any direct share allowed them in the deliberations of government" (*Rights of Woman* [1792], chap. 9, p. 335).

66. Williamson, *Thomas Paine*, p. 68.

67. *Rights of Woman*, chap. 4, pp. 136-49.

68. "His intellectual predecessors . . . had seen in the psychological theory that mind is the exclusive product of sensation, the negation of all moral predisposition. Godwin's extraordinary combination of this view with the Socratic doctrine that vice is error reduced human flesh and blood to a shadow, easily subduable by a reason many times its size." David Fleisher, *William Godwin: A Study in Liberalism* (1951), p. 147.

69. See F. E. L. Priestley, ed. *Political Justice* (Toronto, 1946), 3: 78-81.

70.   See G. S. Veitch, *The Genesis of Parliamentary Reform* (reprint of 1965), chaps. 10-11, q.v. also for a discussion of *Political Justice* in the context of reform politics (pp. 264-69).

71.   Mary Shelley's statement that Pitt opposed a prosecution of *Political Justice* because "a three guinea book could never do much harm among those who had not three shillings to spare" (C. Kegan Paul, *William Godwin: his Friends and Contemporaries* [1876], 1: 80) has often been repeated. In fact, the original quarto edition in two volumes was sold for £1.16s. *(Monthly Review* 10: 311). Upwards of 3,000 copies were purchased (Kegan Paul, *William Godwin,* 1: 81), and "workmen, who alone could not possibly have afforded such a purchase, formed clubs for the express purpose of buying and reading *Political Justice"* (Veitch, *Genesis of Parliamentary Reform,* p. 269).

72.   See Kegan Paul, *William Godwin,* 1: 118; Hazlitt, "William Godwin," in *The Spirit of the Age* (11: 16-18 in *Works,* ed. P. P. Howe [1930-34]).

73.   Priestley, ed. *Political Justice,* 3: 48-50.

74.   Griffiths "was considerably alarmed at the boldness of some of Mr. Godwin's principles, and still more staggered at the accounts he had heard of them. He threw himself on Mr. Holcroft's known attachment to the interest of the Review not to commit its character by undeserved praise" (Hazlitt, in *Life of Thomas Holcroft,* ed. Elbridge Colby [1925], 2: 106-7). Holcroft was certainly the reviewer, and there is nothing improbable about Hazlitt's story.

75.   This is a just criticism of the opening chapters of *Political Justice* as they stood in 1793, showing the influence of Helvétius. These chapters were later modified to conform with Godwin's general conviction that government was a necessary evil and could produce little positive good. See Priestley, ed., *Political Justice,* 3: 28, 82-83.

76.   For this contradiction see Priestley, ed. *Political Justice,* 3: 17-19, 26.

77.   Kegan Paul, *William Godwin,* 1: 83-89.

78.   See John Freeman, *Life of the Rev. William Kirby* (1852), pp. 42-43; Edward Churton, *Memoir of Joshua Watson* (1861), 1: 27-30, 279-85. The account given by John H. Overton in *The English Church in the Nineteenth Century, 1800-1833* (1894), pp. 200-201, and followed by Francis Mineka in *The Dissidence of Dissent* (Chapel Hill, N.C., 1944), p. 51 is mistaken. Nares edited the *British Critic* from the first; the High Church group which did much to found the Review was kept out of its operations.

79.   Bodleian MS. Adds. C.89, f. 97.

80.   Vol. 69 (March 1790): 342.

81.   "Socinianism, moonlight; methodism, a stove. O for some sun to unite heat and light!" (Coleridge, *Anima Poetae,* quoted by Basil Willey, *The Eighteenth-Century Background* [1940], p. 168).

82.   See Carl Becker, *The Heavenly City of the Eighteenth-Century Philosophers* (New Haven, Conn., 1932), pp. 50-51, 60-61.

83.   *Age of Reason,* pt. 1 (1794), p. 37; see also Harry Hayden Clark, "An Historical Interpretation of Thomas Paine's Religion," *University of California Chronicle* 35 (1933): 56-87.

84.   "Revelation is necessarily limited to the first communication. After this, it is only an account of something which that person says was a revelation made to him; and though he may find himself obliged to believe it, it cannot be incumbent on me

to believe it in the same manner. . . . I have no other authority for it than some historian telling me so." *Age of Reason,* pt. 1, pp. 3-4.

85.   Gilbert Wakefield had replied in his *Examination of the Age of Reason* (1794), and added a *Reply to the Second Part* in 1795. Richard Watson's *Apology for the Bible* appeared in 1796 and dealt only with Part 1.

86.   Norman Sykes notes "surprising parallels between the guesses of Paine concerning the literary and historical problems of the Bible and the accepted conclusions of modern scholarship" (*Church and State in England in the Eighteenth Century* [1934], p. 422).

87.   Paine believed that the Hebrew language had no terms for the constellations, and that the naming of the constellations in the Book of Job proved that this was not originally a Hebrew work *(Age of Reason,* pt. 2, p. 38). Moody gives their Hebrew names.

88.   Paine describes it as "one of the most wild and disorderly compositions ever put together, . . . full of extravagant metaphor, without application, and destitute of meaning" (*Age of Reason,* pt. 2, p. 43).

89.   Williamson, *Thomas Paine,* p. 228.

90.   Sykes, *Church and State,* p. 422.

91.   D. S. Wayland, "A Biographical Sketch of Dr. Paley," in Paley's *Works* (1837), vol. 1, p. xxxvii.

92.   *Works,* 3: 3-8. Paley's own argument from the miracles has been satirically summarised by Sir Leslie Stephen: "The man at whose order the clock strikes thirteen must be in the secret of the artificer; and we may trust his account of a hidden part of the machinery" (*English Thought in the Eighteenth Century* [1876], 1: 416).

93.   After the publication of the *Evidences* "dignities and emoluments were showered upon him from every quarter, and at length, with the single exception of the mitre, his talents procured for him all that clerical ambition could desire" (Wayland in Paley's *Works,* vol. 1, pp. xxv-xxvii).

94.   Both quotations are from C. J. Abbey and J. H. Overton, *The English Church in the Eighteenth Century* (1878), 2: 219-20.

95.   Oliver Warner, *William Wilberforce and his Times* (1962), p. 87; Abbey and Overton, *English Church,* 2: 220.

96.   Theophilus Lindsey wrote to Samuel Shore on 12 June 1797: "If you take in the Analytical Review, you will meet with a very judicious critique on Mr. Wilberforce's book; not that I think you woud [*sic*] want any one to point out the weakness of his judgment, his constant misinterpretation of the sacred writings, and overweening partialities to his own and condemnation of the opinions of others" (Dr. Williams's Library MS. 12.57, letter 11).

97.   The immediate cause of Malthus's *Essay* was an essay by Godwin, "Of Avarice and Profusion," in *The Enquirer* (1797), which is linked with wider theories in *Political Justice.* After Malthus's *Essay* had appeared Godwin sought him out, and the two men corresponded politely for some years.

98.   Henry Crabb Robinson identifies his namesake's signature in the *Analytical* as "S.A." in an obituary in the *Monthly Repository,* n.s., 1 (1827): 290.

99.   *Thomas Paine,* p. 150.

Chapter 5: The Reviewing of a History and a Biography

1.   *Memoirs of the Life of Edward Gibbon, by Himself,* ed. George Birkbeck Hill (1900), pp. 122, 195.

2.   Including Robertson, Porson, and Gibbon's editor J. B. Bury, who writes: "If we take into account the vast range of his work, his accuracy is amazing" (*Decline and Fall* [1909], vol. 1, p.x).

3.   See Christopher Dawson, *Edward Gibbon*, British Academy Hertz Trust Lecture (1934), p. 7.

4.   Rose reviewed James Chelsum's *Remarks on the Two Last Chapters of Mr. Gibbon's History* (1776), Richard Watson's *Apology for Christianity* (1777), and Henry Davis's *Examination of the Fifteenth and Sixteenth Chapters of Mr. Gibbon's History* (1778). For these and other attacks see Shelby Thomas McCloy, *Gibbon's Antagonism to Christianity* (Chapel Hill, N. C., and London, 1933). See also J.E. Norton, *A Bibliography of the Works of Edward Gibbon* (1940), chapters. 8, 9.

5.   For John Gillies, LL.D., F.S.A., F.R.S. (1747-1836), see *D.N.B.* Gillies had been introduced to Gibbon in 1779 by a letter from the historian William Robertson. They occasionally exchanged letters, and may have become closer friends during Gibbon's visit to London of 1787-88. Both published with Cadell. See *Letters of Edward Gibbon*, ed. J. E. Norton (1956), 2: 203; 3: 143, 337.

6.   For the Rev. John Whitaker, B.D., F.S.A., Fellow of Corpus Christi College (ca. 1735-1808), see *D.N.B.* He and Gibbon had met at least once, and had corresponded amicably from 1773 until 11 May 1776. Whitaker then wrote rebuking Gibbon for the Deist tendencies of the first volume of the *Decline and Fall*, after which personal relations seem to have ceased (*Miscellaneous Works of Edward Gibbon*, ed. Sheffield [1796-1815], 3: 587-600; *Letters of Gibbon*, ed. Norton, 2: 90-91). Richard Polwhele's story that Gibbon had sent Whitaker the MS of this volume to inspect, withholding the controversial fifteenth and sixteenth chapters (*Gentleman's Magazine*, 1808, no. 2, p. 1035; repeated in Nichols's *Anecdotes*, Chalmers's *General Biographical Dictionary* and the *D.N.B.*) is not borne out by the printed letters; neither is Lord Sheffield's suggestion that Whitaker broke off relations from pique at Gibbon's criticisms of his *Mary Queen of Scots Vindicated* (1788).

7.   See J. B. Bury in his edition of the *Decline and Fall*, vol. 1, p. xiv.

8.   Advertisement to his *Gibbon's History . . . Reviewed* (1791).

9.   *The Autobiographies of Edward Gibbon,* ed. John Murray (1896), p. 300 n. 18.

10.   Norton, *Bibliography of Gibbon,* p. 70.

11.   See Richard Polwhele, *Traditions and Recollections* (1826), 1: 249-51. The articles were reprinted as *Gibbon's History . . . Reviewed* (1791), which runs to 258 octavo pages.

12.   Journal for 9 October 1850, in *The Life of Letters of Lord Macaulay*, by Sir George Otto Trevelyan (World's Classics, 1932), 2: 218.

13.   In his discussion of Gibbon in *The Art of History* (1926), pp. 162-63, 181-82, J.B. Black borrows Whitaker's argument about the misuse of Tacitus, and his stylistic example of the silkworm's "golden tomb."

14.   Most of the *Monthly* reviews of works by or about Johnson were reprinted by John Ker Spittal in *Contemporary Criticisms of Dr. Samuel Johnson* (1923).

15.   Mark Longaker, *English Biography in the Eighteenth Century* (Philadelphia, 1931), p. 408.

16.   Vol. 54 (September 1831), pp. 1-38, a review of Croker's edition of Boswell's *Life;* see esp. pp. 16-19.

17.   Steevens had been active in the *Critical Review* in the 1780s and enjoyed making anonymous attacks on his acquaintances. His malicious habits are well attested in Boswell's *Life.* Boswell was warned early in 1791 that Steevens was depreciating his work. See chap. 1, n. 15; *Boswell's Life of Johnson*, ed. Hill, rev. Powell (1934-50), 3: 281.

18.   *Boswell's Life of Johnson*, 1: 424.

19.   A reference to Boswell's imitation of a cow, and less successful imitation of other animals, at Drury Lane playhouse. The story is told in the first edition of the *Life of Johnson* and reprinted in the Hill-Powell ed., 5: 396 n. 4.

"Upon the Whole Matter"

1.   Bodleian MS. Adds. C.90, f. 100v.
2.   Southey's *Poems* (1797), Godwin's *Political Justice* and *St. Leon*, Holcroft's *Anna St. Ives* and *Hugh Trevor,* Mrs. Radcliffe's *Udolpho*, and Mary Hays's *Emma Courtney.*
3.   J. W. Robberds, *A Memoir of . . . William Taylor* (1843), 1: 127.

Select Bibliography

Where no place of publication is given for a book, it may be assumed that this is London. For a list of works the reviewing of which is discussed in this study, see Appendix A.

The Reviews

The Monthly Review. A Periodical Work, giving an Account, with proper Abstracts of, and Extracts from, the New Books, Pamphlets, &c. as they come out. By Several Hands. (After several short-lived variations the title becomes *The Monthly Review: or, Literary Journal. By Several Hands.*) 81 vols. 1749-1789. (First Series.)

Continued as *The Monthly Review; or, Literary Journal, Enlarged.* 108 vols. 1790-1825. (Second Series. The *Monthly Review* continued in various forms until 1845.)

The Critical Review; or, Annals of Literature. By a Society of Gentlemen. 70 vols. 1756-1790. (First Series.)

Continued as *The Critical Review; or, Annals of Literature; Extended and Improved. By a Society of Gentlemen. A New Arrangement.* 39 vols. 1791-1803. (Second Series. The *Critical Review* continued until 1817.)

The English Review; or, An Abstract of English and Foreign Literature. (Vols. 27-28 as *The English Review of Literature, Science, Discoveries, Inventions, and Practical Controversies and Contests.*) 28 vols. 1783-1796. (Merged with the *Analytical Review.*)

The Analytical Review; or, History of Literature, Domestic and Foreign. 29 vols. 1788-1799. (The final volume, for January-June 1799, was intended as the first of a new series.)

The British Critic, a New Review. 42 vols. 1793-1813. (First Series. The *British Critic* continued in various forms until 1847.)

Sources

MANUSCRIPTS

Letters from various correspondents to Ralph Griffiths. Oxford Bodleian MS Adds. C.89.

Letters from Samuel Badcock to Ralph Griffiths. Oxford Bodleian MS Adds. C.90.

Letters of Henry Crabb Robinson in Dr. Williams's Library, London.

BOOKS AND EDITIONS

Colby, Elbridge, ed. *The Life of Thomas Holcroft, written by Himself; Continued to the Time of His Death from his Diary, Notes, and other Papers, by William Hazlitt; and now Newly Edited, with Introduction and Notes.* 2 vols. Constable, 1925.

Constable, Thomas. *Archibald Constable and his Literary Correspondents.* 3 vols. Edinburgh, 1873.

Curry, Kenneth, ed. *New Letters of Robert Southey.* 2 vols. New York and London: Columbia University Press, 1965.

Grierson, H. J. C., ed. *The Letters of Sir Walter Scott.* 12 vols. Constable, 1932-1937. (Centenary Edition.)

Griggs, Earl Leslie, ed. *Collected Letters of Samuel Taylor Coleridge.* 6 vols. Oxford: Clarendon Press, 1956-1971.

Hill, George Birkbeck, ed. *Boswell's Life of Johnson; together with Boswell's Journal of a Tour to the Hebrides, and Johnson's Diary of a Journey into North Wales.* Revised and enlarged by L. F. Powell. 6 vols. Oxford: Clarendon Press, 1934-1950.

Kegan Paul, C. *William Godwin: his Friends and Contemporaries.* 2 vols. 1876.

Kerr, Robert. *Memoirs of the Life, Writings, and Correspondence of William Smellie, F. R. S. and F. A. S., late Printer in Edinburgh.* 2 vols. Edinburgh, 1811.

Knapp, Lewis. M. *Tobias Smollett: Doctor of Men and Manners.* Princeton, N. J.: Princeton University Press, 1949.

Lonsdale, Roger. *Dr. Charles Burney: a Literary Biography.* Oxford: Clarendon Press, 1965.

Lucas, E. V., ed. *The Letters of Charles Lamb; to which are added those of his Sister, Mary Lamb.* 3 vols. Dent/Methuen, 1935.

Marrs, Edwin W., Jr., ed. *The Letters of Charles and Mary Anne Lamb.* Ithaca, N. Y., and London, 1975-. (In progress; 5 vols. projected.)

Mason, Eudo C., ed. *The Mind of Henry Fuseli: Selections from his Writings, with an Introductory Study.* Routledge & Kegan Paul, 1951. (*Analytical* reviews by Fuseli are listed in Appendix II.)

Nichols, John. *Literary Anecdotes of the Eighteenth Century; comprizing Biographical Memoirs of William Bowyer, Printer, F. S. A., and Many of his Learned Friends; . . . and Biographical Anecdotes of a Consider-able Number of Eminent Writers and Ingenious Artists.* 9 vols. 1812-1815.

———, and Nichols, John Bowyer. *Illustrations of the Literary History of the Eighteenth Century. Consisting of Authentic Memoirs and Original Letters of Eminent Persons; and Intended as a Sequel to the Literary Anecdotes.* 8 vols. 1817-1858.

Polwhele, Richard. *Biographical Sketches in Cornwall.* 3 vols. Truro, 1831.

———. *Traditions and Recollections: Domestic, Clerical, and Literary.* 2 vols. 1826.

Robberds, John W. *A Memoir of the Life and Writings of the late William Taylor, of Norwich.* 2 vols. 1843.

Ryskamp, Charles. *William Cowper of the Inner Temple, Esq.: a Study of his Life and Works to the Year 1768.* Cambridge: Cambridge University Press, 1959. (*Analytical* reviews by Cowper are listed in Appendix C.)

Smiles, Samuel. *A Publisher and his Friends: Memoir and Correspondence of the late John Murray, with an Account of the Origin and Progress of the House, 1768-1843.* 2 vols. 1891.

Southey, Charles Cuthbert, ed. *The Life and Correspondence of the late Robert Southey.* 6 vols. 1849-1850.

Warter, John Wood, ed. *Selections from the Letters of Robert Southey.* 4 vols. 1856.

Studies of the Reviews

Alexander, J. H. "Literary Reviewing in Five British Periodicals, 1800-1808." D. Phil. thesis, University of Oxford, 1968.

———. *Two Studies in Romantic Reviewing. 1, Edinburgh Reviewers and the English Tradition; 2, The Reviewing of Walter Scott's Poetry, 1805-1817.* 2 vols. Salzburg: Institut für Englische Sprache und Literatur, 1976. (Salzburg Studies in English Literature: Romantic Reassessment, 49.)

Bloom, Edward A. " 'Labors of the Learned': Neoclassic Book-reviewing Aims and Techniques." *Studies in Philology* 54 (1957): 537-63.

Clive, John. *Scotch Reviewers: the 'Edinburgh Review,' 1802-1815.* Cambridge, Mass.: Harvard University Press; London: Faber & Faber, 1957.

Erdman, David V. "Immoral Acts of Library Cormorant: the Extent of Coleridge's Contributions to the *Critical Review.*" *Bulletin of the New York Public Library* 63 (1959): 433-54, 515-30, 575-87.

Friedman, Arthur. "Goldsmith's Contributions to the *Critical Review.*" *Modern Philology* 44 (1946) 23-52.

Graham, Walter. *English Literary Periodicals.* New York and London, 1930 (reissued by Cass, London, 1966).

Hawkins, Aubrey. "Some Writers on the *Monthly Review.*" *Review of English Studies* 7 (1931): 168-81.

Hayden, John O. *The Romantic Reviewers, 1802-1824.* Chicago, Ill.: Chicago University Press; London: Routledge & Kegan Paul, 1969.

Hooker, Edward Niles. "The Discussion of Taste, from 1750 to 1770, and the New Trends in Literary Criticism." *PMLA* 49 (1934): 577-92.

———. "The Reviewers and the New Criticism, 1754-1770." *Philological Quarterly* 13 (1934): 189-202.

———. "The Reviewers and the New Trends in Poetry, 1754-1770." *Modern Language Notes* 51 (1936): 207-14.

Jones, Claude E. "Contributors to the *Critical Review,* 1756-1785." *Modern Language Notes* 61 (1946): 433-41.

———. "The *Critical Review* and some Major Poets." *Notes & Queries* 201 (1956): 114-15.

———. "The *Critical Review's* First Thirty Years, 1756-1785." *Notes & Queries* 201 (1956): 78-80.

———. "Dramatic Criticism in the *Critical Review,* 1756-1785." *Modern Language Quarterly* 20 (1959): 18-26, 133-44.

———. "The English Novel: a *Critical* View, 1756-1785." *Modern Language Quarterly* 19 (1958): 147-59, 213-14.

———. "Poetry and the *Critical Review,* 1756-1785." *Modern Language Quarterly* 9 (1948): 17-36.

———. *Smollett Studies.* Berkeley and Los Angeles: University of California Press, 1942. (University of California Publications in English, vol. 9, no. 2.) (Includes "Smollett and the *Critical Review*" and "Attacks on the *Critical,* 1756-1771.")

Klukoff, Phillip J. "New Smollett Attributions in the *Critical Review.*" *Notes & Queries* 212 (1967): 418-19.

———. "Smollett and the *Critical Review:* Criticism of the Novel, 1756-1783." *Studies in Scottish Literature* 4 (1967): 89-100.

———. "Smollett as the Reviewer of *Jeremiah Grant.*" *Notes & Queries* 211 (1966): 466.

———. "A Smollett Attribution in the *Critical Review.*" *Notes & Queries* 210 (1965): 221.

———. "Two Smollett Attributions in the *Critical Review: The Reverie* and *Tristram Shandy.*" *Notes & Queries* 211 (1966): 465-66.

Knapp, Lewis M. "Griffiths's *Monthly Review* as Printed by Strahan." *Notes & Queries* 203 (1958): 216-17.

Lonsdale, Roger. "Dr. Burney and the *Monthly Review.*" *Review of English Studies,* n.s., 14 (1963): 346-58; 15 (1964): 27-37.

———. "William Bewley and the *Monthly Review:* a Problem of Attribution." *Papers of the Bibliographical Society of America* 55 (1961): 309-18.

McCutcheon, Roger P. "The Beginnings of Book-reviewing in English Periodicals." *PMLA* 37 (1922): 691-706.

Mayo, Robert D. *The English Novel in the Magazines, 1740-1815: with a Catalogue of 1375 Magazine Novels and Novelettes.* Evanston, Ill.: Northwestern University Press; London: Oxford University Press, 1962. (See esp. pp. 190-204, "The Criticism of the Novel in the Monthly Reviews.")

Nangle, Benjamin Christie. "Charles Burney, Critic." In *The Age of Johnson: Essays Presented to Chauncey Brewster Tinker* [edited by W. S. Lewis and F. W. Hilles]. New Haven, Conn.: Yale University Press; London: Oxford University Press, 1949.

— — —. *The Monthly Review, First Series, 1749-1789: Indexes of Contributors and Articles.* Oxford: Clarendon Press, 1934.

— — —. *The Monthly Review, Second Series, 1790-1815: Indexes of Contributors and Articles.* Oxford: Clarendon Press, 1955.

Oakes, Norman Edwin. "Ralph Griffiths and the *Monthly Review*." Ph.D. dissertation, Columbia University, 1969.

Patterson, Charles I. "The Authenticity of Coleridge's Reviews of Gothic Romances." *Journal of English and Germanic Philology* 50 (1951): 517-21.

— — —. "An Unidentified Criticism by Coleridge related to *Christabel.*" *PMLA* 67 (1952): 973-88.

Reiman, Donald H., ed. *The Romantics Reviewed: Contemporary Reviews of British Romantic Writers.* 9 vols. New York and London: Garland, 1972. (Many articles reprinted photographically, with brief introductory notes.)

Roper, Derek. "Coleridge and the *Critical Review.*" *Modern Language Review* 55 (1960): 11-16.

— — —. "Coleridge, Dyer, and *The Mysteries of Udolpho.*" *Notes & Queries* 217 (1972): 287-89.

— — —. "Mary Wollstonecraft's Reviews." *Notes & Queries* 203 (1958): 37-38.

— — —. "The Politics of the *Critical Review*, 1756-1817." *Durham University Journal*, n.s., 22 (1961): 117-22.

— — —. "Smollett's 'Four Gentlemen': the First Contributors to the *Critical Review.*" *Review of English Studies*, n.s., 10 (1959): 38-44.

— — —. "The Reviewing of English Literature, c. 1789-1802." B. Litt. thesis, University of Oxford, 1959.

— — —. "Tobias Smollett and the Founders of his Review." *The Call Number* (Eugene, Oregon) 19, no. 1 (1957): 4-9.

Seitz, R. W. "Goldsmith's *Lives of the Fathers.*" *Modern Philology* 26 (1929): 295-305.

Smyser, Jane Worthington. "The Trial and Imprisonment of Joseph Johnson, Bookseller." *Bulletin of the New York Public Library* 77 (1974): 418-35.

Spector, Robert Donald. "Additional Attacks on the *Critical Review.*" *Notes & Queries* 201 (1956): 425.

— — —. "Attacks on the *Critical Review.*" *Periodical Post Boy* (1955) pp. 6-7.

― ― ―. "Attacks on the *Critical Review,* 1764-1765." *Notes & Queries* 202 (1957): 121.

― ― ―. "Attacks on the *Critical Review* in the *Court Magazine.*" *Notes & Queries* 203 (1958): 308.

― ― ―. *English Literary Periodicals and the Climate of Opinion during the Seven Years' War.* The Hague and Paris: Mouton, 1966. (Studies in English Literature, 34.)

― ― ―. "Further Attacks on the *Critical Review.*" *Notes & Queries* 200 (1955): 535.

― ― ―. "Language Control in the Eighteenth Century." *Word Study* 27 (1951): 1-2. (Language in the *Critical Review.*)

― ― ―. "The *Monthly* and its Rival." *Bulletin of the New York Public Library* 64 (1960): 159-61.

Sutcliffe, W. Denham. "English Book-reviewing, 1749-1800." D. Phil. thesis, University of Oxford, 1943.

Ward, William Smith. "The Criticism of Poetry in British Periodicals, 1798-1820." Ph. D. dissertation, Duke University, 1943; on Microcards, University of Kentucky, 1955.

― ― ―. *Index and Finding-list of Serials Published in the British Isles, 1789-1832.* Lexington: University of Kentucky Press, 1953.

― ― ―. "Index and Finding-list of Serials Published in the British Isles, 1789-1832: a Supplementary List." *Bulletin of the New York Public Library* 77 (1974): 291-97.

― ― ―. *Literary Reviews in British Periodicals, 1798-1820: a Bibliography, with a Supplementary List of General (Non-review) Articles on Literary Subjects.* New York and London: Garland, 1972.

― ― ―. "Wordsworth, the 'Lake' Poets, and their Contemporary Magazine Critics, 1798-1820." *Studies in Philology* 42 (1945): 87-113.

Wardle, Ralph M. "Mary Wollstonecraft, *Analytical* Reviewer." *PMLA* 62 (1947): 1000-1009.

Weed, Katherine K., and Bond, Richmond Pugh. *Studies of English Periodicals from their Beginning to 1800: a Bibliography.* Chapel Hill: University of North Carolina Press, 1946.

Whalley, George, "Coleridge on Classical Prosody: an Unidentified Review of 1797." *Review of English Studies,* n.s., 2 (1951): 238-47.

Wichelns, Herbert A. "Burke's *Essay on the Sublime* and its Reviewers." *Journal of English and Germanic Philology* 21 (1922): 645-61.

Index

Graves, Richard, 123
Gray, Thomas, 49, 53, 59; his *Elegy* noticed, 20.n.6
Gregory, George, editor of the *Critical*, 22, 177-78, 183
Grey, Charles, later 2d earl, 177
Griffiths, George: succeeds his father as editor of the *Monthly*, 21, 39, 45,n.194, 259; his review of *A Simple Story*, 162
Griffiths, Ralph: founder, editor, and owner of the *Monthly*, 20-21, 29-31, 34-35, 39, 61, 106, 150, 152, 166, 172, 174-76, 183, 198, 255-57, 259; his review of *Fanny Hill*, 31; his review of Boswell's *Life of Johnson*, 236-41; portrait, illustration no. 2
Grosse, Carl, 141, 144
Gurney, John, 179

Hamilton, Alexander, a *Monthly* review by, 70
Hamilton, Archibald (d. 1793), a founder, owner, and editor of the *Critical*, 21, 177,n.19
Hamilton, Archibald, grandson of the above, 21
Hamilton, Samuel, part-owner and editor of the *Critical*, 21, 178
Hastings, Warren: subscribes to several Reviews, 24; supported by William Thomson in the *English*, 179
Hawkins, Sir John, alleged self-reviewal in the *Critical*, 33
Hayley, William: a subscriber to the *Analytical*, 24; and to the *Monthly*, 24 n.68
Hays, Mary, 146-47; *Analytical* reviewer, 23; her novels reviewed, 156-59
Hazlitt, William, 46,n.203, 47, 68-69, 77, n.41, 94, 198, 259
Heath, William: a writer for the *Antijacobin Review*, 181; his review of *Lyrical Ballads*, 101,n.101
Hellins, John, a reviewer for the *British Critic*, 23
Helvétius, Claude-Adrien, 199, n.75, 202
Henshall, Samuel, writer for the *Antijacobin Review*, 181, n.43
Hill, John, *Monthly* reviewer, 20, n.6
History of the Works of the Learned, 20, n.6
Holcroft, Thomas, 26, n.96, 39, 146-47; *English* and *Monthly* reviewer, 21-22, 150, 176; *Monthly* reviews by him, 39, 84-85,

123, 125, 148, 165, 198-99; his novels reviewed, 150-53; portrait, illustration no. 9
Hollis, Thomas, subscriber to the *Monthly* and *Analytical*, 24
Horner, Francis, 24
Hume, David, 211, 227; *Critical* reviewer, 22
Hurd, Richard, 50

Inchbald, Elizabeth, 136; her *Simple Story* reviewed, 161-63

Jackson, William, of Exeter, his supposed *Critical* review, 33
Jeffrey, Francis: and the *Edinburgh Review*, 40-41, 45-47, 50, 83, 94; his review of Moore's *Anacreon*, 75-76; his reviews of *Thalaba* in the *Monthly* and *Edinburgh*, 45, 108-14
Jerningham, Edward, 82
Johnson, Joseph, editor, owner, and publisher of the *Analytical*, 22-23, 31, 84, 178, 204, 219-20, 255-57; portrait, illustration no. 11
Johnson, Samuel: *Critical* reviewer, 22; invited to review Goldsmith, 33; his comments on the Reviews, 26, 173, 235; *Monthly* comments on him, 235; the *English Poets* with his *Lives*, 51, 61-62; Boswell's *Life* reviewed, 235-41
Jones, William, of Nayland, and the *British Critic*, 180-81
Journal des Sçavans, 19
Justamond, John Obadiah, *English* reviewer, 22

Keats, John, 46
Kenion, James, subscriber to the *Monthly*, 24 n.71
Kennedy, Rev. J., 25
Kinnaird, Charles, 8th baron, subscriber to the *Monthly*, 24, n.69
Kirkpatrick, James, *Monthly* reviewer, 20, n.6
Klopstock, Friedrich Gottlob, 53
Knox, Vicesimus, 203
Kotzebue, August von, 111
Kramer, Carl Gottlob, 140-41

"Lake School," 46-47, 83, 100, 108-13
Lamb, Charles, 43, 98, n.88, 100, 109-10;

"A Charm for a Democracy, Reviewed, Analysed, & Destroyed"
Cartoon by Thomas Rowlandson, published in the
Antijacobin Review and dated 1 February 1799